Frank

FORMOSA
BETRAYED

FORMOSA
BETRAYED

George H. Kerr

HOUGHTON MIFFLIN COMPANY BOSTON

THE RIVERSIDE PRESS CAMBRIDGE

1965

CHESAPEAKE HIGH SCHOOL

5226

FIRST PRINTING **W**

COPYRIGHT © 1965 BY GEORGE H. KERR
ALL RIGHTS RESERVED INCLUDING THE RIGHT TO
REPRODUCE THIS BOOK OR PARTS THEREOF IN ANY FORM
LIBRARY OF CONGRESS CATALOG CARD NUMBER: 65–20221
PRINTED IN THE UNITED STATES OF AMERICA

FOR MY FORMOSAN FRIENDS . . .

remembering the March Affair, 1947.

The Heart of the Matter

"Our experience in Formosa is most enlightening. The Administration of the former Governor Chen Yi has alienated the people from the Central Government. Many were forced to feel that conditions under autocratic rule [Japan's rule] were preferable.

The Central Government lost a fine opportunity to indicate to the Chinese people and to the world at large its capability to provide honest and efficient administration. They cannot attribute their failure to the activities of the Communists or of dissident elements. The people anticipated sincerely and enthusiastically deliverance from the Japanese yoke. However, Chen Yi and his henchmen ruthlessly, corruptly, and avariciously imposed their regime upon a happy and amenable population. The Army conducted themselves as conquerors. Secret police operated freely to intimidate and to facilitate exploitation by Central Government officials. . . .

The island is extremely productive in coal, rice, sugar, cement, fruits and tea. Both hydro and thermal power are abundant. The Japanese had efficiently electrified even remote areas and also established excellent railroad lines and highways. Eighty per cent of the people can read and write, the exact antithesis of conditions prevailing in the mainland of China.

There were indications that Formosans would be receptive toward United States guardianship and United Nations trusteeship. They fear that the Central Government contemplates bleeding their island to support the tottering and corrupt Nanking machine, and I think their fears well founded."

Lieutenant General Albert C. Wedemeyer to the Secretary of State, August 17, 1947. (United States Relations With China, *p.* 309.)

Foreword

IN MANY RESPECTS, Formosa is a living symbol of the great American dilemma. Put in simple and straightforward terms, that dilemma is how to fulfill the awesome responsibilities of being a global power, entrusted with the defense of many societies, and at the same time, remain faithful to the principles that constitute our political-ethical creed. There is no easy answer to this riddle. Indeed, no complete answer is possible, and we should beware of those who peddle simple solutions to enormously complex problems. This does not provide an excuse, however, for ignoring the most crucial challenge confronting American society in our times. Indeed, our success — our very survival — may well depend upon finding more adequate answers than have been discovered to date.

Some eleven million people live on the island of Formosa, approximately nine million of them "native Formosans" who were born on the island and consider it their homeland. The older Formosans grew up under Japanese rule, a fact that has had an impact upon many aspects of their culture. Even the younger Formosans, however, tend to think of themselves as possessed of traditions, values, and a way of life distinct from that of the mainland Chinese. The emergence of a Formosan nationalism is thus a natural development, and despite the

many fissures existing in Formosan political circles, that movement strikes a responsive chord, especially among the intellectuals.

Those who believe that economic determinism is the key to
all political phenomena will not find Formosa a case study to
their liking. In its natural resources, particularly in the fertility
of its soil, Formosa has been amply blessed. The Japanese
legacy and the more recent American largess, moreover, have
combined to give the people of Formosa a much higher standard
of living than that of most of their Asian neighbors. In enterprise as well as in agriculture, the native Formosan has played
an active, dynamic role. Refugees from the mainland, until
recent times at least, were overwhelmingly engaged in government work, military service, and teaching. While not without
its economic problems, Formosa is among that small number
of non-western societies for which an optimistic economic prog-
nosis is reasonable, particularly if the issue of population can
be tackled in serious fashion.

The problems of Formosa are overwhelmingly political. How
long can the Formosans be excluded from any effective voice
in their government in a system that purports to be constitutional and democratic? How long can the myth be continued
that Formosa is China? How long can the estrangement between Formosan intellectuals and mainland refugees continue
without serious political repercussions? Let no one under-
estimate the degree to which the Communists are seeking to
take advantage of the political situation on Formosa. As might
be expected, they are playing both ends against the middle.
To the Nationalists, they urge a return to the motherland, with
all past sins being forgiven. To the Formosans, they promise
the rights of "cultural autonomy" and freedom from "the Ameri-
can-Chiang Kai-shek clique." Presumably, they hope that few
Formosans know the true Communist record in Tibet and
Sinkiang.

Meanwhile, the Kuomintang continues to imprison Formosan

nationalists and dominate the political life of this island. But as the Nationalist leaders grow older and less certain of the future, political tension slowly mounts. Cleavages within Kuomintang circles are sharp and significant. Some mainland refugees would be prepared to accept and even welcome a truly democratic order. Others would prefer to depend primarily upon the secret police and the army. The situation is pregnant with political hazards — and possibilities. Where should we stand?

Few if any Americans are better equipped to present new perspectives on the Formosa problem than George H. Kerr. For some three decades, he has had both a scholarly and a personal interest in the Formosan people. At various critical periods, he has lived and worked with them, witnessing their few triumphs and their many tragedies. No one who reads this book will be unaware of the fact that the author has a deep sympathy with the cause of Formosan independence. No doubt many of his facts and arguments will be challenged by those who support different solutions. It will be impossible to ignore Kerr's case, however; he has marshalled evidence too well to permit that. I find myself in great sympathy with his basic theme. Self-determination for the Formosan people is one of those causes which happily unites our values and our national interests. But in any case, this work should stimulate some serious thinking about American policy toward Formosa both by those who agree and those who disagree with the author's conclusions.

ROBERT A. SCALAPINO

University of California, Berkeley
April 1965

Acknowledgments

MY NARRATIVE HERE is based upon thirty years of involvement with Formosan affairs. It began with a period of study in Japan (1935–1937), led on to a three-year residence at Taipei (1937–1940) and to graduate work at Columbia University.

As a so-called "Formosa Specialist" my civilian service with the War Department (1942–1943), commissioned service with the Navy (1944–1946) and again civilian service with the Department of State (1946–1947) gave me opportunities to see Formosa from the Washington or official point of view.

Since 1947 I have been concerned with the Formosa problem in a rather academic way. My lectures at the University of California (Berkeley) and at Stanford University may have been the first attempts to examine Formosa's historic role on the Western Pacific frontier.

In presenting this account I quote extensively from government sources, from the daily press at Taipei, Tokyo and Shanghai, and from personal letters. I am particularly indebted to members of the UNRRA team who were struggling to bring order out of Chinese chaos at Taipei during my service in the American Consulate there.

I have used official UNRRA reports and many private communications from team members. Some prefer to remain anonymous and some have given me permission to quote directly from their reports, publications and letters. I am grateful to them all and to other members of the foreign community who contributed information incorporated here.

Correspondents still living on Formosa or having family and property there must remain unnamed.

Quotations from Formosan letters which were written originally in English have sometimes required slight editing to make the meaning clear without changing the substance. The changes are indicated with bracketing. Since most of the correspondents were at one time my students I assume responsibility in editing the texts.

Quotations from Formosan and Shanghai papers are taken from daily press summaries prepared at the American Consulate at Taipei. Files are presently on deposit at the Hoover Institute and Library at Stanford University.

The island is known to the Chinese and Japanese as *Taiwan*. I have retained this in direct quotations and in the names of most institutions, agencies and publications of which it is a part. Elsewhere I have used *Formosa,* from the old Portuguese name *Ilha Formosa* or "Beautiful Island."

Dr. K. C. Wu, former Governor of Formosa, has generously permitted me to quote extensively from his open letters to Chiang Kai-shek and to the National Assembly at Taipei. Dr. Ira D. Hirschy, UNRRA's Chief Medical Officer at Taipei in 1946–1947, has allowed me to use his private letters and his published observations. Peggy and Tillman Durdin arranged for me to read portions of an unpublished manuscript entitled *Taiwan and the Nationalist Government* which they are preparing for the Council on Foreign Relations at New York.

Edward Eckerdt Paine, Reports Officer for the UNRRA Office at Taipei and former Major in the United States Air Force in China, collaborated with me in 1948, at considerable personal sacrifice, in assembling raw materials for this record of conditions and events in Formosa in 1946 and 1947. I thank him here again for his cooperation.

Martha and Robert Catto, my colleagues in the Consulate, shared most of the "official experience" and much of the private adventure at Taipei, and have been good enough to read the present text in manuscript.

Dr. Robert A. Scalapino, who honors me with a Foreword here, is Chairman of the Department of Political Science at the University of California (Berkeley) and author of many significant commentaries on the Formosa Question.

Juanita Vitousek, at whose country place this was first drafted in 1958, has read and re-read the manuscript, making many useful comments. Alice Crabbe has done much of the typing, and George Sasaki has prepared the maps. I am grateful to them.

No one quoted in this record may be held responsible for the context into which I have introduced the materials, or for the interpretations which I have given them.

GEORGE H. KERR

Honolulu, Hawaii
February 28, 1965

Contents

PART THREE

CRISIS AND AFTERMATH

PART FOUR

FORMOSA BECOMES "FREE CHINA"

XVIII. *Turning Point*

XIX. *Formosa's "Republican Decade"*

XX. *Behind the Reform Façade*

XXI. *Two Chinas?*

XXII. *Free Formosa*

FORMOSA
BETRAYED

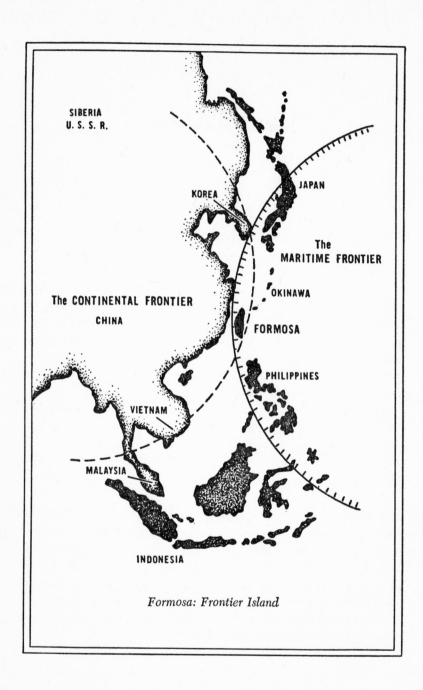

Formosa: Frontier Island

Introduction

A Frontier Tradition

FROM AN AMERICAN point of view on December 6, 1941, Formosa was a mere island-dot on the Western Pacific rim, lost against the vast backdrop of continental Asia. December 7 brought the rude awakening; the Japanese attack upon the Philippines was mounted from Formosan airfields and soon Japanese forces were pouring through and past Formosa into the Indies and Southeast Asia. Formosa had resumed its traditional role as a trouble spot in Asian waters.

It has been many times an international trouble spot because it lies in a maritime world, but always under the shadow of the continent nearby. Here two frontiers meet and overlap. In the days before air power the situation was well defined by the wide channel lying between the continent and the island — much wider, it should be noticed, than the channel which isolates Britain from the continent of Europe. But from a contemporary continental point of view Formosa represents the easternmost thrust of a vast complex of continental interests, of Chinese interests pressing out toward the maritime world. From an oceanic point of view the island represents the westernmost point on the Western Pacific rim, a maritime frontier which embraces Japan, the Ryukyus and the Philippines, a world of seaborne trade and international politics.

A seesaw conflict between this island world and the continent has been in evidence for at least two thousand years. The earliest Chinese notices of Formosa indicate that it was sparsely settled by fierce non-Chinese barbarians long before the Chinese themselves pushed southward from their homeland in the Yellow River basin to settle along the Fukien coast. These savages of a southern origin crossed the channel from time to time to plunder coastal villages or to seek a barter trade. The Chinese in turn sent out expeditions to punish them or to explore the distant island shores. In time a small settlement of Chinese fishermen appeared in the Pescadores but there were no significant attempts to displace the Formosan aborigines or to found permanent Chinese settlements on Formosa until the way had been prepared by others.

Japanese merchants and pirates appear to have been the first to establish small immigrant villages. For centuries they were sailing past Formosa to the China ports, to Southeast Asia and the Indies. In times of storm or when in need of supply or ship's repair they took shelter in the lagoons and inlets along Formosa's western shore. At last a considerable Japanese settlement (which they named Takasago) came into being at a point not far distant from present-day Tainan.

Then came the Spanish and the Dutch. When Japan's great dictator Hideyoshi menaced Luzon, late in the 1500's, Spain's Viceroy at Manila proposed to occupy Formosa. In 1626 Spanish forts and missions were established at Keelung and Tamsui on the island's northern tip. Meanwhile the Dutch had reached the Pescadores, seeking a naval base from which to harass Portuguese trade at Macao and to interfere with the Spanish shipping near the Philippines. In 1623 they abandoned Makung and moved to Formosa proper, founding Anping and the present-day city of Tainan. They sometimes quarreled with the Japanese nearby, but Takasago village faded rapidly after the home government adopted its Seclusion policies forbidding Japanese to travel overseas. In 1642 the Dutch Protestants drove the Spanish Catholics from their narrow foothold at the north, and for twenty years thereafter held the island without serious challenge.

This might well be called Formosa's "European half-century," for the colony prospered as the Dutch created Formosa's first government, established schools and missions for the aborigines, opened up the countryside for agriculture and sent missionaries far back into the mountains. Thus in the second quarter of the 17th century European arms and administration opened the way for Chinese immigration. At that time Ming China was torn by civil rebellion and pressed hard by enemies from beyond the Great Wall. Everywhere local warlords and imperial agents extorted unreasonable taxes and tribute from the common people in an effort to support a tottering central government. Ignoring strict official edicts banning emigration, villagers, farmers and fishermen began to leave the country. The government considered them traitors, renegades and outlaws. Thousands went overseas to Java and Malaya, Borneo, Siam and the Philippines. Tens of thousands made their way across the water barrier to Formosa, so conveniently near — too near, as they were soon to learn.

These "outlaws" were the ancestors of the majority of people living on Formosa today. They were hardy pioneers, bold and adventurous. Those who sought new land beyond the limits of Dutch administration were on a true frontier; their contemporaries in faraway America provide a close parallel if one is needed to illustrate the situation. Going into their new fields they had to carry weapons as well as farm-tools, and they dwelt within stockades. The aborigines contested every advance into the hills, and the Chinese newcomers, on their part, considered the savages to be sub-human, or "non-people" who should be driven back into the highest mountains if they could not be exterminated in the foothills.

Soon enough within the borders of Dutch settlement both the aborigines and the immigrants grew restive, for the Europeans proved to be hard masters who demanded licenses for hunting and fishing and imposed heavy taxes on trade and produce. When at last a merchant-adventurer named Cheng Cheng-kung boldly assembled a fleet in the Pescadores and moved against the Dutch the Chinese immigrant settlers were ready to help him.

Cheng (known in Europe as Koxinga) was the son of a Japanese mother by a Chinese father who called himself and his family "Ming patriots," but when he had driven the Dutch from the island (in 1662) he set himself up in the European forts and mansions as "King of Tung-tu." From this island base he proposed to conquer the mainland, vowing to liberate the Chinese people from Manchu rule. The story here takes on a familiar note, for foreign (British) merchant-adventurers opened an agency through which they proposed to supply these "Ming patriots" with arms in return for substantial commercial concessions once the mainland liberation had been accomplished. This was the first military aid mission on Formosa, but not the last.

After twenty years of independence, however, the island kingdom was threatened by an overwhelming mainland Chinese force, assembled in the Pescadores. A truce was negotiated by the men who controlled the little government at Tainan, and a deal was made with Peking. In reward for a peaceful surrender Koxinga's young grandson the third King of Tung-tu was granted a safe-conduct to Peking, given a resounding title and a pension, and retired to an easy life.

Peking sent a garrison force, magistrates, and a swarm of civil officers into the island. Two centuries of ineffective and abusive rule thereafter generated a local Formosan tradition of resentment and underlying hostility toward representatives of mainland authority. Riots and abortive independence movements took place so often that it became common in China to say of Formosa, "Every three years an uprising; every five years a rebellion." There were more than thirty violent outbursts in the 19th century.

PART ONE

THE VIEW FROM
WASHINGTON

1941–1945

Inland, at a distance from the walled garrison towns, there was chronic disorder. The outlying frontier villages, often at war with one another, were governed by family patriarchs and clan councils who were a law unto themselves within their own territories.

Such were conditions on Formosa when the Western world returned seeking trade in Asian waters after 1800. All nations with shipping in adjacent seas became deeply concerned. The island was considered to be one of the most dangerous and unhealthy spots in the Orient. The coasts were unlighted and unpatrolled; mariners shipwrecked on the eastern shores were at the mercy of headhunters and on the west they were victimized by so-called "wreckers" who plundered stranded vessels and gave no quarter to castaways. It was known that the local Chinese authorities frequently collaborated in these activities.

As international maritime traffic increased the number of shipwrecks and violent incidents multiplied until the situation became intolerable. But when foreign governments demanded corrective action Peking smoothly evaded responsibility. England and the United States in turn attempted to force the issue. In 1853–1854 Commodore Perry wanted to annex Formosa, but knowing that Washington would not approve, suggested a joint Sino-American economic and administrative program, indicating that he thought a well-established American community would in due course petition for union with the United States as the Americans in Hawaii were then proposing to do. He envisioned Formosa as an American outpost guaranteeing peace and order along the Western Pacific rim. England sent in gunboats and became embroiled in a local "Camphor War" in 1868. In 1874 Japan sent an expeditionary force into South Formosa which compelled Peking to admit responsibility and to pay a large indemnity for damages. In 1884 France occupied the Pescadores and Keelung and blockaded Formosa for a year during the Franco-Chinese war in Annam.

At last in 1887 the Chinese Government raised Formosa from the status of a Fukien dependency to the rank of a province although nearly two-thirds of the island still lay beyond the frontiers of local Chinese control.

The changed status and a reform program came too late. In a distant quarrel concerning Korea, Japan defeated China in 1895. As part of the settlement Formosa and the Pescadores were ceded to Japan "in perpetuity." A touch of irony enters here, for China had hired an American lawyer named John Foster, a former Secretary of State, to guide Peking's representatives through the humiliating treaty conference. To lend moral support to his employers, Colonel Foster then proceeded to Keelung to assist in the formal territorial transfer. This was one more adventurous tale he had to tell to his little grandson, John Foster Dulles, then eight years old.

Japanese rule thereafter ensured a prompt suppression of piracy in Formosan waters, produced an efficient coastguard and well-lighted coasts. Soon the island ports were in good order and trade began to flourish. Formosa ceased to be an irritating international problem when it entered upon its "Japanese half-century"; no foreign power challenged Japan's sovereign position in Formosa until the days of the Cairo meeting beside the Nile in 1943. Beyond regularizing a modest trade in tea and camphor and developing a modest market for American products, the United States showed little further interest.

I

The Cairo Declaration

Filling the Empty Files at Washington, 1942

As FAR AS FORMOSA was concerned, Washington was sound asleep on December 6, 1941.

The rain of bombs on Luzon and the rattle of gunfire about Manila brought a rude awakening. Waves of Japanese bombers and fighters flew down from Formosan airfields, striking here and there along the way. Baguio was bombed at 9:30 A.M. All but two American planes were caught on the ground at Clark Field and destroyed at 12:45 P.M. On the next day the great Cavite Naval Base was put out of action. The Grand Marshal of the Philippines Armed Forces, General Douglas MacArthur, had lost his principal shield.

The Japanese military leaders had often called Formosa a "stepping stone to the south" or a "stationary aircraft carrier," and after fifty years of development, it was at last fulfilling its role. General MacArthur on his part, had one radar station at Aparri on the northern tip of Luzon, facing Formosa, and on that fatal day it was not working.[1]

At Washington our Far Eastern military intelligence files concerning Formosa matched the "temporary" buildings in which they were housed, and like them were leftovers from World War I. This was also true of the white-haired Civil Service secretary who had been custodian of the files since 1918.

She had cared for her secrets tenderly, but the files concerning Formosa had not prospered. The "Taiwan Folders" in fact had scarcely been disturbed since the island was ceded to Japan in 1895.

There was a map of Keelung harbor, sent over from the Navy files, dated 1894, and a few photographs of Keelung taken before 1914. We had the standard hydrographic charts available to all navigators and a set of Japanese Imperial Land Survey maps which could be bought at any large stationers in Tokyo. We had a set of topographic maps prepared by the Imperial Japanese Army. The most interesting item in the Army's "Formosa File" was a report on Japan's alleged plan to use Formosa as a base for a push southward into Indochina. This was based on a newspaper series, in French, which had been published at Paris in 1905.[2]

With the strike at Pearl Harbor all this changed. At the Munitions Building in Washington the potted plants went out the door to make room for new files, pending transfer to the Pentagon. The Japan-Manchuria Branch of the Military Intelligence Services (G-2) established subsidiary "area desks" for Korea and Formosa. Area specialists were brought in, and from around the world to these desks came reports having anything to do with the Japanese Empire and its possessions.

The "shooting war" which involved men, ships, planes and guns had to be supported by economic, psychologic and diplomatic warfare requiring an immense range of intelligence data. A bewildering number of "alphabet agencies" sprang into being, each contributing raw data and research papers needed by the established intelligence divisions of the Army, Navy and State Departments.

Our most detailed current information came from British intelligence sources, and from Canadian and British missionaries — doctors, nurses, teachers and preachers — who had served many years in Formosa, knew the local languages and dialects, and had traveled extensively throughout the island. Members of the American Consular Service who had served at Taipei (then Taihoku) were scattered over the world in December, 1941, but their reports, accumulated through some forty years, were on file at the Department of State. They were principally concerned with problems of trade between Formosan ports and the United States. Few reported basic economic development and very few ventured to touch seriously on social and political conditions beyond the routine minimum required by the consular reporting regulations.

As the months passed after Pearl Harbor, Washington's elaborate research apparatus distilled an astonishing quantity of information from Japanese-language sources, from prisoner-of-war interrogation reports, and from documents picked up at every point of contact with the enemy.

Gradually we developed a picture of Formosa's total economic and military position within the Japanese Empire. We found that it was making a major contribution of metals (copper, aluminum and gold), coal, timber, pulp, industrial chemicals, foodstuffs and manpower. Formosan ports and airfields were important way-stations for the immense Japanese military drive into South Asia and Indonesia, toward India and toward Australia. An analysis of captured documents and diaries gave us records of troop movements through this staging area.

But we needed to know more — always more — of the social and political tensions within the island, and of new industrial activity, so that we could develop detailed bombing objective folders and a psychological warfare program. We wanted to know more of new sites, new factories, and the communications system. We needed to know more of production levels and techniques and of labor organization. We needed reports directly from within the island itself.

It was reasonable to look to our allies the Chinese to supply them just as our Western allies supplied us by maintaining a network of fearless agents behind enemy lines in Europe. From the Washington point of view, the rugged Fukien coast with its thousands of tiny islands and inlets, lightly patrolled, seemed an advantageous base-area from which to get agents into the big island across the Straits.

Intelligence Reports — Chinese Style

Our G–2 representatives at Chungking asked for intelligence of Formosa. In due course, back through channels came long reports purporting to tell of conditions within the island, observed by Chinese agents recently returned from hazardous intelligence missions. The papers were signed, endorsed and forwarded by one or more of the thousands of Generals on the Nationalist military payroll.

The reports revealed at once how very little the mainland Chinese knew about any aspect of Formosa, and it suggested how little they cared. It also suggested that high-ranking Chinese officers did not hesitate to misrepresent field conditions to "ignorant" Americans. Obviously we were being told what the Chinese thought we wanted to know; considerations of "face" made it impossible to admit that they had no genuine recent intelligence from the island.

Several Chinese field reports began with assurances that Formosa had been discovered by the Chinese in the year A.D. 607. One (dated August 17, 1943), stated that in January, 1938, the mountain aborigines had swept through the lowlands of Formosa, that there had been strikes in the mines, and that Formosans everywhere had refused to pay taxes. All this anti-Japanese resistance, they said, had been organized by Chinese underground revolutionary agents. In March, 1938, said another report, mammoth oil reserves had been destroyed by Chinese agents — enough to meet Japan's fuel requirements for six years. In September that year Japan's plans to draft Formosans for military service had precipitated a great uprising in the southern part of the island during which twenty-seven Japa-

nese had been killed. This had been followed by uprisings
everywhere. Chinese Nationalist agents, guiding Formosan
revolutionaries, had dynamited railroads and steelworks in November, after which the Japanese garrison had been trebled.
Nine thousand Formosan troops had revolted after killing and
wounding 1200 Japanese officers and men. The insurgents had
taken to the hills, from which they were continuing to foment
riots and strikes throughout the island, guided always by Chinese Nationalist agents.

At Washington I read these reports with fascination; if all
this were true we should have little trouble in bringing about
massive subversion of the Japanese war effort in the rich colony.

But there was a slight difficulty; I had been living on Formosa in these years (1937 to 1940) and had traveled in every
part of the island. These marvelous Chinese tales were inven-
tions, or fabrications based upon incidents — some of them
twenty years in the past — which were well known and had
been reported in detail before 1941. For example, the alleged
destruction of a six-year oil reserve referred to the dropping of
one bomb, far wide of the mark, in the Hsinchu oilfields of
North Formosa on February 18, 1938. At Chungking old reports had been elaborated and twisted to serve the intelligence
requirements of the American command. Chinese face had been
saved.

From Washington we persisted in requests for current information.

Chiang's highest intelligence offices supplied us with a "complete list" of twenty-one airfields and temporary landing strips
on Formosa. We knew that there were in fact more than seventy.

We were then provided with a report prepared by a reconnaissance mission "just returned from Taiwan." The Chinese
agents had discovered that there were five key railway bridges
on the main line linking Keelung and Kaohsiung ports, and that

each consisted of an upper vehicular span which concealed a lower railway deck. One steel and concrete bridge was camouflaged by having it "submerged from three inches to one foot under water." Another report from this reconnaissance mission told of an underground railway tunnel, some eighteen miles long, which linked Kaohsiung harbor with the airbase and factory town at Pingtung. The Japanese controlled only the Formosan lowlands, the report said, for they had been forced to leave the mountainous two-thirds of Formosa to the aborigines. High-ranking Allied prisoners of war (presumably General Jonathan Wainright) had been moved from Formosa to an (imaginary) island lying "one hundred miles east of Formosa."

These last two items read as if they had been reproduced from Chinese reports of the 1870's, when the Chinese themselves garrisoned only the lowlands on the western coast and Chinese geographic information concerning Formosa and the adjacent islets was wildly inaccurate.

A Chinese report prepared in late 1943 stated that a "recent visitor to Taiwan" had seen the Keelung anchorage empty of ships. Our own shipping-intelligence data, analyzed at Washington, indicated that Keelung had an average of forty-eight ships in port per week at that time, traveling under great hazard in order to keep supplies moving southward to Japan's front lines, and foodstuffs moving northward to Japan proper. American photo reconnaissance in 1944 showed a crowded harbor.

In addition to these reports on subversion potential, and on specific communications and industrial objectives, we also received from Chungking a long report on Formosan-Chinese leaders, and on Formosans who were exiles in China. This was prepared by a Formosan "exile" named Hsieh Nan-kuang, whose name will appear again and again in this narrative. Hsieh had left Formosa in the 1920's when police pressure became intolerable to many well-educated young Formosan men and women. Now — at Chungking — Hsieh was seeking favors from the Americans, maneuvering toward what he hoped would be a prominent role in Formosan affairs under a postwar Occupation. To this end he carefully named Formosans who had led in Home Rule Movement organizations after World War I and who were very well known and respected throughout Taiwan. He saw them as potential rivals. Some he smeared as "pro-Japanese collaborationists," and some he labeled "communist." His analysis showed that there were thousands of Formosans-in-exile, prepared to organize for the invasion of Formosa and the post-surrender takeover. He sought large funds to support Formosan organizations then in China, but when pressed for details it became clear that most Formosans were in areas controlled by the Japanese. He was quite willing, however, to be custodian of the American dollar funds until the Formosans could be reached and made ready for post-surrender tasks.

The American research program, the published summaries of Formosa's wealth, and the preparation of more than two thousand American officers for Occupation duty on the island alerted and perhaps alarmed the ruling family and Party oligarchy at Chungking. T. V. Soong (Madame Chiang's brother) as Minister of Foreign Affairs and Sun Fo (her sister's stepson) as President of the Legislative Yuan, began to put forward demands for an immediate reversion of Formosan sovereignty to China, and added claims upon the Ryukyu Islands as well.

Bombing Objective Folders and Propaganda

Chinese intelligence reports were often entertaining but generally useless. It was disturbing to know that our Chinese Allies thought we were so gullible — but we so often were. Nevertheless, our inquiries at Chungking and our reports prepared at Washington sometimes proved to have long-range postwar consequences.

The vast array of data prepared by the Board of Economic

Warfare, the Office of Strategic Services and a host of other agencies enabled the Army and Navy to produce surveys and handbooks concerning Formosa which inevitably passed into Chinese hands at the highest levels. In 1942 the Army (G-2) produced a confidential *Strategic Survey of the Island of Taiwan (Formosa)*. In 1943 the Army Air Force and the Navy began to produce bombing objective folders. In 1944 and early 1945 the Navy produced twelve elaborate *Civil Affairs Handbooks* for the guidance of military government personnel being trained then to follow through an invasion.

The bombing objective folders were of immediate, short-range concern to the Army and Navy. Airfields, ammunition bunkers, and garrison encampments were obviously prime targets. So too were harbor works, industrial plants and rail junctions. But occasionally we had to give thought to bombing as an aspect of psychological warfare. To this end I once suggested preparation of a target folder for the Taiwan Grand Shrine.

The *Rules of Ground Warfare* (written long before the age of nuclear weapons) strictly forbade willful destruction of religious buildings. In this instance, however, I reasoned that the Shinto Grand Shrine in its elaborate gardens near Taipei was not a religious building but a political symbol of imperial Japanese rule. It was a State Shrine which had been constructed at grievous cost to the Formosan people, a "conqueror's shrine" which had no religious significance whatsoever beyond State ceremonial on Japanese festival occasions. In 1939 it had been greatly enlarged. Expansion of the grounds and gardens had required the destruction of one of Formosa's oldest and most revered temples, to the great sorrow and anger of the Formosans. I believed that destruction of the Grand Shrine would be a severe blow to Japanese military morale and would immensely please the Formosan people. The Japanese belief in "divine protection" and the god-emperor would be shaken and the Formosans would joke about it.

I was overruled, and the Shrine was left intact. Rather late in the war the Japanese let it be known that they had established a large prisoner of war camp adjacent to the Shrine, thus giving us a double reason (as they well knew) for not bombing the buildings. We did not discover until after the surrender that the "enlargement" of the Shrine in 1939 was in fact preparation of an elaborate underground headquarters for the Japanese military High Command.

In another bombing-objective folder, however, the responsible officers at Washington were willing to include a red-line overlay on the map of Taipei city showing a general division between the *jonai* or Japanese administrative center, and the Daitotei and Manka sectors, the crowded Formosan shopping and residential areas on the west. It was effective, for when we destroyed the *jonai* area in early 1945 we spared the Formosan quarters. This was noticed and much talked about and had something to do with the post-surrender popularity of Americans among Formosans living in Taipei.

Psychological warfare called for "black" or concealed propaganda designed to undermine morale and to weaken the Japanese will to resist, and for "white" propaganda, designed to appeal directly and openly to the Formosan people. We urged them to rebel, hoping to foster mistrust, uncertainty and fear among the Japanese. We planted misleading stories and rumors here and there around the world, to be picked up (we hoped) by Japan's allies or agents. We tried to suggest that there were elaborate anti-Japanese plots brewing within the island, and that these had secret Allied support. As a matter of fact these "plots" had no more substance than the plots reported to us by the Nationalist officers at Chungking. With such stories we hoped to discourage any move to arm and train Formosans as a Home Guard serving under Japanese officers to repel an Allied invasion. We also hoped to persuade the local government to divert large numbers of Japanese from sensitive labor posts to unproductive guard duty and internal security patrol.

With radio and pamphlet propaganda we attempted to play

on well-known Formosan grievances and to appeal openly for an uprising at an opportune time. By giving the islanders a fairly accurate report on the progress of the war we sought to discredit Tokyo's boastful stories and to destroy confidence in the imperial government. We urged Formosans to be ready to come over to our side if an invasion took place. We hoped at least to secure Formosan neutrality and cooperation if a long military occupation became necessary before Japan surrendered the home islands.

Formosa's Future: The Battle of the Memoranda

Psychological warfare agencies were preparing to air-drop millions of leaflets over the Formosan countryside. The message-content called for high-level policy decisions. What should we promise the Formosans? What could we imply?

The Armed Services were concerned principally with the neutralization of Formosa. Could it be knocked out of the war? Could we deny Japan the advantages of its wealth, its manpower and its military bases? Could we convert Formosa into a base for our own further attacks against Japan proper? We anticipated a very long push; would the Formosans cooperate or resist during a long occupation?

Beyond this, the Army and Navy were also concerned with the prospects of the postwar settlement. Could we make certain that Formosa would not again become a threat to American interests in the Western Pacific?

In early 1942 I prepared a memorandum which explored the possible alternatives for postwar settlements, advocating some form of international control, the creation of a policing base on the island at the south, and the use of Formosa's abundant resources in postwar reconstruction programs. I ventured to suggest that China would not be able to assume exclusive control of Formosa for two reasons; there were not enough Chinese administrators and technicians available to manage such a complex economy, and there were the ever-present dangers of an intolerable exploitation by the Soongs, the Kungs, the Chiangs and other families, and Army and Party cliques who were a curse to China. I had visited China in 1940. It was evident that Formosa was many years in advance of mainland China in terms of technological organization. Certainly general standards of living for townsman and peasant alike were superior on Formosa. China had no surplus of trained manpower to spare for the job which would have to be done in Formosa.

In July, 1942, the Chief of the Far Eastern Division of the Military Intelligence Service was asked to state the Division's views concerning an occupation of Formosa as part of general strategy, together with comment upon propaganda required in advance to secure conditions of least local resistance to an Allied invasion.

A memorandum dated July 31 was the first in a series prepared for use within the Division. Discussions took place intermittently until October, 1944. In sum, it was assumed by the military offices that Washington's decisions on postwar policy would be guided by "enlightened self-interest." America's long-range interests should have priority, but sympathetic consideration should be given to China's claims, and to the interests, rights and welfare of the Formosan people. Plans for Formosa's ultimate disposition should condition all propaganda addressed to the Formosan people *before* surrender.

Three alternatives were evident. In theory the island might be made independent and given self-government, but in practice this would be difficult to bring about, even if the Formosans wanted it and the Allies agreed. (Surely China would object.) A second course would ensure the prompt transfer of Formosa to China, to satisfy loud Chinese claims that it was a "lost province." A third program would provide for a temporary Allied trusteeship, during which the Formosans themselves would prepare for a plebiscite to determine their ultimate political fate.

As a "Formosa specialist" I urged the need at Washington for a recognized "Formosa policy." The island was potentially too important to be treated merely as an ordinary Chinese province, only lately overrun by Japanese troops. History had long since demonstrated its military importance at a strategic point on the Western Pacific rim and its wealth and technological development placed it too far ahead of the mainland Chinese provinces to permit an easy return to Chinese control.

Formosa was an island, a maritime area which had always been agitated by separatist sentiment, and for half a century it had been entirely cut off from the Chinese mainland and the Chinese civil wars. It was not *Japanized* but *modernized*.

A Formosa policy, as such, should be worked out after careful consideration of the historical, social and economic developments of the 20th century. When a policy had been devised, it should be agreed upon by our principal allies in Asia (China, Great Britain, and the Philippines Government-in-exile), well in advance of invasion and occupation. Pending final decisions and commitments, it was suggested that all propaganda directed to Formosa should make a *geographical* rather than a political or racial distinction in all references to island people.

I record these views here at some length, because there has been a tendency in recent years to present the "Formosa Question" publicly as something new, an embarrassing recent development rising out of changed military and political circumstances on the mainland.

"China Firsters"

These memoranda setting forth the "enlightened self-interest" proposal that Formosa be given special consideration, and be held under a temporary trust arrangement, carefully noted that any postwar arrangement would have to provide for China's participation so long as we proclaimed Chiang Kai-shek to be

the great Leader of Democracy in Asia, and China to be a
"Great Power." But most Far Eastern specialists in wartime
Washington were under no illusion concerning Chiang's capacities and strengths. He was a "Leader of Democracy" and
China was a "Great Power" only because the Washington Administration said so, and gave him money and arms to keep him
in the field against the Japanese.

China was an enormous problem. Nothing in the Nationalist
record as of 1942 would support a belief that Chiang Kai-shek's
Party bosses could assume control of the government of Formosa without massive aid, or that American interests there
could rest secure in Chinese hands.

This was well known in the Department of State, but even so
early as 1943 the policy lines were set; Formosa would be returned to China, with no reservations of American or Allied interest whatsoever. Although enlightened self-interest required
some guarantee that all of Formosa's human and material assets
should be conserved for Allied use pending a general and satisfactory settlement in Asia, suggestions to this effect evoked
cries of "imperialism!" "What would our Chinese friends
think?"

Prominent officers in the State Department assumed (with
much justification) that the outstanding issues affecting Sino-
American relations in Asia could not be solved until China
achieved unity under a strong central government, whatever
political complexion that government might have. Arguing
from this, they held that no central government could survive
which failed to recover Formosa. Nationalist and Communist
Party propaganda alike held that it was a "lost province," stolen
by the Japanese. They conveniently forgot that China had
ceded Formosa to Japan in 1895 "in perpetuity," and that only a
postwar treaty of peace could effect a legal retrocession.

But, alas, there was more to State Department opposition
than this reasonable analysis.

Some opposition came from the standard bureaucrat who

wanted to avoid all bothersome problems, and saw in the Formosa Question just one more (and a minor one) in a vast array of emergent problems for which the book of regulations had no index entry. My wartime experience in Washington — in the office, in the conference rooms, and in the cocktail hours about town — soon made clear that an important number of China specialists in the State Department were incurably "missionary" in their approach to Chinese problems. The Chinese could do no wrong (at least outsiders were not allowed to say they could or did) and the Japanese could do no right. The more I stressed the modernizing progress made on Formosa under Japanese rule and the need to preserve the benefits of it, the more vindictive grew the condemnation of such "imperialism." Proposals to delay or qualify the return of Formosa to full Chinese control evoked astonishingly sharp criticism. It was as if I had suggested withholding food from starving children. The ultimate argument turned on the point of population statistics. The Formosans were of Chinese descent. There were only five million of them. Therefore, no matter what their views might be, they were a very small minority among the total hundreds of millions of Chinese on the mainland.

I found it useless to point out that the Formosans' ancestors had left the mainland centuries ago in an attempt to escape from intolerable conditions there.

The tragedy of the Formosans was that their island lay not far enough away from the continent to make the separation permanent and their frontier life secure from interference. The island was too small to be independent, and too big and too rich to be ignored.

As early as 1943 the State Department had adopted the "continental view" of Formosa. It was to be considered the easternmost area of Chinese interests, unfortunately but unimportantly cut off from the mainland by the Straits of Taiwan. There could be no admission that it might also represent the westernmost point on the Western Pacific frontier.

The Fateful Cairo Declaration

As of late 1943 no formal public commitments concerning Formosa had been made by the United States. There was then serious danger that Chiang Kai-shek might reach some sort of understanding with the Japanese. Or he might declare China neutral, ready to sit by while the United States brought about Japan's defeat from the sea. Admiral William D. Leahy must be presumed to have known what the situation was; as he put it "Chiang might drop out of the war . . . if the Chinese quit, the tasks of MacArthur and Nimitz in the Pacific, already difficult, would be much harder." [3]

In late November, 1943, President Roosevelt, Prime Minister Churchill, and the two Chiangs met near the Sphinx at a moment when Allied fortunes were at low ebb. Tired England was entering the fifth year of war, and the Chinese had been more or less at war with Japan and among themselves since 1937. After the fateful blow at Pearl Harbor America was steadily building up its own forces while sending to the Western front all the arms and equipment we could spare. We were rebuilding our naval forces in the Pacific. There was little to spare for the land war in Asia. The Burma front was very far indeed from the heart of the Japanese Empire.

To the British Prime Minister's regret the American President insisted upon hailing China as a "Great Power" and Chiang as a great leader. At Cairo the Generalissimo demanded attention befitting his international status. He wanted more arms for his stockpiles in southwestern China. He wanted the back door to Chungking to be widened by an Allied campaign so that military supply would reach him in massive quantities and not in driblets. He would have had a better case to argue if he could have shown more efficient use of the supplies which had already reached him over the Hump at tremendous cost to the Allies. Neither of the Allies was much interested in Chinese demands.

The Cairo meeting was designed in fact to mask the impending first top-level conference with Russian leaders at Teheran, to which the Chiangs were not invited. Britain's delegation expected Cairo to be a major Anglo-American conference on the conduct of war in Europe, during which Prime Minister and President would prepare for the vital talks with Stalin. Over Churchill's vigorous objection, Roosevelt gave precedence to the problems of China in order to soothe the Chiangs and enable them to hurry back to Chungking. As a shrewd politician soon entering an election year, the President knew that an affront to the Chiangs would be taken to heart by every American missionary society in every parish in the United States, whereas a reward to China's Christian leaders would receive the widest possible publicity and everyone would be pleased. Unfortunately, the Chiangs, too, knew what pressures they could exert within the United States. We had encouraged Madame Chiang to appeal directly to the American people; she had been invited to address both houses of Congress, and now we were about to pay an installment on the price for Nationalist cooperation in the war against Japan.

The American delegation at Cairo included General George C. Marshall, Admiral William D. Leahy, Admiral Ernest J. King, and Mr. Willys Peck, a former YMCA worker, born in China, and now senior China Specialist in the Department of State. Prime Minister Churchill's suite included Admiral Lord Louis Mountbatten, and Field Marshal Sir Allan Brooke. The Chiangs were accompanied by Lieutenant General Joseph Stilwell and by Major General Patrick Hurley.

Something had to be done to soothe the Nationalist leaders at this time, something to give them face among their own restless countrymen and to stiffen their will-to-resist. Something must be done to assure Asians in occupied lands that they were not forgotten.

As we read now unofficial but authoritative accounts of the

Cairo Meeting — the Stilwell Papers, for example, and Admiral Leahy's memoirs — we see that President Roosevelt's highest military aides were deeply concerned lest we lose China as a base from which to cover our seaborne attack upon Japan. At worst Chiang might be pushed aside; his restless subordinates, tired of privation, might be ready to come to terms with Tokyo, and join the puppets which Tokyo had already established in Manchuria, Peking, Nanking, Manila, Bangkok, and Indonesia. Or Chiang himself might declare a truce in order to conserve his weapons stockpiles for his own continuing civil war.

Roosevelt made little use of his State Department advisors at Cairo, and made no serious effort to examine the China problem with Lieutenant General Stilwell. He had jaunty self-confidence that he could manage men and affairs on an *ad hoc* basis.

On December 1, 1943, the President, the Prime Minister, and the Generalissimo issued the Cairo Declaration, over their joint signature.

This was not a carefully prepared State Paper but rather a promise to divide the spoils, dangled before the wavering Chinese. It was a declaration of intent, promising a redistribution of territories held by the Japanese. None of the territories mentioned in the document were at that moment in Allied hands. The Allied leaders had to show a bold face before the world, but in truth no one then knew what ultimate course the war might take.

But once these Heads of State had committed themselves to paper, the damage was done, setting in train a long series of events which are now cause for deep regret. Upon the Cairo Declaration there soon rose a superstructure of reaffirmations, enlarged promises, and further commitments made at Teheran, Yalta and Potsdam. None could foresee that nine years would pass before the Cairo terms were fulfilled, in part, by the Treaty of San Francisco, and that twenty-two years later (1965) the Formosa sovereignty issue would still be in hot dispute.

It is difficult now to understand the offhand manner in which the Conference produced the document. Both Churchill and Roosevelt were sensitive students of Anglo-Saxon history. Both knew the force of precedent and the need for scrupulous legality to counterpoise the lawlessness of the Hitlers, the Tojos, and the Mussolinis. Perhaps Roosevelt was simply too eager to get on to the talks with Stalin. For whatever reason, the Cairo Declaration is as noteworthy for historical inaccuracies within the text as for its rhetorical flourishes. The latter made good propaganda, but the former set a dangerous trap. Some of the damage to American interests will never be repaired.

Korea, properly enough, was promised independence "in due time," but the text refers to the Kurile Islands as having been "taken by force." The sentence which lies at the heart of our postwar Formosa Problem reads as follows:

> All territories Japan has stolen from the Chinese, such as Manchuria, Formosa, and the Pescadores, shall be restored to the Republic of China.

Here expediency led the three Heads of State to ignore distasteful facts; treaties again had become "mere scraps of paper."

Japan acquired undisputed title to the Kuriles by a treaty carefully and peacefully negotiated with Russia in 1875. (In return Russia received undisputed title to the entire island of Saghalin, only to lose half of it, by treaty, at the close of the Russo-Japanese War in 1905.) The Korean Kingdom had been simply expropriated in 1910, but at the time Great Britain, China, and the United States conceded Japan's sovereignty and gave it full legal recognition. Manchuria undoubtedly had been seized by aggression, but the Liaotung and Shantung Concessions held by Japan had been taken from Russia and Germany, respectively, in 1905 and 1914, and Japan's position in each of them was recognized and unchallenged by London and Washington in the intervening years. It was somewhat late to cry "thief."

Peking ceded the Pescadores and Formosa to Japan in 1895 in the Treaty settlement made after China's defeat in the Sino-Japanese War.

Britain's Minister to China (Sir Thomas Wade) and a former Secretary of State for the United States (John Foster) were in effect "god-fathers" to the ceding treaty, and the first President Roosevelt presided at the cession of Russian territory to Japan in 1905. The Cairo Declaration therefore seems to imply that these three worthies were parties in grand larceny.

Japan acquired the Pescadores and Formosa as a "war-prize," stolen in precisely the way the United States acquired the Southwest Territory after the Mexican War, or the Philippines and Puerto Rico after the war with Spain. Above all, in 1943 Formosa was not "just a province of China," lately overrun.

Did no one in the Department of State venture to call the President's attention to the dangers inherent in such unqualified promises to alter boundaries and transfer millions of people from one sovereignty to another without due precaution and reserve? The published record suggests that neither the President nor the Prime Minister took Cairo very seriously, and as Robert Sherwood put it "The agreement . . . did not stick for more than ten days." Before the Chiangs had reached home Roosevelt and Churchill had changed their minds about some of the secret commitments made on the Generalissimo's demand.[4] Unfortunately the mind-changing had to do only with active prosecution of the war. Nothing was done to modify the promises of postwar territorial transfers.

Roosevelt, Churchill and Chiang had "divided up the bear-skin before the bear was dead."

II

"Island X"

Operation Causeway: The Nimitz Plan to Seize Formosa

RUSSIA WAITED. In the name of "neutrality" Moscow denied her allies use of Siberian airfields which were needed for an airlift from Alaska to China. We were forced — at enormous cost — to go the long way around by way of India and over the Hump. Once there, our men, planes and supplies were swamped in the morass of Chinese factional policies and corruption. It is little less than a miracle that we were able to achieve what we did in that enormous Chinese hinterland, far from the sea.

General Douglas MacArthur insisted upon a return to the Philippines, a drive northward, island-by-island, to Luzon.

Admiral Chester Nimitz had a double responsibility. MacArthur's forces "Down Under" — in Australia and the southwest Pacific — depended upon Navy support, and while supplying this, Nimitiz was concurrently driving the Japanese from the northern Pacific, clearing the way for direct attack upon the Japanese home islands. He proposed to strike directly westward, seizing Formosa and the adjacent Chinese coastal regions. The cost would be high, for Formosa was protected by extraordinary natural barriers and lay near the Japanese homeland, but this bold move would cut Tokyo's lines of supply to the over-extended Japanese warfront. A successful operation should paralyze the Japanese effort at every point from the borders of India and Burma through Indonesia, Malaya, and Borneo to New Guinea, and throughout the Philippines. In Allied hands, Formosa could then be used as a base from which to cover fleets moving directly to Japan proper, and for air strikes against Japan's industrial cities. We could paralyze all Japanese movement on the mainland.

In late 1943 the Navy began to prepare intensively for the attack upon Formosa, dubbed "Operation Causeway" for code purposes. Undoubtedly the Japanese would put up a fierce defense, and the Formosan people would be caught between hammer and anvil.

Much might depend upon the popular reaction to an Allied appeal for support — for sabotage of the Japanese defense effort and for riots and rebellion within.

The invaders, once ashore, could expect to find a shattered economy, and must be prepared to control and rehabilitate a population of more than five millions. If possible, Formosans should be won to friendly cooperation, to protect the bases which we would use in the final assault upon Japan proper. No one knew how long the Occupation might continue.

With these problems in view the Chief of Naval Operations established an elaborate training program for officers destined for Occupation duty in Formosa. We needed officers ready to assume control and direction of every aspect of the civil economy — a police force, public health and medical services, transportation, education, commerce, and industry affecting essential civilian supply.

The Schools for Military Government at Harvard, Chicago, and the University of Virginia noticed Formosa as part of the Japanese Empire study series, but this was not enough. A special research center was created at the Naval School of Military Government and Administration at Columbia University, and here in the so-called "Formosa Unit," a series of ten *Civil Affairs Handbooks*, operational field maps, and a large body of unpublished training materials were prepared for Operation Causeway.*

From December, 1943, until November, 1944, the Formosa Research Unit supplied basic information to agencies concerned with the anticipated invasion.

We called our island "Island X," thanks to an admiral who shall remain unnamed. Having been "piped aboard" the house on 117th Street, he made a thorough inspection of the five floors, all devoted to research concerning Formosa. He saw a staff of twenty-one officers, eight enlisted personnel and twenty-one civilians working under my general direction. But among the civilians were ten Japanese-Americans — "inscrutable Orientals." Before "going ashore" the admiral carefully closed the doors to my office and in hushed tones directed Captain Cleary and me to diversify the translation work so that the Japanese translators would not know what our prime interest might be, and to refer to Formosa only as "Island X."

Our detailed studies revealed how rich "Island X" was, and how highly organized. The Navy's Occupied Areas Section in the Office of the Chief of Naval Operations was well aware that the Chinese would demand a share in the administration as soon as American forces made it possible for Chiang's representatives to venture in. The Cairo promises were there to haunt us. If Chiang insisted on exclusive control of the civil administration, he would intrude just as attacks upon Japan were rising to a climax, and Formosa itself would be under heavy counter-

* Captain Francis X. Cleary, USN, was in charge of the Officers Training Program. Dr. Schuyler Wallace (Public Administration) and Dr. Phillip Jessup (Law) were co-Directors of the curriculum. Fifty officers, enlisted personnel and civilians formed the Formosa Research Unit, with Lieutenant George H. Kerr, USNR, officer-in-charge and editor-in-chief of the *Handbooks*. Lieutenant Francis Cleaves, USNR, supervised translation of data upon which the series was based. The Department of Commerce prepared an *Economic Supplement* for the Handbook series, and the Department of Agriculture contributed a *Handbook on Fisheries*. The operational maps (on traffic control, public health, water supply, etc.) were based upon Japanese military and land survey maps, supplemented by aerial reconnaissance photos and translated information.

attack from Japan proper. This would create intolerable confusion.

It was therefore proposed to reach an agreement with
Chiang *before* the invasion began. If possible we should secure Chinese acquiescence to an exclusive American military administration pending Japan's surrender and a general postwar
settlement. At most, no more than a token Chinese participation could be tolerated. This was to be a naval show, on an island from which the Chinese had been cut off for fifty years.
True enough the Nationalists had many admirals on the payroll
in the mountains, but they had no navy on the sea. No Chinese
could reach Formosa unless we agreed to take him there.

A special Naval Mission prepared to go from Washington to
Chungking to review the problem. Suddenly, in November,
1944, it became obvious that the high command was no longer
focusing attention on Formosa. The Military Government
training program dropped from high priority to a level of casual consideration. The Research Unit was disbanded, and the
officers and men scattered to other schools and to the field. The
Mission to Chungking was abandoned.

Behind this lay a prolonged and acrimonious inter-service
debate preceding the decision to bypass Formosa. Admiral
Nimitz wanted to cut Japan's supply lines to the south; General
MacArthur insisted that the Philippines must first be liberated.
President Roosevelt, the Commander-in-Chief, must approve
the decision, and this was an election year. MacArthur's not inconsiderable personal following would count heavily at the
polls.

A series of meetings of the Joint Chiefs of Staff brought a
compromise proposal on March 11, 1944. The Navy would undertake a triple thrust; one would carry MacArthur into Mindanao, one would strike at the Japanese in northern Luzon, and
the third would become the main assault upon Formosa. The
occupation of Formosa would be followed quickly by a push to
the China coast. The invasion of Okinawa, dubbed "Operation

Iceberg," would begin as soon as we were well established on the neighboring island.

President Roosevelt decided to visit the Pacific theatre of war to demonstrate that Asia was not "forgotten" as the Chinese charged. Chiang was clamoring for more supplies and more money, but it was clearly evident that he was not using to our advantage what he received by the long, hard route over the Hump. We flattered him with titles — he was "Supreme Commander" of Allied Forces in China — and we put him forward as the leader of a World Power, but there was accumulating evidence of his reluctance to push the land war against the Japanese. His policy was to "trade space for time" while waiting for the United States to defeat Japan by an assault from the sea. Nevertheless, his demands for ever more arms and economic help began to look like an ill-disguised form of blackmail. We needed secure forward bases near the Fukien coast and in north China, but there were hints that "exhausted China" might separately come to terms with Japan.

At Honolulu, July 26, Roosevelt heard Nimitz and MacArthur present the "Luzon *versus* Formosa" arguments. Navy partisans hold that the President appeared to incline toward the Nimitz plan which emphasized Formosa, but at the conclusion of the conference the General asked for a private word with the President. What passed between them is not a matter of public record; if they talked about the autumn season, Roosevelt may have remembered how cold the wind can be about election time. At the termination of the meeting, Roosevelt declared in favor of MacArthur's return to the Philippines.

Detailed logistic plans were ready on August 23, but by this time the Navy's successes in the North Pacific made it possible for the Joint Chiefs to accelerate the program. On September 15, MacArthur was directed to bypass Mindanao and to seize Leyte by October 20. Nimitz reviewed "Causeway" plans and called for reports from his Army and Air Force colleagues. Lieutenant General Simon Bolivar Buckner, commander-designate for ground troops in the Formosa operation, reported that he faced critical shortages, and that he believed the occupation of Luzon after Leyte would diminish the need for the costly assault upon Formosa.

Nimitz then reviewed his plans with Admiral Ernest King, who proposed to the Joint Chiefs of Staff (on October 2) that the occupation of Luzon, Iwo Jima, and the Ryukyu Islands should be given priority, deferring "Causeway" for a later action. On the next day Admiral Nimitz was directed to bypass Formosa and to seize positions in the Ryukyus by March 1, 1945.[1]

This, in brief, is the story of military decision concerning "Island X," where Japanese and Formosans alike awaited in dread expectation an assault which never came.

Bombs Away!

American reconnaissance planes flew over Formosa in the autumn of 1943. The first major bombing strike (on the Hsinchu airdrome) took place Thanksgiving Day. Tokyo could no longer conceal the direct threat of invasion.

The Japanese High Command ordered its forces in China to sever all rail connections leading to the Fukien coast and to destroy all forward bases from which American planes could attack the island. In 1944 a powerful Japanese drive threatened the major American base at Kunming, vital point on the Burma-China airlift route. Chiang's intelligence organization failed to alert the Americans, important forward airstrips were lost and great stockpiles of fuel, equipment and arms had to be destroyed at Kweilin on November 10 as the Japanese actually moved onto the airfield.

Our relations with Chiang went from bad to worse, the Generalissimo's excuses — his doctrine of "defense-in-depth" — were wearing very thin. Even his ardent supporters found it difficult to justify his manifest shortcomings as a warrior. Said one, "defense-in-depth meant simply running away until the enemy is tired out chasing you . . ." This was not the American style of warfare, and since we were paying for the show in China, we wanted positive action. President Roosevelt, tired of Chiang's *prima donna* behavior, in thinly veiled terms demanded active Chinese cooperation or a termination of American aid and supply. But we were preparing for the great push directly against Japan proper and we could not leave our seaborne forces exposed to attack from Japanese bases on mainland China.

At this juncture Washington began to explore means to bring the Chinese Communists into the war on our side. The Red Russians were our unavoidable allies in Europe, and there was no sound ideological reason why the Red Chinese should not be used in the war against Japan. Washington was warned repeatedly of the risks we were then taking in giving all of our military support to one side in China's civil war, under the guise of "aid to China" in the war against Japan. If the Chinese Communists did not become dependent upon us for the supply of arms, they would surely turn to Russia.

An effort was made to involve them in the war with Japan, and to this end Major General Patrick Hurley began a long series of negotiations at Moscow, in Yenan, and at Chungking which finally brought Mao Tse-tung to Chungking — but too late.

Meanwhile Tokyo was well aware of the crisis in Sino-American relations. Shigemitsu Mamoru, Japan's Foreign Minister, proposed that Tokyo should find a formula for truce with Chiang. If Chiang were a neutral, he would have to deny bases to the Americans. Moreover, Tokyo was much more concerned with the Chinese Communists than with the Nationalists, who were "paper tigers." A China divided was to Japan's ultimate advantage.

Japan's High Command knew that spectacular successes in

South China in late 1944 brought only temporary relief. Formosa would soon be the Empire's first line of defense. In a dramatic move to woo Formosan allegiance at this late hour Tokyo announced that, by Imperial Grace, the island would become a prefecture of Japan proper and that prominent Formosans were nominated to the House of Peers at Tokyo. Elections in 1945 would give Formosans full representation in the National Diet.

The Formosan Home Rule leaders had at last won the battle for political recognition within the empire structure, but Japan had lost the war.

With most unusual candor Tokyo announced one day that more than one thousand American planes had attacked the principal Formosan cities on November 14, 1944. The Emperor is said to have exclaimed "So they have come at last!"

This first massive strike was made from carriers ranging far at sea, with some support from aircraft based deep in southwest China. Allied submarines prowling about in Formosan waters rapidly reduced the strength of Japan's merchant fleet. Keelung and Takao (Kaohsiung) were clogged with cargo waiting for ships that never came.

Formosa's skies were seldom free of hostile planes after the great November raid. In late May, 1945, the administrative center of the capital (the *jonai* district) was laid waste by a spectacular "fire-carpet" laid down upon Taipei. The harbors were choked with burned and capsized ships. Keelung and Takao were virtually wiped out. Rail centers were heavily damaged. Hangars, runways and airfield maintenance areas were mauled.

Industrial targets, on the other hand, were only lightly touched. One power plant on the East Coast had been destroyed by storms and floods in 1944, but the major generating plants on the western coast remained in operation. The majority of mills producing sugar, pulp, and industrial chemicals were intact, and so too were the extensive surface installations at the principal mines in the mountains near Keelung.

Hundreds of thousands of leaflets were scattered over the island. These the Japanese feared more than the rain of steel and fire, for they carried messages in Japanese and Chinese urging the Formosans to withdraw support from the Japanese war effort, and promised "liberation." The preamble of the United Nations Charter was reproduced, and added to all the other declarations of human rights.

One leaflet, for example, showed the island of Formosa grasped by a huge octopus, dressed out as a toothy Japanese army officer. Flanking it were idealized portraits of Chiang Kai-shek and Franklin D. Roosevelt. On the reverse, in both Chinese and Japanese, was this message: "The Two Allied Powers in the Pacific Area [the United States of America and the Republic of China] jointly give a firm promise to all Formosan people that their freedom shall be restored by driving out the Japanese Armed Forces."

The Japanese police made frantic efforts to confiscate these subversive materials, but sheer numbers and the wide area of distribution made this impossible. It was entirely unsafe to discuss the crisis, but Formosan eyes were bright with anticipation.

Russia had remained neutral until this time, and so the Japanese sought Moscow's help in exploring the possibilities for a cease-fire, a truce, or a surrender. Thus Moscow knew that Japan could carry on the war no longer.

On July 26, 1945, came the Potsdam Ultimatum, and on August 6 the blow at Hiroshima.

Stalin now thought it safe and profitable to declare war, and on August 9 Russian armies crossed the border into Manchuria. This cynical "declaration of war" five days before Japan accepted unconditional surrender gave the Japanese new cause to hate, fear, and distrust Russia as never before, but it gave the Russians a legal claim upon territories which Roosevelt had promised them, and it gave Moscow a place in the councils, commissions and conferences which would determine the fate of the Japanese Empire.

All Japanese territories were surrendered *to the Allies* on August 14.

Who Will Get the Prize?

There were prizes to be distributed, but no one knew then how many months or years would elapse between capitulation, a peace conference, and an accomplished treaty settlement. The Cairo Declaration had created a series of commitments but had set no time-limit within which they must be fulfilled. At Yalta President Roosevelt had promised the foggy Kurile Islands to Stalin as bait to draw Russia into the Far Eastern war, and Russia was to recover the southern half of oil-producing Saghalin Island as well. Without a by-your-leave from Washington the Russians proposed to strip Manchuria of an immense booty — industrial equipment including factories, mills, mining equipment, laboratories and raw material stockpiles. Theoretically Korea was to have independence "in due course," but in fact it would soon revert to its old unhappy role as a stage for the quarrels of Russia and China, both pushing toward Japan.

The United States piously disclaimed territorial ambitions (were we not giving up the Philippines?) but we decided to take over all the islands in the northern Pacific as an exclusive "trust" and to these we considered adding the Bonin and the Ryukyu Islands.

China recovered Manchuria (stripped of assets worth two billion dollars), and all the highly developed Foreign Concessions were returned to Chinese control. But Formosa was the great prize.

Technical installations and port facilities on Formosa had been badly hit, but the wealth of forests, fields and mines lay undisturbed. There was no threat of famine, for huge stock-piles of unshipped rice and sugar had accumulated during the last twelve months of war. The island was not over-crowded. The normal economy was temporarily disrupted, but the people were well disciplined, well organized, and well trained. By all Asian standards these were a modern people, eager to resume work within a modern technological framework. There would be enormous demand in nearby countries for foodstuffs, chemicals, metals, timber, ceramics, pulp and fiber during a long period of postwar rehabilitation.

All of these Formosa could produce in abundant surplus.

Best of all, for a half century the island had been cut off from the confusion of civil war on the Chinese mainland. There were no local warlords, and no Communist organizations. The few avowed Communists on Formosa had long been in jail, at hard labor, or on probation under surveillance. After many years of intensive anti-Communist indoctrination, a fundamental distrust of Communist promises and ideology had taken root. There were no "hungry masses" to which the Communists might appeal.

When surrender took place there was an upsurging good will in Formosa, an emotional anticipation of return to China, but it was expected to be the "New China" of our propaganda sheets, a China delivered from the past by American power, and guided now by an American alliance. At that moment — brief enough — Americans could do no wrong. In Formosan eyes the defeat of Japan and liberation of Formosa were *American* accomplishments.

Formosans expected that henceforth the island would elect its own government, and that elected representatives would represent the island in the National Central Government at Nanking.

In 1934 the Japanese had granted a mild form of local elective representation in government at about the time the United States promised independence to the Philippines. The Formosans had not been allowed to develop well-organized political parties. There was a minimum of faction at the time of surrender. The elderly and revered Lim Hsien-tang (Rin Kendo) was the recognized spokesman for the Home Rule Movement whose leaders were prepared to assume any tasks the Allies might require of its members during an Occupation.

They were soon to be disillusioned.

The Washington View in 1944 and 1945

The immense sweep of global events in mid-summer 1945 obscured one technical point of importance. Japan was surrendering her empire *to the Allies* and not to China alone. Formosa was Japan's sovereign territory, and sovereignty could not be transferred until a peace treaty could be worked out, agreed upon, and signed.

President Roosevelt's sudden death had shifted to President Truman's shoulders an inhuman burden of worldwide responsibility, and Roosevelt had done virtually nothing to prepare him for it. The new President turned perforce to his supreme military commanders for advice and briefing. Many fundamental decisions of long-range political consequence were made within a *military* rather than a *political* frame of reference.

In the West General Eisenhower's decisions to permit Russia to occupy Prague and Berlin were examples leading on to grave political consequences remaining with us even now. In the Far East General MacArthur's decision to allow the Chinese to occupy Formosa offers a close parallel.

For this the Department of State must be held to account. President Truman knew nothing of Formosa, nor did his Secretaries of State. Younger men in the Department — the "China Firsters" — appear to have made no effort to raise the Formosa question to levels of serious policy discussion for they were determined that there should be no such thing as a Formosa Question.

The Formosa Problem was just as real in 1944 as it is today

— and its development was quite predictable. As an island, settled long ago by Chinese who had left China proper to get away from it and with a centuries-long tradition of *separation* and pioneer independence, Formosa had been easily ceded by China to Japan in 1895. Fifty years of intensive social and economic development under Japanese direction had made it wealthy and had given the Formosan people a standard of living far beyond that of any province in China. Formosan leaders had turned toward the Western world. The separatist tradition had been given form and direction by Woodrow Wilson's *Fourteen Points* and the doctrine of self-determination for minorities. Well-educated young Formosans who could not be reconciled to Japan's harsh colonial police administration left the island in great numbers, but the conservative and moderate leaders — members of an emergent landholding middle class — formed a Home Rule Movement through which they had steadily pressed Tokyo for local self-government within the Japanese Empire frame of reference. They were making progress along these lines — painful and too slow — when Japan approached defeat.

All this was known in the Department of State, but by 1944 it had already taken the decision that China itself must be unified — under whatever government — before outstanding Sino-American problems can be solved. The problem was, of course, "What Government?"

For a century or more the American people had been enamored with China; China's woes had become the White Man's Burden — at least America's burden — in a very special way. Again and again when China's interests were weighed against America's interests, China came out the winner. Our national relations with China had become so intermixed with missionary enterprise and emotional interest that we were no longer capable of an objective valuation. Whenever one suggested that the least we could do would be quietly to reserve American and Allied interests in Formosa until the treaty was drawn up, or until a general settlement had been reached on the Chinese mainland, the suggestion was heard and rejected with a peculiar attitude of moral indignation.

By midyear 1944 competent observers at our embassy in China had concluded that short of a miracle, Chiang Kai-shek was doomed as a "national leader." We might keep him afloat with loans and military supply, but the common people throughout China were tired and disillusioned, and eager to be rid of him. Some other leadership and a viable program had to be found to replace the Generalissimo and the Nationalist Party organization. The Communist leaders who had maintained themselves and their organization in defiance of Chiang since 1927 were still there in the Northwest and were growing stronger, offering the only apparent alternative to Chiang, and promising "reform." Chiang saw to it that no Third Party, non-Communist leadership could emerge within the territory under his control.

But our military leaders in China were intent upon fighting the war with Japan; they wanted no disruptive political upheavals within "Free China," no fuzzy uncertainties in the established Table of Organization or the Chain of Command. Although the Generalissimo was not a very distinguished military figure, by any standard, he controlled the Nationalist Army and maintained at least the outline of an organization. Military men wanted to keep the lid on the Chinese civil war until Japan's defeat.

In 1944 our Ambassador to China was Clarence E. Gauss, a career diplomat intimately acquainted with Chinese affairs and Chinese intrigue. He was surrounded by very able younger officers, conversant in the Chinese language and familiar with the sprawling provinces and their many problems. Although they were not all in accord on proposals to bring about change, they were in general agreement that Chiang Kai-shek was a very weak reed upon which to rest the whole of American policy and interests.

Into this confusion President Roosevelt projected Major General Patrick J. Hurley as "Personal Representative to the President of China." Hurley paused, en route, in Moscow. Foreign Minister Molotov persuaded him that Russia was friendly to Nationalist China and would not support the Chinese Communists in a civil war. Hurley — a singularly vain man who "knew all the answers" — then paused to talk with Communist leaders hiding out in northwest China, at Yenan. Finally at Chungking he conferred with the Nationalists. Out of all this he reported his conclusions:

> (1) the Communists are not in fact Communists, they are striving for democratic principles; and (2) the one party, one man personal Government of the Kuomintang Nationalist Party is not in fact fascist, it is striving for democratic principles . . .[2]

Hurley reached Chungking on September 6; on November 1, 1944, Ambassador Gauss resigned. Hurley, who took his place, learned that he did not enjoy the confidence of career officers at the Embassy. They were prepared to let Washington know that they disagreed with his interpretation of events and policies. Conditions within the Embassy became tense and at last intolerable. It was a situation designed to delight the Nationalists, past masters at fishing in murky waters. Soon the Ambassador was expounding a vigorous pro-Chiang policy. For a year confusion reigned in the Embassy at distant Chungking, and at last, on November 26, 1945, Hurley resigned.

In an extraordinary letter to President Truman the Major General presented a savage indictment of Foreign Service officers who had dared to disagree with him on China policy. This opened a fantastic era in American relations with China, the era of witch-hunts led by Congressmen of the Opposition Party, too long out of power, and in desperate need of issues with which to embarrass the Administration. In his outburst Mr. Hurley excepted a few career men whose views he approved, but others he proposed to drive from government service.

Within a fortnight of his resignation some were summoned to appear before an unfriendly Congressional Committee. The persecution had begun.

It was soon recognized that only colorless reporting and subservient conformity to a pro-Chiang policy would do. Otherwise a Foreign Service officer risked public humiliation, the taint of "loyalty investigations" and possible dismissal from the Service.

With utmost unreality Hurley had advocated a "Nationalist-Communist coalition policy" to bring an end to the civil war in China. General George Marshall was sent to China to try to bring it into effect, but neither side had any desire to honor commitments made at the conference table under General Marshall's patient mediation. When the coalition policy at last proved hopeless and General Marshall condemned both Nationalists and Communists for duplicity, Hurley heaped blame on the Foreign Service officers who had foreseen the failure. Soon all critics of Chiang were cried down as traitors to American interest and probable fellow travelers.

Against this background of impending civil war across the face of China the Formosa problem was scarcely visible from Washington. The Chinese had demanded immediate and exclusive control of the island, insisting that the Cairo Declaration automatically restored sovereignty to China. When surrender came on August 14, 1945, no significant voice was raised in the State Department to dispute the Chinese claim. Well-informed senior naval officers were reluctant to see the United States abandon, without reservation, all Allied rights and interests in Formosa pending a general settlement, but the War Department and the White House were under irresistible pressure to "bring the boys home." Fathers and mothers believed the war was over, Congress agreed with them, and it would have been impossible to win support on Capitol Hill for the development of a new "unnecessary" occupation force in Formosa. Overseas commitments were to be reduced, not expanded. Faced with the immense problems of the occupation in Japan, the Supreme Commander for the Allied Powers at Tokyo, MacArthur, was glad enough to assign to one of these powers the task of taking over. The island was promised to China anyway, so the sooner we rid ourselves of the problem the better. China's cities were seething with vicious anti-American propaganda; any delay in reversion would inflame China's anti-foreign feeling to a dangerous degree.

So at least ran the arguments, correct enough insofar as they went. But it was a dangerous course of reasoning; we were obviously treating the island as a piece of real estate, recently overrun by Japanese forces, and we were treating five million Formosans as chattel property, to be transferred from one sovereignty to another without reference to their wishes.*

The "China first" or "missionary policy" prevailed.

A Struggle for Place in the New Island Government

Meanwhile some arrangements had to be made immediately to ensure order within the island, to arrange for the demobilization of Japan's military forces, and to begin repatriation of the Japanese civil population. These were essentially military matters, and the military establishment in China was not concerned with the political and humanitarian problems involved; the "Japs" were the enemy, and what happened to the Formosan people was their own concern and the concern of the Chinese government.

Major General Albert C. Wedemeyer had replaced General Stilwell as Commander-in-Chief of American Forces in China, and fractious Patrick J. Hurley had replaced Clarence E. Gauss as American Ambassador at Chungking. Gauss and Stilwell were "old China hands"; the Generalissimo and Madame

---

* The Japanese in 1895 had allowed Formosans two full years in which to make the choice of nationality.

Chiang found it less embarrassing to work with newcomers.

General Wedemeyer was directed to arrange with Chiang the immediate post-surrender transfer of Formosa to Chinese control. A new government at Taipei was to be entirely of Chiang's own choosing. There were no strings attached, no reservations made, pending the legal transfer of title. From Wedemeyer's point of view Formosa was merely another Chinese province from which the Japanese had to be evicted, and on this point the Generalissimo and Madame Chiang were not ready to confuse him with the petty details of history.

Formosa's future was a dead issue at the State Department in Washington. At Chungking the Chiang-Wedemeyer Agreement brought to focus a Chinese struggle for power in the proposed new island administration.

Although Formosan expatriates played no significant part in the war, we must look back briefly to understand their position at Chungking in 1945, clamoring for attention as the island's "true representatives."

A majority of Formosan exiles had grown to manhood under Japanese rule in its harshest years. They had supported Lim Hsien-tang's Home Rule Movement, seeking a measure of local self-government within the framework of the Japanese Empire until Japanese police oppression and harassment had proved too much for them. Many left the island in the mid-1920's. In China again a serious division took place; when they could reach no agreement among themselves on "expatriate" policy or programs some simply settled down to earn a colorless living in the larger cities, some, more ambitious, joined with the Nationalist Party, others threw in their lot with the Communists. Now after a score of years in exile, Japan's defeat brought the prospect of an early return to Formosa.

There were dozens of expatriate leagues, parties and societies. The Formosa Comrades Society (formed in 1925) was perhaps the oldest of these. There had been a great proliferation of associations in 1942, on the eve of the Third Peoples'

Political Council Convocation at Chungking. Here the exiles had hoped to win political recognition.

To their chagrin, it was found that laws regulating the Convocation did not provide for representation on behalf of Formosa. It was not considered a Chinese province by the Chinese. Disappointment was sharpened by the fact that all mainland provinces then occupied by Japanese troops were well represented at the so-called PPC meetings.

Here is an early hint of the discrimination shown toward Formosans by their cousins on the mainland, a legacy from centuries of official and scholarly discrimination before the island was ceded to Japan.

In 1943 six principal expatriate groups formed a loose association known as the Formosan Revolutionists League. No prominent Nationalist Chinese gave it the patronage it required. League leaders represented all colors on the political spectrum. On the extreme right stood General Chang Pang-chieh of the Formosa Revolutionary Party, a graduate of Japan's Waseda University (Tokyo, 1921), and a strong supporter of Chiang Kai-shek in Fukien in the 1930's. Working with Chang was Wang Chen-ming, who had been styled "Director of the Kuomintang's Formosa Party Headquarters" in recognition of Party work among expatriates. General Chang hoped to be made first Governor of postwar Taiwan Province.

Toward the other end of the political spectrum stood General Li Yu-pang, a Formosan graduate in the second class of Chiang's Whampoa Military Academy. Li had opposed Chiang during the Great Schism of the Nationalist Party in 1927, and had been detained under a mild arrest until 1935 when he was restored to some favor and given duties in the Political Section of the Nationalist Army organization.

Far to the left within the League stood Hsieh Nan-kuang, vocal and mercurial Chairman of the Formosan People's Revolutionary Federation. He too had left Formosa in the 1920's and later for a time served the renegade Wang Ching-wei, who became Japan's puppet at Nanking. But Hsieh had deserted Wang early enough, and soon showed himself an ardent supporter of Chiang. We have already noticed him in his role as an informant serving American intelligence officers at Chungking and his forehanded effort to belittle potential rivals for high office in post-surrender Formosa.

There were many other less important factions within the League which claimed a membership of 140,000. But when Hsieh and his friends pressed for a share of American aid at Chungking (money, arms and political support) they admitted that only 1000 League members could be found in unoccupied China.

The majority, they said, were scattered about behind the enemy's lines, ready to do the Japanese great hurt if only the League's Chungking members were granted substantial aid on their behalf.

No Formosan carried weight with the Generalissimo. He had other plans and other candidates in mind who had much larger claims upon his patronage.

Chiang's personal power within China derived from his consummate skill in playing off one powerful Party or Army faction against another and his family alliance with the leading industrialists and financiers. In mid-year 1945, the so-called Political Science Group was the faction momentarily in the ascendant at Chungking. When a temporary committee was established to plan for the "Provisional Government of Taiwan Province," a member of this group became the Chairman.

This was Chiang's friend General Chen Yi.

The Chen Yi Appointment: Chiang Shows his True Colors

The appointment had a certain superficial logic to it, for Chen alone among higher Party officers and generals had had a first-hand look at Formosa. From 1934 until 1942 he had been Governor of Fukien Province. In 1935 he had been a guest of the Japanese Government at Taipei, summoned there to attend the ceremonies and Exposition celebrating the fortieth anniversary of Japanese rule in Formosa. On this occasion he had publicly congratulated the Formosans on their "fortunate" position.

On September 20, 1945, organic regulations governing a new administration for the island of Formosa and the Pescadores (Penghu) were promulgated at Chungking. These appeared to give the new Governor-General more sweeping powers than the Japanese governors had ever enjoyed, but soon other branches of government and other Party factions secured special privileges beyond the Governor's direct control. In theory all lines of authority were to be concentrated in his hands, with a few minor exceptions — exceptions that could be cited conveniently if it became necessary to rebut criticism. The Governor would be appointed by the Generalissimo "on the recommendation of the President of the Executive Yuan." The President of the Executive Yuan was then T. V. Soong, Madame Chiang's brother. Obviously Soong Family interests were not to suffer.

Soong recommended, and Chiang appointed, General Chen Yi.

We may point to this as one of the revealing and fateful decisions in Chiang's career. In mid-year 1945, Formosa was a clean slate, as far as the Nationalist Party was concerned. Here was a unique opportunity to show that the "Three Peoples Principles" and the "New Life Movement" were something more than empty slogans used *ad nauseum* to mask incompetence, corruption, and the brutality of totalitarian Party rule. Formosa was rich, orderly, and modernized. There was no Communism and there were no rival political parties. Here during fifty years of hard work, Japan had demonstrated that any province of China, given orderly and relatively honest government, could be brought forward successfully into the 20th century. True, it had been done without Christian missionary guidance, and with no thought for the individual, but this material and social progress was what the missionaries and their friends in the United States for a century had dreamed of achieving for China proper. The keys to the future of Formosa lay in the choice of personnel to fill the top ranks of the new administration.

In making the Chen Yi appointment, the Generalissimo coolly demonstrated that he could not possibly care less for either Chinese or American public opinion. Ultimately, of course, he was obliged to shoot Chen Yi in an attempt to appease the Formosans and thus make the island a little more safe for himself, but these two events (in 1945 and 1950) bracketed a fateful period in which Formosa was abused and squeezed in typical Party fashion. Washington was disturbed by Chen's record, which we must here briefly review.

Chen and Chiang were natives of the same district in Chekiang. Both had attended military school in Japan, both had had Japanese mistresses, and both had been long associated with the Shanghai underworld.

In 1927 Chen Yi was serving with the warlord Sung Chuanfang in his native province, Chekiang, lying southeast of Shanghai. Chiang, then known as "The Young Red General," was in rebellion against the recognized Government of China at Peking. He drove northward from Canton to the Yangtze River, and from there proposed to move on to the national capital far north. Shanghai lay along the way, one of the world's largest cities and the very heart of China's international commercial life. Here lived the bankers and industrialists, in (or conveniently near) the safety of the International Concessions.

Chiang needed money, a great deal of money, to retain the support of his generals, to pay his troops, and to support his faction of the Nationalist Party. The bankers of Shanghai were fair game, and they knew it. But to be useful he must squeeze them, not kill them; he must take Shanghai with minimum violence.

Every city in China in those days knew what to expect if an ill-disciplined, unpaid army came within its walls, and Shanghai was the greatest prize of all.

Chen Yi served Chiang Kai-shek well at this moment. On the one hand he betrayed his colleague, General Sung Chuan-fang, and on the other he is said to have worked out a satisfactory settlement with powerful gang leaders in the Shanghai underworld, ensuring a quiet entry into the great city. Chiang's forces moved through Chekiang Province, unopposed, to enter Shanghai's "back door."

The bankers and industrialists of Shanghai, led by the brilliant Soong-Kung Family group, had now to come to terms with Chiang. His rivals in the Nationalist Party were forming a Leftist government at Wuhan, upriver. Apparently Chiang made a bargain. In return for financial support on a large scale he agreed to exclude left-wing elements and Communists from the new "National Revolutionary Government."

The bargain was cemented by a marriage between Chiang and an "unclaimed jewel" of the Soong Family, the beautiful Soong Mei-ling, aged twenty-six, the youngest sister of T. V. Soong.

Since this extraordinary marriage-alliance lies at the heart of contemporary Chinese history, and has had such a profound though indirect effect upon the fate of postwar Formosa, we must take some note of it here.

The very wealthy Soong family specialized in brilliant and advantageous marriages. Soong E-ling's marriage with Dr. H. H. Kung, a wealthy banker, established a useful link with the oldest and most conservative tradition in China, for Kung is recognized as the "seventy-fifth lineal descendant of Confucius." Soong Ching-ling's marriage to Sun Yat-sen, on the other hand, had established a link with the most dynamic revolutionary-political movement in modern China. In effect, Ching-ling married China's "George Washington," worshiped on every Monday morning throughout the country as "The National Father." Now — in 1927 — the youngest daughter, Mei-ling, through marriage associated the Soong Family with the most prominent young Nationalist Party general. Henceforth the Generalissimo's Party and Army organizations looked after Soong-Kung Family interests within China, and the brilliant leaders of the Soong-Kung Family cultivated and advanced Chiang Kai-shek's interests abroad — especially in the United States — with astonishing success. H. H. Kung, T. V. Soong, and the three Soong sisters were all graduates of colleges and universities in the United States, and as representatives of "China's leading Christian Family" they became the symbols, in American eyes, of all that might be done and must be done to evangelize and transform China.

Promptly following the fateful marriage at Shanghai — a marriage of military ambition with the keenest financial brains in China — members of Madame Chiang's family assumed control of China's economic life. While the Generalissimo marched up and down the country with only modest success as a military leader, he dominated the Nationalist Party Government as *Tsungtsai* or "Leader," the *Duce* or *Führer* of China.

A bald record, in outline form, may suggest the manner in which this small family group concentrated authority within its grasp. The key offices were Transport (Communications), Finance, and Industry, with Foreign Affairs becoming important when opportunities came to manipulate the massive foreign aid programs upon which the regime became dependent in its later years. The Legislative Yuan made the laws, and the Executive Yuan — the Civil Administration — applied them.

Madame Chiang's Family and the Chinese Economy 1927–1948

Brother (T. V. Soong)		Brother-in-law (H. H. Kung)	
Finance Minister & Vice President Executive Yuan	1928–31	Minister for Labor, Commerce & Industry	1927–30
Acting President Executive Yuan	1932–33	Minister for Industry	1930–32

CHESAPEAKE HIGH SCHOOL 5 2 2 6

Brother (*T. V. Soong*)		*Brother-in-law* (*H. H. Kung*)	
Governor Bank of China	1930–33	Governor Bank of China	1933
Board Chairman Bank of China	1935–43	Vice President Executive Yuan	1933
Minister Foreign Affairs	1942–45	Finance Minister	1933–44
President Executive Yuan	1945–47	President Executive Yuan	1938
Governor Kwangtung Province	1947–49	Vice President Executive Yuan	1939–45
		Advisor to President Chiang	1948–

Another member of the family — Sun Fo — served as Finance Minister in 1927–28, as Minister of Railways from 1928 until 1931, and then for sixteen years (1932 to 1948) held the Presidency of the Legislative Yuan, China's law-making body. In 1948 he became President of the Executive Yuan, succeeding T. V. Soong. Minor posts elsewhere in the Government were held by less prominent members of the Family.

Soong, Kung and Sun Fo held concurrently seats in the highest councils of the Nationalist Party and were in strong positions to influence appointments throughout the Administration.

Chen Yi was not often spoken of as a direct agent for the Soong Family, but the record suggests that an association did exist through which, for suitable rewards, Chen advanced and protected the Family interests.

The ease with which Chiang took Shanghai in 1927 placed him in great debt to Chen. Once he had the city well under control, he made Chen Yi Director of the Shanghai Arsenal, a lucrative post, and soon thereafter made him Vice Minister of War.

In 1932 the Japanese attacked Shanghai, anticipating no great difficulties. To their astonishment, however, they met formidable resistance offered by the Chinese 19th Route Army. The Japanese broke off the attack and came to terms with Chiang. Foreign observers reported that the 19th Route Army was the best disciplined and most effective fighting force in China, but it was not one of Chiang's personal organizations, and its commanders were not his men. Instead of rewarding them and using the 19th Route Army in his further campaigns, he ordered it to disband. The commanders refused, and retreated into the rugged Fukien coastal regions. At this Chiang sent Chen Yi to Fukien Province as Governor (or "Chairman") with orders to destroy the rebels. Since they were now cut off from an adequate military supply, Chen found it rather easy to break up the units, and in time exterminated the leaders.

Chen Yi remained in Fukien for eight years (from 1934 until 1942) which was a very long time indeed for an appointment of this sort in China. He had powerful patrons and acted for them as "front man" covering clandestine trade between China and Japan, long after the second Japanese invasion of China had been launched in 1937. Powerful interests in Shanghai were dealing with powerful interests in Japan. They were under the protection of the Japanese Imperial Navy which patrolled the China coast from Shanghai southward toward Hongkong and Canton. (There was an old Sino-Japanese agreement guaranteeing Japan's "special interests" here.) British firms along the coast were aware of a continuing, extensive trade with Japan through Fukien ports. The Japanese invasion of China in 1937 was an "incident" and not a declared war.*

* After 1937 China kept appealing to the United States to "do something" to force Japan to leave China, and cried for economic support and arms. But there was no Chinese declaration of war upon Japan until after Pearl Harbor and after the United States had declared war. A formal declaration would have embarrassed the great Chinese commercial interests, trading secretly with the enemy. I remember with what anger a young Japanese friend at Osaka (in 1939) told me he had just discovered correspondence within his firm disclosing an important private arrangement whereby certain Chinese firms ex-

Governor Chen's principal aide in financial administration was Yen Chia-kan, a soft-spoken, charming personality who is today (1965) Premier of Nationalist China.

Yen Chia-kan, who used to be known as K. K. Nyien, followed Chen Yi into Fukien — or was sent there — in 1938. The 19th Route Army by then had been wiped out, and the province was under a harsh administration. This was a "side door" into China, conveniently kept open until 1942. Trade with Japan was brisk and immensely profitable, but for the average shopkeeper and peasant of Fukien Chen Yi's "Necessary State Socialism" meant harsh exploitation.

Yen served as Chen Yi's principal economic advisor, holding in turn posts as Reconstruction Commissioner, Tax Bureau Director, Finance Commissioner, and Chairman of the Board of Directors of the Fukien Provincial Bank. *

Chen Yi and his Japanese mistress (the "First Lady of Fukien") enjoyed cordial relations with the Japanese naval representatives along the Fukien coast. When at last the Generalissimo ordered General Chen to withdraw (in 1942) it was arranged for them to leave the province with their personal property intact and without interference before the Japanese forces took over the administration at Foochow. At Chungking General Chen was made Secretary-General of the Executive Yuan, under its Vice President, H. H. Kung. After a time Yen Chia-kan became Director of Procurement for China's War Production Board.

---

ported pig-bristles to Japan by way of Foochow in exchange for shipment of small arms and ammunition to the Chinese. My friend's brother had just been killed on the China front.

* His subsequent career, in brief: Director of Procurement, War Production Board (1945); Communications Commissioner, Taiwan Provincial Government (1945–46); Finance Commissioner, Taiwan Provincial Government (1946–49); Chairman, Board of Directors, Bank of Taiwan (1946–49); Member, Council for United States Aid, Executive Yuan (1948); Minister of Economic Affairs (1950); Deputy Chairman, CUSA, (1950–57); Finance Minister (1950–54); Governor of Taiwan (1954–57); Chairman, CUSA (1957); Premier of China, (1963–).

Governor Chen's questionable relations with the enemy might have been tolerated in Fukien if he had not developed "Necessary State Socialism." This was a complex system of state monopolies designed cleverly to drain off local wealth into the pockets of the administrators, with just enough passed to the National Treasury to satisfy officials along the way. Here was perfected the system which Chen Yi later introduced to Formosa, provoking the Formosans to rebellion.

In the period of Chen Yi's governorship the Province of Fukien was systematically looted. Hot-headed students demonstrated, rioting broke out again and again, and Chen Yi reacted without mercy. The brutality with which students were tortured and killed in Fukien set something of a record even for China.

I observed in Washington that some of the most ardent "China First" men in the Department of State were shaken by Chen's appointment to Formosa, for his Fukien record was well known. But by then it was too late; the Chiang-Wedemeyer Agreement had been made. We could only wait and see.

Meanwhile in China the announcement provoked an extraordinary outburst of criticism. The press at Shanghai was filled with outraged comment. Important Fukien guilds joined with expatriate Formosan organizations at Chungking, Kunming, Kweilin, and Liuchow in begging the Generalissimo to cancel the appointment. Open letters of exceptional bitterness were addressed to Chen in the press, demanding that he withdraw, and forecasting disaster if he took the post. There was an undercurrent of disbelief; now at last the Japanese were defeated, and the Government was allied with the most powerful country in the world — the United States of America. There had been so much talk of the future and reform. And now this.

It was charged that Chen would "create a hotbed of fascism in Taiwan, leading to future war." His crimes in office as Fukien's governor were reviewed in great detail — they were horrifying and, alas, they were for the most part true. Chen's traitorous relations with the Japanese were reviewed; he had openly traded with the enemy, inviting Mitsui capital to enter his province, and permitting the (Japanese) South Manchurian Railway Company to exploit the mines and operate the harbors of Fukien. The commercial monopolies (Necessary State Socialism) had bankrupted thousands of small traders. In 1935 Chen had congratulated the Japanese in Formosa, and when war came in 1937, it was alleged, he openly expressed an opinion that China could resist no longer than three months. He had arrested protesting members of the Fukien People's Political Councils, and he had put to death scores of patriotic anti-Japanese students who demanded an end to trading with the enemy and greater resistance in Fukien Province. When at last the Japanese advanced on Foochow city, Chen had surrendered it without a shot, in exchange for an opportunity to withdraw, unhindered, with his ill-gained wealth and his Japanese mistress.

These were the public charges, and Formosa's prospects were grim.

Chen Yi and the Generalissimo ignored the protests. Nevertheless, in his usual method of operations, Chiang took great care to create checks and balances within the new administration. Here and there Chen had to accept subordinates who were not of the "Political Science" clique, and key military command posts went to generals who were not Chen's men. In theory the Governor-General's authority was supreme, but in practice he knew that unfriendly eyes were watching him, and that he had to share out the loot. Chen was above all a political general; with his superior knowledge of Formosa's wealth he was in a position to offer splendid bribes wherever they were necessary to buy support at Chungking, and on the island he could be expected to soothe rivals and silence important critics by "filling their mouths with gold." Small fry could be shot.

The fighting war ended in mid-August, but the formal surrender had not yet taken place. Formosa lay in a strangely unreal state of suspension between two worlds. The island people saw that the United States had defeated Japan, and therefore looked to the Allied High Command.

What lay in the future?

PART TWO

THE CHINESE TAKE OVER

III

The Surrender on Formosa,
1945

Formosa in Limbo

ON AUGUST 15, 1945, the Japanese Emperor broadcast an appeal to his subjects to "bear the unbearable," to accept defeat, and to obey and cooperate with the Allied forces.

On Formosa Formosans heard this with excitement and happy anticipation. Japanese civilians heard it with awe and regret, not unmixed with profound relief. But throughout the Empire, members of the Japanese Military High Command were angry and bitter. To them (on August 17) the Emperor addressed a special rescript using terms carefully chosen to suggest that they had not surrendered to "China" but to "Chungking," where the Chinese *and the Americans* had their military headquarters.* The distinction was a fine one, it was not calculated to please the Chinese, and it was not lost on either the Formosans or the Japanese in Formosa.

Key Japanese officers met at once in Taipei to consider the situation. What "attitude" should military leaders adopt? Some intransigent young officers refused to believe that the surrender broadcast was genuine, or assumed that the Emperor, speaking under duress, would secretly expect them not to obey.

---

* The precise words were ". . . we are about to make peace with the United States, Britain, the Soviet Union, and Chungking" (". . . *Bei, Ei, So narabi-ni Ju-kei*").[1]

They would fight to the death. More than 170,000 well-armed, well-fed and rested troops were there to defend the island. They would be supported by 330,000 Japanese civilians who would certainly retreat to the hills and never surrender. The Army had sworn never to accept defeat. The situation was not only unbearable — it was unthinkable.

For nearly twenty-four hours the Taipei government was gripped in fearful debate. General Ando Rikichi, now commander-in-chief of all military forces and chief of the civil administration, insisted upon a peaceful capitulation. A majority of his officers accepted the imperial decision. A few made their farewells and committed suicide.

Tokyo directed General Ando to consider himself henceforth under General Okumura, Supreme Commander of Japan's military forces in China. This was the first formal indication that Formosa must look thereafter toward mainland China for authority.

From this moment the island people began to build up profoundly emotional attitudes toward China on the one hand, and toward the leading Allied powers — America and Britain — on the other. The Chinese would occupy Formosa. Tokyo could no longer protect the Emperor's subjects. The center of power and authority for fifty years had vanished overnight. Many Japanese had reason to remember and regret the early days of ruthless subjugation — the days and years of Governor-General Sakuma's brutal administration, for example — and many remembered the more recent occupations of Shanghai, Canton and Hankow which followed the rape of Nanking. Aged Formosans for their part recalled vividly conditions which prevailed under Chinese garrison rule in the late 19th century. Everyone knew something of conditions on the mainland, and of the Chinese Army's reputation.

Thus a sense of profound insecurity began to pervade the island. Japan's propaganda had painted British and American soldiers as monsters eager to rape, kill, and plunder, but there had been no demonstration of this. On the contrary, Allied broadcasts and pamphlets promised Formosa a new era of peace and good government — at least something better than life under the Japanese administration.

Here is one of the keys to our present dilemma in Formosa; we had persistently raised hopes and made promises which we could not fulfill.

A veritable flood of American propaganda and world news poured into Formosa after August 15, for it was no longer forbidden to listen to shortwave programs, and local rebroadcasts from Japan covered the island. Fifty thousand radio receivers were tuned in, night and day. This was not an inland province of China cut off from world events, but an island frontier, listening to the capitals of the world. Every pronouncement by the Allied High Command and the least statements of Allied opinion and news commentary were examined with intense concern.

Our compulsive mass-production frame of mind caused Washington to assume that propaganda for any one people in the world was equally good for another. In our eagerness to rally the non-Communist nations, Washington said the same things and made the same promises to Persia and Peru, France and Formosa. Everyone on our side would have freedom, self-government, and a higher income. Too many people around the world believed that we meant to guarantee Utopia and to pay for it.

The ideals set forth in the United Nations Charter were assumed to be promises, underwritten by the United States. Europeans, lately liberated after temporary occupations, merely expected to revert to prewar status and to rebuild shattered economies with American help. The colonial peoples of Southeast Asia demanded independence. The Japanese, at that moment did not know what to expect, and were fearful. The Formosans were filled with great hope; they assumed that having freed them from Japanese rule we were about to restore them to a "New China," sponsored, guided, and brought forward into world affairs by the United States. They knew well enough that Formosa was far ahead of any mainland province in physical development and social well-being, and they looked forward with pride and zest to the part they might play in building a new country.

Few educated Formosans accepted the picture of China so persuasively presented to the American public by Madame Chiang Kai-shek and her public relations agents in the United States, but they did expect Washington to accept responsibility for the arrangements now to be made. The argument ran in this fashion: China had survived as a nation, thanks to American aid, and would continue to be dependent upon American support for a long time to come. Americans would be welcome if they helped China assume control in Formosa. America's sponsorship of China in world affairs was taken as a guarantee that at last the island people would attain political dignity and equality, and that Formosa would become China's most modern model province, a "showcase province" on the maritime frontier.

In the period 1937 to 1940 I had often discussed Formosan aspirations with friends at Taipei, and immediately after my return to Formosa in 1945 I heard these hopes and expectations expressed again many times. Wilson's idealism after World War I (they believed) had led to freedom for the neighboring Philippines; Roosevelt's idealism, they said, was reflected in the UN Charter and must certainly lead to a new and better life for Formosa.

The Japanese on Formosa had a much more immediate reason to hope that the United States would take part in the formal surrender at Taipei. This might be their only guarantee of personal safety. They felt keenly that Japan had been defeated by the United States, with some aid from Britain. They held the Chinese in traditional contempt. Their own adventure in China had been frustrated by time and distance, they felt, and by the unfortunate "accident" at Pearl Harbor. They had not

been defeated by Chinese arms. Allied victory was a consequence of the Anglo-Saxons' superior technology. They de-
spised Chiang and had every reason to fear a Chinese military
occupation. Many prayed that the Americans would be the
first to appear.

In this frame of mind the Japanese prepared for the "unbearable." A career diplomat (Moriya Kazuo), formerly chief of
the Government's Foreign Affairs Section, now became chairman of a Joint Liaison Office established to represent the armed
services and the civil administration. Concurrently a Postwar
Civil Affairs Office was established to register all Japanese
properties and to represent Japanese civilian interests. The
Japanese Army and Navy each created a unit to account for
military property, direct demobilization, and cooperate in repa-
triating officers and men.

Rumor spread that some intransigent Japanese officers proposed a "Formosa Independence Movement." General Ando
branded the idea "a mischievous and dangerous suggestion,"
leading Japanese civilians scoffed at it, but the denials and
scoffings themselves added something to the tension prevailing
everywhere.

General Isayama, Japanese Chief of Staff on Formosa, flew to
Nanking in the first week of September to represent General
Ando at the formal surrender ceremonies in China. Suddenly,
on September 9, the venerable Lim Hsien-tang and four other
prominent Formosans received a surprising message from the
Commander-in-Chief of the Chinese armies, General Ho Ying-
chin, inviting them to represent the Formosan people at Nanking on this day of China's triumph.

At Nanking there were conferences behind closed doors, but
no public disclosure of their nature. Years later (in 1952, at
Tokyo) I attempted to draw from Lim some explanation of this
interlude, but he would say nothing of substance. It was evident only that the Formosans were prompted to petition China
for a special status for Formosa including a proposal that Japanese residents and Japanese technical and economic interests

66   THE CHINESE TAKE OVER

should be given special consideration "in order to assure the continued prosperity of the island." It has been alleged, without documentary proof, that General Ho wanted to isolate Formosa, not unaware that the island would be an exceedingly rich prize for the men who held it if Japan's exit from China prompted a renewal of the mainland civil war. Any one of Chiang's rivals would have been delighted to have a base there, and Chiang, of course, knew this as well as they.

Throughout September the interim "lame-duck" Japanese government at Taipei functioned with remarkable efficiency. Formosan villagers here and there took revenge on hated individual local Japanese policemen, but these isolated beatings were not numerous and none was fatal. Public order was well maintained.

Economic controls remained in force, keeping a tight rein on inflationary pressures. American forces preparing to enter Japan announced an Occupation exchange rate (fifteen yen for one American dollar) which was to apply throughout the Empire, including Formosa. This prompted many island people to convert their money into goods as a hedge against spiraling prices; rationed and restricted goods were released slowly.

There was an intensive drive to clear the way for rebuilding. High employment rates were ensured by shifting mobilized wartime labor forces to the immense tasks of reconstruction. City Planning Commission engineers and draftsmen worked long hours overtime to perfect blueprints for projects which could be undertaken as fast as the rubble could be cleared away, public services restored, and homes reconstructed. Evacuees streamed back into town. The railroads were soon in operation, keeping to regular schedules. A major effort was made to clear the waterfronts at Keelung and Kaohsiung and to restore service at the principal airfields.

When would the first Allies arrive? What would they demand? Who would they be?

September Liberators

On September 1 the first Allies appeared in Keelung harbor aboard a Japanese subchaser which they had commandeered at Amoy. Three young Americans came ashore with two Chinese who called themselves "colonels." They were followed by a retinue of cooks, body-servants, bodyguards and signal men. Two days later a fourth American joined them, coming in with his own retinue aboard a Chinese junk.

The four Americans described themselves as an advanced Prisoner-of-War Contact Team. Each man of the group, from colonel to cookboy, went heavily armed and traveled only in pairs. From the moment of landing they surrounded themselves with an air of conspiratorial secrecy.

Japanese officials hastened forward to greet these first representatives of the conquering Allies. Uncertainty hung over the meeting, for the Japanese did not know what to expect nor did the nondescript newcomers find it easy to relax. It was soon obvious that they carried no great authority but nevertheless they were offered full Japanese cooperation.

They needed housing and housing was found at once. The Plum Mansion, Formosa's most luxurious geisha house, fully equipped, promptly became their "home away from home."

The Chinese took up quarters in one wing set aside for "Colonel Chang" and "Mayor Huang of Amoy," servants and cooks were established in the service wings and the Chinese guards, armed to the teeth, took up watch around the grounds.

Sharp-eyed Formosans and Japanese intelligence agents watched every move made by the members of this strange establishment. Americans went one way and the Chinese went another. None showed more than perfunctory interest in the Allied prisoners of war.

They demanded money for local expenses. After some discussion the Japanese authorities took them to the Bank of Tai-

wan where three million yen in public funds were transferred
to a special account opened for their benefit. This was the
equivalent then of about $200,000 at the official rate; it should
have taken care of most local expenses for the entire group, but
within two days two-thirds of the deposit was withdrawn and
turned over to the mysterious Colonel Chang. *

It was soon established that the Americans were working
with the Generalissimo's dread Bureau of Investigation and
Statistics or BIS, known to Americans in wartime China as
"Chiang's *Gestapo*." Under General Tai Li the BIS investigations were known to be sometimes very brief and at bayonet-
point. On the mainland Tai Li's first duties were to eliminate
Chiang's personal enemies and more important critics and to
weaken political opposition through methods of terror. As a
wartime measure President Roosevelt had approved a secret
agreement enabling certain American cloak-and-dagger groups
to work closely with the BIS.

On Formosa the Americans served merely as a front for the
activities — the "investigations" — of Colonel Chang and
Mayor Huang of Amoy. The latter were probing the local political situation, noting the names and records of Formosan
leaders who had shown themselves bold enough to demand a
voice in local government under the Japanese administration.
Such men would bear watching. They were also taking notes
on wealthy Formosans who might be worth blackmailing at a
later date under charges of "collaboration with the enemy."

While Chang and Huang were furtively busy in the back
streets the young Americans were in the Taipei markets buying
up huge quantities of canned goods, textiles, liquor, matches
and other consumer goods stockpiled at Taipei. The subchaser
shuttled back and forth between Keelung and the mainland for
a period of weeks delivering cargo to starved Chinese coastal
markets. There such commodities commanded astronomical

---

* All monetary values in the text hereafter refer to the American dollar (US$)
unless otherwise noted. The Chinese National Currency dollar (CNC$) and the
Taiwan yen (TY) are indicated as required.

prices at the time. When local Taipei prices began to soar Japanese officers charged with rationing and price controls lodged a protest with the young Americans but were simply laughed off; they were "enemy Japs," and who cared about the Japanized Formosans?

On September 5 an American naval task force stood off Keelung. Planes dropped orders directing preparation for a swift evacuation of all POW's. Destroyers picked their way in through the choked harbor and within two days approximately 1300 men were taken off, to be flown to Manila at once. A British hospital ship came in to receive about 100 men too ill for transport by air.

This activity had the substance of genuine authority and pointed up clearly the character of the mission so happily bedded down in the Plum Mansion.

The Japanese leaders awaited word on Surrender procedures, but none came from the Allied High Command at Tokyo or from the China Theatre Headquarters on the mainland. Formosa had become a lost island.

September 10 brought a third American deputation, a team of fifteen officers and men who flew in from Kunming, China, to represent the U. S. Office of Strategic Services (OSS). They displayed no clear authority, but again the Japanese knew precisely how to extend the most charming hospitality. The OSS team were installed in the Rose Mansion, a suburban geisha house second only to the Plum Mansion in the elegance of its appointments. The Commanding Officer, an Army major, had no authority to deal with the government.

The two teams, wearing the Plum and the Rose as their colors, met infrequently and then only with stiff formality.

The newcomers — the OSS team — made no demand for funds. On the contrary, they were a quite legitimate group, but were not authorized to deal with the Japanese who so eagerly awaited someone — anyone — who could establish a basis for authority in this strange situation.

The OSS team came well supplied with barter goods —

American canned goods, cigarettes, beer, vitamin pills and Atabrine tablets — which were extremely valuable in trade for intelligence data. Soon team members were scouring Formosa for political information, especially anything concerning Communists. Formosans who could speak a little English and Japanese eager to curry favor, began at once to supply notes for OSS reports to Washington. Since genuine Communists were rare (they were still under lock and key) information was in short supply.

When later in Washington I read some of these OSS reports I could see clearly how hard the local informants had worked to supply the deficiency — I could in some instances identify the informant by the stories he told — and again in Formosa in 1946 Formosan friends liked to recall how easy it was to obtain a pack of cigarettes or a can of beer by fabricating a story for the OSS.

Many personal scores were paid off in this way. Unchecked informants were happy to draw attention to any dissident Japanese or Formosan who had been labeled "communist," "radical" or "subversive" under the old regime.

In certain noteworthy cases, I later discovered, the Americans were being guided along basic lines of inquiry drawn from wartime reports obtained at Chungking, and prominent among them were reports from the busy pen and fertile mind of Hsieh Nan-kuang.

A fourth American group followed close on the heels of the OSS team in mid-September. This was the competent and sober U. S. Graves Registration Unit, commanded by an Army colonel. The men settled at once into a modest private dwelling in the suburbs and began their melancholy and difficult assignment. It was their duty to search the mountains and plains for the bodies of fallen airmen and the graves of prisoners of war, retrieving their effects, identifying wreckage, and documenting finds.

The Chinese Take Over — with Some Help

For a full six weeks Formosa was in limbo; Formosan leaders cooperated with the leading Japanese and both community groups got ahead with the stupendous task of clearing up the rubble and getting factories, railroads and power lines into operation once more. The markets were open and food was coming into the towns without interruption. The Japanese policeman — a very polite fellow these days — was still on duty. But the three American groups now on the island, commanded by a naval lieutenant, an OSS major and an Army colonel, had no authority to speak for the American Government, China, or the Allied Command.

At Chungking General Wedemeyer was preoccupied with the enormous problems of Manchuria and North China where the Russians had begun to loot the factories and the Chinese Communists were taking over with Russian help. The transfer of Formosa was a minor affair, a tidying-up after war. Nevertheless, Chiang and Chen Yi needed help. China had no ships and few planes — and there were those well-disciplined Japanese to be faced.

We cannot doubt that both the Generalissimo and Chen Yi recalled the "metal in the islanders" which had given Japan such a rough experience after 1895 — the "cage of wild animals" that must be tamed. And there were 170,000 well-rested and highly disciplined Japanese troops waiting there.

To help the Chinese Wedemeyer created an American "Army Advisory Group" at Chungking, placed it under command of an aging colonel, and directed him to assist in planning for the transport of Chinese troops to Formosa and the repatriation of Japanese forces. As an Assistant Naval Attaché reporting to the United States Embassy in China, I was assigned to this group. The Army's *Strategic Survey of Taiwan (Formosa)* and the Navy's *Civil Affairs Handbook Series* (both of which I had edited) were the group's principal sources concerning the island. It soon became apparent that the Chinese members of the group found these texts invaluable. No such encyclopedic data — more than 1300 pages — could be found in Chinese references.

On September 30 (forty-six days after the surrender) a Colonel Chang of the Chinese Air Force was escorted to Taipei for a brief survey. He found the Japanese not only docile but eager to establish a basis for government. He saw that the several American teams were going about their business without hindrance. It seemed safe enough.

On October 5, therefore, an "advance team" flew to Formosa. The nominal Chief of Mission was Lieutenant General Keh King-en, with his aides and an escort of about one hundred American officers and men, the so-called Advisory Group. A few days later they were joined by about 1000 Chinese gendarmes — a "Peace Preservation Corps" — ferried across the Formosa Straits in commandeered Japanese ships under American direction.

In his first public address General Keh directed the Japanese to "carry on as usual," set October 25th as the date for the formal surrender ceremonies, and then set the tone for the Chinese occupation of Formosa.

Formosa is (he said) a "degraded territory" and the Formosans are "a degraded people." The island was "beyond the passes" (kuan wai), beyond the pale of true Chinese civilization.

Formosans noted this loud echo from the 19th century but its chilling implications were obscured in the general elation with which everyone welcomed the war's end and greeted the beginning of a new era. The day of Home Rule was at hand. Things would be put right on the mainland soon enough, with American help. Vast Japanese properties would now be confiscated, to be redistributed amongst Formosans. Tens of thousands of acres of good land expropriated by the Japanese since 1896, factories which had been built and operated by grudging Formosan labor, and mercantile enterprises which had supplied

Formosan needs through Japanese-held monopoly organizations — all these and much more would now revert to the Formosan government and people. Or so they thought.

It is difficult to convey in print the atmosphere of great expectation which enveloped the island. This was much more than the end of four years of global war, or of eight years of war in China; it was the end of fifty years of humiliation. General Keh's face-saving bombast could be ignored, for it was obvious to one and all that the Chinese were utterly dependent upon the United States. Keh and his Peace Preservation Corps had reached Formosa aboard American planes and ships, they rode about in American jeeps, and surrounded themselves with guards equipped with American arms.

Whatever came to pass hereafter would be attributed by the Formosans to American policy.

Elements of the United States Seventh Fleet escorted troopships into Keelung and Kaohsiung on October 15. Aboard were the 62nd and 70th Divisions of the Chinese Nationalist Army, numbering in excess of 12,000 men. They were acutely conscious of the presence of Japanese troops concentrated inland somewhere near the ports.

They flatly refused to go ashore. At Keelung Chinese officers begged the astonished Americans to send an advance unit overland — an American unit, of course — through the narrow valleys leading to Taipei some eighteen miles away. The Chinese officers had heard that vengeful Japanese suicide squads lurked in the hills. Only a rancorous argument forced the Chinese to accept their fate and go ashore. At Kaohsiung the Americans, eager to empty the transports, had to threaten bodily ejection of the Chinese troops before their reluctant passengers would "venture into the tiger's lair."

It was an inauspicious beginning, made the more so because these incidents were witnessed by the Formosans. Word soon spread, and lost nothing in the telling. Formosans along the way laughed at the shambling, poorly disciplined, and very dirty Chinese troops. It was evident, they said, that the "victors" ventured into Formosa only because the United States stood between them and the dreaded Japanese.

Much evil and many individual tragedies were to spring from these expressions of open scorn, for the mainland Chinese were losing face, dearer than life itself.

A Matter of "Face" at Taipei

At daybreak, October 23, an American plane left Chungking for Shanghai, bearing Governor-General Chen Yi and his official party. Crowded aboard were the General's plump Japanese mistress, his bodyguards, a number of secretaries, interpreters and executive officers. Commissioner Yen Chia-kan was not there, but in the pre-dawn hours at the airfield his wife had smuggled herself, six children and an immense baggage aboard the plane. She stoutly refused to leave. She wanted a free ride to Shanghai and was desperately eager to leave gloomy Chungking. The plane was grossly overloaded, but room was somehow found aboard for the Chief of the U. S. Army Advisory Group and myself, the Assistant Naval Attaché. It was an American plane, but we were obviously considered rather excess cargo.

We paused at Shanghai overnight, off-loading the ladies, the children and much of the baggage. During the "victory" feasting that evening, I found myself singled out for flattering attention by a personable, graying individual in civilian clothes who introduced himself as "Admiral S. Y. Leigh." He was identified to me later as Li Tsu-i, one of a group charged with managing T. V. Soong's affairs in Shanghai throughout the Japanese Occupation. I was to meet him again and again in Formosa.

Agents reported to General Chen Yi that a minor crisis had

already developed at Taipei between the Chinese military and the American supporting group. Again it was a question of face.

General Keh had found the Japanese Army leaders were preparing to transfer lands, buildings, equipment and foodstocks to the Chinese Army, and the Japanese Navy offices were making ready to relinquish properties to the Chinese Navy, which then existed principally on paper and on the Government's payrolls. But the Japanese had no separate Air Force, hence there were no properties lying about to be transferred to the Chinese Air Force, China's most modern and most pampered service.

The Chinese Air Force officers at Taipei were disgruntled. To remedy the deficiency they simply posted notices that the CAF was taking physical possession at once, of the northern quarter of Taipei City, lying near the airport — a huge block of urban real estate — plus hundreds of acres of suburban and rural land nearby. All residents were ordered to get out within forty-eight hours.

It is possible that the Air Force could have had its way somewhere inland in China proper among an illiterate, unorganized, and inarticulate peasantry. Here they took the view that Formosa was enemy territory; had not General Keh himself said that the Formosans were degraded "non-Chinese" people?

At Taipei these arrogant young officers met instant and vocal opposition. General Keh professed astonishment at the outcry. Formosans swarmed in to appeal to him and to the American officers assisting him. The Americans foresaw trouble, they had already had their fill of Chinese Air Force arrogance, and they saw the basic injustice of this outrageous confiscation. They strongly recommended prompt cancellation of the CAF order. General Keh compromised, denied the Air Force colonels the coveted, crowded urban real estate, but left them temporarily in control of a vast tract of rural and suburban property.

Thwarted young officers angrily and loudly denounced "American meddling." The principal spokesman declared pas-

sionately that he would "run every American out of Formosa
— at gunpoint if I have to!" *

In this unpleasant atmosphere we began the joint Sino-American occupation of Formosa. From the very beginning the
problem of face bedeviled the Nationalist Chinese. It was apparent to all — including all Formosans — that the Nationalists
were totally dependent upon the United States. They reached
the island aboard American transports, and American arms and
subsidies enabled them to stay. The Air Force incident set the
pattern for many more to come.

I assume that while General Chen Yi was at Shanghai he was
told that Formosans and the Japanese on Formosa were jeering
at Chinese troops, stumbling ashore in disorder. Worse, the
Formosans were hailing Americans as their "true liberators."

American indifference to the importance of Formosa was reflected in the casual way in which we were sent off to witness
the Surrender at Taipei. On the morning of October 24, as I
stood by our plane at Shanghai waiting to board, the American
pilot strolled over, produced a map, and asked me if I could tell
him at which end of the island we were to land, and at what
field. He had simply been ordered to "Fly a bunch of gooks
to Formosa." He was surprised to find two American officers
aboard.

Our flight across was uneventful. It was a radiant October
day. I was forward in the cockpit as we flew over the Tamsui
estuary, circled the city and came down on the Sungshan field.
Crowds lined the highway leading to the airport, and flags flut-
tered about the terminal building.

---

* Lt. Col. Lin Wen-Kwei, told a different story: Boasting that he was the first
junior officer to become General Chennault's private secretary, and noting
that he was now assigned to the Chinese Delegation at the UN, Lin wrote:

> I was appointed as a commanding officer to lead the C.A.V. to take For-
> mosa before the Chinese Army and Navy could land there. After I had
> built up the first C.A.V. headquarters in Formosa and arranged everything
> for our landing troops (the Chinese army and navy landed two months
> after I took the island) I began to receive the Japs Air Force in Formosa.
> I worked very hard for six months . . .[2]

From the moment our plane touched down at Taipei Chen Yi and his men pursued a course designed to lower the United States in public esteem wherever it could be done.

A great parade had been arranged for the Governor-General's reception. Leading Formosan citizens were on hand to greet the General, office workers were lined up with appropriate banners, and hundreds of school children had been turned out to welcome the "liberators." They had been standing many hours in the sun.

When Chen had taken the salute and had been properly greeted by Advance Party members, we moved on to the motorcade. General Chen quite properly rode near the head of the procession, with the senior American officer somewhere near him, but our own escorts had faded away, eagerly scrambling for space as near the General's car as possible. Other Americans in the Advisory Group and the Americans who had brought him over from Chungking and Shanghai were left to find their way to the fourteenth and last car in the line.

General Chen's car moved off, and as it passed along the highway toward the city the school children and clerks waved their flags and shouted "Banzai!" three times. But when the Americans at last came along, tailing the procession, there was a prolonged roar of applause and acclaim.

Along the way our battered conveyance failed us, stopped, and had to be abandoned. The crowds thought it great fun, crowding about us in cheerful excitement to push it to the side of the road. By the time another car had been found to take us on to town, General Chen and his party had long since disappeared.

The Colonel thought it all very typically Chinese ("What do you expect?") but I sensed in this small incident — a small unnecessary official discourtesy — the presence of a desire to cause the Americans a public loss of face at every opportunity.

The Formal Surrender, October 25, 1945

The military men who had come in to supervise repatriation of the Japanese forces were scarcely aware that they witnessed the end of a remarkable era and the beginning of a new period, fraught with dangers for American interests in China and in Asia.

A few members of the U. S. Army Advisory Group were invited to attend the ceremonies, and quite by chance a roving Presidential economic survey mission flew in for a day's rest and recreation. Each member carried impressive visiting cards which showed "White House, Washington, D. C." as his official address. Edwin J. Locke, Jr., chief of this odd mission, and his Department of Commerce aide, Michael Lee, presented themselves at the Civic Auditorium for the surrender ceremonies.

General Chen Yi was on familiar ground, for in this building, in 1935, he had helped to celebrate the fortieth anniversary of Japanese sovereignty in Formosa, and it was here that he had congratulated the Formosans on their good fortune to be Japanese subjects.

On this second occasion Chen Yi's address in Chinese was to be broadcast, with an English translation to follow. I was asked to check the English text, and politely called the interpreter's attention to the fact that although the speech hailed China's triumph in defeating Japan and recovering Formosa, there was no mention, at any point, of the part played by the United States in this affair. With some hesitation, a sentence was introduced into the English version, acknowledging American participation.

General Ando Rikichi signed and sealed the surrender documents.

The fateful day closed with feasting, fireworks and a great parade. Celebrations lasted for a week. Chinese soldiers erected triumphal arches over the main avenues of the city, hacking down the nearest garden trees to provide frames and leafy decoration. Long afterward, these dilapidated arches stood in the roadways, and when they fell, gaping holes in the macadamized streets were there to remind us of the day of triumph.

General Ando was sent under arrest to Shanghai to be tried as a war criminal, and there, in prison, he committed suicide.

IV

Americans in Uniform

The American Image: the "God-Country"

MANY THOUGHTFUL FORMOSANS greeted the surrender with deep emotion — a mixture of elation, relief, and extraordinary anticipation of good things to come. Between World War I and World War II Formosa's most influential leaders had talked of Home Rule, of self-government within the Japanese Empire frame of reference. Now the dream was going to come true, but even better, it would be Home Rule within the framework of "New China," thanks to the United States Government and the American people.

The United States was sometimes referred to as the "God-Country." Nowhere in the world was American prestige higher — and by the same token, nowhere since then has disillusionment been so keen and bitter.

It must be remembered that the Formosan people knew much more about the United States than the American people ever knew about Formosa. There was a high literacy rate, a varied press, and some 50,000 radio receivers, many of them attached to community public address systems. Just before World War II news concerning the United States came second only to news of Japan proper in the daily press, and far ahead of coverage for news of China and the rest of the world. I recall, for example, that during the presidential campaign in 1936 the newspapers at Taipei had carried maps of the United States showing electoral college divisions and the voting forecasts. In the public schools Lincoln and Washington were schoolbook heroes, and among some conservative older Formosans Woodrow Wilson's ideas of self-determination as a right for minorities were the Holy Writ of the Home Rule Movement. Young Formosans in the higher schools often discussed the "good fortune" of the Philippines as a possession of the United States.

Our wartime propaganda filtered into Formosa through clandestine radio receivers here and there, and millions of propaganda leaflets, air-dropped after 1944, bore pledges of liberation, the text of the "Four Freedoms" and the Cairo promises.

At the moment of surrender the United States was all-powerful. Washington sponsored China before the world and backed the Generalissimo. All eyes were on American representation.

The United States showed many faces in Formosa in 1945 and 1946; there were the military representatives, the Consular group, the UNRRA team, missionaries, and the miscellany of visitors who flew in and out on special missions and private business.

It should be understood that the ordinary Formosan man-in-the-street drew no distinction between American nationals and the nationals of many lands who made up the United Nations Relief and Rehabilitation Administration group (the UNRRA team) or the Spanish, Canadian, British and American missionaries. They all spoke English, hence they all must be "Americans."

At times the "American image" became a little spotty. Individual heroes emerged during the cholera epidemic of 1946 and the rebellion and massacre of 1947, but there were also toadies and thieves, and one practicing sadist to lend a gamey note to the after-hours stories.

There was always, too, the unpredictable behavior of overnight visitors who take leave of good manners when they set foot in a foreign country. Some of us will not forget the day that a prominent Congressman, wandering about Asia, was taken to Keelung on tour. Seeing a ceremonial crowd en route, he insisted upon pushing his way into a home in which a funeral was being held; he had always heard about Chinese funerals and coffins, he said, and he wanted to see one.

All Eyes on the Americans in Uniform

The "military image" was the first to come before Formosan eyes. Inevitably the conduct of Americans in uniform was compared with that of Japanese and Chinese soldiers.

Long before the surrender the Formosans had noted the absence of Chinese soldiers in the long lines of haggard Allied prisoners brought ashore, paraded into POW camps, and put to work on public projects. More than 600 flyers had crashed on the mountains and in the fields of Formosa, or had washed up in wreckage from the sea — but there were no Chinese observed among them. Had the Japanese shot all Chinese POW's out-of-hand? Or did few Chinese take part in forward-thrusting action along the China coast, at sea, and in the air over Formosa?

The Formosans commented on this "evidence" that Formosa had been liberated by the Western Allies and not by the Nationalist Chinese, whose military virtues they were inclined to belittle. Their dislike of the bedraggled, undisciplined Nationalist garrison forces was unconcealed.

American GI's ashore on Formosa offered a marked contrast. Each day the Chinese newcomers saw evidence of the popularity of American officers and GI's alike. The Formosans made no attempt to conceal their preferences. The Americans, on their part, soon enough had many occasions to show contempt for the riff-raff which our ships and planes were dumping on the island, and to show sympathy for Japanese and Formosans who had to put up with the marauding Chinese soldiers.

The Nationalists quite naturally were angered. The loss of face was insufferable. The Chinese Air Force colonel's threat to "run every American off the island" and the small discourtesy at the airport on October 24 were minor indications of a very deep-running emotional resentment. Unfortunately the officers who commanded the Advisory Group could not or did not comprehend the importance of face in the Orient, nor realize that the Group was under the keenest scrutiny at every moment. As far as the Formosans were concerned at that time it *was* the United States.

With an amused "Big Brother" tolerance the Commanding Officer took the view that we were working with a rather childish people; if the silly Chinese wanted to pretend that they had "won the war" it really did not matter very much. After all, Formosa would be their show in the future, we knew well enough how they reached the island, and we were not going to be around very long.

Our billeting difficulties illustrates the problem again, and the ease with which Americans tended to yield to their "Little Brothers." The American officers ignored it — a temporary problem; the incoming Chinese, on the other hand, manipulated the housing question to make public a demonstration of their contempt for the meddlesome foreigners.

The Advance Team had spent twenty days preparing for the Governor-General and his escort. In that period Chinese generals and colonels and civilian officers of the new regime had staked out claims upon scores of large properties. Some were official residences attached to departments of government or the large corporations. Some were handsome private homes.

From my "imperialist" point of view I thought the circumstances justified and required adequate housing for the representatives of the United States. There were dozens of large confiscated houses, occupied by squatters, which would have made dignified temporary headquarters for the Military Advisory Group and adequate quarters for a permanent American establishment at Taipei when the time came to reopen a consulate on the island.

But the American officers made no suggestions or demands, taking what was assigned to them without a murmur. The Colonel commanding and his Chief of Staff were housed well enough in the official residence of the Bank of Taiwan, spacious, well-kept, and — like the Plum Mansion — completely furnished. But the Colonel's effective working staff (the lieutenant-colonels and majors who had so angered the Chinese Air Force) were assigned quarters in the office building of a pineapple company. True enough, the American Government had long ago rented and used the building for the American Consulate, but even then it was inadequate. During the war it had been remodeled. Now officers slept in the old upstairs residence kitchen and shared an outside toilet with the servants. Innumerable hangers-on crowded about to watch the foreigners and tap the food supplies. Our doctor, a major in the Medical Corps, called the place a "pig-pen," but since these were temporary quarters, and the men spent much of the time in suburban hotspring hotels, the problem was not serious. But from the Chinese point of view we definitely had "small face."

Our enlisted men were quartered in the suburban barracks vacated by the prisoners of war, but the junior officers were happily at home in an undamaged downtown hotel-restaurant, not so fine as the Plum or Rose Mansions across the city, but nevertheless served from an excellent kitchen.

Relations between the American military group and the Chinese Nationalist military organization were officially polite but strained, and a series of ugly after-hours incidents left no doubt that our presence was most unwelcome to Chen Yi's men. For example, on one occasion at midnight a number of young Chinese officers, well fortified with liquor, stormed at the doors of the American officers' quarters in downtown Taipei, spoiling for a brawl and threatening to "shoot up the establishment." There were two instances, at least, in which Chinese military trucks attempted deliberately to force American jeeps over embankments on the twisting mountain road to Grass Mountain in the suburbs. At Keelung on one occasion I was taking on tour a visiting Captain from the Office of Naval Intelligence at Washington when our way was blocked by a Chinese Nationalist officer who refused to move from the road, cursing, shaking his fist, and making an obvious play for attention and face before the gathering crowd. He decamped quickly enough when we moved to leave the jeep. The crowd cheered.

The outpouring of gratitude toward America was at times embarrassing. Just after the formal surrender, I was walking in the countryside near Taipei when I saw a child run into the field to alert his mother. She hastened to the embankment, bringing her daughters. Clambering to the road and removing wide straw hats they bowed again and again, hailing me as "Amerika-san! Amerika-san!" — "Mr. America" — and thanking me in Japanese "for what America has done."

Not far away on another day I passed a half-ruined house and family temple, obviously the home of a well-to-do landholder. An elderly man hurried out, urged me to stop for a cup of tea, and offered to show me through the grounds and temple. The damage had been done by an American bomb which had missed its target nearby, one family member had been killed, but there was no bitterness. It could not be helped; thanks to America, said my host, Formosa was now free, and could return to China. He insisted that I accept a handsome glazed tile, fallen from the temple roof, as a memento of our hour together and the family's gratitude.

Some weeks later I climbed a thousand steps to revisit a Taoist temple high in the hills near the city. I had known it well before the war. At the foot of the mountain I paused for a cup of tea and a talk with hospitable villagers. As I went on my way several bearers with shoulder-poles and hampers passed me, smiling and bowing without breaking a quick swinging pace. At the temple I found preparations for a feast going forward. Food sent up from the village had been spread to welcome me. Before it was served, however, the chief priest asked me to stand before the altar. With fellow priests and acolytes he then gave thanks, praying for peace and prosperity in the world and invoking blessings upon the United States. Forming up a chanting procession they burned incense and paper prayers, while moving round and round the sanctuary in which I stood. This was "God Bless America" in a new version and new setting, but it was obviously a very genuine display of emotion coming from the heart. This was only the first of many times in which I heard Formosans speak of America as a "god-country," meaning a nation that has the character and personality of protective divinity.

In the course of feasting on that occasion the conversation turned for a moment to a series of mysterious murders which had taken place on the streets of Taipei in mid-October. Several Japanese women had been waylaid and killed, but neither robbery nor rape appeared to be the motive. Although the Formosans were glad to see the Japanese become the underdogs for a change, they were shocked at the brutality of these killings. It was evident to me that there was no vicious anti-Japanese sentiment infecting the general community.

Months later we learned that the mysterious "colonels," Huang and Chang — General Tai Li's dread Gestapo agents — had approached responsible Formosan leaders at about this time, proposing a general massacre of the Japanese civil population. They set the date for a "spontaneous" uprising to take place on the night of October 27.

The Formosan leaders would have none of it; this was no longer 19th-century China, and the widespread dislike of Japanese was not a deep-seated hatred. Tai Li and his agents had misjudged the Formosan temper, and certainly they seemed to have forgotten the presence of 170,000 Japanese soldiers lying idle in camps not far away.

What Returning Formosan Labor-Conscripts Had to Say

Soon after the war's end labor conscripts began to return to the island. Some came home with tales of American military conduct in the field and of American attitudes toward prisoners of war. Japan's military fanatics had preached the "disgrace" of surrender, insisting that it was better to commit suicide than to be taken prisoner, and that prisoners deserved only the harshest treatment. The treatment accorded prisoners by the Americans, therefore, was a welcome surprise. For example, sixteen young Formosans, taken prisoner in the Netherlands East Indies by the 158th Regimental Combat Team, worked thereafter faithfully for their American captors and earned a letter of commendation from the Commanding General. Of this they were enormously proud. In it the Commanding General (Hanford MacNider) noted that in the course of the Noenfoor operation the boys had rendered valuable service by accompanying American patrols seeking out stragglers, by negotiating the surrender of both Formosan and Japanese troops, by acting as interpreters, and "by engaging in a wide variety of other helpful activities." When the unit left the Indies the Formosan POW's begged to be allowed to accompany the Americans. This they were permitted to do. Thereafter, said the General, "they conscientiously carried out their duties under hazardous conditions and frequently under heavy enemy fire." He concluded his commendation with these words:

> In the light of these PW's long and faithful service for the 158th RCT and because of their demonstrated loyalty toward the U.S. Forces in the course of the war against Japanese militarism, it is recommended that all possible consideration be shown to this personnel, and that preferential treatment be accorded whenever possible.[1]

This commendation — of which any man might be proud — included the names and nicknames of the young men, and these they continued proudly to use on Formosa until the uprising of 1947 brought reprisals. The nicknames themselves tell of an established camaraderie with their American GI friends, for among them were "Smiley" and "Mike," "Dutch" and "George," "Oscar" and "Charley," "Jake," "Joe," "Johnny," "Cookie," "China Boy" and "Nick."

Elsewhere in the Philippines a unit of the U. S. Sixth Army captured two very young Formosan labor conscripts, who were promptly named "T-Bone" and "Wishbone," given miniature GI uniforms, and adopted as "mascots."

At a more significant level was a study group formed among Formosan POW's interned in the Philippines for some months. They had access to American magazines and newspapers, and in one they found an article which I had published in New York on October 10, 1945, entitled "Some Chinese Problems in Taiwan." [2] This they had translated, reproduced, and distributed as a "discussion text" for study groups organized among the internees.

On one occasion, quite by chance, I strengthened belief in the godlike benevolence and authority of the American military organization among the aboriginal people. Soon after the surrender, I went into the mountains to a former Japanese police station on the borders of the aboriginal country. I wished to see what conditions prevailed among the Taiyal tribesmen. The Japanese had withdrawn, but no Chinese had yet appeared. Formosans living near the border and the tribesmen seemed to be having no trouble, and together they gave me a feast at the border village. On the following days I walked through several Taiyal settlements and heard the stories of women whose husbands and sons had been conscripted years before to serve the Japanese Army as mountain bearers and jungle scouts in the Philippines and New Guinea. The few males left were little boys and old men; few new babies were being born, for by the strict codes of the Taiyal people, no woman could remarry unless she had final proof of the death of her husband. I was begged to "send back the men."

I promised to speak to Governor Chen, and to see what I could do about notifying the American military organizations concerned with repatriation. This was on a Sunday morning. On the following Tuesday evening, at Taipei, I saw a file of aborigines moving from a railway station to barracks nearby, accompanied by Japanese officers. I discovered they were from the district which I had just visited, some thirty miles away in the mountains. By Thursday they were home again. And on Saturday, two days later, a large delegation of young men and women, bearing such gifts as they could contrive, appeared in Taipei at my quarters, having made the long journey down from the hills to "Thank America" for so promptly answering their request for help. We had demonstrated (to their satisfaction, at least) that the American military organization was both benevolent and all-powerful.

During 1946 at least three organizations were established in Formosa by Formosans who had been captured at the front and had developed admiration for the humane treatment and friendly behavior of the average American GI. The stories which they had to tell stood in marked contrast with the experience of several thousand Formosan labor conscripts who had been stranded in South China when the Japanese surrendered. Some 8000 were on Hainan Island and were interned there when the Japanese pulled out and the Nationalist Chinese ventured in.

An UNRRA team in China discovered them starving, wounded and diseased. A long, complicated negotiation at last secured homeward passage for some two thousand. But when UNRRA notified the Chinese at Taipei, there was a harsh reaction. These conscripts, they said, were "collaborationists who had helped Japan" and would have to be fed, nursed, clothed, and sent to their homes. It was a waste of money. The port authorities at Keelung emphatically said that they wanted nothing to do with them, and when UNRRA asked the Director of Railways (Chen Ching-wen) to provide free passage for them to Central and Southern Formosa, he snapped, "They are not worth helping." When at last they did reach home (thanks to UNRRA) they had nothing but ill to say of their "mainland cousins" and the Nationalist Government. When the uprising came in 1947 Chen Yi's men (and Chiang Kai-shek himself) again and again named these conscript repatriates as "Communists" and "troublemakers poisoned by the Japanese."

Meanwhile the Formosans at home had ample opportunity to observe American soldiers and sailors in and near Taipei and Kaohsiung, and what they saw they liked. For several weeks some five hundred sailors came up from Keelung each day to play about in Taipei. They were sweeping mines in the Straits of Formosa. Members of the American Advisory Group became well known and very popular in the period October, 1945, through March, 1946. Americans spent freely, they were relaxed, and they were popular. Most of them had seen service for a time on mainland China. Here in Formosa were no signs saying "Yanks Go Home!" The greeting was usually "Hi, Joe!" Their duties were light, they were well housed, and there was ample time to fraternize in the excellent Taipei restaurants or at the hot springs in the hills.

Technically they were present only to help Chen Yi's men establish themselves at Taipei, and to organize the repatriation of the Japanese troops interned in the countryside. But within a matter of days their role began subtly to change; they found themselves becoming buffers between the incoming Chinese on the one hand, and on the other the Formosans and the Japanese civil population. They made small effort to hide contempt for the incompetent Chinese officers who were perforce their colleagues in this Transfer operation. In the officers' quarters and in the GI messrooms the conversations at table invariably became a recital of Chinese shortcomings — of technical incompetence, dishonesty and individual cowardice. As the weeks wore on the Americans in all ranks found themselves drawn into small crises involving Formosans or Japanese who were being victimized by the Chinese "liberators."

Wanted: Permanent Consular Representation at Taipei

Senior officers in the Advisory Group were in an awkward position. Private sympathy lay with the "liberated" Formosans and the dispossessed Japanese; public duty required close association and daily work with Chen Yi's men.

The military duties (the transfer of Japanese military properties and the repatriation of Japanese troops) were relatively simple, but the problems generated by the presence of 300,000 Japanese civilians and the need to secure an orderly transfer of the confiscated industrial complex were far too great, and lay well beyond the authority or the competence of our Military Group. The presence of Americans at Taipei imposed unwelcome restraint upon the rapacious Nationalists but there was no firm basis from which to attack major problems of the civil economy. In Formosan and Japanese eyes the Americans had become custodians of their safety and welfare pending treaty transfer and organization of a stable new administration. With some irony we remarked among ourselves that although the wartime Schools for Military Government and Administration had trained some two thousand men for duty on Formosa only two had been assigned to the island, and one of these soon decamped.

In November it began to be rumored that gold bars worth more than a half-million U.S. dollars had disappeared while in transit from the Japanese military offices to the Chinese headquarters. They were part of a gold shipment which had been sent from Tokyo to pay the Japanese forces in the Philippines but had moved no farther than Formosa. Each gold medallion, wrapped separately, had its own serial number. They had been double-checked carefully before witnesses as they were handed to an American officer. But when they were delivered to the Chinese and again checked carefully they were no longer in serial order and quite a number were missing. The Chinese promptly lodged charges and prepared to sue for recovery. The American officer who had carried them from one headquarters to another suddenly disappeared, secured an emergency "hardship" discharge from the services at Shanghai and left China.

Throughout the autumn I urged friends at the American Embassy to press for civil representation of American interests at Taipei. Billions of dollars worth of Japanese property were to be accounted for, confiscated and transferred to Chinese control. Surely some thought should be given to its importance in any future reparations settlement arrangements. The so-called "gold case" served as a dramatic warning.

At last a career Foreign Service officer flew in for a preliminary survey of American needs, followed in January, 1946, by Mr. Leo Sturgeon, Consul General-designate for Manchuria. The Chinese received him politely but without enthusiasm. The opening of an American consular establishment was not at all to Chen Yi's liking but he accepted the inevitable and promised "full cooperation."

The presence of Americans on Formosa was proving troublesome. Governor Chen complained to Higher Authority that American military officers were "meddling in civil affairs." He really meant that he and his men were losing face; our presence cramped their carpetbagging style, and — worse — it was clear to one and all that the dispossessed Japanese and the "liberated" native Formosans alike were looking to Americans for protection.

Chen's complaints brought a prompt response; General Wedemeyer's Headquarters directed the American Advisory Group to withdraw.

Either this was more than Governor Chen had bargained for, or he had second thoughts; there were all those restive Japanese troops yet to be repatriated. The Governor revised his complaints, and the withdrawal order was canceled. The Americans were directed to call themselves henceforth merely a "Liaison Group," and to confine themselves strictly to the repatriation problem, a military affair.

My presence presented a slightly different problem, for I was an Assistant Naval Attaché, with Embassy connections and a diplomatic passport. I would not necessarily be withdrawn with the Army Group. Moreoever it was well-known to the Chinese that my return to Formosa had created a mild stir among old friends and former students, and that I was being kept well informed of conditions under the Nationalist Administration. The attempt to have me recalled was neatly made, and represents a technique used again and again in the China Theatre. A visiting Vice Admiral, wined and dined during an overnight stop at Taipei, was told privately that I was attempting to "protect Japanese interests." I was soon summoned to the Embassy at Chungking to explain this, and to report upon conditions on the island. I then returned to Formosa.

In earlier conversations with Governor-General Chen Yi, Consul General Sturgeon had asked Chen to assist the United States in finding a suitable property for an American Consulate. Washington would pay for it, of course. The Consul General at Shanghai asked me to take the problem in hand, and the Governor directed his aides to assist me.

In due course I was handed a list of twenty properties. One by one I checked them off, passing as I did scores of large official residences and private houses which were now occupied by incoming Chinese influential enough to acquire them. I knew that in many instances individuals were laying claim to two or more large properties by a simple exercise of squatter's rights, staked out by assigning three or four servants or guards to ward off other possible claimants. Where legal title could not be secured, it was always possible to profit from bribes paid to with-draw one's squatters quietly.

As I checked off my list of twenty properties offered to the American Government for consideration, I saw at once that considerable thought had been given to American face and how to deflate American prestige. Without exception the listed prop-erties were buildings which no Chinese commissioner, general, colonel, or major would have considered, and no incoming Chinese bureaucrat or private person of rank would have contemplated for his own use. The buildings were at the ends of narrow alleys in the slums, and most of them were in an advanced state of decay. Several were former British business properties for which the legal status was not then clear. Some were in distant parts of town, and some could not be reached by car. They were distinctly the leftovers. I rejected them all.

I thought the United States should have at least one of the better properties being vacated by the Japanese and I thought it odd that the American Government should have to pay hand-somely to local Chinese administrators for the favor of a resi-dence among them.

A second list of properties was presented for consideration. They were better but only slightly so. Only one had adequate provison for a combined office-residence arrangement, a solid construction and a central location. It had been built many years earlier for the local representatives of the Standard Oil Company, had passed from owner to owner and now had been confiscated. We were to be allowed the privilege of buying it. In time it became the American Embassy in China.

There were small difficulties. Mayor Huang of Taipei was attempting to establish squatter's rights in the building as he was also squatting in other desirable properties around town. The Governor's Office ordered him to withdraw. In angry re-taliation he promptly seized a large residence adjacent to the old prewar American Consulate which had been a rented prop-erty. The owner was a wealthy Formosan woman who had many American friends. When she protested vigorously the Mayor arranged to have her arrested on charges of "collaboration with the Japanese." During the noisy litigation His Honor unwisely charged, in print, that the United States Government had "stolen" his property. The officers of the American Liaison Group decided that it was time to object to some of the trivial but persistent efforts to cause the Americans loss of face before the public. The Mayor was asked to publish a retraction which he did with poor grace.

Our troubles were not at an end at the old Standard Oil Building. Before we could survey the premises in detail and begin plans for remodeling we discovered that a Nationalist General had taken a fancy to the house and grounds and had moved in a team of squatters. We were invited to get off the property and to stay off. A direct order from the Governor was required to pry the General's representatives from the kitchen quarters.

The Governor was not in a good mood. At about this time the OSS team living in the Rose Mansion made a blunder which the Communists subsequently took up, embellished, and used in propaganda. In a peculiarly inept attempt to conduct a public opinion survey, OSS officers in uniform went on the streets with interpreters to interview people who were stopped at random. The surprised Formosans were asked whether they would prefer (a) continuing Chinese rule, (b) a return to Japanese administration, or (c) a future under United Nations trusteeship, with the United States as trustee.

It was a silly performance, and the Chinese had cause to be indignant. The OSS officers, on their part, believed that local anti-Chinese feeling was rising to a degree which made the enquiry legitimate.

In January, 1946, a Scripps-Howard correspondent (the late William D. Newton) entered Formosa to survey the state of affairs being then so dramatically reported in the mainland Chinese press. He toured the island, hearing all sides of the controversy which had risen between the newcomers and the Formosans who poured out complaints wherever he went.

Chen Yi's agents were alarmed. At an elaborate dinner arranged for the purpose, I heard one of the Commissioners persuade our unperceptive Colonel that Newton's presence endangered "traditional Chinese-American friendship." There were many toasts to "closer Sino-American cooperation," and soon enough the Colonel sprang to his feet, thumped the table, and roared that he would expel Newton and forbid any other newsmen to enter Formosa without his express permission. We knew that he had no authority beyond his Liaison duties, but the Commissioners, his hosts, smiled happily. He had so neatly jumped through the hoop. There would be no U. S. Army support — transportation, billeting and the like — for Mr. Newton after this.

The Japanese military representatives now reported to the American Liaison Group that the Chinese had broken pledges to keep ample food reserves available until troop repatriation was complete. The Americans were aware of rising tensions throughout the island. They knew that the Nationalist Government promises could not be relied upon; if there were a food crisis involving 170,000 Japanese internees, it might trigger a general outburst against the mainland people.

The Colonel therefore alerted MacArthur's Headquarters at Tokyo, recommended an accelerated repatriation schedule, and by April 1, 1946, the last Japanese soldier had left Formosa. The American Liaison Group withdrew, having no further duties to perform.

The American GI's were gone, but they had left behind them a very deep and very favorable impression. Who would look to Formosan interests now? How safe was the Japanese civil population? No one knew and few cared to contemplate the possibilities.

V

A Government of Merchants

The KMT Military Scavengers

FORMOSAN ENTHUSIASM FOR "liberation" lasted about six weeks. Posters began to appear here and there lampooning Nationalist soldiers and showing Chen Yi as a fat pig. He was in fact short and fat, beady-eyed and heavy-jowled, an easy target for caricature. "Dogs go and pigs come!" was scrawled up everywhere on Taipei's walls and heard everywhere in private conversation. "At least the Japanese dogs protected the property!"

There was ample cause for disappointment. Word that Formosa offered unimaginable riches spread quickly on the mainland. Thousands of carpetbaggers streamed in, coming principally from Shanghai. Those who could afford it bought or bribed their way across aboard American military aircraft in our shuttle service, with such success that at times members of the Army Advisory Group, traveling on legitimate business, found it difficult to obtain passage. The majority of Chinese, less fortunate, crossed the rough channel waters aboard junks.

Looting was carried forward on three levels. From September, 1945, until the year's end the military scavengers were at work at the lowest level. Anything movable — anything lying loose and unguarded for a moment — was fair prey for ragged and undisciplined soldiers. It was a first wave of petty theft, taking place in every city street and suburban village unfortunate enough to have Nationalist Army barracks or encampments nearby.

The second stage of looting was entered when the senior military men — the officer ranks — organized depots with forwarding agents at the ports through which they began to ship out military and civilian supplies. Next the Governor's own men developed a firm control of all industrial raw materials, agricultural stockpiles and confiscated real properties turned over to them by the vanquished Japanese. By the end of 1946 these huge reserves were fairly well exhausted, and at last in early 1947 the Governor's Commissioners imposed a system of extreme monopolies affecting every phase of the island's economic life. This was Chen Yi's "Necessary State Socialism" in its developed form and the ultimate cause of the 1947 rebellion.

Some 12,000 rag-tag troops had been brought across the channel and dumped on Formosa in the first mass movement of Nationalist forces. They came aboard American ships to Keelung and Kaohsiung. Later additions brought the total garrison to about 30,000 men — not excessive in a population of some five millions, perhaps, but they were a rapacious lot. At that time Nationalist troops were being paid — if they were paid at all — the equivalent of $33.00 per year, including (on Formosa) a special "overseas bonus" copied from the American system. Inflation soon cut the buying power until a month's wages could not buy a day's rations. We had no reason to be surprised when the ill-disciplined, ill-fed and underpaid men pilfered war-damaged buildings and unguarded private property. They were expected to fend for themselves on Formosa as they did on the mainland, and here they did very well.

The pickings were good, but the dirty, illiterate conscripts were objects of scorn and contempt among the comparatively well-dressed, well-fed, "modern" Formosans.

The majority were from hinterland provinces and were unfamiliar with paved roads, with a developed communications system, or with simple mechanical devices which had long since become part of everyday Formosan life. We saw them frequently carrying stolen bicycles on their backs, wandering about in search of a barter exchange or a buyer. They did not know how to ride. One evening, driving along the Tamsui river-road I found the way blocked and an angry crowd of Formosans quarreling with some soldiers. Newcomers had established themselves that day on confiscated Japanese small craft lying along the seawall. The boat-cables had been carried over the wall and across the main highway to be looped around roadside trees. Then the tide had risen, and the cables had risen with the tide, very effectively blocking traffic on a principal thoroughfare. At Taipei a similar display of unreason took place when the Nationalist Army Signal Corps strung field telephone wires between KMT Army Headquarters and the offices of the American Advisory Group. The wires were laid across the main railway tracks near Taipei station, and of course the first train through put an end to the service. For many weeks crowds of soldiers stood about on the main floor of Taipei's principal department store, gaping at the wonders of an elevator service. There were countless incidents to illustrate the backwardness of the newcomers.

The Formosans laughed, jeered, or were angry by turn. Fortunately few conscript privates carried side arms, and it was not difficult for the Formosans to shout them down in time-honored Chinese fashion. Usually they could be driven off if they tried to help themselves to something without making a proper payment. But dealing with the officer-class was a different matter. The Chinese Air Force — the "modern service" — considered itself an elite, and the Air Force officers were a particularly arrogant lot. Many officers never hesitated to brandish weapons in an argument. There were hundreds of field-grade officers and scores of generals — including the Major General who was on the books and drew pay as "Director of the Taiwan Garrison Symphony Orchestra." * By the end of No-

* There was indeed a Taiwan Symphony Orchestra, formed principally by Formosan graduates of the Ueno Conservatory of Music at Tokyo. Immedi-

vember looting had become well-organized and was on a massive scale. Foodstuffs, textiles, and scrap metals were at a pre-
mium. Officers worked in small gangs, with conscript help. By
sharing a percentage with "higher authority" they could use
confiscated Japanese military trucks to move loot to depots
from which it was shipped on to Shanghai. The "Peace Preservation Corps" arriving in September had promptly commandeered all of Taipei's garbage trucks, for example, and by late
November those that were still able to move were carrying loot
to the ports. A Formosan truck owner or driver had to be quick-
witted indeed if he were to avoid loss of his vehicle. Meanwhile the garbage piled mountain-high in the streets and the
rats had a merry time in the alleyways and houses of Taipei.

Gang-looting was not limited to military officers, of course,
but they were made conspicuous by uniforms and by the bold
assurance with which they worked at any hour of the day, well
armed and confident that they were beyond the reach of civil
law. Japanese were particularly easy targets. Some 300,000 civilians anxiously waited repatriation or some definition of their
legal status.

While awaiting repatriation, families were expected to
remain in their homes until called to the ports for embarkation. General MacArthur ordered the repatriation from Formosa to be delayed as long as possible, for millions of Japanese
were coming back to the homeland in the dead of winter to face
appalling conditions in bombed Japanese cities and towns. But
by the end of December at Taipei hundreds of Japanese had
been evicted from their homes, without notice, and hundreds
more had their homes entered by armed gangs who stripped
the houses of every movable, salable object.

At first the Formosans thought this inevitable, and perhaps

---

ately after the war a Hungarian refugee from Shanghai took over the baton,
and the organization was given the use of an abandoned Japanese Buddhist
temple. Interference by the nominal Director — the Major General — soon
wrecked the organization.

fair enough, in light of their own past experiences with the Japanese. But November and December brought evidence that well-armed newcomers drew no fine distinctions in conquered territory. Formosans who lived in Japanese style houses or in semi-Japanese style were especial objects of molestation. By year's end it was apparent that no private property was immune. Bribes paid to forestall a raid carried no effective guarantee of later security. There were occasions when two officer-gangs fought openly in the streets before a property which each had planned to "liberate."

Soon major industrial reconstruction assets were being "liberated." The great Zuiho copper and gold mines near Keelung had at one time produced 20 per cent of Japan's total copper ore, and the machinery at the mines was developed to match the wartime importance of such production. Solitary conscripts, on foot, first roamed about the silent unguarded premises, picking up supplies and tools from undamaged machine shops. Then the officer-gangs moved in with commandeered trucks. Soon they had ripped out the heavier machines, removed wiring and all metal fixtures, and shipped the whole off to the ports and on to Shanghai. When I visited the site not long after, I discovered that even the metal door-frames and sheet metal roofing had been carried off, leaving empty shells where important industrial installations had once stood.

In Taipei and Keelung Japanese and Formosan crews worked hard by day, attempting to restore bomb-damaged public service facilities. At night roving scavengers in uniform cut down miles of copper telephone wire, dug up new-laid pipes and fire hydrants, tore plumbing from unguarded buildings, or intimidated guards while the loot was carried out to carts and trucks. Several serious railway crossing accidents occurred before the public realized that the "liberators" were carrying off automatic switch and signal equipment to be sold as scrap metal.

The Japanese Army and Navy had relinquished permanent barracks built to accommodate more than 200,000 troops, hundreds of other military-service buildings, and many thousand acres of land. Despite this, by the year's end Chinese soldiers had overrun schools, temples and hospitals at Taipei and it took most of the year 1946 to get them out. Any building occupied by KMT troops became a mere shell. The great Confucian Temple in northwest Taipei was heavily damaged. A Zen Buddhist temple nearby was totally wrecked, and its contents sold or bartered on the streets. The MacKaye Mission Memorial Hospital was occupied for months, stripped of its equipment and all metal fixtures, including doorknobs. Many of the wooden doors, door-frames and stair bannisters were used by the soldiers to feed cooking fires built on the concrete floors. Troops occupied the Mission Leper Hospital near Tamsui.

The higher Chinese civil and military officers were interested in real estate. In the Japanese era every bureau and department of Government maintained handsome official residences, designed to add to the prestige of colonial administrators. The majority of the great private or semi-private corporations — the Taiwan Electric Power Corporation, the sugar corporation, the fisheries organizations, the banks — each maintained a company residence in town as well as a corresponding mountain house or hotspring villa in the suburbs.

These were now taken over by the high Chinese civil and military officers. In several instances ranking Chinese simply moved into the mansions of wealthy Formosans as "guests," letting it be known that the Chinese Government proposed to seek out and punish all Formosans who had collaborated with the enemy during the preceding fifty years. Several of Formosa's wealthiest men were taken into custody, installed in fairly comfortable quarters at the military headquarters and then, throughout 1946, were "squeezed." They were called upon for "donations" to a great variety of causes, not excluding the erection of a gilded statue of Chiang Kai-shek where once had stood the bronze statue of a former Japanese Governor-General.

The military played a leading role in all this for they symbolized the "liberating power"; by New Year's Day, 1946, Formosans saw "liberation" in its true light. A truck at the gate, a gang at the door, and an agent representing himself to have "high authority" meant eviction on the moment. The reorganization of the economy was rather a matter of civilian controls, but the civilian Commissioners around Chen Yi obviously worked against a military background.

Many civilians on Chen Yi's staff distrusted their own military men. By tradition Japanese houses are surrounded by walls. We had not long been on Formosa when we observed that Chinese civil officers living in confiscated Japanese homes were adding a topping of broken glass to the concrete walls, or barbed wire and spikes to the tops of wooden fences. The Japanese had never felt this precaution necessary while they lived among the Formosans; it was an eloquent if silent confession of the mainlander's state of mind vis-à-vis his own military rabble.

Formosan Reaction to the Nationalist Armed Forces

The Governor found that he faced no organized opposition. The Japanese troops were being removed, there were no Formosan military units and very few Formosans in the policing agencies. The Formosan civil population was well disciplined and law-abiding. There was no Communist threat.

There was little need of a large military garrison. Though published figures were notoriously inexact, we believed that there were about 30,000 mainland troops on the island throughout most of 1946.

In January General Chen announced a plan to conscript Formosan youths, beginning in September. They were to have opportunity to serve the Motherland in repressing Communist rebels and bandits on the continent.

There was a prompt public outcry which appeared to astonish the Governor-General. Formosan spokesmen took to the platform to denounce conscription before a peace treaty confirmed the transfer of sovereignty from Japan to China. They assured the Governor they would be happy to form a volunteer Formosan Home Guard for duty on the island, but they were not prepared to see Formosan youth swallowed up in the civil war. They suggested that a Home Guard recruited on Formosa could defend the island, thus releasing the Chinese garrison forces for duty on the mainland. The press kept the issue before the public for many weeks. It was widely believed that Governor-General Chen simply wished to ship out as many young men as possible, for by tradition the Chinese Government sent conscripts and generals into distant provinces in order to discourage thoughts of rebellion on home territory.

September, 1946, came and went and nothing more was heard of the conscription program. Relations between the Formosans and the occupying garrison forces had gone steadily from bad to worse. Here, on Formosa, clearly defined and well reported, was a demonstration of the fundamental reasons Chiang Kai-shek and his Nationalist Party Government and Army were unable to secure popular support on the mainland, and so lost China.

Unfortunately, in the early months of the Occupation the Formosans openly laughed at the incoming officers and men, mocking their lack of discipline and their manifest ignorance of simple modern technology. I once observed an officer on foot, wheeling a bicycle at his side. Behind him stumbled a tearful, angry small boy who shouted to the world that the officer had stolen his bicycle — the precious family bicycle — and he wanted it to be returned for otherwise he could not go home. Older Formosans took note and the officer saw that he was about to be stopped. He therefore suddenly attempted to leap on the machine and ride away. But after wobbling a few feet he fell off into a fairly deep roadside puddle. The crowd hooted with laughter as the officer got to his feet and went off hastily, cursing and dirty, leaving the bicycle where it lay.

On another day I saw a car grossly overloaded with mainland Chinese officers moving along the Keelung highway. One back wheel was about to come off, the car lurched grotesquely from side to side, but the driver made no effort to stop until, too late, it swerved about and collapsed on the roadway. The roadside crowd instantly caught the significance of this odd behavior; the mainlanders obviously knew nothing about cars. As the shaken passengers extricated themselves the Formosans laughed loudly, shouting coarse jokes about pigs breaking out of baskets. The Chinese were beside themselves with rage and moved off, cursing the Formosans. Fortunately they were un-armed. They had suffered an injury far worse than broken bones; they had lost face.

These confrontations were frequent and took place every-where in the islands. For many years the mainland Chinese had had to endure the condescension implied in Western at-tempts to help "backward heathens" develop modern tech-niques, but here they were being laughed at by their own peo-ple, and an inferior people at that. That is, I think, one of the important keys to the situation on Formosa in all that followed.

The Stockpile Bonanza: Something for the Men at the Top

The loot taken in petty theft from local shops and homes by these plodding garrison soldiers was as nothing when compared with the plunder shipped from the island by Chen Yi's Com-missioners and by civil and military officers in the higher eche-lons of Government and Army.

Japan's leading authority on the subject of the confiscated properties — an economist directly involved with the registra-tion and transfer of titles — estimated the total value of mili-tary and civilian properties handed over to the Nationalist Chi-nese. Using prewar "original cost'" figures as a basis (i.e. not the inflated values at Shanghai or Taipei after 1945) a most

conservative estimate showed the value of *non-military* confiscated properties to be in excess of one billion dollars. In addition the Japanese Army and Navy had each accumulated enormous stockpiles of foodstuffs, clothing, medical supplies and
equipment other than arms and ammunition. These had been
destined for the vast Japanese war-front in southeast Asia and
the Indies, but had not moved beyond Formosa. The total
value of military supplies *other* than arms and ammunition was
placed at two billion dollars at local market values in late 1945.
The value of arms and ammunition stockpiled on Formosa is
not known.

These enormous accumulations began to move out of the island in the first months of Chinese administration. Chen Yi's
men claimed that as good patriots they promptly ensured the
flow of military supply to the Nationalist Army fighting Communists on the mainland, but we have ample reason to believe
that there was heavy "diversionary action" along the way to the
official war-front.

A massive raid upon accumulated foodstocks late in 1945
precipitated one of the first major crises in Formosan relations
with the new regime.

At the surrender the Japanese military had supplies sufficient
to feed 200,000 troops for two years, or 250,000 men for a year
and a half. They had anticipated a long siege. In addition
there was on Formosa a very large backlog of unshipped rice
and other foodstuffs which had accumulated near the ports
waiting transport to Japan proper.* The 1945 crops had been
greatly reduced because of the scarcity of chemical fertilizers,
but even so there was an abundance.

On an earlier page we have noted that General MacArthur
wished to delay repatriation of 500,000 Japanese from Formosa. The first postwar winter was grim in Japan proper, a

---

* Formosa's annual prewar production had reached 1,600,000 metric tons.
Roughly 50 per cent of the annual crop was consumed locally by the population of five millions, who lived well.

winter of hunger and hardship and cold. On Formosa the Japanese could be adequately sheltered and fed.

The Chinese entering Formosa demanded the immediate transfer of all military stockpiles, including rations and rice. The Japanese officers hesitated to comply until the American Advisory Group secured a Chinese guarantee that ample reserves would be maintained and would be constantly available until the last Japanese soldier had left the island.

The guarantees proved worthless. We have already noted that in late December senior Japanese officers reported military food reserves were being removed from storage at an alarming rate. Some supply was being sold locally by individual Chinese officers who had access to it, and great quantities were being shipped out. Nonmilitary food reserves, too, were vanishing. Rumors of an impending food crisis were circulating everywhere. Interned and restive Japanese soldiers could not be expected to remain unmoved if word came of violence done to the unarmed Japanese civilians, or that they themselves were about to starve in the midst of plenty. If food riots occurred at Taipei it was certain that the Japanese civilian population would be the first to suffer. As we have seen, for this reason repatriation was completed at the end of March.

Every Formosan household felt the effect of a sudden loss of grain reserves. Rice could be obtained, but only at exorbitant prices. Farmers who had supplies produced on their own lands were in constant fear of confiscation. In truth the Formosans had an ample supply of vegetables, fruits and other grains to tide them over to the spring harvest, but rice was the staple, and this was the first rice shortage in local history. Without rice the people felt deprived — and frightened. China's chronic famine conditions were well known.

The Formosans' ancestors had left mainland China to get away from chronic hunger and bad government, but now the one was following swiftly on the other. There was more anger than fear in their hearts, however; they knew the fields were producing and that huge supplies of grain were leaving Formosa. Workmen at the docks and warehouses carried it aboard ships and junks day after day. The movement of rice from the island could not be hidden.

To loud demands for action the Government first replied with flowery talk of "patriotism" and "food for the Army, defending Formosa from Communism," and then Chen lost patience with the critics. He sharply denied Government responsibility, countering with charges that the Formosans themselves were selfishly hoarding grain. Undoubtedly some Formosans were, but the quantities in private hands were insignificant.

When the Government took action it was not at all what the Formosans expected; Chen launched an island-wide rice-collection program, ordering prominent men to become chairmen of local committees. This was to make them appear responsible for any continuing shortages. The Formosa Garrison Commander (General Ko Yuen-feng) was then ordered to enforce stringent anti-hoarding regulations, and the police were instructed to enter and search without warrant.

With rice-collection in the hands of the police and the Army no more than a hint was necessary in most cases to bring forth cash or material "gifts" from private rice dealers whose records were alleged to be unsatisfactory. Extortion was the order of the day; for example, I learned of one dealer whose stocks were checked and recorded on Tuesday, but on Friday (after he had made and recorded legitimate sales) a second check by a different police unit found his books "unsatisfactory." He was arrested, threatened, and forced to pay over a heavy bribe to secure release. His rice stocks were confiscated.

By this time (early 1946) Chiang Kai-shek's "Blue Shirt" gangsters had begun to come over from Shanghai. With local gangsters known as *loma* or "tiger eels" they were used to incite riots and raids on private warehouses. General Ko promised immunity from arrest to anyone who broke open private buildings and revealed hoarded stocks.

In other words, within four months of the formal surrender we observed Shanghai's metropolitan gangsterism introduced at Taipei, with Party and Army connivance. In retrospect the Governor's anti-hoarding campaign appears to have been one of his earliest moves to discredit and destroy the educated, middle class which had begun to emerge in the late years of the Japanese era. These were the gentry, small, independent landholders who also had modest investments in shops and small industries in the towns. They represented the articulate Opposition. The Nationalist Government, Party and Army were responsible for food shortages and the threatened crisis, but measures taken to cope with the situation were clearly designed to set Formosans one against another.

Military supplies were shipped out to meet the Generalissimo's personal interest in *power*, as such, rather than in wealth. The huge stockpiles of food could be divided and subdivided to pay off the thousands of military officers, Party men and bureaucrats who were involved in the affair. There were other valuable reserves of industrial raw materials and processed goods lying in storage. Japanese economists engaged in the formal transfer of confiscated properties estimated that across the board there were sufficient stockpiles to sustain most industries for about three years, and that within this period, under proper management, the Formosan economy should be recovering its normal productivity-potential. On the other hand they warned the Chinese that under the circumstances reserve stockpiles represented the operating capital required to pay for rehabilitation. They were bluntly told that it was none of their concern.

The sugar industry was of course the great prize. In 1939 Formosa had produced in excess of 1,400,000 metric tons of sugar. In 1947, the first full crop produced under Chinese management yielded only 30,000 metric tons. This was about the amount which had been produced in 1895 before the Japanese developed the industry, and a dramatic demonstration of the fate of the economy in Chinese hands.

Production of sugar had fallen off in wartime because of labor shortages, a reduction of crop area, and lack of fertilizers. Nevertheless, huge quantities of raw sugar were stockpiled in 1945, waiting shipment to Japan's refineries. Most of the great cane-mills had suffered relatively little bomb damage, although they were suffering from wear and tear and from lack of proper maintenance. But in 1946 the sugar reserves which should have paid for rehabilitation were gone.

Immediately after the formal surrender the Executive Yuan (of which T. V. Soong was President) ordered massive sugar shipments. From Hong Kong came reports that great quantities of this raw sugar were brought there directly to private warehouses. The lowest estimate was 150,000 tons, the highest 600,000 tons. Obviously no one knew the exact figure, but just as obviously Formosa's sugar reserves had disappeared.

In this instance the Formosans held Madam Chiang's brother T. V. Soong responsible. Formosan attitudes toward the Chiang-Soong Family were conditioned by such allegations.

Stockpiles of every description left the island in this fashion. For example, in good years Formosa had produced nearly three million tons of coal mined in and near Keelung, the port city. In 1945–1946 reserves which should have been apportioned to local small industries went instead to Shanghai. For one thing the Taiwan Railway Administration was not interested in handling coal when passengers, baggage and other types of freight were more profitable. Other offices in Chen Yi's administration saw in coal a source of enormous profits. As cold winter came on in Shanghai, in late 1945, Formosan coal commanded fantastic prices in the metropolitan market. Mainland Chinese at Taipei and Keelung bought up all the coal they could, but paid absurdly low prices for it. Formosan mine-operators at last threatened to suspend mining until written contracts guaranteed a reasonable percentage of the profits. The Government stepped in, offered to have one Government agency of the Department of Industry and Mining buy up the coal on these terms, establishing in effect a monopoly on the market. The Formosans, satisfied, signed up and began delivering coal to the Government agency which they assumed would sell the coal at a handsome profit and share the proceeds with them. To their great chagrin, however, the Governor's men in the purchasing agency promptly sold the coal to another agency in the Government (a purely paper transaction) at a ridiculously low profit. Then — in strict accordance with contract terms — they paid off the Formosans at the agreed percentages. The second agency of the Department of Industry and Mining then shipped the coal to Shanghai for an astronomical profit.

In Japanese hands the official monopolies of Salt, Matches, Liquor, Camphor, and Narcotics had yielded a very large per cent of the Government's total revenues in Formosa. In late 1945 the stockpiles of raw materials and finished products were handed over to Chen Yi. Here again was a windfall beyond description.

After the Transfer few of these stockpiled materials reached the open market through legal channels. In most instances we have records of quantities surrendered (records made by the Japanese), but only the vaguest indication of what became of them. Of 423,000 tons of camphor surrendered, for example, an official report shows that only 400 tons were actually refined in the first half-year of the Chinese occupation. We do know that very large shipments left the island, assigned to private warehouses in Hong Kong. Nearly 3,500,000 cases of matches were surrendered, but an acute shortage of matches developed in Formosa in early 1946. (At the first People's Political Council, in May, the Government spokesman explained this, saying that the Government had been able to distribute only 1473 cases in the first six months "because of lack of adequate transport.") The match stockpiles, too, had gone to the mainland.

The fate of the Narcotics Monopoly stocks were of the keenest concern to thoughtful Formosan leaders. The very existence of the narcotics industry as a State concern had been always a source of great friction between Formosans and the Japanese administration. In the decade before the war the Japanese government did not publish figures showing the total quantities of narcotics raw materials or finished products produced annually but for a time made public figures showing the stocks carried over from one year to the next. In other words, we know what was *left over* after the year's work was done, and from this must guess the *order of magnitude* of the total production and of the normal stockpiles.*

It is a matter of record that at the end of 1934 the Taiwan Monopoly Bureau carried over a stockpile of 67.9 metric tons of raw opium and 19 metric tons of prepared opium. At the end of 1935 it carried over a stockpile of 4245 metric tons of coca leaves, 606 metric tons of crude morphine, and 125 metric tons of crude cocaine. Ten years later Chen Yi announced that the Japanese had surrendered only 9720 *pounds* of opium and "a small quantity" of cocaine. These narcotics stocks, he said, had been promptly divided into three parts; some had been released to the local Bureau of Health, some had been sent to Nanking for use in the Army medical services, and the balance had been destroyed. Henceforth, he said, the manufacture of cocaine and coca derivatives would be given up. His agents had assumed control of the coca plantations in Taichung and near Taitung.

For many years Formosa was considered one of the great narcotics processing centers in the world and a major source of supply for illicit traffic in drugs. On the assumption "This is China now," our consul on Formosa in 1946 decided that what the Chinese did with the Narcotics Monopoly was a question of

---

* All Japanese figures in this field must be taken with great reserve, for a League of Nations inquiry brought the unsavory Formosan narcotics manufacturing organization to international attention, and Japanese figures after 1932 showed a very sharp decline, not to be taken too seriously. Narcotics were too important as a weapon used on the Asian mainland. Consumption was most strictly controlled within Formosa itself.

no concern to the American Government. A United Nations report in 1949 noted that the Chinese Nationalist Government had failed to submit reports on the stocks, production or use of narcotics in Formosa since the Surrender in 1945.

The Chinese Commissioners Prepare to
Build a New Formosa

On paper, for the public records, a *Table of Organization* clearly defined the new administration. It looked well — on paper — for it provided for all branches of government needed to supply a highly complex, modern technological economy and for all the social services inherited from the Japanese period.

Chen Yi surrounded himself with a remarkable group of Commissioners and staffmen. The majority had been educated in mission schools in China, in Japanese technical schools or universities, or in western Europe or America. Control of the basic economy lay with the Commissioners of Finance, Communications, Industry and Mining, and Agriculture and Forestry.

The Governor's first choice for the Communications post — vital in an island economy — was a man named Hsu, long associated with T. V. Soong's China Merchant's Steam Navigation Company, the "CMSNC," which dominated shipping in the rivers and coastal waters of China. The nomination provoked such an outcry that Hsu's name was withdrawn. He went instead to Shanghai to become Managing Director of the CMSNC, but it was arranged subsequently to have the Shanghai offices of the Taiwan Government-General located in the CMSNC Building on the Bund. To replace Hsu, Chen Yi chose — or had chosen for him — one of his associates in Fukien days, Yen Chia-kan.

Throughout the period of Chen Yi's rule at Taipei, Yen Chia-kan was key man, serving first as Communications Commissioner, then as Finance Commissioner, and at times as Acting Civil Administrator. Formosans liked him as a person rather better than they did any other Commissioner, for he was never arrogant and seemed always sincerely interested in whatever problem was at hand.

Other Commissioners were less successful in personal public relations. Near Yen stood Pao Ko-yung, a rather elegant young man who had been educated in Europe. He was brought to Formosa as Commissioner of Mining and Industry. His wife's sister was the wife of the Managing Director of the China Merchants Steam Navigation Company and his brother was Chief Liaison Officer for the Formosan Government at Shanghai, with offices in the CMSNC building. Chen Yi's Director of Railroads (Chen Ching-wen) was ultimately to become Commissioner of Communications and Chairman of the Board of Directors of the CMSNC.

When Commissioner Yen moved from Communications to Finance (in early 1946) his place was taken by Jen Hsien-chuen who had been educated in Japan and in Italy and had served briefly in the Highway Bureau of the Central Government. The Commissioner for Agriculture and Forestry was Chao Lien-fang, Ph.D., a much older man, who had graduated from the University of Wisconsin.

These were the key men controlling Finance, Transport, Industry, and Agriculture. Their experience abroad enabled them to meet and manipulate American visitors with remarkable success. So many of our fast-moving visitors from Washington seemed to be persuaded that a foreigner's command of English certified a democratic outlook on life and that a period of student life in the United States automatically guaranteed a pro-American point of view. The Commissioners had mastered the art of granting interviews, passing out succinct statistical summaries, and persuading their guests that things were moving forward on Formosa at an encouraging pace. But long experience with them in official business and unofficial social life made it clear that flowery public references to "our Formosan brothers" only thinly concealed a contempt for the "barbarian" island people, and disguised full-time dedication to the task of removing island wealth as rapidly and as thoroughly as possible. It was not what the Commissioners *said* they were doing in 1945 to 1949, but what, in fact, they did.

The Government's printed *Table of Organization* was neatly arranged, but in practice the lines of authority were blurred by intense rivalries and overlapping functions. There were Army groups and Party cliques, civil-military rivalries and factions based on regional origins and interests (Shanghai versus the capital, Fukien versus Chekiang or Kwangtung, for example), and underlying it all was the essential division of interest — the Formosans versus the mainland Chinese.

Each Commissioner had a personal following and a host of friends and relatives on the payroll. Some, however, were much more flagrant than others in nepotism. For example, the Secretary-General or Civil Administrator (General Keh King-en) promptly appointed seven of his family members to important and lucrative posts for which they had not the slightest qualifications. Kaohsiung's Police Chief was shown to have more than forty relatives on the payroll. Some mainland Chinese drew pay for purely ceremonial duties — such as the Major General listed as "Director of the Taiwan Garrison Symphony Orchestra" who was neither soldier nor musician. The Director of the Taiwan Trading Bureau — one of the most lucrative posts — went to a man said variously to be Chen Yi's nephew or a natural son. One prominent Commissioner was alleged to have a concubine on the Department payroll, listed as a "technical specialist."

The Formosans delighted in publishing facts, gossip and allegation, which would cause the newcomers to lose face, but the situation as a whole was too serious for laughter. The economic burden fell on them; they were about to have the "Fukien experience" of Chen Yi's "Necessary State Socialism."

To carry on administrative work for which the Japanese had employed 18,300 people, Chen Yi's reports showed 43,000 names enrolled by midyear 1946, and these lists were believed to be grossly inaccurate and understated.

As window-dressing five island-born men were appointed to offices at the second and third levels of administration. None had lived on Formosa for at least fifteen years. They were strangers among their own people and by the middle of 1946 they were spoken of contemptuously as "running dogs of the Kuomintang." At midyear 1946 Formosan names were shown as a majority on the Government payroll, but these were the messenger girls and janitors in the Taipei offices and the clerks and janitors in the village offices across the island. The effective administrative posts — the jobs that meant something — were all in mainland Chinese hands.

In October, 1945, all Japanese were promptly stripped of authority and dismissed from the Government and industry as a formality, but with equal promptness some 30,000 (principally in technical services) were retained as "advisors" on a temporary basis. This was an admission that the Chinese were not qualified to administer Formosa, and so to save face the Japanese advisors were required to sign petitions begging for the privilege of becoming advisors, and in effect waiving most of the normal rights of a citizen.

As a matter of fact immediately after the surrender some 50,-000 Japanese had voluntarily petitioned for the right to stay in Formosa, their lifelong home. But a few weeks under Chen Yi persuaded them to change their minds; war-torn Japan, public charity, and the American Occupation seemed the more attractive choice. By late 1946 only about 2000 Japanese remained on Formosa in "advisory" services.

Nationalist Party Men as "Tutors" in Formosa

The Governor announced that the "backward Formosans" would be trained to replace Japanese clerks and technicians, and to this end inaugurated a "Provincial Training Corps Program" on December 10, 1945. The ninety-day course included lectures on Chinese literature, Sun Yat-sen's doctrines, the words and deeds of the Arbiter-General (Chiang Kai-shek) and other spiritual nutriment of this high order. There were scattered lectures on national geography, history, politics and economy, and a few on technical subjects such as accounting and meteorology.

This training program, too, proved to be mere window-dressing. Of the first class of 375 Formosans who finished the course, few were actually employed. They complained bitterly that while being required to take these courses, the offices vacated by the Japanese were rapidly filled by newcomers from the mainland.

In early 1946 the Government became top-heavy with inexperienced mainland people, and the Formosans were relegated to menial posts as clerks, office-runners, and the maintenance staff jobs. Gradually they were dismissed from even these positions in order to make room for immigrants.

The Nationalist Party organization actually played a minor role in 1945 and 1946. The mysterious "Colonel Chang" who had arrived on September 5 emerged later in the year as chief organizer for the Kuomintang Youth Corps which was Chiang Kai-shek's version of the Hitler Jugend or Stalin's Komsomol.

There was a brief flurry of interest, of cooperation at the rallies and of enlistment. The Nationalist Party had long been advertised as the soul and conscience of "New China." Chiang Kai-shek was its *Tsungtsai* or Director-General, and Sun Yat-sen's *Three Peoples' Principles* (*San Min Chu-i*) were its Holy Writ.

The three principles sounded just right in Formosa after fifty years of Japanese rule. They were expressions (in slogan form) of Nationalism, People's Rights, and the People's Livelihood. In 1945 this was taken to mean that the Nationalist Party and the National Leader would work energetically to restore Formosans to Chinese nationality, would ensure popular rights by creating a democratic and representative system through which Formosans would govern Formosa and represent Formosa in the Central Government, and, lastly, that the Party would foster the rehabilitation and development of the island economy.

In practice they quickly discovered that lines of distinction between Government interests and Party interests were not clear. The Party members were an elite, and the Government was expected to serve and finance the Party. In its turn the Party was organized to exalt the authority of the Tsungtsai or Director-General. Just as there could be no Nazi Party without Hitler, or Fascist Party without Mussolini, or Falangist Party without Franco, so there could be no Nationalist (*Kuomintang*) Party without Chiang Kai-shek.

The Formosans found many of the Party's ceremonial requirements much too similar to the ceremonial Emperor-worship of the Japanese State cult. That routine had been costly and burdensome, and they were not happy to resume it under a different name.

For example, in the Japanese era a portrait of the reigning Emperor had to be placed in every school. It had to be treated with the utmost show of reverence. And there were weekly services at which all government employees and school children had to bow reverently before the imperial portrait or toward the imperial palace at Tokyo, "worshiping from afar." Now, under the new Nationalist regime, portraits of Sun Yat-sen, the "National Father" or of Chiang Kai-shek, the "National Leader" had simply replaced the Japanese Emperor's portrait everywhere. On Monday morning in every week, all Government offices, all military posts and all Party organizations were required to hold an hour-long Memorial Service. Participants were required to bow three times before Sun's portrait and before the flags of the nation and the Party. They were required to sing the National Anthem which was the Party Song. School children, Youth Corps members and many other groups were required to show the outward forms of respect to these symbols of Party, Army, and Government.

Soon Party offices were opened throughout the island. Posters, pamphlets, slogans, mass rallies and drills were introduced. Leather-lunged speechmakers harangued the meetings, trying to induce "slogan-thinking" and acceptance of a blind conformity to the will of the Party Leader. Too much was said in praise of the Party and the Generalissimo, and too little said concerning the rehabilitation of Formosa or the depredations of the KMT Army.

When goons in great number came in from the back alleys of Shanghai, Party organizers began to use strong-arm tactics in smaller towns. The truth began to dawn on the Formosans. Attendance at Party meetings and Youth Corps rallies melted away. There were too many demands for the payment of dues and of special fees. When organizers began to demand a share in profitable local business ventures they were astonished by the vigor with which the Formosans objected, and the speed with which these attempts were publicized in the local press.

The Party's share in the division of movable properties and of confiscated real estate was considerable. A number of theaters were handed over to the Party — properties which could be made to yield returns when Party meetings were not in session. By late autumn, 1945, the Party had had its day in Formosa, and began to be the object of sharper editorial criticism in the press.

This caused loss of face; Party spokesmen and the Government newspaper charged angrily that the island people were tainted by long association with the Japanese, that they lacked "true national spirit," and that they discriminated willfully against their brothers from other provinces.

Throughout 1946 the Party was not firmly enough entrenched nor sufficiently important to employ forthright liquidation tactics where it wished to silence an opposition press or destroy a critic. That came later. For a time Party officials and unit organizations merely assisted Chen Yi in setting up his disciplinary internment camp in the Taipei suburbs, called publicly a "rehabilitation and guidance center." By a twist of the vagrancy laws some of the most stubborn Formosan landholders and intellectual leaders were forcibly subjected to periods of "political re-education." This meant that their families were subjected to blackmail and thinly veiled threats of worse things to come if proper "appreciation gifts" or other forms of bribery did not change hands while the head of the house was being re-educated.

Nationalist Party officers assisted the police in checking the credentials of all Formosans who wished to vote, or to become candidates for office, or to stand for election to the Peoples Political Councils which came into being in 1946.

By promising these elective councils Chen Yi inadvertently made a major mistake. On the one hand the Governor-General attempted to make great propaganda by generously offering to establish the Councils at once "to hear the people's opinions," but on the other, the first elections were held and the Councils convened before the Party could get a firm grasp on the machinery. Many men who later proved wholly undesirable from the Government's point of view were elected to two-year terms before Party officials could properly check personal records and send the Party goons into action.

For the moment they were too busy dividing the spoils.

The Confiscated Japanese Property Deal

Having organized the shipment of stockpiles, provided jobs for deserving relatives and friends, and placed many Formosan leaders in "rehabilitation centers," the Governor's Commissioners settled down to the happy task of managing confiscated properties. They had found Peng Lai, the fabled islands of gold and silver in the Eastern Sea.

Immediately after the surrender at Tokyo Bay the Japanese at Taipei formed a Property Registration Commission to prepare for the transfer of titles to the Allied Powers or to the Chinese National Government, representing the Allies. Many types of wealth were surrendered. For our purposes we can group them under three general categories.

Government properties included all those owned by the national administration at Tokyo or by the Taiwan Government-General, or by these two acting in partnership. This group embraced all public lands and buildings, the State-owned transport and communications systems including railways, radio stations, public telegraph and telephone systems, the police telecommunications systems, port installations, and many other less notable properties. State-owned productive enterprises included the salt, liquor, camphor, match and narcotics monopolies. The State's share in great quasi-public corporations brought them into this group, which included the Bank of Taiwan, the Taiwan Development Company, the Taiwan Electric Power Company and other large corporate bodies.

Public social welfare institutions and properties made ready for transfer included the schools, hospitals, research stations, farms and forests, laboratories, training institutes and many other small agencies and properties of a public-service nature. Surrendered financial assets included postal savings institutions in which both Formosans and Japanese had deposits, insurance agencies, and many other investment and credit institutions holding the life savings of persons who had considered Formosa to be "home."

Private properties made ready for transfer included corporate and individual shares in companies producing sugar, timber, pineapples, chemicals, and minerals which were the colonial subsidiaries of great Japanese corporations or of the Imperial Household. The petty private holdings of some 300,000

Japanese who lived permanently in Formosa included residential properties, shops, printing presses, theaters, private clinics and hospitals, restaurants, and hundreds of small mercantile and industrial units of every description.

Japanese civilians preparing for repatriation were notified that they could take with them only property which could be carried in two hands and upon the back. All else had to be sold, surrendered, abandoned, or given away. Here was to be no two-year grace period such as the Japanese had granted the Chinese in 1895, but at least they were given an opportunity to register their losses, in the faint hope that someday they might lodge claims against the Japanese Government at Tokyo for restitution or reimbursement.

The most difficult problems arose with those properties in which there was joint Japanese and Formosan interest or title. Many of these partnerships had come into existence by mutual agreement in the last decades of the Japanese era, although there were some noteworthy instances in which prospering Formosan establishments had been obliged, under duress, to accept Japanese partners. All such jointly owned properties — the Chinese insisted — must be subjected to total confiscation on the grounds that they showed evidence of "collaboration with the enemy."

When the Japanese Property Registration Commission completed its work, qualified staff economists estimated the total value of *nonmilitary* property made ready for transfer at two billion dollars at prewar rates of exchange. If we halve this sum (to mitigate the charge that the Japanese must be expected to exaggerate their losses), we are still confronted with a billion-dollar figure. Under circumstances then affecting values at Shanghai and Taipei it was impossible to put a realistic valuation on Formosa as a whole, and upon the confiscated properties. Here was in effect an enormous reparations transfer of four or five billion dollars' worth of properties (excluding arms and ammunition), by Japan to China. Under proper management Formosa's modern economy could have been made to generate great surpluses needed in the rehabilitation program for China proper, and the island could have become an invaluable training ground for tens of thousands of Chinese technicians needed in every mainland Chinese province.

The "China First" men in the Department of State at Washington determined not to have Formosa discussed as a "reparations" payment to China; if it were discussed at all, it was considered "stolen property" now restored to its rightful owner.*

The Government and people of China proper derived very little benefit from this transaction.

---

* On one occasion at Washington I attempted to discuss the question of Formosa as "reparations," but the officer on the China Desk in the Department turned to his phone to discuss at very great length the interior decoration and appointments of a new four-motor plane which we were about to give to the Generalissimo and Madame Chiang. Since the phone conversation had to be worked immediately into a Memorandum for action, I was waved on to another desk and another day.

VI

Chen Yi's "Necessary State Socialism"

The Monopoly Mechanism

FORMOSANS WERE NOT STANDING idly by while the Japanese Property Commission compiled its lists. They took the position that Japanese wealth on Formosa had been created by the application of Formosan labor to Formosan resources. The record clearly showed that a substantial part of these confiscated properties — especially the sugar lands — had been taken from the Formosans at one time or another by illegal or extra-legal means, or by outright confiscation.

What did the Formosans expect or want in 1945?

An important number of local leaders assumed that confiscated property would be (or should be) divided three ways. The Central Government of China would take over Tokyo's share, the Formosan Government would retain its shares, and the balance — all private Japanese properties — would be held temporarily in trust, to be managed for the benefit of the island people. An arrangement could be made (they thought) to provide opportunities for Formosans to buy up these confiscated private assets as rapidly as financing could be arranged.

I do not know on what grounds it was assumed that this division would take place, but to anticipate it Formosan businessmen formed the *Taiko Kigyo Kaisha*, or Greater Public Enterprises Company, capitalized at one hundred million yen, (then about $6.6 million). Shares were bought up eagerly at Taipei. For reasons never explained they were encouraged to pay over to the Company in banknotes of one thousand yen denomination.

When this was well advanced, the Finance Commissioner suddenly announced that all banknotes of one thousand yen denomination in private hands or on deposit would be "frozen" for one year. It was construed that the new company's capital was all in one thousand yen notes. This effectively paralyzed the Formosan investment company and eliminated many Formosans who would have been competitors to the Chinese bidding for confiscated properties. For Japanese real estate, industries and enterprises Chen Yi's men had other plans.

Shanghai newcomers had ready capital — or could arrange to have it run off the presses, crisp and new. (Commissioner Yen one day told me that his solution to the nagging inflation problem was simply to "Print! Print! Print! Print! Print!") The Formosans stood no chance against such competition.

But even the newcomers had to obey new monopoly regulations — or buy their way around and through the maze of red tape which was spun out of the Government offices.

In outline, the arrangements were simple. The Commissioners controlled and directed the operations of the Government's Confiscated Property Commission by creating a new series of subsidiary commissions, each devoted to a specialized category of enterprise or property. For example, the Department of Mining and Industry (under Commissioner Pao) assumed control of more than two hundred organizations, including all major installations relating to power, sugar, metallurgy, chemicals, textiles, machine fabrication, and electrical engineering. The Department of Agriculture and Forestry (Commissioner Chao) took over food-processing industries other than the sugar mills, and to these added lumber yards, sawmills, and the marine products industries, plus hundreds of thousands of acres of productive farmlands, plantations, and forests. The Commissioner of Finance assumed control of all banks, trusts, insurance companies and other financial institutions (including the presses which supplied banknotes in the early months of the Chinese administration). He also controlled organizations set up to manage the rental and sale of small parcels of real estate and the miscellaneous small businesses, homes, and shops which did not fall into the larger categories.

This division of responsibilities was reasonable enough immediately after the transfer took place, but the next move revealed unmistakably the true direction and character of "Necessary State Socialism."

Within each Control Commission the Governor's men reserved for themselves top positions, *ex officio,* and then filled the ranks with friends, relatives, and close associates. Within each Commission special management committees were formed to control specific enterprises. For example, all confiscated tea companies came under one management, all iron works under another, all pulp mills under a third, and so on until the hundreds of small property units were merged or under the control of one agency. In this fashion, for example, Mining and Industry Commissioner Pao had developed at least thirty-three companies by midyear 1946.

The next step was the obvious one. Management committees began to be transformed into "Boards of Directors" and other convenient forms of control. In theory the Government continued to own the capital assets and real property, but the amalgamated companies were run as private enterprises. In one sense efficient Japanese ownership and management had been replaced overnight by inefficient Chinese ownership and management. The Formosans were left to nurse their grievances as best they could.

Now came the ultimate step; the Directors, Board members, managers and operating personnel — mainland Chinese at all levels — were in a position to vote themselves salaries, bonuses and perquisites, including official residences and cars, and inside opportunities to acquire blocks of shares in the new companies.

Thus a major portion of the productive economy passed into mainland Chinese hands. The Commissioners on top — Yen, Pao, Chao — held the power to regulate trade and transport, taxation, and the rehabilitation subsidies. They could grant or withhold licenses to operate and trade, they set the rates on transportation of goods, and issued (or withheld) export licenses. They had established a stranglehold on the confiscated enterprises and properties.

At the same time Commissioners and their associates as *private persons* held salaried positions and dividend-bearing shares. In a thousand public statements the Governor and his men professed dedication to the rehabilitation of damaged industries and a speedy restoration of Formosa to its high prewar production levels. In practice it was clear to all that the payment of private salaries, bonuses and dividends came first; if there was anything left over it might be spent upon long-range reconstruction.

"If You Can't Sell the Product, Sell the Plant!"

The year 1946 was one of unrelieved economic disaster. Prices rose steadily, production fell, and unemployment among the Formosans became a grave problem everywhere. The only happy people on Formosa were the Commissioners and their friends, who spent the year converting the island's industrial assets into good hard gold bars which could be tucked safely away, out of sight, in any part of the world.

The Finance Commissioner controlled three banknote printing presses which hummed busily throughout 1946. I was told by employees in the Bank of Formosa that no one actually had records of the total issue, and that there was much extra-legal printing. There was no clear definition of the channels through which fresh notes went into circulation, and the disclosure of a large-scale forgery pointed to connivance by staffmen in the Finance Department.

Between May and December all banknotes of Japanese design were gradually withdrawn. The replacement issues bore a picture illustrating the first Chinese victory over a European people (the defeat of the Dutch on Formosa by Koxinga in 1662) and the expulsion of meddlesome foreigners from the island. The new banknotes were printed in New York at the Government's order, and were shipped to Taipei by way of Shanghai. On the first day of issue the Bank of Taiwan proposed to release a total of TY 2,600,000. On that morning a mainland Chinese appeared at the teller's window with a suitcase containing no less than TY 3,000,000 in crisp new notes with which he proposed to open an account. My friend the teller summoned Bank officials who demanded explanations. These began with the remark that one of T. V. Soong's aides had made the cash available to him in Shanghai as a private favor. The interrogation was abruptly closed; the magic name had been spoken.

Large bonuses, "overseas pay," and cheap rice rations were made available to themselves by the Government officials. This contributed steadily to inflationary pressures. One by one the factories and other productive enterprises failed, and goods became scarce. Formosa in effect became a huge Thieves Market.

Formosans complained that for every shipload of commodities which left the ports they received in return only a shipload of greedy mainlanders. Few came over with a view to making Formosa a permanent home. Each tried to make the most of a good thing in the shortest possible time. We concluded that as a rule of thumb neither the Government nor private persons were interested in any transaction which yielded less than 100 per cent profit. The Japanese had reached a general conclusion that between ten and twenty years must be required in Formosa for a moderately prosperous business to recover its initial capital expenditure, but the newcomers showed no interest in long-term investment. For example, one of Japan's leading fisheries experts (Maene Hisaichi) was retained by the Government to advise on the rehabilitation of the marine products industry. He prepared plans which called for the development of fleets, technical training schools, markets, and a return of capital investment over a ten-year period. The Governor's men promptly rewrote the proposal, calling for an American agency to provide the capital, but making no allowances for maintenance, expansion, training, or the amortization of the original investment. The profits were to be immediate, and were estimated at twice the figure anticipated by the Maene Plan.

Maene gave up; he knew that he would have great difficulty in securing a release from his position as "advisor," for he knew too much of the smuggling activities being carried on by the Department of Agriculture and Forestry and so one day he simply vanished, to reappear in Tokyo, well beyond reach.

This was exclusively a "government of merchants"; the Commissioners and the majority of office-holders below them were not interested in reviving and enlarging production, but only in buying and selling. Financial policies across the board were being manipulated to advance the interests of newcomers and to eliminate competition offered by independent private Formosan enterprise.

The Finance Commissioner withheld all figures on total revenues, publishing only the budget of alleged expenditures. Statement sheets bore little resemblance to reality. For example the Government budget showed that millions of yen had been appropriated to the Education Department, but when local school administrators and teachers stood ready for operating funds and wages, the Department accounts proved empty. If the total original funds had ever really been transferred to the Education Department (a moot point), too many official hands had been in the till between the Finance Office and the countryside.

The Japanese Monopoly Bureau system offered a superb pas-

ture for the grafters in the Government. Before 1945 ten private companies were licensed to distribute the Bureau's products, and the Government confined itself to processing and
manufacture. Under Governor Chen the Government itself assumed responsibility for the distribution and sale of alcoholic
beverages, matches and camphor. The Salt Monopoly was de-
tached to form a separate bureau administered as part of the
national salt monopoly system. It was announced that the Narcotics Monopoly would be abolished.

Although only five commodities were handled officially by
the Monopoly Bureau, goods of every description were passing
under Government controls, to be bought and sold many times
over *within* and *between* the government agencies before they
reached the consumer on Formosa or at Shanghai. Each paper
transaction was expected to yield a profit to the men concerned.

Some newcomers were unfortunate enough to be assigned to
administrative jobs which were not directly associated with
production and commerce. They had to devise their own ways
of milking the economy. I discovered one of these by curious
chance, a minor one, but important in consequence.

My home lay on the principal boulevard leading from town
to the Shih Lin suburb. One day a heavily loaded bullock cart
broke down at my gate. In passing I noticed that it was loaded
with books which had been stripped of hard covers. They were
being taken, I was told, to a small pulping mill at Shih Lin.
When I discovered that one of my acquaintances was employed there it was arranged for him to set aside and sell to me
any interesting book having to do with Formosa. He told me
that each week the pulping mill received many tons of books
and statistical records — anything made of paper — and that
the bulk came from school libraries and minor office files which
had been taken over by the mainland Chinese. Many, indeed,
bore the stamp of well-known institutions, from primary schools
to high Government offices. The newcomers could see no use
for the books (written in Japanese) and so were selling them

out the back door, to be pulped, pocketing the money for themselves. At the same time, I discovered, many mainland administrators and teachers were making a private business of school supplies by requiring the children to buy paper and pencils from "private stock."

All new paper produced at the confiscated Japanese factories was reserved for the Government's use. After its own needs had been met the remainder was allocated to wholesale and retail distributors. Along the way Government officers acquired substantial quantities which they sold in the black market after paper rationing (which they themselves decreed) had driven the prices to an exorbitant figure.

There was an acute paper shortage. Normal prewar consumption had been about 2400 tons annually, when Formosa's own paper mills were producing 40,000 tons per year. Engineers with UNRRA in 1946 estimated that under proper management the total annual output could be raised to 50,000 tons at that time. The new Taiwan Pulp and Paper Company, founded by the Government in May, 1946, was the largest enterprise of its kind in all of China. One factory unit (at Lotung, south of Keelung) had previously supplied fifty-six press and publication agencies on Formosa.

A Chinese manager took over control in November, 1945, retaining a staff of Japanese technical experts to continue operations. They promptly advised him that the factory had only two months' reserve supply of certain critical materials and parts. When these were gone, they resorted to many ingenious makeshifts to keep the factory in production. Eight months after the manager had been alerted to the factory's critical needs (i.e. in June, 1946), he gave his first reply to the Japanese technical staff, saying that probably nothing could be done until the end of the year. The Japanese gave up, and sought to be repatriated.

Factory after factory simply disappeared. The principle seemed to be that "If you can't sell the product, sell the plant."

Chinese managers would not agree to operate a factory at a temporary loss to ease unemployment or to use profits for capital reconstruction. If a factory was not yielding commodities which could be sold promptly, the working assets were sold, beginning with the stockpiled raw materials and finished products, and then by dismantling the factories themselves. Units which could be sold piecemeal went first, then the very framework went, shipped off to Shanghai as scrap metal.

The fate of the Tropical Chemical Industry Company near Chia-yi was an example. Here cassava root from some eight hundred farms was processed at a factory employing more than one hundred workers. In the face of organized community protest the new management simply dismantled and sold the works as machine units and as scrap metal. The cassava farmers were without a market, and the factory workers without jobs. In a similar fashion the industrial alcohol plant near Chia-yi (the largest of its kind in the Orient) was allowed to fall into complete disrepair and go out of production. From a maximum of 3200 employees the working staff was reduced to a skeleton maintenance crew of about 130 men. Much of the plant fabric was carted away as scrap metal.

Here and there we observed able men in office, but the average was extremely poor. For example, a former YMCA worker from Shanghai was made Director of the Taichung Regional Office of the Taiwan Pineapple Company. In the best years some 25,000 acres of land had been planted to pineapples and Taichung had been one of the world's noted production areas. Pineapple industry experts from Hawaii came in 1946 to have a look. The Director for Taichung took them on a guided tour. As they rode southward from Taipei the route lay through sand dunes near the western shore. Suddenly this important Pineapple Company executive excitedly pointed out the first "pineapples," and the visitors gazed in wonder and disbelief. Mr. Fu was showing them, with obvious delight, the inedible fruits of the pandanus tree, a wild beach growth that has nothing whatever to do with the pineapple industry.

The Taiwan Tea Corporation management was just then operating at about the same level of competence. Formosa had been one of the world's leading tea producers, with a world-wide reputation, shipping 13,200 metric tons of tea in 1939. The new Director was a brother of General Keh, the Civil Administrator. One day he brought to the American Consulate three half-pound bags of tea (one for each officer in the Consulate, we supposed) with a handwritten "advertisement" copied clumsily by a 19th-century gelatin process on flimsy paper. "Would the Consulate please send these to America to help promote the tea trade?"

The Trading Bureau was of special interest to Chen Yi himself. Producers of many commodities were required to sell to the Trading Bureau at fixed prices, and the Bureau in turn sold them on the local market or at Shanghai, thereby "generating State capital." After five months' operation the Governor announced that the Bureau had accumulated a profit of 160 million Taiwan yen "in the public interest." Men working in the Bureau or close to it asserted privately that the profits were at least ten times as great.

Even members of Chen Yi's official family were astonished by the magnitude of corruption within the Trading Bureau. Word reached Nanking that Chen Yi was skimming off a disproportionate share of the profits. Investigating agents from the Central Government ordered the Bureau Director placed under arrest, but the moment the investigating Commission left Formosa, the Director was released "for lack of evidence" and left the island, a free man.

One instance will illustrate the Bureau's methods. Large stockpiles of confiscated crude rubber had fallen into the hands of the Department of Industry and Mining, which resumed local production of bicycle tires, shoes, and other rubber goods. The finished products reached the market at exorbitant prices. Vigorous public protest brought the explanation that the Trading Bureau was receiving only a 10 per cent profit; the public should not complain. Technically, the 10 per cent figure was indeed accurate, but investigation showed that by arrangement with officials in Commissioner Pao's Department of Industry and Mining, the prices of rubber had been marked up 600 per cent *before* the rubber goods were sold to the Trading Bureau, which then so modestly added a mere 10 per cent to the inflated price.

Ships and Rails: Communications in an Island World

Transport and communications are the ultimate controlling factors in an island world. The people of Formosa were entirely dependent upon their railway system for internal economic life, and upon ocean shipping for communication with the larger world.

The Railway Bureau was made responsible to appropriate offices in the Central Government. Wartime damage at key junctions was soon repaired. Rolling stock was in poor condition, but the Taipei (Sungshan) Railway Shops were considered to be superior to any on the China mainland. Although some replacement parts were in short supply, it was clear that the principal damage to railroads in 1945 and 1946 was suffered at the hands of the incoming Chinese themselves. Soldier-gangs made off with all copper wiring and switching equipment they could find, and passengers in the second-class coaches slashed out the plush upholstery. No metal fixture in any coach, baggage car or "goods wagon" was safe.

The new Bureau Director (Chen Ching-wen) was an arrogant "proper pipe-smoking chap" who had acquired an exaggerated British accent at school in England, a dislike of "meddling Americans," and a monumental contempt for the Formosan people, often plainly expressed. Members of the UNRRA Team considered him an able administrator, most fortunate to inherit a well-organized, well-staffed railway system.

But under this new administration nothing was safe aboard

the freight and baggage cars. By midyear 1946 shippers had to assign their own agents to ride with goods in transit from town to town to ensure arrival and delivery at the proper destination.

Director Chen developed a corps of special Railway Police, but they were soon accused of being as unreliable as any of the other special and regular police forces, for despite heavy guards aboard the trains, freight and baggage shipments, if unaccompanied, continued to disappear or were rifled along the way. Because of his arrogance, and the ruthless behavior of his private policing force, Director Chen became an object of special dislike among the Formosan people.

At times the highly developed transport and communications system seemed to baffle the new administration. There was nothing like it in any province on the mainland. On one occasion a Commissioner complained to me "The Formosans have too much and demand too much." Before the war there had been twelve express or semi-express trains each day passing between the ports of Keelung and Takao (Kaohsiung), and with subsidiary services as well. In their peak years the Japanese railways on Formosa had carried approximately one-sixth of the toal freight tonnage carried over the whole of the sprawling continental Chinese railway system in its best year (1936). The Commissioner noted that China got along well enough with two express trains per day running between the national capital (Nanking) and Shanghai, one of the world's largest cities. The Formosans (he said) were making a nuisance of themselves in clamoring for the restoration of "normal" services.

Commissioner Jen controlled warehousing, internal transport, and portside shipping facilities. Few goods could move from the countryside to local markets or from the island to the mainland without paying tribute to the communications monopoly.

This enhanced the profits of smuggling. The laws, rules and regulations on the books of the Communications Department were not there to improve and promote transport services but were there to be circumvented — for a fee. Here the squeeze system flowered in its finest form, for there were few Formosans whose livelihood was not affected, and no mainland enterprise could ship or receive goods without a proper permit, to be had for a price.

The monopoly on sea transport dominated the economy, and was in the hands of the Taiwan Navigation Company, by now a subsidiary of the China Merchants Steam Navigation Company. In the next chapter we will review the effects of this stranglehold upon transport and communications, reflected most clearly in the UNRRA reports for 1946 and in the threatened extinction of foreign private commercial interests on Formosa.

Crisis Behind the Scenes?

It had been obvious from 1941 to 1945 that the Chinese had little understanding of the wealth and complexity of the island economy, and that our American studies of the island had directed Chinese attention to it and stimulated interest in the spoils. T. V. Soong was in wartime Washington occasionally, and his agents and lieutenants kept him well informed. It required some little time *after* the surrender, however, for word to spread through Chungking, Nanking and Shanghai that in Formosa China had indeed inherited "Treasure Island."

The only large-scale foreign investment in prewar Formosa had been a $25,000,000 bond issue floated by J. P. Morgan and Company on behalf of the Japanese Government to finance construction of the first dams and power stations at Sun-Moon Lake. The J. G. White Engineering Corporation had surveyed the power potential and upon White reports the Morgan Company had agreed to promote the enterprise. Late in World War II it is not impossible that T. V. Soong (then Foreign Minister) was approached for assurance that American investments in

Formosa would be respected in the event of a transfer of sovereignty. Be that as it may, Soong had prepared well in advance of the Surrender at Taipei; within a matter of days the J. G. White Corporation had a team based at Taipei to check the power situation and report on industrial potential.

Nothing long remains secret in China; we must presume that the contents of the second White Survey report were fairly widely known early in 1946. The Government moved from Chungking to Nanking on May 1. About that time I was in Shanghai and found myself wined and dined by a number of major bankers and businessmen eager to discuss the situation in Formosa. Questions and comments clearly reflected a keen but new interest in the island, its economic history and its current problems under Chen Yi's administration.

I interpreted some of the remarks to reflect considerable chagrin that the Generalissimo had turned Formosa over to Chen Yi and Necessary State Socialism. My interrogators obviously thought Chen Yi had held the island long enough to reap his reward, and feared that the total economy would suffer irreparable damage if he remained there much longer.

In May and June we became aware of a crisis behind the scenes we believed to be the consequence of a powerful conflict of interests at Nanking and Shanghai — a determined effort to oust Chen Yi and the so-called Political Science Clique which he was supposed to represent. There was great tension and the threat of violence, but we could not obtain a clear definition of the lines of conflict.

At one moment it was rumored that T. V. Soong himself would fly in (several leafy arches were erected near the airfield to frame "Welcome!" signs); and it was rumored that he had someone in the city waiting to replace the Secretary General, Keh King-en (the "Civil Administrator"). Any changes at this level would mean a drastic redistribution of authority, wealth and privilege. Since General Keh was not a "Chen Yi" man, we wondered if Soong was about to eliminate a rival faction which

had brought critical pressure to bear at Nanking. Perhaps
Chen Yi was not sharing the wealth to everyone's satisfaction.

The surface manifestations of crisis were very real. Communications between Formosa and the mainland were obviously a
key to the situation if it came to a show of force. For a month
regular air service to Shanghai was suspended. The Chinese
Air Force suddenly showed that it would tolerate no interference with its properties and prerogatives. Armed Air Force
units seized the principal airfield (Sungshan), surrounded it
with guards and set up sandbagged barricades with a gate at
the main approach. They defied the Governor to take the airport. For a fortnight the Shanghai Bureau of Communications
refused to transmit telegraphic messages to Formosa. Obviously someone near the top of the National Administration was
bringing heavy pressure to bear upon Taipei.

The American Consulate became very popular as a consequence. Commissioner Pao Ko-yung was suddenly seized with
a desire to do pressing business at Shanghai and asked for our
help in getting him aboard an American plane. The former
Taipei Chief of Police (now suddenly transformed into a Special Representative for the Foreign Ministry, according to his
calling card) persuaded the American Consul to help him secure passage aboard a foreign vessel then at Keelung. An
agent from the Governor asked the Consul's help in getting the
Governor's Japanese mistress (Formosa's "First Lady") out of
the island; she too had pressing reasons to reach Shanghai — or
at least to leave Formosa. These were official people and "technical experts," therefore our office was happy to oblige.

For a brief time it seemed probable that Formosans would
witness a bloody clash within the ranks of their mainland
"brothers" and "liberators," but the crisis passed, settled somewhere by compromise.

Cutting the Formosan Pie Another Way

Chen Yi and his men remained at Taipei but the Commissioners had to share the spoils on a wider basis. Nanking directed them to reorganize confiscated properties and to provide a new division of responsibility. Certain major enterprises were to be entrusted to the executive management of the National Resources Commission. The NRC alone was in a favorable position to arrange foreign (American) financial and technical aid on the scale required to rehabilitate the Taiwan Copper Mining Company (all gold and copper mines), the Taiwan Aluminum Manufacturing Company (with plants at Hualien and Kaohsiung), and all island petroleum interests, now brought together as the Taiwan Branch of the China Petroleum Company. The NRC men — technically able and with a reputation for honesty — began promptly to rehabilitate the mines which had been so badly damaged after the surrender, and to reconstruct the bauxite processing plants. The oil refineries near Kaohsiung had been damaged in 1944 and 1945, but could be brought back to their original planned capacity of 100,000,000 gallons of petroleum products annually. The China mainland had nothing to match these three enterprises in scale of operations or in technical development.

The new dispensation called for the formation of seven new corporations to be managed jointly by the National Resources Commission, the Taiwan Provincial Government, and certain private mainland Chinese capital investors, who were not identified. These seven companies brought together all the Japanese power installations, sugar interests, chemical fertilizer factories, paper and pulp industries, alkali industries, machine-manufacturing operations and shipbuilding concerns, including the drydocks at Keelung.

It should be remembered that henceforth any American or

United Nations aid extended to these industries was aid to the unspecified private capital investors then on the mainland as well as to the Nationalist Party Government.

The leftovers (which were by no means inconsiderable) were divided among Chen Yi's Commissioners, and they, too, underwent reorganization. Twelve major companies were combined under one management to be known as the Taiwan Industrial Enterprises Company, directed by Commissioner Pao. Shares in this company were held by the Taiwan Government and private investors, who turned out to be the Commissioners and their associates. The syndicate embraced all confiscated companies having to do with coal, iron, rubber, vegetable oils and fats, textiles, industrial ceramics, electrical equipment, glass, chemicals, printing supplies, and supplies required for the construction, mining, and industrial maintenance activities on the island.

After June, 1946, only eight million yen were made available by the Government to private Formosan enterprises for the second half of the year; Commissioner Pao's new Taiwan Industrial and Mining Enterprises Syndicate was provided with an operating capital of two *billion* yen.

The Formosans were simply frozen out. As they struggled to revive and rehabilitate their own small industries and commercial enterprises they found their rivals were Government men who held the licensing power, controlled transport, and manipulated the capital and credit sources. The Formosans were overwhelmed by the red tape of the licensing system. Few permits or licenses could be obtained without payment of squeeze.

Thus in late 1946 the Formosans found themselves at the mercy of three principal agencies. The Finance Commission very effectively restricted private (Formosan) use of foreign credit and of domestic loans for development purposes. The Department of Transport and Communications exerted a powerful influence on the flow of commodities, and the Taiwan Trading Bureau fixed prices which made black-marketing inevitable and universal. This in itself generated a wealth in bribes for the law-enforcement officers.

Quite naturally the Formosans measured these conditions against the best years they had known in the Japanese era. Using 1937 prices as a base-line of 100, the commodity price indexes prepared at the UNRRA offices and at the American Consulate summarize the story. Foodstuffs rose from 3323 in November, 1945, to 21,058 in January, 1947. The cost of building materials rose from 949 to 13,612, despite the resumption of forest operations, local cement production, and brick-kiln operations, and despite a light need for new housing, thanks to the availability of thousands of vacated Japanese homes.

The farmer, who desperately needed chemical fertilizers, saw the index figure rise from 139 at the end of the war to 37,560 by January, 1947, although local factories were returning to production, and China's Western allies were donating tens of thousands of tons of fertilizer through the UNRRA program.

Unemployment became a grave problem. Manufacturing industries before the war had employed between 40,000 and 50,-000 persons. Fourteen months after the surrender fewer than 5000 were employed. For example, an UNRRA report on one machine-tool shop showed that a normal payroll of 1000 men had been reduced to a maintenance minimum of thirty-five employees by the end of 1946. They could not meet the rising cost of living in the cities. Late in 1946 the unemployed Formosans began to drift back to their ancestral homes in the countryside, to help out on the farm. But they took all their grievances and disappointments with them.

Under these conditions new extremes of wealth and poverty appeared. The small but prosperous Formosan middle class began to vanish. Men and women from Shanghai set unprecedented standards of luxury, and ragged peddlers and beggars — a new phenomenon in Formosa — became a common sight.

My Formosan friends complained bitterly that they might as well give up urban life and go back to tilling the soil. And this,

I suspect, was precisely what Chen Yi's Commissioners hoped they would be forced to do.

The sooner Formosa could be reduced to the familiar conditions of mainland provincial life, the easier it would be to manage the economy, KMT-style.

But the Formosans — and UNRRA in Formosa — took a different view.

VII

Unwelcome Witnesses

The Formosa Problem That Would Not Go Away

"THIEVES AND RASCALS can run faster in the dark." The mainland Chinese who were glad to see the U. S. Army Liaison Group depart in April, 1946, were not happy to see an American Consulate and an UNRRA office established at Taipei in May.

It would be difficult to say who most regretted the necessity for a Consulate — Chen Yi's men or some of the junior officers at Washington who refused to consider Formosa a distinct "problem" and were not prepared to discuss Formosa's legal status.

In prewar days commerce and visa work were the primary concerns of American consular establishments around the world, and so it had been at Taipei. After 1939 Formosa's trade with the United States dwindled to the vanishing point; the State Department proposed to close the office. The British Government — considerably wiser in these matters — thought it worthwhile to keep open a small window here, for it was obvious that Japan was building up Formosa as a forward base for military adventure, and Hong Kong was nearby. The Philippines attack in December, 1941, was launched from Formosan bases. The Vice Consul and his clerk were promptly interned, the consular records and furniture packed off to storage in the

British Consulate at Tamsui. Thus the civil interests of the United States were not represented on Formosa for three and one-half years.

In January, 1946, I was asked to transfer from the Naval Reserve to the Foreign Service. China had virtually no navy and naval interests on Formosa could be looked after by our Attaché's Office at Shanghai.

I reported to the Naval Attaché at Chungking and then returned to Washington to report here and there around town.

My old colleagues in the War and Navy Departments were eager to discuss the situation in Formosa, but not so some of the "China Firsters" in the State Department. It was an astonishing experience. There was manifest an unspoken belief or hope that if Formosa were not discussed, any problems there (real or fancied) would simply vanish. If there was a problem, it was a purely local one of bad relations between two groups of Chinese; it should not be permitted to rise to a level of serious discussions along the Potomac. Gains made in the Japanese half-century were of no interest.

On March 6, an officer called me into his office in the old State Department building, tossed a paper across the desk and said brusquely that he had been directed to show it to me. To forestall any suggestions of change, he said that it was to be in the hands of the State, War and Navy Coordinating Committee (SWNCC) on this very afternoon, March 6. The SWNCC (known as "Swink") was a policy-discussion board from which well-considered policy questions or alternatives were moved forward to higher levels in or near the Cabinet.

The State Department had been asked for a statement of its position on the status of Formosa, and this was to be the answer prepared in the Far Eastern Division.

The Memorandum stated very briefly that after careful consideration it was the Department's view that the Chinese Nationalist Government exercised *de facto* control, hence the United States would recognize China's exclusive claim to sovereignty. So far as we are concerned, "This is China now."

I brought forward my tiresome points (a) that Japan had surrendered Formosa to the Allies, and not to China alone, (b) that the United States was throwing away in advance the legal right to intervene on Formosa if in future the Allies should need the island as a policing base, and (c) the American government was ignoring a moral obligation to see that the "liberated" Formosan people were given just treatment and a guarantee of basic human rights.

As the paper was taken from my hands and tossed into the "OUT" basket, the reply was "Yes, but that's just too bad . . ."

Two weeks later the Department had rather an unpleasant jolt; the Formosa issue was not "going away" as it should. The Scripps-Howard papers in Washington had begun to publish a special dispatch series by William H. Newton under these bold, black headlines:

CORRUPT CHINESE RULE BLEEDING RICH ISLE

CHINESE EXPLOIT FORMOSA WORSE THAN JAPS DID

FORMOSAN PLANTS RUST AS CHINA BUNGLES RULE

U.S. PARTLY BLAMED FOR FORMOSA'S WOES

The *Washington Post* editorialized on the "Formosa Scandal" and asked if the United States could afford to stand by while our ally and protégé, Nationalist China, made such a mockery of all the wartime "liberation" promises. Here and there across the country the Newton series evoked similar press comment. Every Congressman read the Washington stories — or at least saw the headlines.

Newsmen at the State Department asked embarrassing questions and received short answers. "Responsibility for conditions in Formosa, where the war's aftermath has produced corruption, looting, and graft, rests with China and not with the United States, State Department officials said today." On the hasty surrender of all Allied rights and interests to the Chinese, the Department spokesman observed that "the United States has no part in the rule of Formosa . . . the ability of the Chinese to administer Formosan affairs was not a consideration in the arrangement." [1]

I had not seen Correspondent Newton since he had visited Formosa and provoked such an angry roar from our colonel, and I had had no communication with him even then, nevertheless some of my new colleagues in the Department and most of Chen Yi's Commissioners at Taipei instantly concluded that I had prepared or promoted these stories.

Thus the Formosa problem came home to roost in a very embarrassing and public manner at the nation's capital. The need for official American representation at Taipei could no longer be ignored nor action delayed.

Institutional Schizophrenia: The American Consular Establishment

A career consul was sent to reestablish the American office, and to restore, if he could, the prewar consular routines. He was soon to discover that something more than tea-shipment certificates and occasional passport work were to require attention, but he did the best he could to maintain the traditional routine. This itself was a complex job under the circumstances, for the little book of *Foreign Service Regulations* was clearly out of date; the postwar world had not been made to order in Washington, D. C. For some months we did our collective best, as an official body, to ignore unpleasant realities about us, and to deal only with official bodies of equal or higher rank.

Our consular staff numbered three American officers — the Consul, a Vice Consul, and an officer in charge of the United States Information Service. We had a supporting body of devoted clerks, interpreter-translators, radio operators and general errand boys. Some were Formosans and some were mainland Chinese.

The Director of the USIS was in a most difficult position, for he was called upon to pioneer both inside and outside the consular office. The United States had never maintained a formal propaganda agency in peacetime. This new, subsidiary organization at the Consulate was obviously unwelcome and irritating. Its position in relation to bills of lading and visa duties was not well defined in the *Foreign Service Regulations*. Worst of all the USIS program called for some sensitivity to local current affairs and called for a show of cordial interest in local unofficial people that was distressing to old-school bureaucrats.

The USIS was expected to "tell the people about democracy," to explain American policy, and to assure the local population that Washington had its best interests at heart. The basic idea was to persuade people to "join up" with the United States and to close their ears and eyes to anything unfavorable to the American image. We were to show "our side" in the best possible light.

Unfortunately in those early days of USIS operations the USIS representative was expected to maintain a constant flow of radio and press news-release handouts to local radio stations and publishers. Too often these were stale or stereotyped and much too often entirely unsuited for release in the local situation. But instead of exercising local discretion to withhold unsuitable releases sent out from Washington, we were considered bound to distribute them.

The USIS operation at Taipei was extremely popular among Formosans, for it brought in a breath of fresh air. There was a reading room open to the general public and there were mobile units (sound trucks and projectors) which carried films into the distant countryside. The USIS representative took part in many ceremonial activities which had nothing whatever to do with tea-exports, visa problems, or the official activities of the Chinese Government.

But from a traditional Foreign Service point of view this exposed the Consulate to far too many contacts with unofficial bodies. Since the Consulate had become so extremely active in pushing the American point of view, many Formosans assumed that they would receive a sympathetic hearing if they came forward to express a Formosan point of view as well. They brought their troubles to the Consulate with ever-increasing frequency. It was all very irregular.

Irregularity, above all things, was dreaded. If prescribed forms were not available for required reports, nonconformity had to be explained to Washington with meticulous detail. It was really thought better to make no report at all. Reports of "unusual events" brought risk; further reports and elaborations might be required by Higher Authority. Analysis of current events must be undertaken with utmost circumspection, if at all. Official people counted heavily; unofficial people were a waste of time and often a distinct embarrassment.

Within a few months the American Consulate at Taipei was in a schizoid state. The USIS program on the one hand attempted to create a rousing good impression of the United States as China's "Big Brother," and on the other hand the traditional Consulate proper attempted to make it very clear that as an "official body" the American Consulate was not interested in people — trade, yes, but not people. The dread of bureaucratic irregularity and possible censure impeded the flow of information to the Embassy.

We were also conscious of leakage somewhere along the line between Taipei and Washington. On June 5, one of Chen Yi's staff (Ma Hsien of the Secretariat) let it be known that a secret report on the Chinese Army's misconduct in Formosa, (prepared by the OSS team at Taipei), had been brought to the attention of General Chen Yi by the Generalissimo himself. There were other hints that the Chinese had knowledge of confidential and secret reports emanating from American agencies on Formosa. This froze the Consular blood.

My colleague, the Information Service Director (Mr. Robert J. Catto), shared my belief that Washington should have full reports on current events, for tension was growing steadily within the island, and we were keenly aware of misrepresentations sent abroad by the Governor's Office of Information. We knew that Chiang's position on the mainland was most unstable, and that circumstances within the island were prompting Formosan leaders to appeal to the United States more and more often for help. We believed it was important to conserve America's high prestige and influence among the Formosans; the United States might need their goodwill one day.

We were very well aware that the Consulate was not a policy-making body, but we felt that our Taipei office had an obligation to impress upon the Embassy and the Department the nature of the growing crisis.

We were greenhorns who had not learned to let well-enough alone, sleeping dogs lie, and dust settle.

The truth was we were all trying to pick up the bits and pieces of a world that would never be the same again. There was much more to do in the American interest than stamp shipping invoices. The Okinawan problem on Formosa in 1946 was an excellent example.

Okinawans and Other Troublesome People

Officially the Consulate took the position that the problems of nationals of other countries who were also on Formosa were of no concern to the United States of America, and in 1940 this might have been so. But in 1946 General MacArthur ordered the mass repatriation of Japanese living on Formosa. Among them were 14,906 Okinawans. Those who lived far from Keelung port sold or gave away all their properties, including their homes, moved to Taipei and Keelung, and prepared to depart. About one-third the total number had sailed for Okinawa when another MacArthur order directed the remaining Okinawans to stay in Formosa; war-torn Okinawa could not take care of them.

For months thereafter 800 homeless Okinawans camped in the fire-gutted ruin of the Government-General building, and other hundreds camped in primitive shelters in the parks or in any nearby shed. They were forced to use street-side hydrants for water and street-side ditches for latrines. An investigation (by UNRRA personnel) disclosed that more than 2000 were near starvation, that the incidence of disease was rising, the death rate was very high among old people and infants, and petty theft and prostitution were becoming the principal means of economic survival. Desperation was breeding radical agitation among the jobless younger men.

Older Okinawan leaders — some of them doctors and teachers I had known before the war — came to beg for American help for their stranded compatriots. The Chinese took the position that they were Japanese subjects and enemy aliens, obviously the responsibility of Tokyo, and of no interest to the Taipei Government.

On May 27 a principal Okinawan spokesman came to the American Consul asking for confirmation — or denial — of a rumor that SCAP had again begun negotiations for Okinawan repatriation. His people were desperate; if they were not soon to be sent home they would have to scatter over Formosa in search of shelter and food in less crowded areas.

The Consul denied knowledge of SCAP's plans; he made it clear that the American Consulate was not officially interested in the problem; the fate of the Okinawans was a matter of concern to the military authorities alone. The Consulate had received no instructions, and it should be understood that it was not the Consulate's fault that it had no proper channels through which to bring the problem to Tokyo's attention.

The Okinawans then turned to the UNRRA group, which managed to work out a modest relief program, tiding them over until Tokyo permitted repatriation.

In August I prepared the routine midyear report on social, economic and political conditions, called for by the *Foreign Service Regulations*. Lest any whisper of criticism concerning the Okinawans had reached Washington, I was directed to insert this carefully worded disclaimer:

> While the American Government here dissociates itself from the problem of many thousands of Japanese retained for "technical services," and from the problem of the several thousand Okinawan refugees who are living near starvation while awaiting American permission to return to their homeland, the possible development and repercussions of the problem of their presence in Taiwan cannot be overlooked . . .

This bureaucratic double-talk informed Washington of the problem, as a matter of record, but assured the Department that in all correctness we had done nothing about it.

There were foreigners of many nationalities marooned on Formosa at the war's end. The majority looked to the United States for help, whether they might deserve it or not. To our official distress spokesmen for the Japanese who had been retained as technicians made it clear that they looked to the United States for protection in a very chancy situation. Said one, "The fact that there is someone listening to the words of the Japanese remaining on the island with the attitude of impartiality and fairness is a great relief to us." He was referring to the UNRRA staff and not to the Consulate.

Only a demonstration of consular interest in conditions aboard repatriation ships forced the Chinese to abandon plans for grossly and most dangerously over-crowding Liberty ships sent to carry the Japanese back to their homeland, but this demonstration took place only after it was pointed out to the Consul that a disaster at sea would have international attention, and that responsibility for it would rest squarely with the American Government.

During my brief residence as the Embassy's Assistant Naval

Attaché on Formosa, I had made some reports on curious and interesting foreigners on the island at the end of 1945. There were Annamese who had been political exiles here, abandoned when Japan was defeated and driven from Indochina. A large number of Javanese seamen were present, stranded in local ports after a period of service in the Japanese merchant marine. Filippinos were present who had served the Japanese in various ways. Two Russian peddlers were known to have been living on Formosa at the outbreak of war. I could not locate them, but was not much surprised to have delivered to my hands one day a cablegram addressed simply "To the Representative of the U.S.S.R. at Keelung," which created a minor mystery, never solved. Here and there German nationals lived obscurely in the larger towns, teachers of science and of the German language, ready enough to serve Germany's ally Japan when all went well, but now claiming volubly to have been "secret agents" working for the Allies when surrender came. They were a familiar breed all along the China coast. In 1946 a German bearing a Peruvian passport came to me asking for a visa, and for introductions which would help him find scientific employment in the United States. He professed to be investigating microorganisms living in or near hot springs, though we developed reasons to believe that he might be more interested in radioactive minerals. He had been trained in a German science institute, sent by the Nazi Government to Peru, and from there (with a Peruvian passport) sent on to Japan and Manchuria. The war's end found him employed in one of T. V. Soong's vast enterprises, and by the Soong interests, so he said, he had been sent to Formosa. He did not like the prospects of impending trouble there, and so asked us for permission to enter the United States. Our answer was "No."

The presence on Formosa of such a diverse bag of foreign nationals suggested the need for a report to Washington. "No," said the Consul, the presence and activities of other foreigners was of "no concern whatsoever" to the American Consulate.

Late in the year I sent along to the Embassy and the Department a secret coded supplementary report upon prominent personalities about town, and certain evident conflicts within the Taipei Government. My report evoked a telegraphic request for more detail, but this was construed to be a rebuke; I had committed an unpardonable bureaucratic sin by raising an issue which called attention to ourselves.

My second semi-annual report for 1946 on social, political and economic conditions was endorsed, coded, and forwarded through Nanking, to Washington. It carried a warning that tensions within Formosa were near the breaking point, a violent crisis might be upon us at any time. The document was given a number and entered into our secret record book.

Thus throughout 1946 the Consulate was an unhappy "schizophrenic" organization. The career Consul represented the old regime, when Consulates were official bodies dealing principally with official bodies and with commercial matters, according to the *Regulations*. The USIS organization, on the other hand, represented the new postwar order. The world had changed, the United States Government and people were entering upon the long cold war of words, ideas, and human emotions.

We were reminded soon enough of this when we began to see the pattern of Chinese reaction to the presence of prying, spying foreigners on Formosa.

Chinese Reaction to Foreign Critics: "Getting the Facts Straight"

Chen Yi's men resented the presence of foreigners, for it gave them a double task. On the one hand they had to persuade the world overseas that despite occasional unfriendly news reports, they were doing a magnificent job, rehabilitating the economy and leading the Formosans back from Japanese servitude to full and happy membership in the democracy of China.

On the other hand, they had to undermine and destroy, if

they could, the high prestige of Americans on Formosa, and the emotional trust with which Formosans were turning to foreigners with tales of woe. The biggest task was to block development of Formosan appeals to the United Nations or the United States. The American Consul's associates and the UNRRA group were a menace to the success of Necessary State Socialism.

The Department of State appeared to be much more certain of China's legal position than the Chinese themselves seemed to be. Would other nations be willing to subscribe to the views on sovereignty embodied in the SWNCC memorandum? And what if unfriendly press notices abroad prompted the United States Congress to demand an investigation?

Anticipating this challenge, Chen Yi reorganized the Provincial Government Information Service. All references to the "provisional" character of the local government began to disappear from official and unofficial documents and from public statements. All foreign visitors — and especially American visitors — were smothered with evidence of progress, presented by men who knew how to flatter Americans. Steps were soon taken to lower American prestige among the Formosans and to discredit Formosans in the eyes of foreigners overseas. Something had to be done to check this dangerous talk of local appeals to the United States or the United Nations.

A graduate in journalism from the University of Missouri (Stanway Cheng, M.A., '37) was placed in charge. Huang Chao-chin (M.A., Illinois, '26) became "Foreign Affairs Representative" or front man. The Central News Agency of China opened a Formosa office on March 16. A private, confidential press-clipping wire-service in Cheng's office kept the Governor's men abreast of published American comment on Formosan affairs.

Visiting Congressmen, the Administration's agents, and other unwary guests who came to Taipei were at once taken in hand by Cheng and Huang or their deputies, to be given flattering

V.I.P. treatment. For visiting "fact-finders" it was a great convenience to be handed up-to-date statistical summaries which could be read at any time on the homeward journey. These made tedious on-the-spot investigations unnecessary, and left time for delightful suburban tours, hotspring outings and gargantuan Chinese feasts. Over-crowded scheduling for the visitors ensured a maximum insulation from reality and prevented any unfortunate straying from well-marked paths. If a visitor insisted upon talking to Formosans there was always ex-Mayor Huang, a native of the island, and Chairman of the People's Political Councils, to satisfy their curiosity. Delays in transportation, far from Taipei, or mechanical difficulties with cars within the city became standard means of forestalling undue meetings with independent and articulate Formosans or long conferences at the American Consulate. Creating insulation for visitors was a fine art, pursued by talented men.

Manipulation of the news to show "progress under Chen Yi," and America's hearty support of the Chen Yi regime is illustrated in this example, published in Taipei, which purports to have originated in Washington:

GREAT IMPROVEMENT IN REHABILITATION ON FORMOSA
AS TOLD BY RETURNING U.S. ECONOMIC OFFICERS

(UP) Washington, Aug. 5, Relayed by Central News Agency. United States economic officers who have just returned from a tour of the Far East do not fall in with the general belief that the Chinese administration on the island of Formosa is inadequate and that there has been large-scale looting and ransacking.

They saw marked improvement in rehabilitation work in the regions they visited where the Chinese Government seemed to be exercising an adequate management of all industries and local affairs with every possible technical assistance available.

Except those who were retained as technical experts and their families, totalling about 28,000, all Japanese on the island have been duly repatriated.[2]

The Newton articles were not forgotten. To smother unfavorable impressions created by one man's dispatches, Chen's Information Office invited twenty-six correspondents to spend the week of August 31–September 6 on Formosa, with lavish entertainment and all expenses paid.

The *bona fide* correspondents knew that their press credentials for long-term work on the mainland might be lifted if they were too outspoken. They could merely hint that all was not well. For example, Ronald Stead of the *Christian Science Monitor* wrote that "Chinese Government officials and Taiwan provincial administrators say the number of dissidents is very few. So far our time has been so occupied in eating our way down and up the island, receiving the most lavish hospitality everywhere, but making only a wide, superficial inspection, that there has been little time to weigh the situation."

A few foreigners were assumed to be well-paid agents hired to steer the group toward a proper understanding and reportage of Chinese achievements on Formosa, and some frankly confessed (privately) that they were "free-loaders" professing assignments — fictitious or self-devised — from local papers in the United States. Temporary press cards had been issued to them at Shanghai.

Transients could be handled by Chen Yi's agents with marked success, but the presence of UNRRA and Consular people remained always a problem. In a move to concentrate the foreigners' evening activities at one spot, Cheng and the Information Service arranged (behind the scenes) to open the Lucky Bar, thoughtfully designed to appeal to American patronage. Here the Chinese Information Service could keep abreast of day-to-day affairs within the foreign community.

I had doubted the accuracy of the report which told of the origins of the Lucky Bar, but one summer evening, after drinks and dinner at my house, the mysterious Admiral S. Y. Leigh (T. V. Soong's man, Li Tsu-i) asked me why I never went to the Lucky Bar, adding, indiscreetly, that whenever he wanted to know what Americans thought of the situation in Formosa he simply went to the Bar and took the booth next to that habitually occupied by the American Consul, his wife, and their friends, or sat near the favorite booths and tables of the UNRRA members drifting in and out.*

The story of the United Nations Relief and Rehabilitation Administration (UNRRA — Taiwan) is thoroughly documented and rests upon the observations of able men and women from fourteen nations — doctors, nurses, industrial engineers and agricultural specialists.†

A majority had worked in China on earlier assignment. Formosa was a challenge; here was no need for "relief," but an opportunity to bring about speedy rehabilitation and a high production of material needed for relief on the mainland. The Formosan people were well organized, well disciplined, "modernized" and eager to cooperate. And it was refreshing to discover that the Formosans were friendly and that here were none of those signs reading "Yanks, go Home!" Soon the presence of this mixed foreign group exerted an influence upon Formosan relations with the mainland which was out of all proportion to its numbers, or the value of the material and technical aid brought into the island under its auspices.

* Thus in the Lucky Bar we had the forerunner of Madame Chiang's clubs, The Officers' Moral Endeavour Association (OMEA), a series of hostelries which catered to foreign correspondents, businessmen, diplomatic service underlings, and minor military observers, all taken in at a distinctly favorable rate. To the charitable OMEA establishment there were added in due course the Friends of China Club, the Taipei Guest House, and the Grand Hotel, all of them listening posts — Lucky Bars — on a grander scale, befitting the "temporary capital of China."

† Australia, Brazil, Canada, Columbia, Costa Rica, Denmark, France, Haiti, Holland, New Zealand, Norway, the United Kingdom, and the United States of America. One Formosan staff-member later became an American citizen.

The technical and professional fields represented here included medicine, nursing, dentistry, child welfare, public health, dietetics, sanitary, industrial, and transport engineering, and agricultural rehabilitation. There was a small supporting staff for administration.

VIII

The UNRRA–CNRRA Story[1]

The Peculiar UNRRA Program for China

THE UNRRA PROGRAM for China was the latest but not the last of a century-long series of American philanthropic attempts to improve the conditions of the Chinese people. The entire 19th-century missionary effort implied a degree of patronage not very welcome among the great majority of educated Chinese. Missionary success in the 19th century was confined largely to the lowest classes. In the 20th century, aid to China began to be institutionalized, taking the form of support for hospitals, schools, research institutes, and international scholarships. It was not really necessary for a Chinese to become a Christian in order to benefit directly from foreign philanthropy. Japan's invasion of China in 1932, her withdrawal from the League of Nations, and the second invasion (1937) brought American "Aid to China" to an important level of national interest and international politics. The *manipulation* of aid grants and credits became truly big business at the Chinese capital, invariably dominated by the Chiang-Soong group.

When the United States offered Lend-Lease aid to China, T. V. Soong insisted that the "dignity of the Chinese people" required that full legal control of aid supplies must rest in Chinese hands.

Mr. Yen Chia-kan, lately Chen Yi's principal aide for economic affairs in Fukien Province, served at Chungking as Director of Procurement for the Chinese War Production Board. This meant in effect the collection and redistribution of materials produced in China, an operation geared to the procurement and allocation of American aid supplies.

This was not a happy arrangement, for there were often times in China when American military units in desperate need were unable to use supplies — aviation gasoline, for example — stockpiled nearby but held under Chinese control.

When a United Nations Relief and Rehabilitation program was proposed for China late in World War II, the arrangements for it had to be made through Soong, at that moment the Minister for Foreign Affairs. When it was actually carried through, he directed it as President of the Executive Yuan, with his brother-in-law, H. H. Kung as Vice President.

The China Program was the largest "single country" program attempted by UNRRA anywhere in the world, and through it China received goods and services valued in excess of half a billion dollars, including $470,000,000 contributed by the United States. In effect we were trying desperately to salvage something of the ally who had been propped up in the Security Council of the United Nations as a "Great Power" but was in fact rapidly falling apart. Not much aid — as aid — went beyond the warehouses at Shanghai.

The United States, dominating UNRRA operations, adopted a thoroughly unrealistic approach to the China program. In Europe the international organization, cooperating with the host countries, retained control of all material supplies for relief and rehabilitation until they reached the point of "end use." Not so in China. Chinese spokesmen, led by Madame Chiang and her brother T. V. Soong, maintained that only Chinese knew how to operate in China, and again that the "dignity of the Chinese people" would not permit foreign interference. The United Nations organization would be permitted to operate in China only in an advisory capacity. They spoke with convincing sincerity as leaders who understood and could interpret the American way of life; they had dedicated their lives to bringing reform and democracy to their ancient country. We could deny them nothing.

Washington agreed and the United Nations had to accept the terms. It was an extraordinary arrangement; UNRRA would relinquish title to all supplies the moment they left the ship's tackle and dropped to the docks in any port of China.

This was the price of admission to Chinese territory (including Formosa) and was in effect a gigantic blackmail scheme. The probable alternatives were clear, for without massive aid China would slide into chaos and communism. The American public was not told that Madame Chiang's family dominated the warehousing and shipping interests of China, including the China Merchants Steam Navigation Company which managed subsidiary shipping on China's rivers, and most of the principal warehousing facilities along the docks at every important river-port and anchorage in the country. These were the docks at which the UNRRA relief supplies would be unloaded and the warehouses into which they would be carried. UNRRA would be billed for both storage and transport.

Through the Executive Yuan (T. V. Soong, President) the Chinese Government created an organization known as the "Chinese National Relief and Rehabilitation Administration" or CNRRA (pronounced "Sin-rah") which was authorized to take possession of relief supplies and to carry through a rehabilitation program for which UNRRA specialists would make recommendations, but in which they would exercise no authority.

Insistence upon Chinese supremacy in the administration of relief was prompted in some degree by national pride and considerations of face. The Nationalists wanted to demonstrate that at least they were masters in their own house. In the distribution of aid goods *within* China great effort was made to conceal the foreign or international character of the postwar UNRRA supplies. Chiang wanted credit to accrue to the Nationalist Party Government; Kung and Soong wanted funds and materials to pass through the family's banks and warehouses.

Hardly less astonishing than the transfer of legal title (and consequent loss of control) were the arrangements which the Chinese devised to increase the value of the international gifts. Although a half-billion dollars' worth of goods and services were being *donated* to China, the Government complained that it could not afford to distribute relief goods. If anything were to be done at all, UNRRA had to agree that CNRRA could sell relief goods "at a moderate rate" to generate funds with which to pay for distribution.

In subsequent accounting to UNRRA, China charged off $190,000,000 as "administrative costs," and an enormous percentage of relief goods disappeared into private channels once they had passed through those yawning warehouse doors.*

UNRRA's only defensive weapon in these circumstances was a degree of authority to halt the entry of relief supplies into Chinese waters, a weapon extremely difficult to use.

The Fraudulent CNRRA Program

The local UNRRA–CNRRA program began at Shanghai on November 1, 1945, when funds were appropriated for use in Formosa. Ultimately the Taipei CNRRA organization had a central office staff of about one hundred persons, including half a dozen foreign specialists assigned by UNRRA to work within the CNRRA organization.

The CNRRA Director for Formosa was Chien Chung-chi,

* No time was wasted; a Norwegian ship's captain told me that he had docked at Shanghai one morning with an UNNRA cargo including some rather unusual brands of tinned food. He had supervised cargo discharge before noon. In the late afternoon he saw this distinctive food-brand being hawked in the streets near the dock. It was possible that a stray carton or case had "slipped overboard" but he thought not; checking, he observed carters hauling the shipment out from one end of the warehouse as fast as it was being brought in from the ship at the other.

who had been Governor Chen Yi's private secretary for twenty-five years. Three of the divisional directors under Chien had long been associated with the Governor on the mainland, knowing well his views, methods and standards of operation.

Two and a half months after they began to draw pay, the first CNRRA project was inaugurated at Taipei on January 22, 1946. A gang of coolies was set to work repairing broken water pipes, but when the work was finished (on February 11), it was declared unsatisfactory, and was done a second time around; too many pipes laid down in the day had been promptly dug up at night, and shipped off to Shanghai. Nine other projects of a like nature followed this one. All of them had to do with ditch-digging and trash removal.

In the first six months of operations CNRRA-(Taiwan) spent approximately 2,800,000 yen for field projects, and nearly 8,-200,000 yen for "administrative expenses."

The UNRRA-(Taiwan) team, with much prodding, persuaded CNRRA to raise its sights and broaden its program, moving from temporary make-work unemployment-relief projects to long-range, basic rehabilitation programs. The island needed constructive rehabilitation rather than stopgap relief, and here a little relief should go a long way. They were soon disillusioned. As the UNRRA Team Reports Officer later wrote:

> Our earliest surveys of Formosa indicated that the island required little if any relief, despite the rumors which had circulated in Shanghai. The problem was not that there was insufficient food, although food production had diminished through over-working the soil and lack of fertilizers — but a matter of poor government.
>
> The Chinese had failed to understand and make any attempt to continue in operation the Japanese rationing system which had insured not an abundant but an ample amount of food for everyone. The Chinese Government, had, rather, collected a large percentage of the basic food, rice, from the farmers and

was hoarding it itself. The farmers had thought that the collection of rice had heralded a continuation of the rationing system by the new government. They did not like this system, but realized its necessity and therefore willingly sold the food to the government at a very low price (which for the most part was never paid to them). But rather than seeing that everyone received supplies of the rice, the Army and the Chinese Government smuggled the rice from the country to China where it brought high returns from the short coastal markets, or hoarded it on Formosa. This created an artificial shortage, raised prices, so that the government then received large sums when the rice was released, and put the food out of the reach of many.

This was the beginning of the aggravation of the problems of Formosa by the Chinese, a process which has continued up to the present.[2]

In summing up, the Director of the local UNRRA office reported to his superiors that his biggest battles were waged in a ceaseless effort to protect the chemical fertilizer distribution program from the scheming Commissioner of Agriculture and Forestry, and his efforts to outwit the Chinese Director of Public Health. Both were working directly for Chen Yi. One controlled the Farmers' Associations through which fertilizer must reach the peasant in the field, and the other controlled medical supplies, prized in every market in Asia. Underlying these specific areas of difficulty were the general conditions of corruption and waste in the administration of relief.

The picture was by no means sharply drawn in black and white — "good foreigners and Formosans" versus "bad mainland Chinese" — for some CNRRA employees were highly qualified mainland Chinese and of great personal integrity, but they were too few in numbers and too unimportant to present an effective check on "the system." Some had taken employment on Formosa because it appeared to offer an opportunity for genuinely constructive service. By the end of the UNRRA-CNRRA operation they admitted total defeat.

Nor were Formosans all innocent lambs-among-wolves; many found it highly profitable to collaborate with Chen Yi's men in dishonest schemes (it was much safer to cooperate than to criticize), and many were eager, independent, and highly successful operators in the black market for relief supplies.

UNRRA's Chief Medical Officer (Dr. Ira D. Hirschy) summed up the Government's attitude toward public service problems:

". . . the aims of the two organizations UNRRA and CNRRA as well as those of the individuals within them, were not identical. Whereas UNRRA was attempting to fulfill its obligations by philanthropic giving, CNRRA could not get away from the attitude that it was a business organization whose chief concern was selling at a profit." [3]

After May 1, 1946, foreign specialists ranged freely over the island, saw conditions in each district and talked to people at every economic level. Of the Chinese who wanted to do a good job, a social welfare officer had this to say:

Mr. . . . of CNRRA was an unusual person. He said, . . . "We cannot and must not promise anything to these people unless we are sure we can fulfill the promise" and he adhered to this principle . . . He particularly felt that progress for his people was quite impossible unless the corrupt regime was removed.

I talked to many Chinese who told me in whispers that they felt there was no hope for any kind of planning until they could free themselves of the corrupt officials at the top . . . One said that he had given up all hope of accomplishment under his government on the mainland until he was offered an opportunity to work in Formosa. He thought maybe given a fresh start he could do something to get the factories operating again. He saw crime increasing because of hunger and idleness in his city. But when I saw him last he was trying to resign and was in despair . . .

I talked with many Taiwanese women who were hard workers

as well as courageous citizens. They were trying to reorganize
nursery schools and service projects. They were interested in
. . . homes for the aged and sick . . . We helped them to reorganize . . . but we never felt that any of our work would endure . . . The mainland Chinese do not seem able to maintain a
plan even when they have worked on it and understand it. There
are exceptions, of course, but certainly hospitals, schools, and
institutions of public health and welfare were falling apart
under their regime. Formosa could function happily with a
minimum of social welfare planning. The people are responsive
and eager to learn how to solve their own problems.[4]

The UNRRA staff carefully analyzed relief and rehabilitation
needs and formulated recommendations for action. It was reserved to CNRRA to control and distribute relief supplies and
services. In practice UNRRA's advice was received politely
enough at weekly executive meetings at Taipei, but then it was
often enough simply ignored. Many of the mainland Chinese
seemed genuinely astonished that the UNRRA people should
be so naïve as to expect CNRRA to waste supplies on the Formosans. Nevertheless, the UNRRA group, restricted though it
was to an advisory role, exercised some influence as a check
upon CNRRA's actions, inhibiting as far as possible the subor-
dination of relief to business.

Business, nevertheless, was very good. CNRRA's sales policies on wire cable supplied for industrial rehabilitation realized
about 100 per cent profit (nearly six million yen). It will be
recalled that China charged UNRRA $190,000,000 as "adminis-
trative expenses." This figure did not include the "administrative fees" earned in the field. At Taipei CNRRA was ordered to
sell 10 per cent of the relief flour in order to finance free distribution of the balance. UNRRA discovered that in fact 75 per
cent of the relief flour was sold on this pretense, realizing a neat
profit of some $300,000.

The range and variety of fraud and speculation was limitless.
One of Chen's highest officers took control of new breeding cat-

tle imported by UNRRA — and of course took charge of the millions of yen set aside for their care and management. Little was heard of either beef or yen thereafter, but the officer had taken over the confiscated Japanese ice-manufacturing and refrigeration business, among many other things, making these a personal asset in all but name. This led to a frontal clash with UNRRA. There was an acute shortage of ammonia for ice production. Ammonia could be extracted from certain types of chemical fertilizers being imported by UNRRA, and these Chen's commissioners were authorized to allocate and distribute.

We estimated that the Governor-General and his cronies would take millions of dollars in profit from the import, distribution and sale of the chemical fertilizers which were to be received in great quantity.

UNRRA headquarters at Shanghai had agreed that this gift fertilizer could be sold to the farmer on Formosa at a price which would cover the costs of distribution within the island. Chen Yi promptly had his men create a new (and quite unnecessary) organization to handle distribution. Fat salaries and administrative costs would of course have to be charged against the return from sales.

UNRRA (Taipei) demonstrated that the farmer should pay in local currency no more than the equivalent of 3.6 to 5.0 cents per pound, according to the type of fertilizer. Despite this, when CNRRA distributed the first thousand tons they charged from eight to ten cents per pound, thus realizing an estimated profit of about $300,000.

While a second shipment of 5000 tons was entering the island, UNRRA at Taipei tried to make a major issue of this bold exploitation of the Formosan farmer and of foreign aid. It was estimated that Chen Yi's men stood to make a profit of some $500,000 on this shipment. Moreover, CNRRA's loading, unloading, and storage records showed an astonishing 20 per cent loss in transit. Investigation disclosed a real loss averaging 0.4 per cent. Nearly 20 per cent of this gift fertilizer was going into hidden storage and black-market operations — and to the Commissioner's ice-making machines.

To circumvent the foreigners' meddling at Taipei Governor Chen and his Commissioners cleverly proposed to have the Taiwan Government General purchase 200,000 tons of fertilizer from UNRRA at Shanghai under an arrangement which would keep it out of CNRRA's jurisdiction on Formosa, and hence beyond the embarrassing purview of the Formosa UNRRA team. If this move proved successful, Chen and his Commissioners could expect a profit to themselves of not less than $12,000,000 and possibly as much as $18,000,000, depending upon the type of fertilizer sent in as "relief supply."

The proposal was being negotiated when rebellion at Taipei broke in upon the Governor's career.

This vital fertilizer program affected every farming community, hence the UNRRA–CNRRA conflict was discussed in every village and farmhouse. The farmers were eager to obtain the precious chemicals at precisely the right time to apply them in the growing season. Chen Yi's men on the other hand were not at all eager to hasten distribution, for as long as the fertilizers rested in Government's warehouses, storage fees could be charged to the UNRRA–CNRRA budget. The farmers knew that the foreigners were attempting to speed the fertilizer to them, and that the Governor's men were causing the delay. They also knew that the foreigners were trying to check gross cheating in the quantities delivered and paid for.

When the UNRRA records at Kaohsiung showed abnormally high percentages of loss in transit an investigating UNRRA officer (Ray Shea) happened to notice that coolie girls sent into the ships' holds at dockside as "sweepers" seemed always to gain weight while at work. This was odd, and the weight-gain was oddly distributed on the maidens. Further investigation disclosed the widespread use of a peculiar type of pants which served as pockets, usually filled with more fertilizer than girl when the wearer came ashore.

Thus the UNRRA team watched swindle and cheating practiced at every turn in the administration of the rehabilitation program. With angry frustration the foreigners saw standards of living sink toward mainland levels as the basic opportunities for rehabilitation wasted away. There was a surplus of electric power, for example, but services were undependable, and rates were increased to a prohibitive level. One small Formosan mining enterprise which had paid TY 5000 per month for power in November, 1945, paid TY 160,000 in March, 1946. Many small shops and home industries could no longer meet the bills. Many homes returned to the 19th-century use of lamps and candlelight.

Ample supplies of coal were available and many smaller industries were ready to resume operations with minimum assistance if they could obtain fuel. But investigation showed that Chen Ching-wen's railway was doing such a roaring business with passengers it was often refusing to move freight which was more trouble to handle and yielded less revenue. The official excuse was that there was a serious lack of boiler tubes and lubricants, and this lack, of course, was blamed upon the United States and UNRRA.

With the breakdown of power and transport services the island retreated toward the 19th century, but with the interruption of the normal food supply came the real danger of rebellion.

UNRRA's Battle of the Pescadores

The only "famine areas" were in the over-crowded, infertile Pescadores Islands and in fishing and salt-field villages along Formosa's barren southwestern tidal flats. During 1946 seaweeds, potato leaves and the dried remnants of the 1945 sweet potato crop became the standard diet. Many families could afford to eat even these meager foods only once each day. More than half the Pescadores population was left unemployed when the Japanese withdrew from the Makung naval base.

An UNRRA team surveyed the problem, reported to CNRRA, and attempted to speed relief to the channel islands.

The "meddling foreigners" soon found that CNRRA was not interested in an area in which people were too poor to pay even minimum charges for relief supplies, and certainly unable to pay squeeze. The issue of "Relief for the Pescadores" became symbolic of the conflict between the foreign workers and Chen Yi's government.

The total population of the Pescadores exceeded 73,000 persons. There were fifteen doctors on the six small islands, but nine of them were in Makung town which had a population of 25,500. In one rural area there was one doctor for nearly 14,000 people.

At Makung the electric generating plant operated only from seven to eleven o'clock each evening — four hours — because of a lack of diesel fuel. Normally ten tons of diesel oil were required for minimum operations each month, but although there were forty tons on hand when the UNRRA team investigated, they were controlled by city government men (mainland Chinese) who were not interested in "wasting" fuel.

The town had running water only three hours a day, in the early morning.

The public health and medical situation was extreme. Among 200 cholera cases in 1946 there had been 170 fatalities. The isolation hospital was discovered to have two rooms for patients and one for examination. That was all. The Provincial Hospital was inactive. Dr. T. S. King, Director of the Taiwan Provincial Health Bureau, had ordered the local hospital to accept no more than one free patient for every five paying patients. At the time of the UNRRA investigation there were only three in-patients, hence the hospital administrators maintained they could treat no patients free of charge.

It was discovered that private physicians (Formosans) operating private hospitals and out-patient clinics were entirely overworked. One man was doing much more work for free patients than the entire Government medical organization in the Pescadores.

Government and relief supplies were in storage or not accounted for. There were 200 cases of malaria under treatment, but only 60 patients had been able to obtain any of UNRRA's Atabrine tablet supply, although millions of donated tablets were stored away at Taipei. The UNRRA supplies which had reached Makung (after great difficulty) lay about still crated. Of 50 cases of dried soup powder which had been shipped to Makung, only 10 had arrived.

Every pressure was brought to bear to force CNRRA action. Formosan leaders showed outspoken concern and repeatedly made it an issue in the local newspapers. At last CNRRA published an announcement that 7000 sacks of flour had been shipped to relieve Makung, but UNRRA at once called attention to the fact that only 750 sacks had been shipped, that they had been shipped unaccompanied, and that they could not now be accounted for.

On July 1 CNRRA shipped 1400 cases of biscuits from Tainan to Makung, but there Customs Officers refused to allow them to enter, sent them back to Tainan, and reported that the application for a local (Pescadores) import license read "food" instead of biscuits. Five months later (at the end of November, 1946) the head of the Makung Customs Office consented to send the documentation back to Taipei for "correction." Meanwhile hundreds of Makung residents had been starving while government agencies charged "storage fees" on the biscuits at Tainan.

In the course of this "Pescadores Incident" an UNRRA investigation disclosed that all relief shipments leaving the main island (through Tainan port) had to be cleared for export through no less than five offices there, and upon arrival at Makung a second series of five offices insisted on issuing import clearances. This included the office of the Commander of the Makung Naval Base. There were outstretched hands at every clearance desk. Ten agencies required payments of some sort before relief goods, donated by China's allies, could move forward 30 miles to a starving community.

After three months' effort UNRRA secured 500 tons of Siamese rice in Hong Kong, to be delivered to the Pescadores aboard a British freighter. En route the vessel stopped first at Keelung. UNRRA officers were delighted to find room aboard for 800 tons of fertilizer desperately needed by the Pescadores farmers. But CNRRA refused to cooperate, "regretting that all fertilizers have been allocated." Inquiry disclosed the truth; since the Pescadores farmers were too poor to pay anything whatever for relief supplies, the Chinese organization did not intend to waste a valuable commodity at Makung. Furthermore, said the CNRRA officers, "it is illegal for foreign ships to carry cargo between Chinese ports." Domestic inter-port freight services were the prerogative of the China Merchants Steam Navigation Company or its subsidiaries.

The Communications Stranglehold

When UNRRA wished to ship phosphatic rock to Formosa for the hard-pressed local fertilizer industry, the Navigation Company demanded $32.00 per ton for the shipment. UNRRA officials refused to pay such an outrageous sum, and after long negotiation brought the Chinese figure down to $4.00 per ton which even so provided profit. The difference indicated the margin of profit demanded, and suggests the problems faced by individual Formosan shippers who had not the leverage which UNRRA enjoyed in dealing with Soong's agency. A bribe in the right place, however, could always move one's interest a little forward, but by the time squeeze was paid all along the bureaucratic line there was nothing left of profit to justify an initial effort. Small trade withered quickly under these conditions.

Shipments moving either way, to or from Shanghai, were subjected to exploitation. Cement for reconstruction purposes was in high demand throughout China and throughout Asia. A large reserve was surrendered on Formosa. The Kaohsiung Cement Works were quickly rehabilitated and returned to full production of 15,000 tons per month in 1946; nevertheless, cement was available on Formosa usually only on the black market. UNRRA discovered that amounts far in excess of normal prewar and wartime Japanese needs had been turned over to three offices under the Department of Communications, which controlled sea transport.

UNRRA also discovered that it cost three times as much to move bulk cargo by sea between Kaohsiung and Keelung as it did to move it overland by rail. When the Department of Mining and Industry decided to market a trial cement shipment of 1000 tons at Shanghai, it was first shipped overland to Keelung and thence by sea to the mainland. The railway freight charge alone was TY 2500 per ton. To this was added the charges for warehousing, transfer, insurance, and sea-freight, and at Shanghai Formosa's cement was expected to compete in the market with American cement, selling then *in Shanghai* at the equivalent of 3000 Taiwan yen per ton. Each agency along the line from Formosa to Shanghai had taken its squeeze and its excessive profit. The longer the rail haul the higher the profit to the railway officials, the longer the delay in warehouses the greater the profit to insurance and warehouse agencies.

The traditions of integrity which had once marked the China Customs Service (under foreign management, to be sure) did not survive under Nationalist control in Formosa. Of ten agencies squeezing UNRRA relief shipments from Tainan to the Pescadores Islands on one occasion in 1946, at least four were branches of the China Customs Service. Government agencies, UNRRA, and private concerns were charged heavy "import duties" when they attempted to ship materials from one Formosan port to another.

This scramble for bribes choked overseas trade. In November, 1946, it was announced that clearance for ships desiring to leave Keelung port could be completed only during certain limited office hours, and not at all on weekends and holidays. Ships' captains and foreign shipping agents soon discovered that key officials often "stepped out of the office" at critical moments within the posted working hours, but underlings made it known that with special consideration (i.e. bribes) the difficulties of port clearance could be surmounted promptly. The alternative, of course, was equally expensive, for high port fees had to be paid as long as a ship lay in harbor.

The Customs, the Quarantine Services, and the Harbor Police were each under a different agency. Complex and sometimes quite contradictory regulations offered many opportunities to confiscate goods on the pretext that import or export rules had not been observed. For example, on one occasion supplies for UNRRA personnel were confiscated and then offered for sale to the UNRRA consignees with an additional charge laid on for "interim storage."

By late 1946 an orderly import and export trade was no longer possible, the entire island economy lay at the mercy of newcomers who controlled the ports and were able to interpose regulations profoundly affecting the use of relief and rehabilitation supplies.

But where regulation was most needed, there was none; the Quarantine Services were neglected and the offices stripped of medical supplies and equipment. As the entire economy sickened, there was a general breakdown of the health and welfare services, most dramatically demonstrated when cholera and bubonic plague entered Formosa in epidemic proportions.

Here was a threat to life itself.

The Break-up of Public Health and Welfare Services

Doctors, nurses, food specialists and welfare workers on the UNRRA team promptly won the respect and cooperation of Formosans and of some CNRRA colleagues, but they had come late — seven months late — to the scene. The cities had slowly begun to take on the appearance of China's squalid towns. When Chiang's "Peace Preservation Corps" commandeered Taipei's garbage truck fleet in 1945 to transport stolen goods to the waterfront, huge piles of rubbish accumulated in the parks, side streets and alleyways. A primitive system of handcart collection, substituted for the motor trucks, could remove only about one-tenth of the daily accumulation of trash. The rat population multiplied fantastically.

Formosa's larger towns had at one time maintained regular sewage disposal and house-to-house disinfecting services, carefully supervised, paid for out of taxes, and available to all. Now under the mainland Chinese the work was farmed out on the concession basis. Each householder had to negotiate for service and pay directly to the collectors. As living costs soared the collection fees increased, and if not paid promptly upon demand there was no collection. Overflowing cesspools raised a stench and led to dangerously unhealthful conditions.

In 1937 there were no less than ninety-eight city and town waterworks in operation, with an additional twenty-eight planned or under construction. These supplied 1,270,000 people or a quarter of the island population.

UNRRA representatives were deeply disturbed by the Chinese failure to rehabilitate these public water systems. CNRRA's first feeble attempts to restore Taipei's water supply failed because of the widespread theft of plumbing fixtures, including both public fire hydrants and faucets and piping from unguarded private homes.

Unchecked loss of water made it impossible to maintain ade-

quate pressure in crowded areas. Unfiltered water was turned
into urban systems to mix with treated water. In some instances the chemicals intended for use at the reservoirs and
pumping stations went instead into the black market.

Malaria, smallpox and tuberculosis were serious problems.
An UNRRA survey showed that from 60 to 90 per cent of
the schoolchildren examined were suffering from malnutrition.
Wartime privation had lowered physical resistance in the urban population, and thousands of teen-age boys, sent in 1944
and 1945 to keep watch on the beaches, had developed either
malaria or tuberculosis, or both, after long exposure in dugout
shelters or inadequate tents and shacks hastily constructed in
the countryside.

Port quarantine services were disrupted in the last days of
war, and whatever was left of equipment or supplies went the
way of all movable loot in the late 1945 "scavenger period" of
petty pilfering. The new Government was not much interested
in the enforcement of quarantine checks and restrictions upon
traffic to and from the mainland. Incoming Chinese brought a
particularly virulent form of smallpox which became epidemic.
Despite public clamor, nothing was done to resume the compulsory vaccination system which had been in force before surrender. UNRRA doctors ascertained that some Chinese garrison troop units had a venereal disease rate of 90 per cent and
that in some areas 25 per cent of the civil population was now
infected.

Medical supplies were scarce, equipment was obsolete, and
the Government showed little interest in repairing heavily
damaged hospitals. There were approximately two thousand
registered doctors available, including many newcomers, but
there were few adequately trained nurses. Fortunately the
Formosans — trained in Japanese medical schools and short-
term institutes — cooperated well with the Japanese doctors
and public health officers who wished to remain in Formosa if
they could. Both groups were eager to welcome UNRRA spe-

cialists bringing in new ideas, new techniques, new equipment and medical supplies. Here and there Japanese trained in the old German tradition offered resistance to change, but on the whole the foreign specialist could rely upon support at every level of activity.

In developing an UNRRA–CNRRA medical program only the Chinese Director of Public Health — a Johns Hopkins man — refused cooperation.

Reasonably enough the Governor had transferred the Public Health and Welfare services from the Police Bureau to the Department of Civil Affairs. The new Director, Dr. T. S. King (trained as a physiologist and pharmacologist), had been running a drug concern in Shanghai in which the Governor was interested. He had no previous experience in public health administration. Soon he showed that he had no interest in public health; he had been brought to Formosa to look after Chen Yi's drug interests as General Manager of the Taiwan Drugs and Surgical Instruments Company, a subsidiary of the Department of Mining and Industry.

In his public capacity Dr. King controlled the licensing of doctors, nurses, pharmacists, and medical services. He controlled confiscated hospitals, clinics, medical supplies and equipment. It was within his power to license drug imports and the local manufacture and sale of medicines. He was therefore in a strong position to exclude or restrict the local use of medical supplies (including relief supplies sent in by UNRRA) if they competed in any way with his own or the Governor's private interests.

In his "private capacity" Dr. King promptly organized a new pharmaceutical manufacturing center and a distributing company on behalf of Chen Yi. The sale of patent medicines and prescriptive drugs was an enormously profitable business. To the management of these enterprises the Director of Public Health and Welfare devoted most of his time. One of his first private undertakings was the production and sale of a patent curative for tuberculosis, put on the market under his own name.

It was inevitable that the UNRRA specialists should come into open collision with the Director of Public Health. He in turn took every occasion to belittle UNRRA's services and the qualifications of foreign personnel, bringing pressure to bear upon the University Medical School, the hospitals, and the Taiwan Medical Association in jealous efforts to restrict public or professional access to lectures, demonstrations, and films which the foreign specialists were prepared to offer. For example, during the 39th annual meeting of the Taiwan Medical Association some seventy papers were presented, after which Dr. King caused the following comment to be printed in the Government newspaper:

. . . However, the article by Dr. Hirschy of UNRRA entitled "The Prevention of Contagious Diseases" is comparatively of a preliminary nature. It is merely common sense. It seems to be unsuitable to be read at the meeting of a medical association, for it is a waste of time. Some of the people are of the opinion that foreign medical doctors should try to acquaint themselves with the medical standards of the province.[5]

In another context Dr. King strove to impede the free distribution of Atabrine tablets in the anti-malaria campaign, and to prevent competition which freely distributed foreign aid supplies offered to his private mercantile interests. Some 45 million Atabrine tablets were in the warehouses, but Dr. King proposed to put his Pharmaceutical Company into the quinine business. King's successor as Director of Public Health, on the other hand, later proposed that the 45 million tablets be handed out to everybody on Formosa — about six tablets per person — thereby "quickly wiping out malaria throughout Formosa." They had been lying in the warehouses for more than one year, while the Government collected storage fees indirectly charged to UNRRA.

The so-called Mukai Incident profoundly disturbed relations between Formosans and the incoming Chinese. Dr. Mukai, a Japanese gynecologist, maintained a private hospital long conceded to be the best in Taipei — certainly the best there in 1946. The wife of a prominent mainland Chinese official became a patient, underwent a Caesarean section, and then refused to abide by Dr. Mukai's instructions concerning postoperative care. She died. The husband then refused to remove the body, making huge demands upon Mukai for "consolation money."

Soon other patients had to leave; Dr. Mukai was arrested, his hospital was confiscated, and promptly turned over to an incompetent woman from the mainland who was supposed to have a medical degree.

Formosan and Japanese doctors throughout the island saw the dangers implicit in the "Mukai Case"; banding together they gave financial and legal support to Dr. Mukai on the one hand, and on the other threatened to withhold all medical attention from all mainland Chinese unless guarantees were forthcoming that there would be no more incidents of this type.

A vigorous legal defense secured Mukai's release. He was then "hired for operations" in his own hospital, but it was quickly apparent that he could not work under the new management. Although Formosan women organized an appeal to him and petitioned the Government to retain him and restore his hospital, he had had quite enough.*

Private hospitals and clinics were extremely valuable properties; the majority were swiftly taken over, sometimes by presentation of a handful of red-sealed confiscation orders, or more abruptly by raiding parties who simply walked in. Doctors about to be repatriated to war-torn Okinawa petitioned to be allowed to take their medical kits with them so that they could

---

* The Formosan lawyer who successfully conducted Mukai's defense caused the Government prosecutors and their client the official to "lose face" by airing the truth. As a consequence he lost his life in 1947.

contribute their skills to rehabilitation there, rather than to reach Naha without a means of livelihood. The American Consulate refused to consider such appeals or to raise the question, even informally, with the Chinese authorities.

Plague and Cholera Return: "This is China Now"

In midyear 1946, four cases of bubonic plague were discovered at Tamsui and in the Hsinchu district. The victims had come in aboard Chinese junks and had not been quarantined.

The Formosan press broke into an uproar of protest; there had been no bubonic plague among the civil population for nearly thirty years. Here indeed was a threat, directly traceable to the collapse of the quarantine system so strictly enforced under Japanese administration. Houses which had sheltered the plague victims were burned to the ground. Some feeble steps were taken to reactivate quarantine services at the ports, but in these no one had confidence.

As summer approached cholera reappeared in Formosa.

Within a few days it had spread beyond control in the southwest. It had not been known in epidemic proportions since 1919. The Director of Public Health made no move to recognize the threat, but UNRRA doctors and nurses, aided by CNRRA personnel, Formosan doctors and public health employees, promptly moved to Tainan and Kaohsiung, cut through extraordinary official red tape (deliberately spun out to embarrass them) and promptly reduced the death rate from 80 per cent to 29 per cent of all known cholera cases. After a long summer fight cool autumn weather brought relief, but by November 1 the UNRRA team had recorded 2690 cases, with 1460 dead.

The Public Health Director's studied indifference was shared by the men he placed in control of government hospitals at Tainan. At the height of the epidemic, which centered there, they continued to observe regular office hours, refused to receive or treat cholera patients brought in between five o'clock in the afternoon and eight o'clock in the morning and flatly refused to release medical supplies beyond the allotted issue — small enough — indicated for "normal" times.

The UNRRA team set up special isolation barracks, but when it was discovered that human excrement from these wards was being dumped into nearby commercial fishponds, the Director of Public Health was asked to have something done about sewage disposal. He was also asked to ban the sale or distribution of fish from local sources until the epidemic came to an end and the polluted fishponds were properly cleansed. He refused to do more than to have a press statement issued advising the public to be careful in cleaning fish.

Dr. King's undisguised obstructionism prompted UNRRA doctors to threaten to make an international issue of it. To one, the Director of Public Health blandly observed that "after all, only the poor people are contracting the disease."

The "official American attitude" during this crisis was very little better than Dr. King's. UNRRA team members and consular employees were besieged with appeals. Formosans in every walk of life sought American help. Some leaders suggested that we should bring the Generalissimo's attention to conditions in Formosa through the good offices of his friend, the American Ambassador, and others asked us to appeal to the United Nations.

For example, we received a postal card bearing this brief appeal, painfully spelled out:

Alas the enemy of civilization, pest, penetrated into Taiwan. Very sorry much. It is regrettable story. We cry to America [for] the prevention of epidemics formation.

But appeals such as this, from "unofficial persons" embarrassed the Consulate, and reinforced a view that the natives were an ignorant lot.

American members of the UNRRA team, the Vice Consul and the Director of the United States Information Service considered this merely a small straw among thousands that were beginning to stir in the winds of popular resentment. Political tensions, already dangerous, were heightened perceptibly by the intrusion of cholera and plague. After so many years of well-publicized American investment in public health and medical services in China, this seemed hardly the time to present an official show of studied indifference. Self-interest alone seemed to dictate some concern that cholera and plague had reappeared in an area adjacent to Occupied Japan, where the United States had stationed very large forces, and had assumed a monumental responsibility for some eighty million Japanese people. The dread diseases should not be allowed to spread there.

I was directed to incorporate a notice of the epidemic in the routine monthly report. When I urged the need for a telegraphic report to the Embassy in China, to Tokyo, and to Washington, the response was curt; it was explained to me that a telegram would be irregular; the newly opened Taipei Consulate had no official questionnaire forms to guide us in making a public health report.

When I insisted, a compromise was reached; I was to sign my name rather than the Consul's to the irregular telegram, and in a follow-up report I was to explain carefully our failure to conform to the printed questionnaire required by Foreign Service Serial No. 188, of June 9, 1944, of which no copies, alas, were available at the Taipei office.

Popular concern with public health problems roused by this intrusion of plague and cholera was heightened when it was realized that Formosa's lepers were no longer being confined, registered, or treated. An American on the UNRRA staff reported on a visit which she had made to the Government Leprosarium some distance inland from Taipei. It had been established by the Japanese and was well organized to provide schools and work in addition to medical care. Provision was made nearby for the children of leprous parents and there was an inn for visiting relatives. Periodic clinical examination of all registered lepers was a legal requirement. At this Leprosarium there had been about 700 patients when UNRRA staff members first visited it in 1946. Nine months later there were less than half the number, the clinics were closed, and no provision was made for the non-leprous children of the patients. Said the UNRRA officer:

> The Director (a Chinese without interest in lepers and with no training for the job) said "They just wandered away."
>
> I reported the above facts [to the UNRRA Medical Director, who took up the matter with Chen Yi's Director of Public Health, Dr. King]. Dr. King felt that all lepers should be shipped to some far away island, existing only in his mind, and left to shift for themselves.[6]

As the months passed the Formosan people looked more and more often to foreigners to represent their interests and to press for change. The heroic effort to stem the cholera epidemic earned a measure of profound gratitude, often and freely expressed. Efforts to compel CNRRA to make an honest distribution of relief goods and to carry through a constructive rehabilitation program were widely appreciated.

Inevitably the UNRRA team was considered an American group, and credit for its good work accrued to the United States, for American members were in the majority, and most relief supplies entering Formosa were of American or Canadian origin. As the Formosans saw it then, this "American" team was attempting to give substance to all the propaganda which had promised a "New China." Thus the "good things" of postwar life were inescapably identified with the West, and principally with the United States, and the "bad things" — the hardships and disappointments — were identified with mainland China.

Chen Yi's men — led principally by American college graduates Stanway Cheng and Huang Chao-chin — did all that they could to undermine the popularity of the UNRRA group. With the full cooperation of the CNRRA office they gave credit for relief supplies to the "generosity" of the Nationalist Party and Government, and when things went wrong they blamed "foreign employees of CNRRA." When there was outspoken Formosan criticism of the quality, quantity, price or distribution of CNRRA supplies, Chen's Information Office or its agents placed blame on the "meddling" UNRRA team or upon the United States. In its own defense UNRRA prepared a series of stories for the local press, explaining the origin and purposes of the United Nations program, but when they at last appeared in print, the "United Nations" identification was deleted, and the stories significantly tampered with. As the year wore on the attempts to blame the United States for worsening conditions within Formosa became so flagrant that even the American Consul endorsed a report to the Embassy on the issue.

The UNRRA team continued to function at Taipei until December, 1947. Relief supplies worth approximately $25,000,-000 *before* delivery to China had been off-loaded at Formosan ports. The UNRRA team watched the distribution and sale of these donated materials, and saw that the Formosans were required to pay exorbitant prices in many instances. Relief goods sent to Formosa generated profits many times 25 million dollars in value for the China National Relief and Rehabilitation Administration, responsible to the Executive Yuan (T. V. Soong, President).

But UNRRA team members had brought into Formosa something far more valuable than bulk shipments of fertilizer, mine cables, or flour; they had provided an image of democracy at work far more important than material supplies.

PART THREE

CRISIS AND AFTERMATH

Korea
Japan
CHINA
Okinawa
FORMOSA
The Philippines

Taoyuan
Keelung
Taipei City
Taipei
Hsinchu
Ilan
Ryukyu
Islands
Miaoli
Taichung
Changhua
Nantou
The Pescadores
(Penghu)
Yunlin
Hualien
Chiayi
Tainan
Tainan City
Kaohsiung
Taitung
Lu Tao
(Green Island)
Kaohsiung
City
Pingtung
Lan Yu
(Orchid Island)

FORMOSA
(TAIWAN)

IX

The Formosans' Story:
A Year of Disenchantment

Law and Order Under the New Regime

JAPAN'S GREAT CONTRIBUTION to Formosa was the intro-
duction of a rule of law and order. Police rule was often harsh,
and the application of law often unfair when Formosan interests clashed with the interests of the ruling Japanese, but nevertheless the legal system provided an essential foundation for
economic and social advance. This was understood. The chaos
and uncertainties of the 19th century gave way to orderly process. If questions of subversion or rebellion were not at issue,
every Formosan enjoyed a reasonable degree of security for his
person, property and livelihood. The courts were respected and
the right of appeal was there. If a Formosan challenged a Japanese in court (or even in argument at the local street-corner
police-box) the scales of Justice were often out of balance, but
in normal village life every individual enjoyed protection of the
law.* After the surrender these safeguards vanished.

As we have seen in an earlier chapter, the greatest confusion
reigned in the first months of the "Take-Over Period." Japan's

* The dispossession of the small landholder in favor of the great sugar corporations could be brought about — and often was — by the manipulation of
available water supplies through State-owned or -managed irrigation systems,
and there were other forms of economic pressure under which the individual
or family became helpless, but the individual as such everywhere in Formosa
enjoyed an unprecedented degree of protection.

post-surrender Premier Shidehara announced that Japanese property overseas would be transferred to the Allies as reparations, but the formal Japanese Property Custodian Board on Formosa was not set up at Taipei until December, 1945. Representatives of the U. S. Army Advisory Group were active Board members whose presence strengthened Japanese attempts to make an orderly business of the legal transfer. But this impeded Chinese who sought to lay hands on confiscated property before legal controls were too highly developed in the transfer system. We have noted earlier that at this point complaints went "up the back stairs" to American authorities at Chungking, accusing Americans at Taipei of undue "meddling." American attempts to support an orderly transfer of property titles became "attempts to protect the Japanese," and orders came down from Wedemeyer's headquarters directing his officers to consider themselves no longer an "Advisory Group" but merely a "Liaison Team," concerned only with repatriation problems.

The confusion of this so-called "Take-Over Period" was easily exploited by thieves and racketeers of every stripe, some of them highly placed in the Governor's official family. In their view the law was a nuisance, and it came as a distinct surprise that "degraded Formosans" dared to expose them in the press and attempted ceaselessly to bring charges into the Courts.

This involved a painful loss of face.

An incident which took place immediately after the surrender may be said to have set the tone for Chen Yi's administration of legal affairs. His Chief Procurator for the Supreme Court (i.e. his "Attorney General") was found to be using the High Court's vermilion seal upon forged orders with which his agents expropriated private property. In this instance they were compelling Tamsui motor-craft owners to engage in illegal transport of stolen goods to the mainland. The case came to light when a small-craft owner, ordered to load stolen sugar for a hazardous cross-channel trip, pleaded a mechanical breakdown, removed the motor to a hiding place, and then boldly went up to Taipei to enlist the help of well-known Formosan lawyers and the local press. He won his case, and Chen Yi's Chief Procurator had to leave Formosa, for the Governor was not yet sure of himself, and it was too early in the Occupation to defy public opinion in a case given such wide publicity.

In another example Governor Chen's Commissioner of Agriculture and Forestry ordered Formosan fishermen along the East Coast to deliver their craft to Keelung "for safekeeping during the winter months." This would have been virtual confiscation, and few owners complied. It was known that the "protected property" might merge with a large fleet of confiscated Japanese craft then being employed in clandestine trade with the Ryukyu Islands and Japan, and in smuggling "liberated" goods to Shanghai.

The daily press was happy to publish details of alleged or proved dishonesty in every department of the administration. Such examples of official malpractice in high places could be cited almost without number. The effect was to place before the Formosan public a picture of corruption in Government, from the highest to the lowest office. This was the "new democracy."

Under these circumstances law enforcement would have been difficult for the most honest law agency; Chen's Department of Legal Affairs faced an enormously complex task, for all legal documentation was in the Japanese language. Codes peculiar to Formosa must be collated with Chinese law.

Lawyers and judges, to function at all, had to be literate in both the Chinese and Japanese languages, and conversant with one or more of the local dialects. The use of the Japanese spoken language in official business was technically forbidden, but in many instances it had to be employed. Although few mainland Chinese had both the linguistic and legal qualifications, they were given the highest appointments at Taipei.

Circumstances compelled Chen Yi to appoint qualified Formosans as district and local judges and procurators. The majority were bilingual, having studied literary Chinese while passing through the higher schools, and having taken law degrees at the Japanese universities. I knew many, including several very able men who had been my students at Taipei before the war and were graduates of Tokyo Imperial University. They enjoyed the confidence of the Formosan layman, and they kept me well informed of many incidents affecting Formosan interests under the new dispensation.

Standing against them were Chen Yi's civil police force, brought in from the mainland. At the surrender in October, 1945, the police organization numbered 13,000 officers and men, but of these only 5600 were Formosans, in the lower ranks. The Governor ordered Japanese members of the force to remain at their posts until December 10, but under the circumstances the Formosan public treated them indifferently. Formosan police employees found it very difficult to obey "lame-duck" Japanese superiors, and the incoming Chinese paid them no heed whatsoever.

But to fill the 7400 posts vacated by the Japanese, Chen Yi did not promote experienced Formosans and recruit others for "freshman" jobs. Thousands of newcomers were placed on the rolls, inexperienced relatives and friends of mainland Chinese already established in the Administration. Many policemen could speak neither Japanese nor the local Chinese dialects, and hundreds were mere boys in their teens, younger brothers for whom lucrative jobs must be obtained. The authorized pay was of much less interest than the prospect of bribes and perquisites. When all police jobs vacated by the Japanese had been filled, the Government began to discharge Formosans to make room for more newcomers.

And here again, as with the Army, Formosans at first were tempted to jeer at blundering novices. But questions of face were involved, the policeman took courage in arms, and soon there was no laughter to be heard at police expense. I one day

witnessed a shouting argument between some Formosan hecklers and a trio of policemen near the Round Park Police Station
in Taipei. A tense crowd gathered near. Suddenly one of the
policemen drew his revolver and, firing, lunged at his torment-
ors. But his aim was poor; as the crowd scattered one of his
wild shots felled an innocent bystander. The three police
made no effort to pursue the hecklers, but satisfied themselves
by dragging the bleeding corpse to the station steps, flinging it
there to remain through the day, an example and warning to all
"degraded Formosans." It had been a question of face.

City mayors controlled the urban police forces. At the surrender Chen Yi made expatriate Huang Chao-chin the Mayor
of Taipei, and Huang made one of his cronies (Chen Shang-
bin) the new Chief of Police. They had been associates in the
Nationalist Chinese Foreign Service.

Soon after he took office and assumed control of the police
organization it became evident that Huang's officers were collaborating with the underworld gangsters known locally as
loma or "tiger eels."

Years earlier the Japanese in Formosa sometimes gave habit-
ual criminals a choice between long penitentiary terms at hard
labor or employment along the China coast as subsidized dope-
peddlers, racketeers and rabble-rousers in the ports. They had
an evil reputation from Shanghai to Hong Kong, tainting the
reputations of all Formosans at that time. Now in 1945 they
swarmed back to the island to prey upon their own people.

At Taipei each "tiger eel" gang had its own sphere of influence, its city ward, and its police affiliation. They were rivals in
petty theft, dramatic robberies and extortion. By night the
streets were unsafe; *loma* gangs broke into shops and dwellings,
noisily ransacked the premises, and trucked away the loot, assured that no policeman would show his face unless it was to
give a helping hand. Frightened victims stood by helplessly,
knowing it was useless to summon aid. It was dangerous, too,
for any complainant became a marked man. The police stations

were crowded with people brought in under false accusations, to be imprisoned, fined, or released according to the size of the bribes they were able to pay.

For example, in early 1946, a Formosan employed in a textile company charged that a Chinese colleague was embezzling large funds. The accused bribed the police to allow him to decamp for Shanghai. Then the police jailed the plaintiff, who was held under arrest for many weeks, on the grounds that he had "held administrative responsibility." He was released only after his family was bankrupted paying bribes.

Day after day the Formosan press recorded incidents involving the police as irresponsible incompetents, law-breakers, or racketeers. My notes for the first three weeks of February, 1946, show some typical cases.

On February 1 several inexperienced young mainland police burst into a crowded theater, firing wildly. The terrified audience poured into the streets. It was learned that the officers were searching for a suspect who "might be in there," but none was found. On February 8 a Chinese merchant from Keelung paid four policemen to accompany him some thirty miles inland to the town of Taoyuan, where they attempted to force a local shopkeeper to sell his stocks at a ridiculously low price. Angry townspeople discovered these "negotiations" in time to drive the policemen and their friends from town. This involved a loss of face.

During the night of February 17 some thirty police officers — Mayor Huang's men — drove from Taipei to suburban Keibi village, forced their way into a prominent landowner's home, and announced that they were there to "conduct an examination." Household members, fleeing through the back door, shouted "Thieves!" which brought out the neighbors armed with makeshift weapons, and the local Formosan police unit. The sirens wailed, whereupon a nearby Nationalist Army unit dashed into the village in a truck, from which a mounted machine gun fired wildly into the night. The Mayor's officers took cover, sending two men back into the city for reinforcements. When dawn came at last the absurd and dangerous character of this three-way battle was revealed, and as a Keibi villager later remarked to me, the whole thing recalled conditions of the 19th century.

On February 16 a member of the Police Training Institute Staff — a Foochow man — was caught robbing a house, and on February 18 the Chief of the Kaohsiung police forces shot up the premises of a Formosan who refused to sell goods to him at a ruinous discount. This had caused him to lose face before a crowd of onlookers.

We need not linger on the question of prison administration and the treatment of anyone so unfortunate as to fall into the hands of the police. An UNRRA officer inspecting the Kaohsiung prison in September, 1946, found that accommodations built for one hundred persons now held seven hundred, and that fifty prisoners had died recently from lack of medical care. The prison dispensary had used a total of $18.00 worth of medical supplies in a period of seven months. In the view of Chen Yi's Public Health Director, Dr. King, one does not waste a salable commodity on prisoners.

This recital of petty theft and systematic police-gangster operations suggests the setting in which the ordinary Formosan citizen attempted to pick up the threads of everyday life after war. Abuses of the "scavenger period" in late 1945 were felt most keenly in and near the ports and the larger towns, where the ill-disciplined Nationalist Army conscripts wandered about, but abuses of the regular police system were felt in every town and village across the island.

Throughout 1946 Formosan leaders addressed themselves to the problem of police control, which rested in the hands of town mayors and district magistrates. These men were appointed by the Governor. Obviously the solution lay in an elective system whereby the public could choose the Governor, the mayors, and the magistrates.

Representative Government and the Kuomintang

It was evident to us that Army, Party and Government entered Formosa in confidence that they would have no difficulty controlling representative assemblies in this "backward area." Flushed with the prospects of his new opportunities in Formosa, Governor Chen repeatedly promised Formosans a large share in government.

His "Training Classes," inaugurated on December 10, have been described. They neatly entangled leading Formosans for a month or two just as the Japanese left their posts, thus giving mainland Chinese an opportunity to fill them.

On December 26 the Governor announced plans to establish "Organs for Hearing the People's Opinion." These were Peoples Political Councils (PPC's) to be made ready to assist the Government by May, 1946.

All citizens who fulfilled registration qualifications would be eligible to vote. Any citizen who desired to become a candidate for membership in the Councils must satisfy certain conditions and be approved by the Government and Party. Only natives of Formosa were eligible and each man was to be elected for a two-year term. Certain large occupational guilds were to be represented, and each Council was expected to have a proper percentage of women among its members. District and Municipal Councils would elect representatives to the Provincial Council, and in due course the Provincial PPC would send elected delegates to the National Assembly.

All these arrangements looked well on paper — especially when set forth in English summaries for visiting American V.I.P.'s. But the mainland Chinese, in practice, adopted the "tutor's" attitude, as if all this business at the polls was a new experience for the Formosans. No references were made to the fact that for ten years Formosan voters had been going to the polls and candidates had become thoroughly familiar with all the necessary campaign business of posters, public addresses, and the shepherding of votes. It was true that before 1945 the end-product was a very limited voice in district assemblies in which half the members had been nominated by the Japanese administration. But for this very reason the Formosans now looked forward eagerly to truly representative voting privileges. Many who prepared to stand for election in 1946 had been agitating for just such island-wide Assemblies since Woodrow Wilson stirred them with the notion of self-determination for minorities at the end of World War I.

Thoughtful Formosans promptly objected to the oath which required them to swear allegiance to the Nationalist Party, the Kuomintang, in these words:

> I promise, with sincerity, to keep the Peoples Three Principles, to support the Kuomintang Government, obey the National laws and ordinances, perform the citizen's duties, and bear one part in the foundation of Great China.

On the strength of this oath and a certificate of registration, all citizens at least twenty years of age were granted voting privileges. According to official figures a total of 2,393,142 persons had become eligible to vote by midyear 1946. This number was not to be accepted at face value, for it was well known that registration procedures had not been carried through in many places at the time the figures were published.

To qualify as a candidate for elective office was not so easy. A *curriculum vita* had first to be submitted to the local government office. If the Governor's representative or a Party official approved of the candidate's educational qualifications and his "attitude," his application might be approved. If it were rejected, there was no appeal. The difficulties here were two; the Governor's man was usually a Kuomintang member and approval often had a price tag attached to it.

The next hurdles were the Civil Service examinations. Formosans becoming candidates for provincial, district or city PPC's had to pass Class A examinations, and those who were candidates for the lower village, town or regional assemblies must pass Class B tests. Here again, money and favor carried weight. As of October, 1946, said the Government, 10,671 persons had passed the First Class examinations, and 26,803 had passed the Second Class tests. With Party proctors controlling the enrollment lists and examinations, they anticipated docility in the Assemblies.

But the Government and Party had not established a firm enough grip upon the system in early 1946, nor were the individual Party workers from the continent accustomed to working with such an alert and well-informed electorate.

The first local elections were held in February and March, 1946. Eight district and nine municipal councils convened in April, and were to meet thereafter for a few days at intervals of three months.

The public paid little attention to these familiar local convocations. All eyes were on Taipei, where for the first time in Formosa's history there would be an island-wide Assembly.

The First Peoples' Political Council
Assembly versus Chen Yi

The first session opened on May 1, 1946. It was to be in session ten days, and then adjourn for six months. In a transparent attempt to control the agenda Governor Chen arranged to have expatriate Mayor Huang Chao-chin made Chairman of the meetings. This caused keen popular disappointment; the public felt that Lim Hsien-tang, the Home Rule leader now sixty years of age, should have enjoyed the first Chairmanship after his lifelong fight to establish such an Island Assembly.

Governor-General Chen addressed the ceremonial opening session, with the usual worn references to the National Father,

Dr. Sun Yat-sen, the National Leader, Chiang Kai-shek, and to democracy, progress, and the peoples' rights.

The oldest councilor present rose to respond. He had been a youth of twenty-two years, he said, when the Imperial Chinese Government ceded Formosa to Japan, he had witnessed the confusion of the short-lived "Republic" in 1895, and the full course of Formosan development under the Japanese. Now in this keynote address he wished to warn the new Government that its actions and achievements would be compared not only with the achievements and shortcomings of the Japanese during the preceding half-century, but would be compared as well with the confused and corrupt administration by men sent from the mainland in the 19th century.

These remarks were not welcomed by the Governor or his representatives, but otherwise the occasion went off well enough. That night, however, Taipei seethed with stories of an incident which had taken place elsewhere in the city. The Commissionor for Education (Fan Shou-kang) had addressed a Youth Corps rally in the afternoon. Speaking in a mainland dialect few Formosans could understand, he had an aide translate into the Formosan vernacular. As his remarks became plain, a storm of anger swept through the audience. According to subsequent press accounts, he asserted that Formosans "have thoughts of independence; they are slave-converts [of the Japanese], they are discriminating against people of other provinces, and they are indifferent to public affairs." He then branded all Formosans as "backward people, unfit to be considered true Chinese."

He had been goaded to this outburst by sharp criticism of his own incompetence in office and by frequent editorials and Formosan speeches which discussed the legal status of Formosa, Formosan rights under international law, and the legality of Nationalist claims that the island had become Chinese territory before a Japanese treaty had been signed, ceding it to China.

His remarks were promptly reported in the Council. An indignant Formosan (Keh Kuo-chi), retorted in these words:

There is a notion of independence in this province. Formosans have revolutionary ideas and spirit. The arrival of Chen Cheng-kung [Koxinga] in Taiwan was motivated by a patriotic, revolutionary desire to overthrow the Manchu dynasty and to restore the Ming Government. What was meant then as an act of independence was but for the national salvation. The Formosans have this revolutionary national idea. When Formosa was ceded to Japan, it was done to save the whole mainland of China.

As for the thought of alienation from China, we love and respect natives from other provinces who come to work on our behalf, and truly work for the reconstruction of Formosa, but if they come for the purpose of making money and for high official positions, we certainly want to get rid of them . . . to govern Formosa by Formosans is an obligation incumbent on Formosans . . .[1]

The first day's business session set the tone of rancorous discord and conflict marking all subsequent debate. Day after day the Governor's Commissioners and Bureau Chiefs were called before the Council to report upon the "transfer period," the administration's activities during the first six months of the new era, and upon future plans. One by one they were subjected to sharp interrogation.

The performance of two Government representatives will illustrate the general character of these interpolations. The Commissioner of Education was called upon to explain and to apologize for his remarks at the Youth Rally. He protested that it was all a matter of misinterpretation due to language difficulties. He was asked to outline Chen Yi's plans for free, universal compulsory education. He explained to unbelieving councilmen that the Central Government would provide the necessary funds. This they knew it could not do. The Commissioner could not explain why the Finance Commissioner's budget showed large appropriations had been made for education, although there were virtually no funds actually being spent for the schools. When pressed to provide the Council with statistics on current educational affairs, he said hesitantly that he "thought" there were 10,690 students enrolled in higher schools in and near the capital, but that "poor communications" prevented an accurate survey elsewhere. He had no way, he said, to calculate the total number of children in school, but he guessed that "each school has two classes, and each class has fifty pupils."

Council members accused him of presenting a report drawn from ill-digested and misunderstood prewar Japanese records. They noted that the trains were running and the long-distance telephone system had been restored, hence "poor communications" was no excuse. Commissioner Fan left the assembly rooms in anger when twitted on recent disclosures that he had illegally "borrowed" school funds for a private business venture in Shanghai, and had managed to survive the incident only by making restitution of one millon yen.

A more chilling atmosphere surrounded the address and interrogation of the Garrison Commander, General Ko, who chose his words very carefully to show his complete contempt for "the people." The Army, he said, was under no legal obligation to report to the People's Council. This was a concession to the forms of democracy, and the Council must appreciate his readiness to present a statement to them. He asked the Formosans to realize that the Army assumed no responsibility for civil law and order, and would tolerate no criticism concerning Army discipline and behavior, for these were not of public concern. Any charges that officers or men behaved in a lawless manner or any general criticism of Army morale must be made in writing and bear the signature of the persons making such charges.

When General Ko had finished, Council members who ignored his warning leaped up to vie with one another in laying on the record, with names, dates, and places, instances in which persons and properties had been subject to abuse by military men. After a few minutes the Garrison Commander, pale with anger, abruptly left the Council chamber.

The testimony of Commissioner Fan had betrayed the incompetence which marked Chen Yi's administration, and General Ko's address had underscored its ruthlessness.

As the sessions drew to a close a list of grievances — in effect, a general indictment of the Nationalist administration — was drawn up, with recommendations and suggestions for the Governor's guidance through the forthcoming months. Summarized, the issues fell under four headings. Economic abuse led the list; the Formosans demanded an end to the monopolies of production and commerce exercised by quasi-official companies. They demanded that something be done to restrain the violent and abusive conduct of police and military personnel, and they asked that the Government make a greater effort to fulfill its promises. Capping these, they attacked the Governor for his refusal to employ Formosans at effective, policy-making levels in the administration.

On this last point the Governor announced (on May 12) that he had permission from the Central Government to employ Formosans under *Provisional Rules and Regulations Governing Qualifications For Appointment of Government Personnel in Bordering and Remote Provinces,* i. e., in "backward" areas; here was an explicit statement of the Central Government's attitude toward "remote" Formosa.

These May meetings provided the first real opportunity for Formosan leaders to emerge in a quasi-political character. Many members used the forum as a means of personal advertisement, which was unfortunate, and the traditional fragmentation of Formosan community life was strongly evident. Prominent men bickered among themselves and local cliques failed to submerge their differences in unity for a common cause.

For ten days the Council chambers had been made a focal point for discontent, and an irresponsible press eagerly exploited every sensational verbal clash, scandalous rumor and factual report discrediting Chen Yi and his Commissioners.

The Development of Opposition Leadership

One group of the Opposition (led by Keh Kuo-chi) made violent nationalistic speeches, attacking Chen Yi and his associates for weakening China's position on Formosa. He demanded that Formosans be armed to protect the island from any aggression. "After all," said he, "Formosans have no Chungking to which they may retreat!" Another group spoke with greater moderation, suggesting that reforms in local government must be hastened to prepare for nationwide constitutional government.

After the Council meetings moderate opposition leadership was assumed informally by a few articulate, well-educated men. A new Chinese national Constitution was being prepared, and it was expected that when this went into effect — perhaps by the end of 1946 — Formosans could claim full rights as citizens under its terms. They looked forward to election of Formosan representatives for the nationwide Peoples' Political Councils to be convened at Nanking.

Public attention focused upon the lawyer and editor Wang Tien-teng, who was expected to represent Formosan interests in the National Assembly. As he campaigned he made no secret of his plan to impeach Governor Chen at Nanking or of his hope to persuade the Generalissimo to reform and clean up the Taipei administration. Using Wang's editorials as evidence of subversion, the Governor had him seized and tried on charges of "inciting to rebellion." The arrest was timed to interfere with Wang's campaign activities.

The story of the Liao brothers is instructive. They were sons of a wealthy Christian landowning family in south-central Formosa. The brothers had left the island in the 1920's to study abroad. Both held doctoral degrees from American universities and each had a Caucasian wife.* Upon returning to China Joshua (the elder) entered Government service and academic life at Shanghai and Nanking. Thomas, the younger, became a chemical engineer on Formosa. When Formosa was handed over to Chiang Kai-shek in 1945 they had every reason to anticipate appointments at high levels in the new administration. But they suffered certain disabilities; they were honest men, and they believed in the principles and practices of democratic representative government — not notable qualifications for employment under Chen Yi. Just after the Surrender Thomas Liao was given charge of the Taipei Municipal bus services, an honor he soon relinquished.

Throughout 1946 the brothers devoted themselves (and the family fortune) to a campaign of public political education in Formosa. Joshua remained principally at Shanghai lecturing, writing, and conferring with liberal "Third Party" non-Communist Chinese who wanted to see the Nationalist Party leaders driven from power at Nanking before it was too late to rally the country against the Communists. Formosa seemed to offer an ideal opportunity to demonstrate the possibilities of "New China" under fresh leadership. In the Liaos' view, Formosa, properly administered, could become a major asset in the rehabilitation of continental China.

Thomas Liao spent the year 1946 carrying forward a campaign of lectures and organization of public opinion on the island itself, appealing principally to well-educated younger Formosans to demand effective constitutional administration. Both Liao brothers made it perfectly clear that to secure good government and to preserve the freedom and rights of the Formosan people within a Chinese national structure, every educated Formosan leader must expect to incur grave personal risks to life and property. They condemned totalitarian Party

* Joshua Wen-ki Liao: M.A. Wisconsin, Ph.D. University of Chicago (Political Science). Thomas Wen-yi Liao: M.A. Michigan, Ph.D. Ohio State University (Chemical Engineering)

rule in the strongest terms, whether it be Communist or Nationalist in name. We will meet them again in a later chapter.

With the lawyer Wang Tien-teng, Thomas Liao stood for election to the National Assembly at Nanking, and made "constitutionalism" the basis of his appeals to the voter.

When the ballots were counted in the autumn election Liao had a majority, but the administration announced that "too many Liao ballots were marked with "imperfect calligraphy." His election was declared void.

Lim Hsien-tang, the old hero of the Home Rule Movement, was too frail to take a vigorous part in the year-long political struggle. He was often accused of having been too willing to accommodate himself to the Japanese Empire system, but his critics conveniently forgot that until the Western Allied Powers came along in 1945 there had not been the slightest prospect that Formosa would ever leave the Japanese Empire organization. He had argued for the realities of his time, but now there had come worldwide change; leadership of a new Home Rule Movement lay with younger men. The struggle for recognition was no longer with Tokyo but with Nanking.

In 1946 the Formosans wanted no change in the *form* of government, but simply a change in personnel representing the Central Government at Taipei, a return to government by law and to reasonably conservative economic policies. They wanted an end to ruthless exploitation by their Nationalist Party "brothers."

The First Session of the Peoples' Political Council Assembly (held in May) had defined the major areas of popular discontent. The December meetings made it clear that the Government had paid not the slightest heed to warnings and recommendations set forth in May. In the second half of 1946 public antagonism intensified; the Second Session of the PPC Assembly served as a burning glass, bringing popular anger to focus on the National Party record of incompetence and abuse. Henceforth the elected representatives of the people faced the Government in undisguised hostility.

X

The Search
for Recognition

Intervention: Nanking, Tokyo, Washington, or the UN?

FAITH IN THE Central Government died hard. Formosans wanted to see their problem as a local one which could be corrected if the Generalissimo would take note of conditions on the island. They had entered 1946 continuing to declare loyalty to Chiang, and with faith in the future of "New China." By the end of the year they were seeking desperately to invoke some form of foreign inquiry or intervention. In this chapter we will review the change in attitudes toward the Generalissimo and China.

Here and there a voice publicly expressed belief that if Washington, through the American Ambassador, would draw Chiang's attention to Taipei he would at once decree a change for the better. Others who sought to avoid any suggestion that China's allies should become involved, noted that China's new constitution would sufficiently guarantee Formosan interests by providing for election of the governor. Some Formosans heatedly rejected the idea of an appeal to Washington or the United Nations, wanting no shadow of the old "foreign intervention."

In January, 1946, General Chen announced conscription of Formosan youths for service with Nationalist forces on the mainland. In the outcry which greeted this, local leaders declared that their sons were eager to train for the defense of their island home but raised the question of Formosa's legal status. Editors and orators took the position that it was technically "occupied enemy territory" and as such not subject to conscription by the "Occupying Power." Behind this, of course, lay a profound reluctance to commit any Formosan youth to the Nationalist Army organization for service on distant mainland frontiers. The Formosans had seen quite enough of undisciplined Nationalist troops, half-starved and ragged. They had no faith whatsoever in the future of the National Army. Many believed the move was designed to strip Formosa of able-bodied young men who could defend their homes vis-à-vis mainland Chinese if things went from bad to worse on the continent and on the island.

Voices proposing an appeal to the Supreme Commander at Tokyo grew louder, and then came suggestions that appeals should be addressed to the United Nations. Some suggested direct appeals to the United States.

Governor Chen saw that conscription was premature, and quickly dropped the subject. The Central Government was extremely sensitive to any mention of the sovereignty issue and deeply resented any suggestion of intervention however friendly the foreign power or powers might be. Every means was taken to quench the issue. The official line was firmly established for propaganda guidance: Japan's surrender automatically brought about the return of "stolen territory" to China. The Cairo Declaration had done the trick. Formosans were united in support of the Nationalist Government. Only communist malcontents criticised the administration.

But among the Formosans wishes fathered thoughts; in growing alarm they watched the disintegration of Chiang's mainland military, political and economic position and the failure of the Marshall Mission. More or less subconsciously they turned toward the United States, and by midyear the island was swept with rumors of an impending American intervention to prevent a Communist invasion. Word spread that Washington was about to establish trusteeship for a ten-year period, or for the duration of the Communist threat. Rumor said that Chiang was about to hand Formosa to the United States in payment for war debts, or surety against huge new grants of military aid.

Because it was widely believed that American Armed Forces were about to move in, alert businessmen approached the American Consulate for aid in securing commercial concessions near bases which they understood were to be taken over by the U. S. Army, Air Force, and Navy. At the same time the Consulate had many requests for information concerning prospects for direct Formosan-American trade which could be arranged to bypass Shanghai. It was rumored, too, that a new university would soon be established, under American auspices, to develop local intellectual and political leadership.

Our Consul thought the whole business distasteful, embarrassing, and rather silly; there was no substance to all this — ("This is China now") — hence it could be dismissed. He did not seem to understand the strain this drift of affairs placed upon the United States Information Service. Our USIS program, after all, was the "other half" of the Consular organization, and it was required to pour out a flood of propaganda praising American aid to "democratic China."

The expectation of American aid was a deeply emotional phenomenon; the Formosans had expected so much, and as things now stood (in 1946) some act on the part of the United States — as China's sponsor before the world — was believed to be the only possible solution to local difficulties.

The Formosan Press Formulates the Issues

Obviously, if Formosa turned to the United States for help, it would be profitable to know the English language. Study of the Chinese "national language" (*kuo yü*) so popular in 1945, was now put aside. English conversation classes flourished, radio programs offered English instruction, and a spate of new publications eagerly reprinted American stories and news commentary.

Many of these reprints — perhaps a majority — were provided, gratis, by the United States Information Service. American concepts of a brave new postwar world were projected eagerly by young Formosan editors. The slogans "Freedom of the Press" and "Freedom of Assembly" became prime topics for public debate.

In January and February, 1946, Dr. Lin Mou-sheng (a Columbia University man) published a series of articles in which he developed the theme that "If in Formosa the *Three People's Principles* [of Sun Yat-sen] cannot be carried out, then the future of the Republic of China will indeed be dark." His blunt comments were timed to reach the attention of an official deputation which the Central Government proposed to send to Formosa for an inspection tour. In time-honored fashion it was announced that these representatives would receive petitions addressed to them by "the People." The Formosans knew enough of Chinese history to know that this was traditional "window-dressing," something to look well in the historical record; they proposed more incisive action. Public discussion of current issues led quickly to political organization.

On February 2 a Formosan People's Association came into being, reorganized soon after as the Taiwan Political Reconstruction Association. On March 11, 1946, the newspaper *Min Pao* (edited by Lin Mou-sheng) published names of its officers and members, a representative cross-section of substantial landholders and professional men. Contrary to later Nationalist charges, this was not a secret, subversive organization but rather a revival, in new form, of the Home Rule Association which had struggled so long to represent Formosan interests under the Japanese administration.

Concurrently there began to appear "Citizens' Freedom Safeguarding Committees" which were in effect vigilante units formed by men determined to defend local interests wherever they were threatened by mainland Chinese newcomers. The first Committee appeared at Taipei on March 5, 1946, only five months after the surrender. Others soon appeared throughout the island, letting it be known that they felt they could no longer look to the local police to maintain law and order.

The Government did all that it could to impede the growth of these popular bodies, and a running battle of words filled the press. In this the *Min Pao* took the lead in a series of editorials entitled "Safeguarding the People's Freedom" which bitterly commented upon the need to take such measures of self-defense so soon after "liberation."

The Formosans were prepared to fight for freedom of expression, so long denied them under Japanese rule, and the mainland Chinese were equally determined to repress criticism. Before the war the Formosan journal *Minpo* had been suppressed, and five Japanese-language dailies were consolidated and published as the *Taiwan Shimpo* from 1942 until the Japanese surrender on October 25, 1945. Literate Formosans were starved for a means of expression, and among all the glittering promises rained down in American propaganda pamphlets and broadcast by American stations, none was more attractive than the assurance "freedom of the press" would be theirs.

The mainland Chinese at Taipei, on the other hand, were baffled; they had expected to have no more trouble in controlling the provincial Formosans than they normally experienced in outlying illiterate mainland provinces. Throughout 1946 they underestimated the significance of a well-developed island-wide communications system and of widespread literacy.

Within a few weeks after the surrender ten newspapers came into being. The old *Taiwan Shimpo* — with the best technical assets and largest organization — was taken over to serve as a Government mouthpiece, under the name *Hsin Sheng Pao*. Circulation soon dropped from 170,000 to less than 56,000 or one-third. The Opposition was led by Lim Hsien-tang's old Formosan newspaper, revived as the *Min Pao* or "People's Journal." Under the editorial guidance of Lin Mou-sheng it promptly began crusading on behalf of Formosan interests.

Aligned with the *Min Pao* was the *Jen Min Tao Pao* or "People's Herald" founded on January 1, 1946, by several Formosans who had returned after years in China, and who were somewhat left-of-center in political ideology. It failed, and on the point of bankruptcy the noted local lawyer, Wang Tien-teng, took it over, reorganized it, and soon made it popular through his spirited attacks upon corruption in Chen Yi's government.

Representatives of the wealthy Lim Clan undertook to publish Formosa's only evening paper — the *Ta Ming Pao,* or "Great Light," designed to appeal to local intellectuals. It was a progressvie paper urging reform within the Government and an early development of liberal constitutional government throughout China.

All independent Formosan newspapers were subjected to government and Party interference. On March 7 the Government suspended publication of the only East Coast journal, at Hualien City, because the editor had dared to criticize a speech made by an official newly arrived from the mainland. For a time "Freedom of the Press" was a dominant theme, and on May 23 General Chen took note of it in conversations with representatives of the American Consulate. We were told that he wished to stress his desire to ensure full freedom of speech and press. Three days later, however, we learned that representatives of the Bureau of Mining and Industry had attempted to seize the building of the *Ta Ming Pao* and had severely manhandled Formosan pressmen attempting to hold them off.

One quotation will suggest Wang Tien-teng's approach to the problem of relations with the mainland. A Government editorial (in the *Hsin Sheng Pao*) had stressed Formosan obligation to compare local conditions favorably with contemporary conditions on the mainland, rather than unfavorably with high prewar standards which prevailed under Japanese rule. Wang's editorial rejoinder was often quoted thereafter. He said:

> Does this mean that because China has corruption, Formosa must also have corruption? And because China has widespread famine, Formosa must also have famine? . . . The problem is that the common people here have their own viewpoints, quite different from the Chinese view.
>
> Of course, in the process of reconversion various difficulties are inevitable. Rome was not built in a day. These are facts. But we cannot rely upon corrupt officials to save the situation. Guarantees of success depend upon wise administration and an upright people. We favor the Sinification of Formosa, but this does not mean that Taiwan should also be corrupted and poor . . .[1]

Is the U.S.A. Responsible?

There were many smaller newspapers and magazines, a number of which were published in English, or in English and Chinese. The *Taiwan Youth Report* (English edition of the *Taiwan Chinglian*) encouraged English-language studies and stressed the need for strong international ties to advance Formosa's development. The *Liberty Weekly* or *Tzu Yu Pao* of Taipei, was filled with hopeful plans for the future of Formosa as China's most progressive and well-developed province. The *Formosan Magazine* (subtitled "The Magazine for New Formosans") was the most elaborate of the "youth" publications.

The founders and editors of these journals were young men whose well-to-do families had sent them to Japanese universities. In 1946 they looked upon the United States as the leading modern nation and upon English as the indepensable "international language" through which they must keep abreast of world affairs and technical developments. But they held to the proposition that Formosans must be citizens of China, enjoying local self-government while contributing to China's growth as an independent constitutional state. American aid must be welcomed throughout China, for it was obviously essential to national political security and economic recovery. At the same time they looked to the United States to assume moral responsibility for the actions of Chiang's Nationalist Government in Formosa because of Washington's unlimited support for the Generalisimo.

After the bloody March crisis, 1947, Chen Yi's propagandists (Stanway Cheng and his men) charged that the *Formosan Magazine,* the *Taiwan Youth Report* and the *Liberty Weekly* were "Communist journals." Here is the record: Of thirty-seven items published in the first issue of the *Formosan Magazine* (September, 1946) no less than thirty-four concerned the United States. The leading article was a biography of President Truman, followed by one entitled "Japan's Fatal Mistake" (reprinted from the *U. S. Infantry Journal*), and an essay by E. R. Stettinius, Secretary of State, entitled "In the Cause of Peace." There were articles on the United States armed services, on the English language, American industrial know-how, and the names of the forty-eight states. A Saroyan short story and the reflections of a Gold Star mother were among the diverse offerings of this "Communist" journal.

The leading editorial in the first issue took for its background a commentary entitled "Formosan Scandal" which had appeared in the *Washington Post* on March 29. Responsibility for conditions within Formosa were laid at America's door.

With the unconditional surrender of Japan, the transition of the Jurisdiction of Taiwan to her original Chinese owner had been carried out swiftly and smoothly. America, that supplied us with men and vessels, took an important part in the period of transfer. Chinese troops and officials were shipped over into this island by American ships to replace the Japanese. The repatriation of the Japanese from Taiwan, too, has been carried out by American vessels . . .

Noting Japan's tireless prewar efforts to estrange Formosans from China, to suppress news, to discourage the use of English, and to censor English and Chinese texts which the Formosans wanted to read, the editorial continued:

> Our Generalissimo Chiang sent to Taiwan Governor Chen, although an upright man, we regret to say that some of his followers misbehaved themselves, thereby incurring much misunderstanding among the Taiwan brethren who believe their coming here is for the sake of finding riches rather than doing good work for the Province of Taiwan . . .

The editor notes China's failure to press toward rehabilitation of public services which had so distinguished Formosa from the mainland provinces.

> Communications on land and sea are becoming more difficult. On land we find decayed old locomotives and bad trucks running over bad railways and unrepaired roads; and at sea we have very few steamships plying among our ports . . . Two centuries ago our ancestors came by junks to this island, and we find our brethren are resorting to the same means to come over [today].
> Now we wish America to help us immediately with vessels to import raw materials that we urgently require for our factories, and we hope that our provincial government would consult with American Authorities to help us solve this important problem . . .
> Taiwan is now under the Chinese flag, the islanders should adopt everything Chinese, and cast away the hypocritical ideas of the Japanese. Since the retrocession of Taiwan to China, many officials did not make a thorough study of the intention of patriotic and aspiring youths, under the plea that they are disqualified for lack of Chinese learning, and of knowledge of the

National language. Learning does not mean knowing of the
writing of Chinese characters and language; it means the understanding of things in general — as the knowing of Science,
Philosophy, Politics, etc. . . .

With the advancement of Science, the Pacific Ocean voyage
separating the two big Powers — America and China — has
been made much shorter . . . The people of the two continents
are becoming intimate friends.

America does not hesitate to help China, for the Chinese are
a peace-loving people, and to understand American civilization
and how Americans of late have made tremendous improvements, the first thing for the Taiwan people to learn is English,
and then American books in every branch of learning. If opportunity offered, go to America at once, and you shall conceive
how our American friends are going on in their daily life, and
adopt what is good for the improvement of the nation. It is
shameful to everyone of us if we cannot keep step with our good
friends; in case if we cannot keep pace, at least we must follow
as closely as possible the improvements of our friends.[2]

This, in Nationalist eyes, was a "Communist line," or so it
was represented to be by American-educated Chinese on Chen
Yi's staff in 1947.

The third issue of the *Formosan Magazine* (November,
1946) was devoted principally to a discussion of international
interests, including articles on the British Government and people, and upon UNRRA. A series entitled "The Great Dream"
attempted to outline Formosa's potential as a proving ground
for both technological development and democracy in China.
Several articles were critical of the Nationalist Government.
The situation in Formosa was compared to the breathless period preceding a great typhoon, and warned of coming chaos
if conditions were not improved and mainland policies not re-
versed. One discussion of Formosa's fate ended with these
words: "Struggle on, Formosans! Yield to nothing, but go on to
our goal! But I wonder what will become of Taiwan???"

The American Consulate was fully aware of Formosan opinion; members of the UNRRA organization reported profound

discontent in every island community, and the Formosans themselves tried again and again to bring their problems to the
attention of foreign residents. On July 2 I dined with seven Formosans who had been well known to me before the war. They
had returned to Formosa with firsthand knowledge of colonial
systems as diverse as the British, Portuguese, French, Dutch
and Japanese. Several had observed the Philippines preparing
for independence before 1942, and the fate of the Filipinos who
had remained loyal to the United States during the Japanese
occupation. Now they discussed Formosa's peculiar fate as a
"liberated" territory. All agreed that the island must be considered a province of China, but felt that a federated relationship
would serve the island's interests to best advantage. They
agreed that Formosa lacked strong leadership, political sophis-
tication, and organization, and that few Formosans were of
sufficient stature to command island-wide support and respect.
But, said one, "If civil war breaks out in China proper, then a
ten- or fifteen-year trusteeship under the United States is the
only salvation. The people of Formosa trust the United States
to give them freedom to return to China when the Chinese government has been reformed. Look at the Philippines."

On August 2 a petition was addressed to the American Consulate by an organization of Formosans who had been taken to
the Philippines as wartime conscript labor, and there made
prisoners of war by American forces. Having outlined their experiences, they concluded with these words:

> We have returned to Taiwan with mixed feeling. We feel
> happy and we also feel sad, because we are compared to the
> slaves, and we find our former abodes occupied by others. We
> earnestly hope, therefore, that the U. S. Government will give
> us speedy relief in view of our lot . . .

A more emotional appeal, made in a letter dated September
30, reflects the heightened sense of insecurity disturbing Formosa as we entered the autumn months of 1946:

Many silent prayers be given to those American soldiers who sacrificed themselves for the sake of world peace, and at the same time may we give thanks unceasingly to the United States of America.

To tell the truth, when I read [an American magazine article, published on June 10] which stressed that if the Formosans are permitted to choose their own sovereigning nation by vote, by all means they will first of all choose the United States of America and then Japan; we perfectly in sympathy with them. When we read this latter one, we felt that what was said was too much of a truth, and we could not but to thank them . . . We could imagine how much the United States of America is just like a God who will not only lead us but the whole world. The government we have now is a ruinous government which takes us as slaves and which will lead the whole race to hell.

At the time of retrieving [i.e., return to China] we clapped our hands to welcome the arms of Chiang, the Chairman, but at present we are somehow equivalent to be in a state where after a dog (Japanese) is being driven away, a swine came into its place here in Taiwan.

This suffering, this lamentation! For the release of our 6,700,000 people we must first of all lean upon America and next on Japan, which is of the same yellow race. This is our intention.

The Government shouts of "The Three Principles," "Equality" and for "A World for the Public" but is it not true that it takes an attitude of a squeezism in secret? Our desire is to make the present government retire, and to build a powerful, responsive government; for this we shall pray without ceasing. The usurping of goods which the UNRRA sent for relief and the distribution of them at the market price are certainly rotten.

I will introduce you our present government; its name shall be "The Great Chinese Joint-Stock Company, Unlimited." Chiang Kai-shek is the Chief of the Trustees. T. B. Soong the Vice Chief of the Trustees, Chen Yi, the swine, is the Manager of the Branch Office.

Please communicate this to the God of Salvation, the American people, for their reference.

The Chiangs Visit Taipei

A few Formosans did think of the American people in terms of "divinity" — or at least omnipotence; the majority placed a less exalted valuation upon those indestructible symbols of "Chinese-American Friendship," the Generalissimo and Madame Chiang. This they made clear on October 25.

At Nanking General George C. Marshall patiently continued to seek some basis for a lasting truce which might save China from civil war, and the Nationalist Government from disaster. But Chiang refused to take the advice of American military advisors and was even then losing North China. Now he refused to make a serious effort to solve his problems through negotiation. He had persuaded himself that soon enough the United States would move in to defeat the Communists on his behalf, just as the United States and Great Britain had moved in to drive the Japanese from China.

General Marshall persuaded Communist leader Chou En-lai to agree to further negotiations at Nanking. Obviously Marshall needed Chiang there, too, for only the Generalissimo could speak with an authority binding upon the Nationalist Government.

Chiang would have none of it; it was announced that he must visit Formosa to celebrate the first anniversary of Japan's surrender there, and would then retire modestly to a quiet mountain resort to celebrate his own sixtieth birthday.

From a propaganda point of view, the visit was a blunder for the Nationalists. Commemoration Day (October 25) was chosen for the official triumphal entry into the island capital. A general holiday was declared, and hours before the event students, teachers, government employees and many others were marched into place along the principal boulevard leading into Taipei. The tedium of waiting was broken only once, when a truck and a jeep bearing UNRRA officers sped down the high-road. Enthusiastic acclaim swept the Formosan ranks, flags waved, a spontaneous shout went up, and on all sides one heard "Banzai! Banzai! Amerika-jin! Hi, Jo!"

Half an hour later the Chiangs passed along the same route. For the better part of the way they were met by silence, broken only here and there where embarrassed mainland teachers or government officers prompted their charges to make a show of greeting.

Throughout the ill-timed visit the National leader and his wife were received with notable coolness, and suffered thereby a painful loss of face. But everywhere they went the way was smoothed; roads were repaired and buildings refurnished, and only the "right" island people were brought forward to be received by the Chief of State.

In public addresses the Generalissimo noted the evidence of successful reconstruction which he professed to see on every side. To the American Consular staff Madame Chiang made her usual remarks about dear orphans, designed to show her interest in little children and good social works, but added — when we spoke of Formosa's wealth — that she would like to be Governor of Taiwan for ten years.

The Chiangs' visit perceptibly heightened Formosa's sense of disillusionment; the National Leader had found everything in Formosa to his satisfaction — so he said — and praised Chen Yi for the quality and progress of local administration.

It is just possible that the Generalissimo believed what he said, for even at the end of a year of rapacious administration the general conditions of livelihood upon uncrowded Formosa stood in sharply favorable contrast to conditions on the war-torn and exhausted mainland. But local Army and Party leaders were well aware of the swift decline of the Chiangs' prestige. Moderate Formosan leaders could no longer hold forth the assurance that conditions would improve "if the Generalissimo only knew the truth."

In an attempt to reach the Generalissimo's eye, on October 28 the *Min Pao* editorialized:

Taiwan has every possibility of becoming a model province of China. However, present conditions on the island prove to us the contrary . . . We fully appreciate the good will of the Governor, but regret that many of his men are corrupt. The increasing number of unemployed indicates that the social crisis is approaching, followed by a political and economic crisis. Every day we see youths looking for jobs while all positions high and low are filled by strangers. News of robbery and theft is ever-present in the papers, and we even hear that some of the brothers from the mainland have organized looting parties.

The thoughts of the unemployed youths are deteriorating daily. Dissatisfied with the corruption of the officials and the extravagant rich, many of them become robbers and thieves. This year is coming to an end, and we must take steps to prevent the final crisis.[3]

On the previous day a number of prominent Formosans had announced the formation of a Constitution Promotion Association of Taiwan. They anticipated the promulgation of a new constitution for China on December 25, to become effective one year thereafter. As the year drew to a close the island press devoted many columns to discussions of constitutional problems and procedures, and conservative editors and public speakers referred often to the American federal structure, which recommended itself to advocates of maximum Formosan autonomy within the Chinese provincial system.

American Propaganda Feeds the Fires of Discontent

Less experienced younger men, however, were beginning to think in terms of direct action, and in this they were prompted by the inappropriate propaganda being distributed on the island by the United States Information Service.

The situation in Formosa at this time — and the tragic events that were about to take place — foreshadowed the rebellions of a later date in Poland and Hungary, where other distressed minorities took American promises of sympathetic support and America's "Liberation" propaganda at face value.

Propaganda directives emanating from paneled offices along the Potomac often bore little or no relevance to areas for which they were issued. The Formosans, for example, were in no position to enjoy the luxury of political self-expression which American propagandists piously assumed was every man's prerogative. Much against the better judgment of the local United States Information Service Director at Taipei, Washington required distribution throughout Formosa of propaganda preaching the "American Way of Life," and "American-style democracy."

As an example, in late 1946 the Consulate received from Washington thousands of copies of a well-illustrated pamphlet entitled *The Story of the United States Government — How it Started . . . and How it Works.* This purported to show the growth of American representative political institutions, beginning with migrations from England in search of freedom in new lands, the development of pre-Revolutionary New England town meetings, and the final development of the legislative and judicial systems under constitutional protection. Colonial protest against taxation without representation was illustrated, and so, too, was the ideal of the individual prepared to die for the cause of local self-government.

The pamphlet — like many others — took the form of a pictorial appeal to young people of middle and high school age, that age of political unsophistication when all things seem possible to achieve through direct action. Formosans reading it could see the parallel distinctly — their ancestors, too, had left mainland China for an open frontier, and they, too, had tried again and again to protest taxation without representation. (The taxation of tea was a very familiar issue.) For a quarter century their fathers and elder brothers had struggled under the Japanese to achieve local self-government through elective assemblies; now it was their turn to take up the self-sacrificing struggle.

A few quotations from this Washington production will indicate how extraordinarily inappropriate and irresponsible American propaganda was at this time in this place, already ripe for rebellion:

> John is an American citizen . . . He learned how the people of early American colonies fought and won their independence and freedom to govern themselves . . . and that each of these colonies had a separate government.
>
> He learned that under each of these colonial governments were many local governments . . . and that many of these local governments were formed by vote of the people at a mass assembly.
>
> John understood that self-government made it easy for public officials, reflecting the will of the people, to act according to the needs of the community . . . and that it was easy for the people of the community to see that the public officials performed their duties . . .
>
> [*The pamphlet then described the evolution of the Constitution, and continued*]
>
> Political parties were organized under the Constitutional guarantee of the people's right to assemble peaceably . . .
>
> The party organizations help in many ways to stimulate interest in government, and to develop leadership. It is possible, however, for these organizations to fall under the control of unscrupulous politicians who then select candidates to serve selfish interests instead of the best interests of the people . . .
>
> And it is a result of these experiences that John's form of government has become precious to him — a government which permits freedom of religion, freedom of speech, freedom of press, freedom of assembly, and freedom to choose those who govern. Today John and millions like him all over the world are fighting to keep these freedoms alive.[4]

This sort of thing was construed to mean that the United States Government and the American people were standing by ready to support a "fighting effort" to make democracy come true in Formosa.

The United States Information Service Director realized that propaganda headquarters in Washington was paying not the slightest heed to our consular reports. These had been grave enough in early 1946, but as the year drew to a close they carried warning that a sense of crisis filled the island. November brought many new reports of conflict between the Formosans and the mainland Chinese, and some of these incidents — in retrospect — were to take on special significance. Not least were reports of a series of verbal clashes between Nationalist Army officers charged with the military training program at the higher schools, and Formosan students, most of whom had received some training during the last years of the Japanese administration. Students at the University took delight in jeering from the ranks, calling out offers to show the incompetent Chinese newcomers how to conduct close-order drill "in the Japanese manner." The furious instructors retired from the field in confusion, shouting threats of revenge for an intolerable loss of face. The possibility of violence was present; the ill-considered propaganda was inflammatory, but the Consulate continued to distribute it.

The Second PPC Assembly Brings the Crisis Near

As we have noted, December 12 brought the second convocation of the Taiwan Peoples' Political Council. In an obvious attempt to reduce the effectiveness of meetings and to limit public debate, Chen's officers withheld permission to use the wide stage and large auditorium of the Civic Center. The sessions therefore opened in the narrow chambers of the Educational Association Building, far from the center of town. There was scarcely space for the participants, virtually no room for spectators, and the public-address system conspicuously failed to operate at critical moments when Formosan delegates rose to speak.

For ten days the Council Chambers rang with angry debate. The Government presented its formal reports, but it was evident that they were no more accurate or truthful than those made to the First Council session in May, and that the Governor had pointedly ignored most of the recommendations made in the spring.

Formosan leaders at last realized that the organization of the council system itself was mere window-dressing, mocking the democratic process which China's leaders professed to uphold. Many intemperate exchanges took place. Formosan demands that the mainland garrison troops be replaced by a Home Guard, recruited on Formosa and trained to repel any future threat of invasion, were singled out by Chen's officers as "proof" that the Formosans harbored rebellious thoughts. Council members made it unmistakably clear that they had no faith in Chiang's ability to establish order on the mainland or to defend Formosan interests. Army spokesmen retorted that Formosan youths were "disloyal" and "subversive."

Council meetings broke up in an atmosphere of unbridled anger. Formosan councilors heaped abuse upon the Governor and his men, and left no rumor undiscussed. No solid support could be given to many of the charges, but so much was true and so widely observed that Formosans were prepared to believe the worst of any mainland Chinese. Since each stormy meeting was given full press coverage throughout the island, tensions were heightened everywhere. Wang Tien-teng, then President of the Tea Merchants Guild, told me in mid-December that he was being urged to organize demonstrations, but that he refused, hoping that as soon as the new constitution for China came into effect it would automatically modify the autocratic powers of the Governor-General and provide a peaceful road to reform. Liberals and conservatives alike would then have representatives at Nanking, lobbying for national recognition of Formosa's problems under Chen Yi. If the new constitution (to become effective in 1947) brought no relief, it might be necessary then for Formosans to take stronger action.

A wave of disillusionment engulfed Formosa at the year's end. The island-wide Assembly, so long anticipated, had failed to shield the people from an abusive government. Leading members of the Council were caught in a cross fire between an angry Government and an angry electorate. The public had expected too much of the Council, believing it to have greater power and authority than it actually possessed. The Government, on the other hand, had trifled with the electorate, underestimating the Formosans' profound determination to secure representative government, and the effective strength of widespread literacy. Chen was not dealing with yokels of an interior province but with an island people who had been exposed to the Western world long ago, and for fifty years had been governed by the most advanced nation in Asia.

The American position was awkward. Formosans were proud to think of themselves in association with the people of the United States through China's status as an ally. China's prestige in Formosa in 1945 derived from this association quite as much as from any emotional ties with a "mother country." The Allies — led by the United States — had delivered the island from colonial servitude — and now, at the end of 1946, Formosans looked to the American people to help them escape a new tyranny. They were baffled by the situation at the Consulate, from which poured out a flood of printed materials advocating the "1776 approach" to oppressive government. At the same time the Consul made it unmistakably clear that as an official body the Consulate was not interested in the Formosa problem. Its official relations were with Chen Yi and his Commissioners.

We realized how quickly a complaint by Chen Yi to the

proper Higher Authorities at Nanking could cause our recall from Taipei. This could be done by a word at Nanking hinting American sympathy for "rebels" and "Communists." We were acutely conscious of the Department's decision that "This is China now," but in our eagerness to make this clear to Chen Yi's Commissioners, we sometimes rather overdid it both in social cordiality (Sino-American friendship was given many a toast) and in "sterilized" reports going forward to the Embassy and Washington.

We consistently underplayed the significance and gravity of events about us. Every statement was qualified or hedged about by bureaucratic phrases such as "Formosans claimed . . ." or "It was alleged by Formosans . . ." as if neither the Consular staff nor the Americans in the UNRRA group had eyes or ears with which to perceive the incidents and record the circumstances leading to crisis. The whole was to be treated as a petty misunderstanding within the Chinese national family.

In December the Consul flew off to Shanghai and Nanking for a brief holiday which also provided opportunity to discuss informally, the situation in Formosa. Perhaps things were not so bad as they might seem in formal reports. We had excellent working relations with Governor Chen's Commissioners, he thought, and the American posture in Taipei was "correct." But during his absence our "official friends" at Taipei staged an anti-American demonstration designed to show the world how much *Formosans* disliked the U.S.A.

The Government's "Hate Foreigners" Campaign

We were now in a most awkward three-sided confrontation. The Formosans were looking to the foreigners to help them rid the island of Chen Yi, the American Consulate was assuring the Nationalists of its firm support, and the Nationalists were doing all that they could to destroy Formosan trust in Washington's promises and leadership.

By midyear 1946 Chen's advisors and propaganda officers had become alarmed by the impact of United States propaganda in Formosa and by the popularity of the UNRRA team and program. The American military group had made a favorable impression on the Formosans, too, throwing the condition and behavior of the Nationalist military into high relief.

By contrast, the Commissioners were acutely conscious that Formosans held mainland Chinese in contempt, and equally sensitive to the fact — obvious to all — that the Nationalist Government was wholly dependent upon the United States for political and economic support if it were to stay in power. Here again was a matter of face.

Governor Chen's office began a campaign to undermine Formosan trust in the United States Government and people, and the United Nations. It was as obvious as it was vicious. Stanway Cheng knew that Formosans had grown indifferent to the study of mainland Mandarin or *kuo yü*, and were intensively pursuing the study of English, reading anything in English that came to hand. He therefore launched a new English-language journal, the *New Taiwan Monthly* with a dual purpose. It could be used as a vehicle for anti-American propaganda within Formosa, and it could be used abroad as a counterfoil to the popular *Formosan Youth Magazine* and *Liberty*. Since the new journal could be printed and circulated at Government expense, it could smother the struggling Formosan papers.

The October, 1946, issue established the official line. The Governor was pictured as a man much too generous and indulgent, a father to his people; his critics were represented as either pro-Japanese Formosans, or Communists. The American people were represented as cruel, calculating, bigoted and avaricious, but very skilled at hiding all this behind a façade of good works.

On this first point, said the Editor:

Opinion on the Chinese administrative policy on Taiwan seems to be sharply divided into two camps of thought. One school tends to believe that a maximum amount of freedom and rights should be given the Taiwanese who should live under a local government pretty much autonomous if not independent, from the Chinese National Government. Taiwan should be Taiwanese is their slogan. Everywhere they complain and charge the present administration of exercising too much control over them both economically and politically. This group, led mainly by those local gentry and intelligensia [sic] who used to be friendly with their Japanese masters, believes in a closed door policy and insists that Taiwan can be best governed by themselves only.

The other school [the mainland Chinese] points out that complete democratization of Taiwan after fifty-one years of slavery and iron rule by Japan, can not be successful without first undergoing a period of de-Nipponization and Chinese nationalization. If an unprepared people such as this are given democracy at once it can do more harm than good, they point out. A wise administration should grant democracy bit by bit. This will help the people keep control of themselves. This group is equally critical of the present [Chen Yi] administration, for being too rapid in pushing democratic ideals and instruction to the local people . . .[5]

A long article entitled "Memoirs of a Japanese Professor in Taiwan," (a transparent fabrication) embodied a vicious attack upon the United States and the American armed forces. With heavy sarcasm it implied American contempt for all Asians ("Surely there is something in American psychology which is beyond our sluggish Oriental minds!"), and suggested that the failure to stage an Allied invasion of Formosa was to be attributed to American cowardice in the face of strong defenses. It alleged that American flyers took pains to bomb nonmilitary targets, but that it was American policy to spare industries which the United States could acquire after the surrender. Formosan suffering during the last months of the war was caused by careless, mischievous and callous American airmen. Chen Yi's difficulties in rehabilitating Formosa must be attributed to wanton American action, a love of destruction for its own sake.

While Stanway Cheng directed this outpouring of anti-American propaganda in print and on the radio programs emanating from Taipei, Chairman Huang Chao-chin of the Peoples' Political Councils took the lead in making newsworthy anti-American remarks in public. Having lived long in the United States he represented himself as an authority on the American political system. American-style democracy, said he, was most unsuitable in Formosa, which was being offered the opportunity to enjoy "true" or Nationalist democracy. The Formosans, he said, had no capacity to understand democracy as he had observed it in the United States, and he implied that, at best, American-style democracy was a sorry business.

The Governor's agents planted rumors and stories designed to disparage the United States and its Western Allies. The argument usually suggested that the Americans and the British were no better than the Axis partners had been, and that the only difference was this — Japan and Germany had been straightforward in their conquests, whereas the United States and Britain were devious, using UNRRA supplies and other relief measures to further imperialist ambitions in an underhand way.

The Formosans found most of these propaganda efforts absurd, but affairs took a more serious turn in December when the Governor's agents attempted to stage a "Formosan attack" upon the American Consulate.

For this they thought to exploit popular reaction to an incident at Tokyo of which grossly distorted reports were being spread about in Formosa. A number of Formosans living on the edges of the underworld in Tokyo were encouraged to exploit their new status as "Chinese citizens" in Occupied Japan. There was a clash with the police and a riot in the Shibuya ward, in Tokyo. The ringleaders were arrested, tried, and sentenced to deportation by General MacArthur's Headquarters. Stanway Cheng's office seized this "Incident" as evidence that the United States proposed to revive Japanese militarism, and that there was imminent danger Formosa might again be subjected to Japan's control. Formosans were encouraged to protest the verdict brought against their "brothers" in Japan.

At Taipei, on the morning of December 11, the Acting Secretary-General, Yen Chia-kan, sought an appointment with me, for I was then Officer-in-Charge at the Consulate. With an air of secrecy and deep concern, Yen reported that the Governor's agents had uncovered a Formosan plot to stage a great anti-American demonstration on the following day. The Taiwan Political Reconstruction Association (under "communist" leadership, according to Mr. Yen) was scheduled to hold a mass meeting at the nearby Civic Auditorium, after which the demonstrators would march upon the Consulate.

The Governor, said Mr. Yen, deeply regretted this state of affairs. An adequate force would be provided to ensure protection for the Consulate.

This offer of armed protection I declined, with thanks, assuring the Acting Secretary-General that most Americans on Formosa felt no apprehension of danger at Formosan hands. I did not add, however, that the "communist" leader of the forthcoming mass meeting was in fact well known to me, and had already forewarned the Consulate of a plan, hatched in Government offices, to make the proposed mass meeting appear to be a demonstration against Americans on Formosa.

Before bidding Mr. Yen good day I observed, offhand, that it was rather odd the Governor would permit a Communist rally to be held in the Civic Auditorium, which was Government property. That, said Mr. Yen, was simply a demonstration of the Governor's sincere desire to ensure freedom of speech and assembly.

On the next morning (December 12), truckloads of gen-

darmes and civil police appeared at the Consulate gates, set up
machine guns covering the nearby streets, and formed a double
line — a distinct channel — reaching from the Consulate to the
plaza upon which the Civic Auditorium stands. To the unin-
formed it looked indeed as if the American Consulate were in
danger and had called in Chen Yi's men to provide protection.

Toward noon, however, the scene changed suddenly. Without a word to us the unwanted guards decamped; gendarmes
and police hurried away in the direction of the Governor's
office. As the mass meeting broke up, and the crowds poured
forth upon the plaza, the leaders had ignored the channeling
lines prepared for them and had turned instead toward the Gov-
enor's office to which they marched under banners protesting
the Chinese Government's weakness in defending national interests and the interests of its new citizens (the Formosans) at
Tokyo.

That afternoon the leading demonstrator, the "communist"
Chairman of the Formosan Political Reconstruction Association, called upon me in person at the American Consulate to ask
that a "Memorandum of Protest" be forwarded to the Supreme
Commander at Tokyo. This document held that the Formosans
who had been expelled from Japan had not been properly represented by the Chinese Nationalist mission there. This business accomplished he then thanked the Consulate and the
American Government for all that was being done by America
on Formosa's behalf in this difficult period of postwar adjustment. He was especially grateful for American guidance for
Formosan youth. It was a remarkable speech for a "communist."

About this time a new mainland Chinese phenomenon — the
professional student agitator — appeared on the island. It will
be recalled that the "Go Home American!" campaign was then
being vigorously promoted at Shanghai and in other cities
throughout China proper and in these demonstrations the professional student-agitators took the lead. Now they entered

Formosa. Drab, blue-gowned mainland Chinese girls began to make rabble-rousing speeches in the classrooms, on the campus, and in the public streets and parks. They were a new and unwelcomed phenomenon in local academic life. Formosan students were urged to join their mainland "brethren" in a drive to expel foreigners from China.

Formosans were unaccustomed to a noisy role for women in the classroom; the nationalist slogans had little appeal; island students were more interested in the Western world than in China proper, and were in fact beginning to believe that only an appeal to the Western powers would restore the academic standards they had known before 1945.

They found now, however, that if they refused to take up the anti-foreign cry, they were subjected to torrents of abuse and accusations that they were "slaves of imperialism," "running dogs of the Americans" and the like.

At the year's end these professional agitators found a fresh cause in the so-called "Christmas Rape Case" or "Peking Rape Incident" involving an American serviceman in North China. Stanway Cheng's office and Chen Yi's Department of Education were delighted to exploit the affair. A new "anti-American Demonstration" was arranged for January 9. Nationalist Party agents ordered teachers to march their classes against the American Consulate. Those who protested this unwarranted interruption of class schedules were berated, humiliated, and thoroughly intimidated by the professional student-agitators who had infiltrated the major schools.

On January 9, therefore, the streets were filled with marching youths carrying flags, banners, and stickers bearing anti-American slogans prepared in advance in great quantity. Several thousand people were led through the streets near the Consulate, passing its gates again and again in what might appear to be an endless procession. Small primary school children waved slogans they did not understand, and chanted whatever they were told to chant.

With a great show of embarrassment, members of Chen Yi's government conveyed to the receptive and understanding Consul their regret that the "backward" Formosans should show such signs of anti-American sentiment, but that evening — and for days thereafter — older Formosan students and their teachers privately sought out foreigners to apologize for the "anti-foreign" demonstration in which they had been compelled to participate.

The "anti-American demonstration" had been staged with careful timing. Stanway Cheng's office made sure that it was well reported in the foreign press, where it might be expected to provoke American anger, to create anti-Formosan prejudice at Washington, and to quench any flickering concern in what was about to follow at Taipei.

XI

On the Eve of Disaster

How the Match Was Laid

DISILLUSIONED LEADERS looked about for help at the end of 1946. The Nationalists from the mainland had quickly proved their true character, but the Formosans were not at all prepared to turn to the Communists for help.

Communism had made no headway in prosperous prewar Formosa. There were no concentrations of industry to produce a radical urban proletariat. There had been full employment and a slowly rising standard of living in town and countryside alike. This was not the proper soil for communism.

Between the two world wars the Japanese had hunted down agents and agitators who entered from Shanghai or Canton or Tokyo, driving them from the island or thrusting them into jail. Organizations suspected of leftist sympathies were kept under strict surveillance. It should be recalled that the Japanese drive to suppress communism began with the Russian revolution, and that it continued with unwavering zeal while Chiang Kai-shek and his son, Ching-kuo, in turn studied communism and communist techniques in Moscow.

When MacArthur's orders freed all political prisoners in the Japanese Empire in 1945, the Communists held in Formosa were released. There were no cheering crowds awaiting them at the penitentiary gates. Some left the island promptly and some returned quietly to their village homes. Events were soon to show that some sixteen months after Japan's surrender there were fewer than fifty self-declared Communists on Formosa in a population exceeding six millions.

But by late 1946 the Nationalists had created conditions altogether favorable for the intrusion and growth of communism.

The Industrial Rehabilitation Officer for the UNRRA team (Allen J. Shackleton of New Zealand) traced the rapid increase in unemployment and the number of strikes, and had this to say:

> As I went round the Island, I noticed the tension rising, and reports of strikes due to the Formosans being replaced by mainland Chinese became fairly common. On October 10th in the Takao factory of the Taiwan Steel Manufacturing Company all the workers, comprising 960 men, went on strike as a result of trouble with the police. The workers objected to Chinese being put over them and capable Formosans being replaced. When the police were called in they came with drawn revolvers but they were attacked and disarmed, the Formosans expressing the hope that the matter could be settled amicably and with justice. Further police were called in and the workers walked out. Agreement was reached after two or three weeks.
>
> In the Taiwan Alkali Company's plant at Takao on October 28th, 1946, 2,000 men struck for reasons similar to those in the steel manufacturing company, and demanded equal treatment with the Chinese. They returned when the management acceded to their requests. Similar action took place in the cement factory at Takao.
>
> In the Taiwan Development Company much higher officials were evidently involved. This Company was organized by the Japanese to develop agriculture, commerce and engineering, and under the Chinese regime, in September 1946, a thousand employees struck against the reorganization of the Company with Chinese heads and high officials . . .[1]

Labor was bitter and restless; the Government maintained that the unemployed numbered no more than 10,000, but the

UNRRA specialists placed the estimated figure at more than 300,000, which did not include *under-employed* Formosans who had lost normal means of livelihood and had withdrawn to the shelter of family homesteads upon the crowded farms.

The sense of crisis was particularly acute at the capital; the worst administrative abuses were felt there, but the exodus of Formosans to the countryside carried word of conditions at Taipei into every outlying community.

Strikes and demonstrations grew in number and variety. Employees began to walk out when wages were not paid, or paid only in part, or when the Government management refused to entertain petitions for improved working conditions. Within a short time scores of important plants were shut down, or were working on schedules reduced by strikes and temporary walkouts. Public Health Service employees went on strike. Bus drivers at Taipei struck when they were told that henceforth they would have to pay out-of-pocket for any damage suffered by their vehicles, regardless of the circumstances involved. Workers at the Government printing plant walked out. Students rioted in Kaohsiung in a battle with the Government Railway guards. Elsewhere students refused to attend classes and parents supported their demands for reform in the school administrations. As with students everywhere in the world when caught up in economic and social crises of this magnitude, Formosan student leaders proposed direct action and radical, prompt solution to problems whose complex and remote roots they could not apprehend.

By mid-February, 1947 food shortages were felt again, and rice riots occurred with increasing frequency throughout the island. Here was tinder for rebellion.

Are Formosans Brothers, Cousins, or Enemy Aliens?

The immediate application of the new constitution after December, 1947, was understood by Formosan leaders to be the final test of Chiang's "sincerity" and the Chinese Government's policies. Warnings were going up everywhere that Nanking would have to extend to Formosa some semblance of equal treatment or risk the emergence of a belligerent "autonomy faction" which could easily be transformed into a Formosan faction demanding "independence." This might be the signal for a minor maritime war on Chiang's flank while he endeavored to hold the Nationalist lines across north China.

There was no agreement among Formosans as to the best course of action. Joshua W. K. Liao published bitter attacks upon Nationalist policy which had turned Formosa over for exploitation by factions within the Party and Government. He warned that past history suggested the dangers of Formosan separatism; the Formosan desire to be reunited with postwar China was very rapidly wasting away.

On December 20, 1946, Formosan representatives to the National Assembly at Nanking addressed a letter to the Minister for Foreign Affairs (Wang Shih-chieh) noting that Formosans overseas (meaning here, Tokyo) were being treated contemptuously by diplomatic and consular officers of China, and were not always recognized as Chinese citizens by the governments of foreign states. Wang's reply contained this paragraph:

> Since the restoration of Taiwan, this Ministry has instructed all Chinese consular services by telegram to consider Formosans as overseas Chinese and given them protection. This Ministry has also notified all foreign national authorities that all Formosans have been restored to their Chinese nationality since October 25, 1945. A reply was received from the British Government stating that it will consider Formosans as nationals of a friendly nation before the signing of the peace treaty with Japan. The U.S. Government has not yet agreed as to the official restoration of the Chinese nationality for the Formosans and negotiations are being carried out.[2]

Meanwhile the *Central Daily News* at Chungking had written editorially (on December 25) that Formosa was thinking of

independence or of "subjugating itself to the United States."
This provoked a prompt and indignant reply from many quarters. The Taiwan Political Reconstruction Association and editors of the local Formosan press most vehemently denied the
allegation. Formosan representatives to the National Assembly
had this to say:

> Nothing can be further from the mental state of the Formosans
> [than thought of subjugation to the United States]. Such re-
> ports are certain to impede the unification of our nation. We
> have heard such rumors and are greatly afraid that the con-
> tinual repetition of this false information may cause the rumors
> to materialize into truth. But these are the facts:
>
> 1. Taiwan was the base for the Chengs' struggle against the
>   Manchu dynasty for the restoration of the Ming dynasty,
>   [in the 17th century] and was also the base for the strug-
>   gles safeguarding our territory against Japan in 1894. For-
>   mosan's love of our fatherland and its people is by no
>   means less passionate than that of the people of any other
>   Province. Thoughtful Formosans deem it most shameful
>   to be pro-American or pro-Russian.
> 2. Taiwan is prepared for the Constitution; the fact that For-
>   mosans requested the early realization of local autonomy
>   and the public election of magistrates and mayors means
>   that Formosans are zealously desirous of a constitutional
>   administration, and does not mean that Formosans are
>   anti-Government.
> 3. It is the corrupt and greedy officials from the mainland
>   that Formosans abhor most. We are always enthusiastic
>   in our welcome, and loath to part with good officials and
>   intelligent people who come to Taiwan. It is greedy and
>   corrupt persons who, in fear that they may not be able to
>   maintain their positions under severe criticism, insist as a
>   camouflage for their own faults, that Formosans are ex-
>   clusivists.

By spreading such groundless rumors as those that the Formosans are thinking of becoming independent, are pro-Ameri-

can, are Bolshevised, or respect only force, such persons are instigating the Government to resort to high-handed actions against Formosans in order to fortify their own prestige.

In addition, those prominent people who come to inspect Taiwan have had very few opportunities to approach local residents and in that way may open the way to the alienation of the Formosans from the mainland because of prejudiced observations carried away which are very obnoxious to our people . . .[3]

Commenting on the issue later (January 20) the editor of the *Ta Ming Pao* at Taipei observed that "These arguments can be summarized in one sentence, that while Formosans are requesting complete local self-rule, the Government is afraid of losing its control over the people." He noted that caution was necessary on both sides, with compromise and genuine effort to reach mutual understanding.

Confusion of thought among younger Formosans was illustrated in the January issue of the *Formosan Magazine*. It carried as its cover a full-page picture of the Chinese national flag, but its leading editorial was a long and bitterly worded catalogue of grievances. In describing the disillusionment which had overtaken Formosa in 1946, it called for "reflection on the part of our countrymen from the mainland," and for patience as well as action on the part of the Formosans. The *Taiwan Youth Report* for January, 1947, hinted at the underlying desire for autonomy inherent in a frontier island:

Now that Taiwan has been returned to China . . . darkness, corruption, counter-revolution and anti-democracy are not out of existence. The present literati, scholars and intellectuals are waging a determined fight against these evils, until they are wholly destroyed. They understand the fight is the inheritance from this traditional spirit of Taiwanese Culture.[4]

On January 3 the Government newspaper *Hsin Sheng Pao* said that "as far as Taiwan is concerned, we are now badly in need of political and administrative personnel due to strong Japanese suppression in the past," and urged the Formosans to humble themselves and learn the techniques of democracy from national leaders who had come over from the mainland to guide them. To this, the Formosan paper *Ta Ming Pao* retorted that all the fine talk of democracy merely clothed the personal ambitions of Chen Yi's Commissioners and their ilk.

Thus far the conflict remained only a war of words, but the words were becoming increasingly sharp. Appeals to members of the Central Government often contained thinly disguised hints that if Nanking did nothing to improve the situation soon, there would be serious trouble on Formosa. As we reported to Washington (through our Embassy at Nanking) "Published articles, telegrams and editorials reflect the confusion which has arisen from a desire to become at once a model province of China, but one with a large degree of autonomy, cleansed of the corrupt administration of Chen Yi. Above all, the Taiwanese wish to remain aloof from the mainland civil war, which they feel the Central Government can ill-afford."

About this time Thomas Liao traveled about the island delivering a series of public lectures on "Questions in Practicing the Constitution." Constitutional right to criticize the Government was the keenest issue of the day. The Superior Court just then dismissed charges of libel which had been preferred by the Government against Chiang Wei-chuan, President of the Chamber of Commerce, but the Courts at the same time resumed trial of Wang Tien-teng on charges of "undermining public confidence in authority," through his campaign to expose extreme corruption in the Kaohsiung Police Department.

Much of the conflict which began as bitter personal and individual dispute became generalized antagonism. A prominent doctor in Tainan City with great good will had attempted to help the new Mayor of Tainan in 1946. Soon becoming aware of the Mayor's character and of his administration, he rose at last in the City Council to air a list of charges of incompetence and gross corruption. He began his interrogation with these words:

> I worked many months close to you. I greatly admire Chinese from Foochow in general, like yourself, for three reasons — your ability to use scissors, your ability to use a knife, and your ability to use clippers [i.e. all Foochow men are tailors, cooks, or barbers].
>
> In these fields no Formosan can compete with you. But I don't know why you put so many able Foochow people in office, displacing even the lowest Formosan workers.

The Municipal Council meeting broke up in a tumult, the story of the Mayor's loss of face instantly became the talk of the town, and on the following day a crowd of Foochow immigrants attempted to mob and kill the doctor, who was soon enough to lose his life.

On January 9 it was announced that the Land Tax would be increased 30 per cent "to conform to the Central Government's regulations." The increased revenue would be used for educational purposes, said the Governor.

No one believed this for a moment. During 1946 the physical assets of the island-wide educational system had been looted thoroughly, there was no money left in the local treasuries, and the posts vacated recently by the Japanese teaching staff and administration had been filled by mainland riff-raff — the hangers-on too unimportant to merit better opportunities for graft. "Shoes can't be repaired in Shanghai; all the cobblers are on Formosa." From this day until the outbreak of the Incident, student strikes increased in frequency throughout the island.

No Constitution in 1947?

On January 10 — the day following the staged "anti-American demonstration" at Taipei — the Governor-General delivered the first of three great blows. He announced that China's new constitution would not apply to Formosa when it went into effect on the mainland on December 25, 1947. The mainland Chinese, he said, were advanced enough to enjoy the privileges of constitutional government, but because of long years of despotic Japanese rule, the Formosans were politically retarded and were not capable of carrying on self-government in an intelligent manner. Two or three more years of Nationalist Party "tutelage" would be required to prepare them for full citizenship.

On January 12 it was announced that "for economy's sake" more than 20 per cent of the Government's employees would be discharged. The Formosans knew that this was intended to cover the discharge of island natives who remained in the government service, in order to make way for newcomers.

Formosan discontent was very near the bursting point. Foreign observers found it incredible that the Chen Yi Government could be so blind to the signs of crisis. What lay behind this?

Formosa and the Crisis at Shanghai

January had brought a major crisis at Shanghai. Chiang was seeking desperately to obtain another half billion dollars as a "loan" from the United States, but Washington was not showing much enthusiasm. There was a growing possibility that the whole Nationalist Party and government structure would collapse. Each faction, and each man, would then take what he could and run for safety.

At Taipei we were dimly aware of a second behind-the-scenes struggle concerning Formosa. If the Nationalist Government collapsed on the mainland, Formosa would be a most advantageous place; in a time of general civil war, the island could be cut off, to achieve the autonomy so desired by the Formosans, but certainly not under their control or in their interest.

We were aware that the conflict between the local Government and the Chinese Air Force was continuing, with serious clashes from time to time. Who would control the principal airfield at Taipei?

There was a flurry of visitors, men of high rank from Nanking. The Vice President of the Executive Yuan (Wang Yun-wu) flew in, the Minister of Communications (Yu Fei-peng) appeared, the Chief of the Military Service Bureau arrived, and the Acting Commander-in-Chief of the Chinese Navy (Kuei Yung-ching) showed up.

A series of administrative conferences were held on January 10, 13, and 16. We wondered if they were here to prepare the way for a retreat from the mainland.

The very delicate subject of conscription was brought forward again, shadowed — like the constitutional issue — by the question of legality in an occupied territory. High officers of the Nationalist Army addressed a convocation of mayors and magistrates. On the transparent excuse that enforced conscription would be "worse than Japanese methods," the Army proposed to avoid the legal issue by having "voluntary" conscription, to be handled through the Governor's Civil Affairs Department rather than through the Army.

This was awkward. On the one hand the Formosans had been clamoring for an opportunity to form a Formosan Home Guard for service limited to the island itself. For obvious reasons Chen Yi was not ready to arm Formosans who might drive the whole lot of carpetbaggers out of Formosa. On the other hand, there had been ugly rumors that the few Formosan volunteers who enlisted with the understanding they would be used only on the island, were in fact being shipped out and those who had deserted had been summarily shot. The Army's proposal was generally interpreted as a Central Government move designed to empty Formosa of hot-headed youths, thereby making it a safer place for Chiang's retreat.

February was to bring other evidence that Chen Yi's official family was seeking an arrangement to ensure complete control of the local economy if Shanghai slid into the vortex of mainland civil war.

The Administrative Conference also produced the Governor's announcement that local popular elections would not be held until sometime in 1949. The outcry was keen, prompting the local Nationalist Party organization to propose a compromise — an indefinite delay, with elections to be held before 1949 "if the public were ready and preparations were complete."

The Taiwan Political Reconstruction Association promptly appealed to the members of the Central Government at Nanking, saying in part:

> In Taiwan there were once complete census records, detailed cadastral surveys, complete police nets, good sanitary conditions, convenient transportation, and popular education. The guild system was popularized, and all waste land brought under cultivation. The general cultural level in Taiwan is high, and Formosans are possessed of sufficient comprehension of, and ability for, local autonomy. In other words, we were quite safe to leave the doors open at night; things lost in the road were not pocketed; every piece of land was fully utilized and merchandise well-distributed.
>
> At present, due solely to the administrative inefficiency of the Government, a peculiar situation which is strange to Formosans has been brought about, and thus opportunities are not available to able Formosans.
>
> For the purpose of restoring a comfortable and civilized Taiwan, the Provincial Government authorities have only to reform their own inefficient system and noxious attitudes, and to try to recover swiftly the pre-war conditions. At the same time they must be more reasonable in the appointment of officials . . . the Government need not begin everything from the very beginning.[5]

This idyllic picture of prewar conditions of security and contentment was not precisely accurate, but it did show that by the beginning of 1947 the Formosans looked back on the Japanese era as the base line against which to measure the performance of the Nationalist Chinese regime. While the older leaders protested devotion to Mother China, the younger ones began to look elsewhere for alternatives.

On January 15 a group of angry young leaders — representative of the financial and educated elite of the island — drew up a petition addressed to General George C. Marshall, who had recently become Secretary of State at Washington. More than one hundred and fifty signatures were attached, of which some represented spokesmen for organizations or groups of private citizens, numbering about eight hundred in all.

But when it was ready, and a suitable number of copies had been made, the leaders decided to delay presentation to the American Consulate; appeals to the National Assembly, to the Central Government and to the Chinese public might even yet induce the Generalissimo to intervene at Taipei.

The February Monopolies

On February 1 Chen Yi delivered a second great blow to Formosan hopes. The Government's policy for the sale of confiscated Japanese properties was announced. Instantly it was apparent that few Formosans would be able to compete with mainland Chinese either through cash purchases or through credit arrangements.

A great protest rally was proposed. Chen Yi promptly forbade it and doubled police patrols under pretense of "cleaning up the city," "enforcing traffic regulations" and "preparing the celebration of the New Life Movement."

The traditional Chinese landlord system was too well known to be welcome again on Formosa; it was evident that the relatively efficient Japanese landlords, the Mitsuis, Iwasakis and Imperial Household agents, would soon be replaced by agents for the Kungs, the Soongs and the Chiangs. A petition was addressed to the Governor, asking him to alter the auction plan to permit Formosan tenants to have first chance to buy, applying rents already paid through 1945 and 1946 to the final purchase price, or to allow them to bid in properties at 30 per cent less than the highest bidder. If these failed, then let the Government retain ownership of confiscated lands, leasing them on long-term, low-rental contracts.

Chen Yi countered with the specious argument that modern times called for big machinery and big land-units, and that Formosans and mainland Chinese should form collective farms.

When public protest continued, the Governor on February 25 condemned Formosan criticism of land policies as "immoral," and angrily brushed aside all further argument.

We have noted the long-established relationship between Chen Yi (as Governor of Fukien Province), wartime coastal trade with Japan, and the powerful China Merchants Steam Navigation Company.

Obviously in a time of national crisis at Nanking, basic control of the island economy would lie in the hands of the men who controlled shipping, and were in a position to cut off Formosa from the mainland.

On February 1, 1947, all seaborne commerce entering or leaving the island — including all foreign shipping — was brought under rigid control. The Taiwan Navigation Company (based on the confiscated Japanese shipping interests) was now reorganized with a capital of two billion Taiwan (Formosan) yen, jointly subscribed by the Taipei government and by the China Merchants Steam Navigation Company. Chen Yi's Commissioner of Communications (Jen) became the second in command, under Hsu, the Managing Director of the CMSNC.

It was a neat arrangement. What the *quid pro quo* may have been for Chiang's approval we do not know, but at the moment he was desperately in need of more money, and was negotiating with a mixture of begging and blackmail, for a half-billion dollar "loan" from the United States.

The new corporation was authorized to control all export

trade carried in vessels of more than 100 tons capacity, and all import trade destined for use by any government agency, including all the confiscated Japanese agricultural, industrial and commercial establishments. All incoming UNRRA shipments would be subject to its control. All foreign merchants and all agencies for foreign shipping companies fell under this new administration. Nothing would move in and out of Formosa without paying toll. If foreign companies wished to carry cargo in their own ships, they would have to secure costly licenses from the Government shipping syndicate, and to pay heavy fees on each transaction. Furthermore, a percentage of the value of all export and import cargoes had to be handed over to the Taiwan Trading Company.

Concurrently another syndicate was announced which would control all internal transportation and warehousing. It was in business, but it was also empowered to grant or to withhold license for all independent rival carriers and warehousing agencies, and to collect a percentage of the value of services rendered by private agencies.

On February 12 the Finance Commission announced new regulations governing foreign currencies and new rates of exchange. Persons who applied to the Bank of Taiwan — the only legal source — found that there were no dollars to be had, but it was soon recognized that the best black-market source for dollars lay within the body of government officials themselves. Scarcity drove the price of dollars upward, but any Formosan who dealt secretly with a government official on a private basis instantly made himself liable to prosecution, and confiscation of his properties. There was no guarantee that hush-money paid to one officer (or a clerk privy to a transaction) would prevent another from attempting blackmail.

The situation prevailed throughout the island; palms had to be greased and squeeze had to be paid.

On February 15 the British agent for Jardine-Matheson, one of the largest and oldest foreign firms, went down to Keelung to greet an expected British ship. New sets of regulations had been issued that morning which required clearances, in advance, from the Customs Office. The Harbor Office would not act until it received a set of clearance papers from the Taiwan Navigation Company. These were issued without inquiry or apparent reference to the new regulations, but when the foreigner returned to the Harbor Master he met with verbal abuse and an order that the papers must also be cleared by the Mayor of Keelung City.

In due course, the Mayor was found, already aboard the ship, searching it. There were no Customs Officers in sight, but the vessel swarmed with the Mayor's police. Soldiers at dockside and aboard blocked the foreign agent's entry upon his own ship.

The Mayor now disclosed that he was responsible for currency control in the Keelung area, but that the police had final authority in all port affairs, and that they must be satisfied, which of course meant satisfied with suitable informal payments.

The Mayor could produce no documentary evidence or written authority for this new position, blustering that the instructions had come directly from the Governor-General who had "made them up himself."

Meanwhile all through-transit passengers remaining aboard as well as those coming ashore were forced to disclose all currencies. There was no confiscation, but those landing were forced to exchange Chinese National Currency at a ruinous rate. The individual policemen then offered to be "bankers" in the cheaper black market.

While this confusing search was in progress, the foreign agent was notified that all cargo had to be discharged into the warehouses of the Tung Yung Company, a subsidiary of the Transportation Commissioner's organization. There it would lie until it was sealed over to a Forwarding Company warehouse, under police certification.

The cargo in question had already been sold to the Taiwan Customs organization for use in repairing the Customs building, but under police orders the stevedores refused to discharge it into the Customs warehouse. Nevertheless, the Taiwan Trading Company now offered to release the cargo to the Customs at the Trading Company's price. If the price demanded were not met, then the cargo must be returned to the point of origin aboard a Taiwan Navigation Company ship, with suitable charges for interim storage and transport.

When this fantastic procedure was announced, the Mayor stated blandly that he was acting under instructions which could not be revealed.

If the reader is confused, he simply shares the confusion of the foreign shipping agent and of all others attempting then to do business in Formosa. It meant in essence that every department and agency in Chen Yi's government was becoming infected with the feverish uncertainty then sweeping Shanghai. The principle of the day was to make what money one could, in whatever fashion, and to be ready to run when the great crash came. In this instance various units of the local Government were trying to squeeze one another, the National Government, and the foreign trader.

On the day following this performance at Keelung (i.e. on February 16) the Taiwan Navigation Company published its own version of the new shipping regulations, dubbing them an announcement of the Taiwan Trading Company. To rub it in a bit, Jardine-Matheson's agent was presented with a copy of the required new regulation forms by a representative of a rival tea trading company. Jardine's — so long the dominant trading company in China, the "Princely Hong" — was being put in its place on Formosa.

Thereafter (according to the new rules) the Taiwan Navigation Company would handle all of Jardine's business and Jardine would no longer have control of its own ships and cargoes while in Formosan waters. The new Navigation Company would allot cargoes and establish rates, and all passengers and freight-shipments would be booked only through the Taiwan Navigation Company offices.

On February 18 the Government newspaper published four new regulations "to facilitate clearance of commodities and collections of bills of exchange," and three additional new regulations notified to the public by the Navigation Company.

Meanwhile on February 15 the Bank of Taiwan had moved one step further to eliminate all competition from private Formosan interests. On the Governor's orders, the Bank was instructed to recall 20 per cent of all loans outstanding to private merchants for commercial purposes. Formosans who lacked good connections within Finance Commissioner Yen's office were unable to pay, many went at once into bankruptcy, and by late February private commercial enterprise throughout Formosa was virtually paralyzed. Many merchants closed shop; those who had capital funds prepared to live on them while they lasted, and many individuals began to stockpile food and fuel. Many more retired from the cities to ancestral homes in the countryside, there to "wait and see."

At this critical moment in mid-February Yen Chia-kan himself was in Nanking, conveniently absent when these extreme blows were struck at private enterprise.

It was widely speculated that Chen Yi and his men were preparing for a break with the mainland, anticipating a final chaotic dissolution of the economic and political structure at Shanghai. Some of the underlings — in the third and fourth levels of the government hierarchy — had been too hasty in issuing the ultimate monopoly regulations at Taipei. In the event, before the end of February, the crisis at Shanghai eased temporarily, Nanking was still in control, and both the United States and Britain could be expected to lodge strong protests concerning interference with legitimate trade in Formosa. The extravagant orders were rescinded or modified almost at once but the psychological damage had been done. Public confidence had fled.

While these economic moves and countermoves were taking place at Taipei I had occasion to proceed to Kaohsiung (on

February 14) with the Reports Officer of the UNRRA group. There was one first-class compartment aboard the express and this we shared with five Nationalist Chinese Navy officers led by Commander P. H. Hsu. Commander Hsu promptly let it be known that he had spent two years training in the United States, that he did not like America or Americans, and that he wished we would all get out of Formosa. To underscore the point he bluntly asked us to move out of the first-class compartment. "It is too crowded," he said, "for us to put up with you."

I was on my way to Kaohsiung in my consular capacity, to meet the U.S.S. *Frank Knox*, due in port for a "courtesy call' on February 15. According to arrangement, therefore, we were at the Kaohsiung Customs Shed at seven-thirty in the morning, having been advised that the ship lay off port and expected to dock at eight o'clock.

But to our surprise it lay beyond the harbor entrance for three hours, unable to get clearance from the Harbor Master who refused to grant entry until he had special orders from the Commandant of the Chinese Naval Base five miles away. There had been ample notification that the *Frank Knox* was coming to Formosa. At last it was signaled in, but despite Captain Berthoff's courteous message to Captain Kao, Naval Commandant, we received no response.

I was piped aboard and piped ashore again before an entertained crowd of Formosans lounging on the pier, but the official atmosphere about the town was frigid; perhaps the Chinese were interpreting this unwelcome naval show to be a hint that the United States Government was indeed in a position to interfere on Formosa if need be. In point of fact the U.S.S. *Frank Knox* had delivered to my care nothing more than twelve cases of liquid "consular supplies" which had been waiting for space-available transport from the Consulate-General in Shanghai. Perhaps it was a "show of force," but there were no deep plots and no secret messages involved.

A Formosan Appeal to General Marshall,
Secretary of State

In mid-February the young Formosans (Stanway Cheng's "communists") at last brought to the Consulate the long petition which they had addressed to General Marshall. It was addressed only to the Secretary of State, and not to the President; according to the *Regulations* it would not automatically have to be forwarded to Washington. Nevertheless, it would have to be reported, and someone in Higher Authority might desire to see it.

If someone had presented us with a leper's bell and begging bowl he could not have been less welcome.

The English was opaque, but the meaning was crystal clear. The text follows:

> We are young Formosans. We'll shout our sorrows from the bottom of our hearts, in order to appeal [to] our respected United Nations and all brethren abroad.
>
> Our fine island, beautiful Formosa, now are trampled away by Chinese maladministration. The misery are full . . . [such as] we never experienced before.
>
> . . . our own democratic organization must be reconstructed. This is all our target mark . . . Before the Constitution are took in effect we should take notice of the nationalities of Formosans are still a pending question among the United Nations. With this unshakeable fact, are there any [obligations that] we have to obey their order to dig our own graves?
>
> We are afraid the United Nations recognizes Formosans as similar to Chinese. We are sure that Formosans have the blood connection with them, but you should inspect our nature [which] have already been [changed] and promoted for 50 years [through] Japanese culture in every sort of scholarship. Especially we have learnt patriotism and anti-tyranny [because] of them.
>
> The Cairo Congress drove us into this "Living Hell." We

6,300,000 Formosans since half a century have not been blessed. The representatives at Cairo should take responsibility to this fact that we struggle with our misfortune at this moment. We strictly protest the decision, which meant to put all Formosans into slavery life.

The United Nations should pay attention to overseas Dutch Indonesia, French Indo-China, Burma and our neighboring Philippines. For what are they struggling? Exactly, they are fighting for a freedom alive. In our case is the same.

The revolutional gun and atomic bomb against the incompetent government is the pen at first. Adding the United Nations sympathy and friendly intervention to the Chinese authorities is the only way. Because Formosa is not yet perfectly returned to China before the Peace Treaty concludes between the United Nations and Japan . . .

In these circumstances we fortunately found Formosa still has a hope; the young Formosans mostly have been educated and have a fighting spirit which are the most essential in order to decide our own destiny.

Please give these young Formosans a chance in political training under your protection and let them have a self-confidence. Then we are sure that a misgovernment would be replaced.

In conclusion we dare to say that the shortest way to the Reformation of the Provincial Government is wholly to depend upon the United Nations Joint Administration in Formosa, and cut the political and economical concern with China proper for some years. Otherwise we Formosans will become the stark naked.

We hope we shall have a good reaction from you in the near future. We are thankful for your kind help and wish you have a good luck.

The petitioners were led by young men who were at the heart of the Formosan Youth Movement and were quite prepared to "throw the rascals out" — or at least to try. They saw no reason to accept Chen Yi's racketeers; Sun Yat-sen and Chiang Kai-shek were by now names symbolizing all that was reactionary and backward in contemporary China.

Some, unknowing, had only a few more days to live, but it was in these days they prepared the March issue of the "radical" *Formosan Magazine* using for the most part materials provided at their request by the United States Information Service. In this March issue Joshua Liao continued his series entitled "Whither Formosa?" in which he was developing the theme of historical separatism as a traditional character of Formosan relations with the mainland.

But there were other articles concerning the Queen of England, rural education, and Free Speech in the United States, one concerned Errol Flynn. A featured article was entitled "A Citizen Speaks at U. S. Town Meeting." There was — in this "radical journal" — even an article by the American Consul himself entitled "Taiwan in Transition." Letters to the editor begged for more opportunities for the public to hear Englishmen and Americans speak in public address.

A number of UNRRA team members were happy to volunteer instruction in the English language for which there was an eager demand. One series of "American and English Conversation Association Classes" was conducted in two concurrent sessions while the Formosan sponsors tried to find meeting space large enough for a third. There were daily English Conversation Classes broadcast from Taipei.

By late February, however, some of the more restive and impatient young men began to question American propaganda. The American Consulate was showing two such different faces, there was no sign that the Embassy at Nanking nor the Government at Washington had given the slightest attention to the state of affairs in Formosa.

Divisions began to appear among some of the older leaders as they all sought for a way out of the dismal situation. Other voices in China proper were urging them to beware of the United States, saying that Washington would merely use Formosa in its own interests as it was using Chiang as a puppet on the mainland. Old friends came to me in despair to warn that it was "now or never" if some gesture by Ambassador Stuart, some expression of interest by General MacArthur at Tokyo, or some pronouncement at Washington were to provide a check upon the Nationalists and Chen Yi before true disaster struck the island.

The tinder was there, the train was laid, and the explosion came late in the evening of February 27, 1947.

XII

The February Incident,
1947

Murder in the Park and Mobs in the Street

ON THE EVENING OF February 27 a cigarette vendor and her two small children set up a portable stand under the banyan tree in Round Park. On it were a few packs of cigarettes and several coins with which to make change if she were lucky enough to make a sale.

Monopoly Bureau agents appeared, accused the woman of handling untaxed cigarettes, and seized her small stock with her tiny reserve of cash. People began to gather round. When she screamed in protest, seizing the arm of one of the agents, she was brutally struck down and pistol-whipped about the head. At this the angry crowd moved on the agents. Firing wildly, they opened a way for themselves to escape to a nearby police box. Behind them one person lay dead and the vendor appeared to be dying.

When gendarmes appeared, summoned by the civil police, the crowd permitted them to take the Monopoly Bureau agents away, but then promptly burned the Monopoly Bureau truck and its contents in the street.

On the next morning (February 28) a crowd estimated at about 2000 marched in orderly fashion from the Round Park area to the Monopoly Bureau Headquarters, carrying banners and slogan-placards which had been prepared during the night.

They had also in hand a petition addressed to the Monopoly Bureau Chief which demanded a death sentence for the agents who had committed manslaughter on the previous night, and the resignation of the Bureau Chief as an admission of responsibility. It also demanded reform of the Government's overall monopoly practices.

The demonstrators passed near the American Consulate in late morning. It was a long, long walk, and when they had reached the gates to the Monopoly Bureau they found them closed, under heavy armed guard. The Bureau Director was "officially absent," and no deputy was forthcoming.

After waiting about for a tedious period it was decided to turn northward to the Governor's office to present the petition directly to Chen Yi.

Meanwhile there had been grave trouble elsewhere in town. In a street not far from the UNRRA offices, Monopoly agents were discovered abusing two children who had been vending cigarettes. This was too much; an angry crowd beat the Chinese agents to death within a few hundred feet of a Monopoly Bureau Branch Office. In a moment the Formosans began to sack the storerooms. Military police trucks sped to the scene. The Formosans stood back until mainland Chinese employees had been escorted to the trucks and taken away, then surged into the building, spilling the contents into the streets and setting them afire. There had been one tense moment when a military policeman threatened to shoot an UNRRA staff member taking photographs and another when a Formosan in the crowd was caught pocketing some of the cigarettes. He was beaten severely, made to kneel and beg forgiveness "from the Formosan people," and then sent scurrying away, glad enough to be alive.

I had been lunching nearby with the Director of our USIS program and with Formosan friends. We were attempting to weigh the gravity of the Round Park affair and its consequence when suddenly we heard the rattle of machine-gun fire. Leaving the table we drove at once toward the Monopoly Bureau, knowing that the morning demonstrators had intended to go there, but the plaza and streets nearby were empty. The marching crowd had moved on to the Governor's office.

As our jeep came into the intersection dominated by the Generalissimo's gilded statue, we found ourselves running between a line of heavily armed Nationalist soldiers, before the Governor's gate, and a silent crowd of Formosans, facing them across the plaza.

On the macadam roadway between lay the bodies of unarmed civilians who had been shot down as the demonstrators approached the entrance to the Government grounds.

The anticipated crisis had come at last.

We were in an awkward position. No time must be lost in reporting the incident; we knew how pleased some of the Governor's men would be to charge that we had been seen "leading a Formosan rebellion," but on the other hand something had to be done to break the tension, prevent further violence, and give aid to the wounded.

Fortunately at that moment the UNRRA Reports Officer (Edward E. Paine) drove into the plaza; with great presence of mind he appraised the confrontation, drove his jeep to a position between the Governor's guard and the muttering crowd, and leaped out. He signaled the soldiers to stand off. They were amazed at this bold action and shuffled back to positions within the gateway as Paine checked the six bodies. When he found that two showed signs of life, he summoned help from the crowd, commandeered two rickshas, and sent the wounded men off as fast as possible to a nearby hospital. When the crowd realized what had so swiftly taken place, it broke into a cheer for the lone American who had so boldly stood off the Governor's armed guard.

Meanwhile my colleague and I sped to the Consulate; this violence at the Governor's gate probably meant general rebellion and must be reported at once to the Embassy.

Just after noon — about the time the Governor's guard fired upon the petitioners at his gate — a Formosan member of the broadcasting station staff broke into a program to say that a demonstration was taking place, that a petition was being presented to the Governor, and that all Formosans should give it support. Then the station went off the air.

By late afternoon normal activities throughout Taipei were suspended. Crowds surged through the streets, forming here at this intersection, dissolving, reforming wherever someone had a fresh bit of "news" or a new version of the day's incidents. Mainland Chinese took to cover. Occasionally one would be discovered hurrying through the alleys trying to look as much like a Formosan as possible. Japanese-style footgear known as *geta* — hitherto condemned by the mainland Chinese — now became popular with them. Formosan schoolboys had an old joke in which they referred to the island as "Japan's sweet potato." Now mainlanders on the street were challenged "Are you sweet potato or are you pig?" and if the proper answer were not promptly forthcoming a hot chase took place, and sometimes a beating.

It should be noted here that from Taipei the rioting spread to nearby towns and in a day or two mainland Chinese were in hiding everywhere in Formosa. But foreign observers in all parts of the island reported later that they saw no Formosans carrying weapons. Mainland Chinese were occasionally stoned, or beaten with sticks, but no guns, knives, or swords were seen in the hands of the angry Formosans. Moreover, there was no looting. Occasionally the contents of a house or office were burned in the street, but we noted that overturned official cars and heaps of furniture were left strictly alone throughout the following week, serving to remind one and all of the bloody events of "2–28," and of the spontaneous public reaction.

By late afternoon the majority of mainland Chinese had barricaded themselves in office buildings or in their homes, or in the homes of Formosan friends — if they had any. The Garrison troops were intensely busy. Barbed wire and sandbag barricades were thrown up before the principal government buildings, machine guns were mounted to cover gates and major intersections nearby. Military trucks, with machine guns or with squads bearing rifles aboard, began to move about the main streets, firing now and then at random.

Martial law was declared at six o'clock as winter dusk settled over a tense, unhappy city.

The radio broadcasting station was one of the first government buildings to be heavily guarded. Early in the evening came a broadcast by a doctor, a woman born in Formosa but reared on the mainland, who was often put forward by Chen Yi as a "spokesman for Formosan women." With great indiscretion she now tried to tell the radio public that she had been present and that no shooting had taken place before the Governor's office that afternoon. Within the hour angry neighbors sacked her house and office, burning the contents in the streets. She herself vanished into the security of a Government compound for the duration of the Incident.

How to Settle the Incident?

Formosan leaders recognized at once the extreme gravity of the position in which they found themselves. On the morning of March 1 at ten o'clock, the Chairman of the Municipal Peoples Political Council, with representatives from the National and Provincial councils, called on the Governor to form an official "Committee to Settle the Monopoly Bureau Incident." When the Governor's guards fired upon the unarmed crowd, the issues had become much greater than the mere punishment of Monopoly agents and a financial settlement for the wounded and the dead. If Chen Yi now made no satisfactory effort to break the monopolies, to place the police under firm control, and to reform the general administration he would face open, island-wide rebellion. The issues would have to be taken up with the Government with delicacy as well as with firmness.

They urged Governor Chen to lift martial law promptly in order to avert further dangers of a clash between the unarmed civil population and the military. This he agreed to do, at midnight. On his part he forbade all public meetings and parades.

But Chen was not going to waste the precious hours until midnight; military trucks appeared in the street as fast as they could be made ready, carrying riflemen and machine-gunners, and the volume of shooting increased steadily through the day. It was an obvious attempt to terrorize the city and to make Formosans receptive to whatever further the Governor might have to say.

At about five o'clock Chen Yi angered the public by a radio broadcast in which he declared the Monopoly Bureau Incident already settled by a generous payment of money. He made no reference to the shooting which had taken place before his own gates, but accused the Formosans of "increased rioting." Nevertheless he generously promised to lift martial law at midnight.

"There is one more point," said the Governor. "The PPC members wish to send representatives to form a Committee jointly with the Government to settle this riot. This I have also granted. If you have any opinion, you can tell me through this Committee." [1]

"Formosans Attack the American Consulate!"

While the Governor was broadcasting assurances that the Incident was settled by a generous money payment, the American Consulate became directly involved for the first time. Our walled compound lay near a major intersection, the North Gate crossing. On the east lay the Central Post Office, to the northwest nearby stood the walled compound and principal buildings of Chen Ching-wen's Railway Administration. From the North Gate traffic circle a main street led into a Formosan section of town, crowded with shops and homes. From our balconies we watched the crowds surging about in the streets.

As one of Chen Yi's armed trucks came past the Consulate gates riflemen aboard, shooting at random, killed two pedestrians and drove on. A crowd gathered, and just as the bodies were about to be carried away several students from the countryside entered the Railway Administration Building a few yards distant, to ask when train services would be resumed; they had been marooned in the city on the previous day and they wanted to get home.

The Railway Director's private guards were nervous; gunfire was heard, and the boys were not seen again. Then the special Railway Police, hidden within the walled compound, turned their guns to the street outside and two more pedestrians were killed.

By this time a very large crowd had gathered at the North Gate intersection, and would probably have stormed the Railway Offices, but just then a military truck approached, summoned, perhaps, by the Railway Offices. Its way was blocked, but a sudden burst of machine-gun and rifle fire sent the crowd scattering. At least twenty-five persons were killed at once, and more than a hundred were seriously injured. No one knows how many others were struck, but able to walk away.*

This bloody diversion gave twenty-five Railway Office employees a chance to make a dash for safety across the street into the American Consulate. Raising a cry, Formosans gave chase.

Among the mainland Chinese it was each man for himself, and devil take the hindmost. The hindmost here were the women, clerks from the office; some of the first men to burst in through the Consulate gates promptly tried to close them in the faces of their fleeing colleagues. The last ones came in over the

---

* Doctors, treating the wounded, found that soft-nosed dum-dum bullets had been used in some guns, creating horrible wounds.

fence as best they could, and as they did someone in the street crowd threw one stone after them. It struck the Consulate wall with a thud.

A small crowd lingered in the street nearby until night fell; some of our own Formosan employees, returning to the compound through the crowd, reported that bystanders were cautioning one another, saying that they had no desire to involve the American Consulate, and regretted the fact that a stone had been thrown into the grounds.

Confusion reigned within the Consulate. Twenty-five pale, frightened mainland Chinese were taken to the second floor, to the Consul's living quarters, and there given tea and some light food.

The Consul of course was indignant. He promptly put through a call to Stanway Cheng at the Governor's office, requesting him to have the refugees removed at once. It was all very irregular. Moreover, a stone had been thrown into the Consulate grounds. Cheng assured the Consul that the matter would be taken care of as soon as possible.

Six hours later two buses, under heavy guard, pulled into the Consulate grounds. The Formosan crowds had long since gone home to mourn their dead or to care for the wounded and to discuss what next must be done.

We soon realized why the Governor's Information Officer had been too busy to expedite the removal of the refugees, for in less than an hour after he received the Consul's call, and five hours before the buses came, the Government radio broadcast a report that Formosans were attacking the American Consulate at Taipei, but the world was assured that all Americans on Formosa were under the protection of the Governor's men. It was a neat propaganda coup, designed to place the Formosans in the worst possible light in the international press.

When the Incident was reported to the American Embassy in Nanking, the response was brief: "Look only to established authority."

But who represented "established authority" in this first week of March?

March 2: Chen Yi Concedes a Need for Change

Sporadic gunfire was heard throughout the night. Morning light disclosed a rash of posters and placards and handbills, hastily composed and now widely distributed. "Pigs! Go Home!" was a common theme. The Monopoly Bureau Incident was entirely overshadowed now by the issue of general reform in Chen Yi's administration.

We also saw that the wide-ranging patrols of March 1 had covered an intense activity on the north side of town, near the airport. There an encampment had sprung into being, under heavy guard, and to this spot the mainland Chinese who had sufficient influence were removing personal property. Here they proposed to stay until the crisis had passed. There was a steady rumble of trucks transporting an immense amount of household gear, goods, cash, other valuables and of course, the women and children. How many actually took refuge there we never knew.

The Governor-General's office and a few key buildings nearby (including the broadcasting station) were under very heavy guard, but for the remaining days of that week, the camp and the administrative headquarters were in effect the only area in Taipei actually under Chen Yi's "established authority."

At noon, March 2, the Governor received the "Untaxed Cigarette Incident Investigation Committee of the Taipei Municipal Peoples Political Council," and with this began an attempt by Formosan leaders to clarify fundamental political and economic problems forming the background of this crisis.

With the Governor sat the Secretary-General and the Commissioners for Civil Affairs, Communications, and Industry and Mining. Yen Chia-kan, the Commissioner of Finance, had been caught down country, at Taichung, and had taken refuge in the home of Lim Hsien-tang.

Martial law had not been lifted at midnight March 1; the Governor was therefore warned that there could be no peace in the city while roving military patrols were sweeping the streets with gunfire. This paralyzed all normal activity, and soon there would be a food crisis.

The Governor and the Committeemen knew well enough that without large reinforcements, the Government was power-less. If further provoked on this day the people of Taipei could overpower and destroy the patrols which were operating only in the heart of the city and between the Governor's offices and the suburban camp.

The Governor had no choice but to accept several conditions to be maintained while the people organized fundamental demands for reform. He had invited them to express public opinion; they were determined to make the issue clear. These "temporary demands" were as follows:

1. The Governor agrees that a schedule of fundamental reforms should be prepared for discussion by March 10, after representatives of the people throughout the island can be consulted;
2. The Governor promises that he will not bring additional troops into the city while these consultations are in progress;
3. A volunteer student organization, cooperating with other youths under supervision of the Mayor and the Municipal Chief of Police [a mainland Chinese], will maintain law and order temporarily;
4. Communications will be restored at once in order to avoid a food shortage.

The Governor accepted these stipulations, and agreed to broadcast his acceptance at three o'clock in the afternoon. He also agreed to reduce and withdraw the street patrols — meanwhile the patrols were to place rifles and other arms on the truck floors, and to use them only if they found Formosan crowds beating up mainland people or otherwise disturbing the peace.

It should be noted here that after March 1 there were few instances reported of bodily harm done to any mainland Chinese at Taipei. Once a formal Settlement Committee was established, the spontaneous outburst of anger gave way to a new public mood and a rather remarkable show of public cooperation with Formosan leaders who, for nearly one week, formed the effective government.

At the Consulate, meanwhile, we had a busy morning on March 2, checking the whereabouts of American citizens, discussing the tense situation with UNRRA staff members, and preparing our reports for Nanking. Our work was interrupted by the arrival of a Formosan doctor, with several friends, bringing us a dum-dum bullet. On the previous afternoon this random shot, fired by a passing patrol, had entered the doctor's office and lodged in a heavy medical volume on the clinic shelf. Would the Consulate please lodge a protest with the proper authorities? The use of dum-dum bullets was outlawed by international agreements. Here were the book and the bullet, evidence that the Nationalist troops were using them.

The Consul took the position that this unfortunate incident was strictly an affair between two Chinese groups; the United States had no reason to take cognizance of trouble between a provincial governor and his people. This was China now.

The doctor and his friends, rebuffed, took the dum-dum bullet to the UNRRA offices, leaving it there in safekeeping with a request that it be sent to the United Nations as evidence of the lawlessness of the Chen Yi regime. They were heard with sympathy but the Taipei UNRRA Office had no regular channels through which to raise such an issue with the international organization at New York.

Just after noon a great crowd filled the Civic Auditorium. At two-thirty o'clock the Governor's representatives sat down with the Settlement Committee on the broad stage before the assembly. Chen Yi had asked the Taipei Mayor to join the Commissioner of Civil Affairs, the Commissioner of Communications and the Director of Police, acting as his deputies.

It was announced that as a result of the morning conference the Governor had decided to readjust the Committee, bringing into it representatives from the Chamber of Commerce, the Labor Union, student organizations, other popular organizations, and the important Taiwan Political Reconstruction Association.

At this afternoon meeting these additional "temporary demands" were formulated:

1. All people arrested in connection with the riots in the preceding three days were to be released;
2. The Government will pay death gratuities and compensations to the wounded;
3. The Government will not hereafter prosecute the persons involved;
4. Armed police patrols will be stopped immediately.
5. Communications will be restored at once.

A number of leaders wondered why the Governor sought to draw in such a very wide representation. The Committee might become unwieldy, and such a generous interest in widely representative opinion was not in character. We were to realize later that by this device Chen Yi learned exactly where the individual Formosan leaders stood vis-à-vis the National Government, the Party, and his own regime. Huang Chao-chin served as his secret ears-and-eyes during Committee deliberations.

The meeting was disturbed repeatedly by gunfire on or near the plaza outside. When the Governor's promised three o'clock broadcast was postponed, and postponed again, disquieting rumors spread through town saying that Chen Yi, violating his pledges, was trying to get troops into the city from the south. If they reached Taipei before the broadcast, he would not have to make this humiliating public acceptance of the Committee's demands. If they could reach the city before the crowd had left the auditorium, he would be in a position to seize all the most prominent members of the Opposition.

But at last, at five o'clock, March 2, Governor Chen again went on the air, concluding his address with this statement:

> A Committee will be organized to settle the incident. Besides Government officials and members of the PPC, representatives from the people of all walks of life will be invited to join the Committee so that it may represent opinions of the majority of the people.[2]

In the evening the city learned that despite his pledge Chen Yi had called troops from the south, but alert people of Hsinchu along the way had removed rails on the main line just outside the town. Troop trains were unable to proceed, and at a narrow place on the highway nearby barricades prevented ten truckloads of mainland soldiers from passing round the rail-break.

This was the first noteworthy example of the importance of well-developed local communication by telephone and telegraph during the crisis week, and of the effectiveness of Formosan organization.

March 3: An Appeal for American Understanding

Communications, as such, played a peculiar role in this tragic affair. On the one hand Formosan leaders skillfully took full advantage of all the public and private telephone lines and telegraph services within the island — the public system, the network of police wires, and the private systems which the Japanese had installed to serve the power corporation and the sugar companies. Chen Yi and his henchmen had never before tried to ride down an unarmed provincial population technically so well prepared to organize and maintain close communication throughout the area. This was not "backward" China.

On the other hand the Governor's man Stanway Cheng controlled the radio stations and the cable services, and knew precisely how to manipulate rumor, plant stories, and twist facts. The exploitation of the stone-throwing incident at the Consulate was a foretaste of shrewd publicity management. On this day (March 3) the Manila radio carried an extravagant story of a Formosan attack upon the American Consulate, of organized Formosan troops with machine guns, and of a serious attack upon the Central Government. Broadcasts from Osaka, Japan, on the other hand, repeated a face-saving story; all was quiet on Formosa, according to this, and the Governor-General had firmly rejected all Formosan demands. In the news dispatches sent to Japan it could not be admitted that the Chinese were unable to govern Formosa.

Formosan leaders were acutely conscious of these misleading broadcasts and of the damaging effect they would have on appeals for American intervention, or for an inquiry by the United Nations.

At 10 o'clock in the morning, March 3, the Settlement Committee sent a delegation — a subcommittee — of five prominent Formosans to the American Consulate with a petition that the Consulate should cable the truth to Washington, and help them correct the record. They desired above all a clear and sympathetic American understanding of their position.

They were promptly turned away. "This is China now."

The general meeting in the Civic Auditorium heard a report on Chen Yi's attempt to bring troops in through Hsinchu. This confirmation of rumor produced great excitement. Moderate and conservative elements — the Settlement Committee members — were willing to accept the Governor's word and to proceed with negotiations. Younger, more skeptical men agreed to support the Committee in its efforts, but reserved the right to prepare resistance to any military action that might be taken against the Formosan people.

Public security was discussed. One passionate speaker proposed to rally 100,000 men to form a defense corps which would maintain public order and be ready to confront any mainland Chinese force sent against them. He warned the audience that "you must not follow the old track, allowing yourselves to be utilized by the police force and then afterwards be disposed of as gangsters as happened just after the restoration of the island."

The delegation treating directly with the Governor was now enlarged to some twenty members, including a representative of the Women's League and several additional popular organizations. It was clear that every organized group on Formosa wished to join in this search for a reformation of government.

Meeting with five of the Governor's Commissioners and with the Chief of Staff, General Ko Yuen-feng, the Committee stressed again the need to withdraw military patrols from the streets. They were still roaming about, firing wildly, three days after the Governor-General's promise to call them in.

After prolonged discussion the Governor's representatives (including the Chief of Staff) agreed to seven points:

1. All troops will be withdrawn by six o'clock that day (March 3);
2. Public order is to be maintained by a temporary Public Security Service Corps, including gendarmes, police, students, and other youths;
3. Communications will be restored by six o'clock p.m.;
4. Military rice stores will be released to avert a food crisis;
5. Any military personnel making a disturbance will be sent to General Ko for punishment;
6. Any civilians disturbing the peace will be punished according to law, on the guarantee of the Committee;
7. Troops absolutely will not be brought from the south to the north.

On reaching this last point of agreement, General Ko vowed to "commit suicide" if his personal guarantee were broken. Nothing was said of troops coming in from abroad.

The Formosans were treating in good faith, but this "vow" was a bit difficult to accept at face value. General Ko, an unusually small man, smartly uniformed, had established a reputation for ruthless action, cruelty, and diamond-hard contempt for "the People." He was not one of Chen Yi's men, but was assigned here by the Generalissimo as a counterbalance to Chen; it was an illustration of Chiang's technique of government through the counterbalance of clan, clique, and economic faction.

At this point General Ko began gradually to emerge as the symbol of the National Army and Central Government, and in retrospect we see the design. The Formosans were to be made to appear as rebels against the authority of the National Government rather than in protest against the maladministration of Chen Yi.

To fulfill the second requirement in the day's agreement concerning public order, the Settlement Committee recommended members to key posts in a "Loyal Service Corps," the Taipei City Provisional Public Safety Committee which would be dissolved on the day normal conditions were restored. The Settlement Committee members themselves promptly subscribed 770,000 yen to finance the Corps.

Of all the organizations formed in this first week of March this was the most significant, and the fate predicted for it on that day was the most tragic. The mainland Chinese police had disappeared, for they were the first objects of popular wrath. Formosans who were on the police force now formed the nucleus of a new, temporary force. Young men of high school age or recent graduates of the Japanese Middle Schools eagerly joined up, for they had been well drilled under the Japanese and could quickly grasp what was required of them. "Loyal Service Corps" armbands gave them a sense of authority, and the pent-up angers of a year fired them with determination to show the mainland Chinese how a proper police force should conduct itself.

Had the Formosans at this point really wanted to overthrow Chen Yi and drive the mainland Chinese from the island, it could have been quickly done, leaving the National Government with a second war — a maritime war — on its hands. This Chen Yi and General Ko well knew.

By March 5 the Formosans were in control throughout the island except within Chen Yi's office area at Taipei, and within the garrison compounds and camps.

They wanted reform and not civil war. "We should acknowledge the aim of this action, that there is no other desire except to demand a reformation of Government." [3]

XIII

Town Meetings, American Style

Island-wide Mobilization of Public Opinion

ON MARCH 4 General Ko shed a number of crocodile tears in public. Addressing the Settlement Committee he touched indirectly upon the problem of Formosan confidence in the United States of America or the United Nations, a "shameful embarrassment."

> Both the Government and the people should feel ashamed on behalf of the nation and the Chinese race because of this Incident. On the first day . . . I received two reports. The first one was that Americans were taking pictures of the Incident, and the other was that Japanese were celebrating it.
>
> I was much more hurt by this information than by reports on the casualties of both government employees and civilians. I feel so badly that tears gather in my eyes.
>
> As to this Incident, everything can be settled if we do not diverge from our national and racial standpoint. I will rather die here than to do anything or make any promise that departs from our national and racial standpoint. This is my duty as a soldier. This is the duty charged upon us by our nation, for us to perform.[1]

More than one thousand people packed the Civic Auditorium throughout the day to hear Committee discussions and the Government spokesmen who met with them on the wide stage.

By this time Formosans were beginning to focus attention on specific grievances of an island-wide nature. Basic utilities and public services must be maintained while reform proposals were being drawn up.

The principal resolutions of the day reflect the situation at the capital:

1. The Settlement Committee invites the formation of branch committees throughout the island. Representatives will be drawn from the elected Peoples Political Councils, and distinguished private persons in every city and District. These branch Committees will forward to Taipei the recommendations and resolutions having to do with reforms in local government.

2. The Government is asked to fulfill its promises to restore communications. If there are "accidents," the responsible people must be called to account.

3. A Committee of Three [including Huang Chao-chin] will negotiate with General Ko concerning soldiers in the streets. If they are on the streets in search of food, they must be unarmed. [Five days had passed since the Governor General promised to withdraw the roving troops.]

4. There must be broadcasts to China proper and overseas "explaining that the Formosans only demand reforms in the provincial government and nothing else."

5. "All information broadcasts will be exclusively released by the Information Section of the February 28th Incident Settlement Committee."

6. The Taiwan Electric Power Corporation will be asked to maintain constant services so that full communications can be maintained.[2]

The problems of public utilities services were acute, and first among these was the railway problem. The Director of Railways (Chen Ching-wen) was especially disliked and mistrusted. His monumental contempt for the island people had been undisguised. Although his administrative capacities were recognized, his arrogance was intolerable. Mechanical operations were handled skillfully enough, but the hated Special Railway Police Corps, responsible to Director Chen, were a ruthless lot. It was widely believed that they were either totally inefficient as a Guard unit, or were actually covering well-organized, systematic cargo-looting in transit between the ports and cities.

The slaughter of high school students in the Railway Offices on March 1 made Director Chen a first object of "reform." A delegation met the Commissioner of Communications (Jen), in the presence of a Lieutenant General representing the Taiwan Garrison Headquarters. It was agreed that Director Chen would be removed from office, that the Railway Police would be temporarily inactive from March 5, while reorganization of the police system went forward, and that a Railway Workers Service Corps (Formosan employees of the railway) would maintain order pending the general administrative reorganization. The Railway Bureau personnel who had taken refuge in the American Consulate should be dismissed from the service. All Formosan assaults upon employees from other provinces will be stopped.

Meanwhile a report on the electric power situation was brought before the general meeting at the Auditorium. All mainland Chinese were absent from their jobs, the island-wide system was being maintained solely by Formosan personnel, and the public was asked to cooperate in every way to enable them to keep the power services in full operation, for they were vital to public security.

Elsewhere in the city the All-Taiwan General Labor Union met to hear passionate speeches in support of the Settlement Committee. It was voted to have each union send two representatives to cooperate with the Committees.

About noon, March 4, a delegation of Settlement Committee representatives, representatives of the Taiwan Cultural Promotion Association and representatives of student organizations

met with the Governor-General to explain arrangements to
have youth organizations temporarily take over police functions. They then met with five of the Governor's Commissioners to discuss details of this, and at 3:30 P.M. reported again to
the Governor. In summary, they requested his views, and
asked him to direct the Settlement Committee to draw up a
Reform Program for negotiation with the Government. They
then asked him to have more direct contact with the public,
explaining his own views and policies so that the common people would understand. These requests were of course designed
to get Chen Yi's direct commitment to a Reform Program negotiation. There was the polite implication that he did not really
know what was going on, and that if he did he would certainly
desire reforms to be made.

The Governor's answers were suitably vague. He felt that his
political and economic policies were good, "but not yet perfectly carried out." As for unemployment, relief measures were
being taken. All views on the matter were welcomed. He was
eager to keep in close touch with the people. On the matter of
arms in the hands of a temporary youth corps for policing purposes, he had already ordered all the gendarmes and police to
refrain from carrying weapons, therefore there was no need to
place weapons in student hands.

Buried in the heart of the affable discourse was a statement
which foreshadowed events to come. The Governor noted the
difficulty he had in adjusting local problems and policies with
national problems and policies. He asked the Formosans to de-
vote more attention to local problems.

The delegation left the Governor at 4:00 P.M. to report to the
Civic Auditorium.*

* The efficiency with which Formosan leaders organized for island-wide representation is noteworthy. At Taipei the Committee had the following Sections,
each reporting its deliberations and recommendations to the full Committee
sitting on the platform of the Civic Auditorium.

   1. *General Affairs Section* — to digest letters and formulate recommenda-
     tions;

The Taiwan Association at Shanghai meanwhile had sent an urgent message to Chiang Kai-shek requesting him to undertake a thorough investigation of conditions which led to the February 28 Incident, and on that day (March 4) the Control Yuan of the Central Government ordered the distinguished educator Dr. Yang Liang-kung to investigate and report. At Taipei Chen Yi sent deputies to "comfort" the wounded in various hospitals.

Toward the close of the day's meeting Wang Tien-teng announced that a telephone message had been received saying that a Branch Committee had been formed at Taichung and that the city there was now entirely in Formosan hands, to be governed by the Committee during the negotiations for reform. The Taipei Committee was requested to ask the Governor to restrain and withdraw the armed troops which were shooting up the streets of Taichung as they were continuing to do in Taipei.

The "Star-Spangled Banner" and All That

Fortunately for the record we have eyewitness reports of events in this week, compiled by members of the UNRRA staff who were scattered over the island on their several errands. These

---

2. *Liaison Section* — to communicate with Government offices;
3. *Investigation Section* — a fact-finding group;
4. *Organization Section* — to coordinate the work of the diverse sections;
5. *Public Order Section* — to maintain order through an organization of students, Formosan policemen, etc. — the "Patriotic Service Corps";
6. *Relief Section* — to provide "Red Cross" services; to meet sanitary corps problems and related welfare problems;
7. *Finance Section* — to rally contributors and to request the Government to meet its share of the costs;
8. *Information Section* — to counter the gross misrepresentations being broadcast by Stanway Cheng's office on behalf of Chen Yi;
9. *Food Section* — to handle ten million yen contributed by Committee members to buy rice, and the twenty million yen promised by the Government Food Bureau. An additional thirty million yen would be available if needed, from the Provincial Food Bureau. The Food Section was authorized to buy rice from the liquor manufacturing companies.

are supplemented with letters sent to foreign friends at the UNRRA headquarters and in the American Consulate in that week.

We now know that we witnessed a most remarkable attempt on the part of the Formosans to put into practice the democratic principles which Washington put abroad in wartime and postwar propaganda. Had the Formosans behaved in March, 1947, as their ancestors would certainly have behaved in the 19th century, they would have wiped the mainland Chinese from the face of the island. They were in a position to do so, for the Nationalist troops on the island could have been overcome or driven into hiding. There could so easily have been a general massacre of mainland Chinese.

But the Formosans were attempting to bring about reform within the existing political framework. For one week they had the upper hand, but they chose to conduct themselves with a scrupulous regard for "correct" procedures, hoping throughout that the United States or the United Nations would show interest, that the American Ambassador in China would persuade Chiang to recall Chen Yi and send in a new man to undertake a thorough reform in the administration.

Events at Taipei were made known at once in all parts of the island. Here and there civilians clashed with military squads or with the mainland police. In many places mainland soldiers simply surrendered their arms; they had no stomach for a fight when it became clear that the Formosans were prepared to resist. The Formosans, on their part, developed a propaganda line urging the mainland soldiers not to aid in a civil war.

Government offices and private enterprises were taken over with little difficulty, for the mainland Chinese wisely remained within doors wherever they could.

Street fighting was brief but fairly severe in Taichung and Chia-yi, and at Kaohsiung a hard core of military force (commanded by General Peng Meng-chi) held its own base and continuously made trouble in the city, despite the Governor's promises and the guarantees of Ko Yuen-feng, the Chief of Staff.

All mainland people in the Hualien district on the East Coast surrendered local controls voluntarily and without incident. The people of Hsinchu District undertook to guarantee that food would move steadily into Taipei city. Commissioner Jen reported to the Settlement Committee that all rail services were restored on March 5.

Down from the hills in the central districts came aborigine leaders and young men, offering to assist the Formosans in any way they might, and in mid-week a delegation of Taiyal and Ami tribesmen called on me at the American Consulate to "seek direction." I advised them at once to go back to the mountains to look after their own families and village interests, and to stay as far as possible from trouble centers.

Our sources of information indicated that the mainland Chinese were suffering a peculiarly unsettling fear of "what the aborigines might do." Rumors of the wildest sort were circulating in Taipei, relaying reports that "thousands of headhunters" were coming down from the mountains and had already reached the suburbs of the capital city. This was nonsense, but it represented the survival or reactivation of traditional Chinese mainland views of Formosa, the savage island.

Just as the aborigines called at the American Consulate to "seek direction," the people of Pingtung, far to the south, were responding to Taipei's call for organization and recommendations for the reform program. Two Canadian nurses directing an UNRRA training program at the local hospital, watched with interest as local leaders convoked a general town meeting to prepare proposals for administrative reform in southern Formosa.

A truck carrying a loudspeaker toured the town, making announcements at suitable street intersections and public gathering-places. While moving from place to place the public address system blared forth "The Star-Spangled Banner" — the

American national anthem — although no American citizens were anywhere near the Pingtung District at that time. The Formosans were determined to have a town meeting in "true American style," and here, as everywhere else, showed deep confidence that the United States was prepared to back up its urgent propaganda on behalf of democratic institutions.

Miss Snow Red and the Communists

Where, meanwhile, were the Communists?

They had failed to make an impression on the Formosan people in 1946, and for more than a year had been keeping to themselves working in secret principally in the Taichung countryside. But now they came into the open, believing they could capitalize upon the crisis and perhaps seize the initiative and direction of a general rebellion.

From Taichung — from a former student — I received this letter, dated March 7:

> Allow me to report the present accident in Taichung prefecture.
>
> At first I did not believe the matter which took place in Taipei would effect so big influence all over this island. But early in the morning on 28th Taichung City Hall was opened and soon crowded with fanatic citizens and councillors. They debated zealously and agreed that this time the case is past endurance and they would demand rapid disposition of it by the government.
>
> A representative was sent to Taihoku [Taipei] and a close comunication [i.e. consultation] was taken all around Taichung prefecture. But without any relation with City and Prefecture Council, radical element which had been concealed, abruptly appeared at that night and lead students and daredevils.
>
> The head of this was Miss Sha Shets Ho [Hsieh Hsueh-hung], a good fighter and suspected communist.

Then in the street an inquiry "Are you pig or sweet potato" was begun, and any passerbys who look like pig was knocked [i.e. anyone looking like a mainland Chinese was beaten].

But what incurred citizens indignation most and gave them a chance to explode their stayed rage, was that two boys were shot down by guards when they went to the Prefectural Governor . . .

Next morning Taichu people were already united, they rose up, student corps was formed, help was telephoned to the neighbor district. They seized [the] 8th batallion, [the] 36th air corps and police offices.

In accord with Taichung City, districts and villages commenced their work. They arrested ill-famed and suspected Chinese and the unfortunates are imprisoned. Concerning about Taichung prefecture, it seemed they got through very fair. Most of the Chinese force are under our disposal and a good deal of weapons are now in our hands.

But one thing I am afraid is so many pistol and gun are scattered in the confusion among people, and it is sure there are wicked persons who would take advantage of confusion. For this a new borned Public Peace Section was hoped [i.e. requested] to the people that arms should be gathered in one spot and reserved for better use.

I tried to catch the movement of communists these days, but except some demagogy, the communist intrigued, I don't think they would influence so potential power upon peoples. It is none of their business this time, every educated person would rightly think so. For them [the Communists] the trouble is they have no foundation in this island, and this chance is too big [for] their weak power.

Of course at some spot in the country we can see poor people flock before the rich gate demanding rice distribution, but they don't know what communism means exactly, and they have no leader.

Nevertheless the food problem before us is very serious. This accident is very smart, it is sure [i.e. advantageous for the Communists] but how far would the country wives and poor people understand it? For them the dominant element to determine what is good or bad largely depends on how more or cheap rice is. Could not UNRRA's flour in the godown meet this problem?

Yesterday Taichung Prefectural emergency Committee which was resumed for a time being, held a meeting and concreted its stuff [i.e. organized its activities]. The representatives of all institutions gathered and discussed earnestly and elected fifteen executive committee. You would see the resolution at the following pages. The meeting was serious itself, you only see it and you would understand how the people of Taiwan longed for democracy. The dominant opinion was Taipei Prefecture Committee should be more bold and be more careful lest they would not fall a prey to the Chinese intrigue. They insisted that now they had [taken] a step they should advance more steps and carry through.

It seems Taichung men are rather stubborn and irresistable. At first time since this accident I saw a group of Mandarin wearing a Formosan-like shabby cloth walked in the street. Chinese in Taichung City are now divided in four parts — soldiers, ill [i.e. rascals or evil persons], good, [and] wounded. The ill and soldiers are under our guard, wounds [wounded] and killed are not clear, but appeared the killed are extremely little both Chinese and Formosan.

Sir, you know quite well the cause of this regrettable accident, I am sure. So I don't like to mention this any more. But I would like to know how America thinks. Has America any disposal [i.e. plan] if the matter go bad? Is Taiwan legally returned to China from the point of view of international law? I also love my country, I mean China. But a mere love is heartfailing in this case. Love should be substantial. What do you think? [3]

Here before our eyes was repeated the drama of bitter choice which the American colonists had had to make in 1776. There were those who loved England, but loved freedom more. In Formosa the expectation of a new postwar life in a new China, guided by and in association with the United States was now cruelly destroyed. What indeed, did America think?

The answer was brief: "This is China now."

The Youth League and Local Political Expression

The March 4 delegation which demanded dismissal of Chen Ching-wen, Director of the Railway Administration, represented the gradual organization of specific demands within particular offices of Government. The Settlement Committee leaders rather hoped that it would not have to be concerned with such issues until larger issues were settled — issues having to do with the mechanics of developing a reasonable reform program after the widest possible reference to representative organizations. They had begun to feel the need of unity — a common front — in meeting the Government.

There were disquieting rumors that troops might come from the mainland. A forceful younger element urged the Committee to seize all mainland military personnel on the island, a move, the Committee realized, which could have the most grave consequences. That would indeed be rebellion, whereas they sought only reform within the existing offices of Government.

As the Committee worked long hard hours to bring about careful organization (there were seventeen local subdivisions created throughout the island) conditions at the capital greatly improved. The Monopoly Bureau cars overturned in the streets remained untouched, as reminders of the incident at Round Park, but shops were again open and the primary schools resumed classwork.

An amateur radio operator was in touch with someone on the Fukien coast. It was evident that troops were being concentrated at Fukien ports and were presumed to be destined for Formosa. It began to be rumored that the Governor-General had set March 10 as the date for the presentation of a reform program because he believed he could get troops into the island before that time, and thus make it unnecessary for him to recognize the reform documents.

Each rumor strengthened the argument of the "activists,"

and made more difficult the task of the Settlement Committee.

A new organization appeared, a Taiwan Youth League, founded by Chiang Wei-chuan.* It had a platform of six principles:

1. Formosa must achieve the highest degree of autonomy, to enable it to become the leading model province of New China;
2. Formosa must insist on the general popular election of a governor, and of magistrates and mayors, "in order to fulfill the program of National Reconstruction outlined by Dr. Sun Yat-sen";
3. Formosans must demonstrate a law-abiding spirit, and lead in the promotion of democracy;
4. Formosa must promote Chinese culture for the benefit of China and of mankind;
5. The Government must revive industry and increase production in order to stabilize the local economy and enrich the lives of the people;
6. The Government must encourage the people to achieve a high social standard.[4]

Chiang Wei-chuan broadcast to the mainland on March 5, saying that the vendor's death at the hands of the Monopoly Bureau agents was the immediate provocation, but that the underlying cause was profound dissatisfaction and bitterness after months of Chen Yi's rule. He assured his audience there was no thought of rebellion nor of independence in the island; the need was for immediate and widespread reform. Chiang then addressed the Youth League assembly at Taipei in these terms.

We absolutely support the Central Government, but will eradicate all corrupt officials in this province. This is our aim which

---

* The founder, Chiang Wei-chuan, could appeal to Formosan youth with special force, for his brother Chiang Wei-sui had died in a Japanese prison in the 1930's because of his work for the Taiwan Home Rule Movement at that time.

I hope every one of you fully grasp. At the same time we must realize our present situation. We need organization, but we must try our best to bring about a peaceful settlement, and never indiscreetly resort to force.[5]

The Taipei Settlement Committee received the "Declaration of Taichung Prefectural Administrative Committee for Emergency" which represents a fair sample of opinion being expressed by each of the seventeen Committee centers now established throughout the island. I quote the text as translated and sent to me from Taichung on March 7.

OUR POLITICAL PURPOSE

1. We would recover order, maintain political peace and welfare, and work for political reconstruction.
2. We would dispatch ables [i.e. able men] and cooperate to all institutions, private and official.

OUR CLAIMS [I.E. DEMANDS]

1. We claim for the immediate enforcement of Constitution and election of the Governor of Taiwan Province, prefectures, cities, districts. Our objective is self-government.
2. We claim for the reorganization of the officials of Taiwan and raise men of ability to higher position from the people of this island for the building of New Taiwan.
3. We claim for the distribution of official and military provision stock to meet the food shortage of this island.
4. We claim for the abolishment of the monopoly system and any factory belonging to it would be facilitate [i.e. managed] by we Formosan.
5. We claim for the juridical independence and the strict purge of the tyranny of soldiers and policemen. We are serious to have the respectability of public rights and public seven freedoms — of live, of speech, of thought, of publish, of gathering, of formation of association, of residence.
6. We claim any juridical pursuit [i.e. prosecution] should not be

applied for persons who righteously take part in this 2–28 accident.

7. We claim Government should take means for [i.e. to combat] soaring commodity prices and unemployment problem.

OUR SLOGANS

1. Build New China Republic.
2. Guarantee democratic policy.
3. We support National Government. Our aim is to eliminate corrupt briber.
4. An immediate enforcement of the election of all in chief [in administrative office] in Taiwan — province, prefecture, and city.
5. We [are] against civil war.
6. Hell to the autocracy.
7. Do away with undemocratic administration.
8. Abandon weapons; we want a peaceable government.
9. We disgust [i.e. decry] armed intervention, and would deem it as our enemy.
10. Gentlemen, ables [i.e. men of ability] honest and peace-loving person from all corner of our China, take share of us and cooperate our brilliant future.

The China Republic forever!

The Taiwan Province forever!

On March 5, about the hour Chiang Wei-chuan was addressing the Youth League rally, a delegation representing the Taiwan Political Reconstruction Association came to the American Consulate bearing a brief letter and a "Manifesto" which restated the Formosan desire for reform within the existing political structure — a reform of personnel and policies, and not a break or change in Formosa's relations with China. The petition addressed to the American Consul said this:

Sir:

For the protection of the lives of the six million Formosans we cordially request you to forward the enclosed letter to Am-

bassador Dr. Leighton Stuart for transmission to the National
Government of the Chinese Republic.

/s/ *The Political Reconstruction*
Promotion Association of Taiwan

The petitioners were not received by the Consul, and at Nanking, at a later date I was unable to discover any record of the
"Manifesto."

The "Thirty-two Demands" —
What the Formosans Wanted

Ugly rumors from the mainland spurred the Settlement Committee to hasten work on the Draft Reform Program to be
offered to the Governor-General for his consideration *and for
transmittal to Nanking.*

Chen Yi had set March 10 as the day for the program to be
presented to him, but it was now suspected that he would land
troops, making it unnecessary for him to endure this humiliation.

The Committee's Executive Group acted as direct sponsors
of the Reform Program. The group included four members of
the National Assembly, two members of the National Peoples
Political Councils, six from the Taiwan Provincial PPC, five
from the Municipal PPC's, and two "reserve members" or
"members-at-large."

It must be stressed again that this was not a group of irresponsible radicals; every member had been cleared and approved by the Government as PPC candidates in 1946, and for
the most part they represented the senior economic and professional men in the island. The Settlement Committee had been
appointed by Governor-General Chen Yi himself, and to the
Governor they now presented these "demands."

Obviously much thought had been devoted to these issues
long before the crisis of February 28. It remained only to bring

them together in a text. The document was presented to Governor Chen well ahead of the March 10 deadline. Thanks to carefully organized communication with the seventeen branch Committees, the final draft embraced reforms needed in every part of the island and at every administrative level. On review we see that the items could be grouped roughly under six general categories. The full text, with notes, is presented in Appendix I (pp. 475–479) as I presented it to Ambassador Stuart at Nanking.[6] Here it is summarized.

The minimum reforms required to ensure equality and honest representation of the Formosan people in island government were ten. These included reforms which would guarantee freedom of speech, of assembly, and of the press. Major appointments to administrative office must be approved by the elective Peoples' Political Councils. The Nationalist Party must no longer be authorized to control the election process through control of candidates and management of the polls.

A second category of "demands" — seven in number — listed reforms required at once to ensure security of person and property. These touched upon control of the civil police, administration of the law, and the composition and administration of the local courts.

Economic reforms — the third category — numbered six and were designed to secure a revision and liberalization of general economic policies, to eliminate the abusive monopoly system, and to guarantee an equitable solution to the confiscated Japanese property problem.

A fourth category included three reforms affecting military affairs on Formosa. They are of special interest because the Generalissimo later justified his harsh and vindictive policy, his "punishment" of the Formosans, by reference to these three demands. Formosan leaders demanded that the military police should be forbidden to arrest anyone other than military personnel. They asked that the armed forces — the Army, Navy and Air Forces — should employ as many Formosans as possible on

Formosa. And they demanded that the Taiwan Garrison Head-quarters should be abolished in order to put an end to the misuse of military privilege. Formosa should not be treated as a gar-risoned occupied territory.

Reforms affecting social welfare included a demand that la-borers be protected by law and that the wealthy men and noted leaders must be released who were held as alleged "war crim-inals" and "collaborators." The political, economic and social rights of the aboriginal peoples must be recognized and guaran-teed.

At least three of the "demands" were subordinate items offer-ing opportunity for face-saving concessions and compromise. One concerned the Vocational Guidance Camp for political re-education "and other unnecessary institutions." Another called for payment by the Central Government for 150,000 tons of foodstuffs exported after the surrender in 1945. A third de-manded payment for the huge sugar reserves which had been shipped out of Formosa by order of the Executive Yuan when T. V. Soong was President. Formosans believed that the sugar had gone into private warehouses.

In presenting these "Thirty-two Demands" the Settlement Committee was profoundly aware of its responsible official character and acted with great restraint at a time when Chen Yi was militarily helpless and his government paralyzed.

The Committee's work was greatly hampered when many impossible demands were made upon it by individuals and groups not authorized to develop a reform program for the Government's consideration. It was most seriously embar-rassed by published demands that *only* Formosans be allowed to hold arms on Formosa, and that all Central Government troops must be withdrawn. It was also embarrassed by extreme threats against individual members of Government which ap-peared in handbill and poster form.

Reform — Not Rebellion

By now (March 6) rumor ran everywhere that Chen Yi was bringing in military reinforcements from the mainland despite his pledges.

Until the very last the leaders at Taipei and at the seventeen subordinate "town meeting" centers worked feverishly to prepare this reasonable program. There was no ultimatum involved, no challenging "either-or" threat to declare independence. From among newspaper editorials and published declarations of the day we need here quote only two which clearly state the Formosan grievances:

> First . . . we admit that the cause and spread of the affair was nothing but a reflection of the constant alienation of public sentiment since the restoration. This sufficiently explains that the political and economic arrangements of the last one and a half years have caused a universal and intense dissatisfaction on the part of the people, and that the Incident was nothing but an inevitable outlet of such discontent.
>
> For over one year the people's discontent has daily increased, the popular opinion organizations have been doing their part in giving reports, criticisms, and suggestions; to this the authorities can make no denial of ignorance. Nevertheless, the authorities have not paid much attention.
>
> As a result, today's most tragic situation has come into being. Once it had burst, it became something which cannot be denied; indeed, we cannot but blame the authorities for their lack of sensitivity to political matters. Hence we hope that the authorities, having learned a lesson from the Incident, will give some sincere reflection, will put into practice the Settlement Committee's demands, will work out an immediate solution to the Incident with us, and will listen to public opinion, reform the Government, restore people's confidence, and lead the six million Taiwanese brothers back to a closer relationship with the Government, so as to cooperate with one heart in rebuilding Taiwan.

Therefore we [Chinese] cannot but give our urgent cry to these six million Taiwan brothers saying that "We are all Chinese and descendants of the Great Han race," that from our origin we are brothers of the same blood, that we have been separated because of Taiwan's half-century under the Japanese.

At this date after restoration, when there has not been sufficient time even for families to be reunited . . . is no time for us to have hostile feelings. Even worse is it for us to engage in slaughter! No matter what is the right or the wrong of the situation, brothers, mutual slaughter is to our shame. This sort of disgraceful action will not only cause foreigners to jeer, and the frantic joy of the Japanese, but will cause us to stain the history of this glorious island . . .[7]

An editorial in the influential *Min Pao*, at Taipei (March 6) noted that the Settlement Committee had adopted the principle of no discrimination toward people from other provinces, so long as Formosans are properly represented at all levels of the local administration. It too raised the issue of civil strife:

Foreign countries have been given much wrong information regarding this Incident. There is also a misinterpretation of other purposes and wishes. However excited the Formosans become, their conception that they are a part of the Chinese race will not change. Since we belong to the same race, we should have brotherly regard for one another. How can we meet each other with arms?

We hope our [Nationalist] soldiers will lay down their arms so as to give our Formosan compatriots a calm moment to deliberately discuss problems of the situation. Perhaps an earlier enforcement of the Constitution and an immediate preparation for the general election of provincial chairmen and magistrates will contribute somewhat to the settlement of the situation.[8]

This, of course, was whistling for courage. An amateur radio operator on the mainland was continuously warning friends on Formosa that a punitive force had been assembled there. Chen

Yi had set the date for presentation of the Reform Program — March 10. The Formosans presented it to him on March 7, and made public the text. He was therefore obliged to accept it as a document for consideration, but he pointedly warned that he could act only in matters affecting Provincial administration; all matters touching on the National administration would have to be referred to Nanking.

Ships bearing Nationalist Army units left the mainland that night, heading eastward to bring in Chiang Kai-shek's solution to the Formosan problem.

By Saturday morning, March 8, the Settlement Committee learned, beyond shadow of doubt, that a force — a very large one, heavily armed — was about to land, and that Nationalist Army units were continuing to assemble at embarkation points along the China coast. Obviously Chen Yi and his men — and the National Government — had betrayed them.

Some members began to issue retractions and modifications of statements made earlier in the week, or denials of acts and proposals emanating from Settlement Committee Headquarters after the February 28 Incident. It was much too late.

XIV

The March Massacre

The Betrayal

AT NOON on Saturday, March 8, Major General Chang Wu-tso, Commander of the Fourth Gendarme Regiment, called on the Settlement Committee at its Headquarters to make the following statement:

> I can guarantee that there will be no social disturbances if the people do not try to disarm the soldiers. I want especially to report to you that the demands for political reforms in this province are very proper.
>
> The Central Government will not dispatch troops to Taiwan. I earnestly entreat the people of Taiwan not to irritate the Central Government, but to cooperate to maintain order.
>
> I can risk my life to guarantee that the Central Government will not take any military actions against Taiwan.
>
> I speak these words out of my sincere attachment to this Province and to the nation. I hope Taiwan will become a model province after these political reforms.[1]

In mid-afternoon several foreign businessmen at Keelung were startled by the crackle of machine-gun fire near the docks. With growing volume it soon spread into the streets leading back into the city proper.

The Nationalist troops had come. Chiang Kai-shek had responded promptly to Chen Yi's call for help.

Ships from the mainland lay in the harbor. Local military units ashore, by prearranged signal, began to clear the streets near the docks. Indiscriminate gunfire was directed at no particular objects or groups.

A fairly reliable Government source later told us that 2000 gendarmes were first put ashore to control the Keelung dock area, after which 8000 regular troops came off. Concurrently at Kaohsiung some 3000 troops landed from the ship *Hai Ping*. With these troops came suitable equipment, most of it of American origin. This was China, now, but a hasty paint job did not hide the clearly marked original lettering on the vehicles.

Was this to be the *American* answer to Formosan pleas for help?

That evening after dinner we sat discussing with friends the dread implications of the word from Keelung. Suddenly the night silence was shattered. The rattle of gunfire could be heard not far away on the boulevard leading into the city from the north. Soon thereafter — a matter of minutes — Nationalist Army trucks rolled slowly along the road before our house, and from them a hail of machine-gun fire was directed at random into the darkness, ripping through windows and walls and ricocheting in the black alleyways.

The crack of rifle-fire and the chatter of machine guns could be heard throughout the night, across the town. The troops had come in from Keelung.

This was to be the Government's answer to proposals for reform. Dawn on that Sunday opened a week of naked terror for the Formosan people.

During a lull in the action on our boulevard, we made our way to the Mackaye Mission Hospital close by, to join there the Director of the USIS, his wife and baby, and other foreigners who realized that the large walled mission compound might offer some security from random gunfire in the streets.

From an upper window we watched Nationalist soldiers in

action in the alleys across the way. We saw Formosans bayon-
eted in the street without provocation. A man was robbed before our eyes — and then cut down and run through. Another
ran into the street in pursuit of soldiers dragging a girl away
from his house and we saw him, too, cut down.

This sickening spectacle was only the smallest sample of the
slaughter then taking place throughout the city, only what
could be seen from one window on the upper floor of one rather
isolated house. The city was full of troops.

At one moment from our vantage point we saw the Canadian
nurse in charge of the hospital (Miss Hildur Hermanson) run
out accompanied by two Formosan nurses and three assistants
with stretchers. They boldly crossed the boulevard to enter a
warren of alleys beyond. Soon they returned, carrying a desperately wounded man. As they entered the hospital building
soldiers leveled fire from the street, but missed the nurses,
merely knocking chunks from the cornice just under a large
Canadian flag. This time there were no official news broadcasts
to tell of Nationalist troops attacking a Canadian Mission hospital.

Throughout that grim Sunday patients were brought into the
mission compound, some shot, some literally hacked to pieces.
A well-known Formosan teacher had been shot in the back
while trying to reach her home and had been robbed as she lay
in the street before someone managed to bring her into the hospital nearby.

Night came, but no rest; gunfire continued to be heard, and
was especially heavy that evening in the Manka quarter of the
city, a crowded slumlike area.

What were we to see next day?

General Chen's Monday Morning View
of the Situation

The Taiwan Garrison Headquarters published an ambiguous communique saying that "all illegal organizations must be abolished before March 10, and meetings and parades are prohibited." [2] Only the Government's own paper, the *Hsin Sheng Pao,* appeared on March 10.

With the landing of troops Governor-General Chen and his henchmen had suddenly regained great courage. He now took the line that the whole activity had been rebellion directed not against himself but against the Central Government and Chiang Kai-shek. Given Chiang's vengeful character, this would ensure full support for what was about to follow; it was to be a "Fukien Settlement" once more.

On March 10 General Chen issued the following statement to the press and public:

In the afternoon of March 2, I broadcast that members of the national, provincial, and municipal PPC's, Taiwan representatives to the National Assembly, and representatives from the people may jointly form a committee to receive the people's opinion concerning relief work for the February 28 Incident.

Unexpectedly, since its formation, the Committee has given no thought to relief work such as medical care for the wounded and compensation to the killed and so forth. On the contrary, it acted beyond its province, and on March 7 went so far as to announce a settlement outline containing rebellious elements. Therefore this Committee (including *hsien* and municipal branch committees) should be abolished. From hereafter, opinions on political reforms concerning the province may be brought up by the Provincial PPC and those concerning the *Hsien* and municipalities by their respective districts or municipal PPC's. People who have opinions may bring them up to the PPC or to the Government General by writing.[3]

While the indiscriminate slaughter was at its height in Taipei, the Governor-General went on the air with this statement:

Brethren of Taiwan —
Yesterday I declared temporary martial law again. Now with the utmost sincerity, I want to tell our good and virtuous brethren who constitute the vast majority of the population of the island, that my declaration of martial law is entirely for your protection. You must not listen to the rumors of wicked people. You must not be suspicious or afraid. There shall not be the slightest harm to our law-abiding brethren. You must feel at ease.

I have declared martial law again solely for the purpose of coping with the very small number of the desperate and rebellious. As long as they are not annihilated there will be no peace for our virtuous brethren.

Since the occurrence of the February 28 Incident, I have broadcast three times. Regarding the Incident, I have had the Monopoly Officer who caused the manslaughter tried by the court, the families of the dead have been indemnified, and the wounded compensated and taken care of, and those who have taken part in the beatings [of mainland Chinese monopoly employees] are exempted from prosecution.

As to political reforms, I have promised that the Government General may be reformed to absorb as many as possible of the people of the Province, that mayors and magistrates may be elected by the people, and that other political reforms may be discussed and decided upon later, according to law. Thus, what is expected and requested by the majority of the people, as far as it is within the boundary of law, has nearly been accepted. Anyway, I believe that from now on order will be completely restored without further trouble.

However, since martial law was lifted on March 1, plundering of property, seizure of arms, and storming of government organizations and godowns has continued to occur in Taipei, and statements against the State were publicly announced. In other places looting, seizing of arms and arresting of government employees, and besieging of government institutions has also occurred. Please reflect whether such deeds are proper and legal. I believe that every one of you, my good brethren, will realize that such actions are far from legal, and are in fact rebellious.

Brethren, since the occurrence of the February 28 Incident, what you have wanted to settle is the question of manslaughter by the Monopoly personnel, and the question of political reform.

But a small minority of ruffians and rebellious gangsters have taken advantage of the situation to invent rumors, sow the seeds of dissension, tell lies, and make threats in order to attain the aims of their plot. All good citizens have suffered a terrible life during the past ten days.

Brethren, such suffering has entirely been created by these ruffians and gangsters. In order to relieve you from this suffering, the Government cannot but declare martial law so as to obliterate these gangsters who are harmful to you. This point I hope you will thoroughly understand.

The transference of national troops to Taiwan is entirely for the protection of the people of the province and for the eradication of rioters and rebels and no other purpose. There is an exceedingly small number of rebellious people in this province; most of the people are exceptionally good and virtuous, and they have provided various means of looking after those from other provinces who have been beaten. Such manifestations of brotherhood I have deeply appreciated.*

To these good people of Taiwan I express my sincere gratitude. I further hope they will rally their courage and display their sense of righteousness, and love one another in order to build a new Taiwan.[4]

The Governor's soothing words were printed up in pamphlet form and scattered by plane over the cities and towns of the island. This statement set the general framework in which both the local and national governments developed later public explanations of the February 28 Incident and its aftermath. "A few wicked gangsters had terrorized the island in the first week

---

* This may allude to the protection given to Yen Chia-kan by old Lim Hsien-tang, in whose Taichung house Commissioner Yen took shelter. Or did it refer to the assistance given the Governor by such virtuous Formosan natives as Huang Chao-chin who had served him in the Settlement Committee meetings?

of March and had rebelled against the Chinese Government; Chinese Nationalist troops had come in to protect the righteous people, and were now soothing and protecting all honest and upright Formosans."

The roadways, the river banks and the harbor shores were strewn with bodies at that moment, and the Nationalist troops were spreading out through the countryside, to bring "peace and protection" *à la Kuomintang*.

What the Unwelcome Foreigners Saw

In later days when UNRRA members, missionaries, foreign businessmen and our consular staff men could come together to compare notes for that week, the stories were much the same from every part of the island. For the Government had decided upon a policy of pure terrorism. Anyone trying to hide or to run was doomed. For example, one foreigner saw a youngster riding his bike at breakneck speed through the streets, evidently trying to reach home, or perhaps speeding to his grandparents' home with messages. He was knocked off his bicycle. He was then forced to hold out his hands which were cruelly slashed, after which the Nationalist soldiers made off with the machine, leaving the boy bleeding and helpless in the street.

Looting began immediately. The soldiers made it a practice to beat upon closed doors, and then to cut down whoever chanced to open them. Other occupants of the house were fortunate indeed if they escaped unhurt.

On Sunday night I found my house crowded with friends seeking shelter which I gladly gave them. It was "irregular," of course. Throughout the following week came a steady stream of messages, queries, and entreaties addressed to members of the foreign community. All of the UNRRA staff and most of the consular community were left heartsick and bitter and angry.

The Government promptly undertook an intensive search for

members of the Settlement Committee, and for all editors, lawyers, doctors or businessmen who had taken an active part in preparing the reform program. Some were killed with great brutality. Unlike the few local Communists, Formosan leaders had had little or no experience in the arts of escape and concealment. Some managed to remain at large briefly, hiding in the outlying villages or skulking in the hills, and a few managed to leave the island. The majority, however, were captured promptly.

Wang Tien-teng, Chairman of the Committee, is believed to have been executed on March 13. Tan Gim, Columbia University graduate, banker, and head of a large Trust Company, was taken from a sickbed and done away with. The *Min Pao* editor, Lin Mou-sheng, another Columbia University graduate and former professor of the English and German languages, was dragged naked into the night and not heard of again. Gan Kin-en, owner and director of important mining interests, was seized and killed.

One Committee member, Huang Chao-chin, not only emerged unscathed from the "2–28 Incident," but greatly enriched as well. He was made Chairman of the Board of Directors of the First Commercial Bank of Taiwan, he remained Speaker of the Taiwan Provincial Assembly and became a member of the Central Committee of the Nationalist Party. He had acquired an almost professional status as the "representative Formosan" whose views all visiting Americans must hear. He would be an asset for days and years to come explaining away the "Incident.'

On March 11 I was informed by a most reliable Formosan source that while the Settlement Committee was intensively busy in the preceding week, a substantial number of younger men had concluded it was hopeless to treat with Chen Yi, and had begun to develop an underground organization. When the troops began to land on Saturday night these youths were much better prepared to escape. While the more conservative older leaders were being captured, tortured and killed about town, the more determined resistance group leaders managed to go into hiding and ultimately escaped to Hong Kong, Shanghai or Japan, where they had developed contacts.

After the Committeemen on Chen Yi's vengeance lists came members of the youth organizations — the Loyal Service Corps, the students and teachers who had volunteered to take over policing duties when the mainland Chinese abandoned their posts on March 1.

A systematic search was made, based on the Service Corps enlistment rolls. If a student could not be found at once, either a member of his family was seized or a fellow student was taken to serve as hostage or as a substitute in death. Orders were issued requiring that all weapons be turned in, with a deadline for compliance. But simultaneously orders of equal weight were issued which forbade anyone to carry a weapon in the streets. How, then, was a young man in good faith to comply with these contradictory orders? If the house-search revealed a weapon, the entire household might suffer disastrously, and certainly the responsible youth would be shot. But if he were discovered in the streets on his way to turn in the weapons which had been issued to him by the Service Corps, he was equally certain to be liquidated.

After three days of random shooting and bayonetting in the Taipei streets the Government forces began to push out into suburban and rural areas. Machine-gun squads, mounted on trucks, were driven along the highroads for fifteen or twenty miles, shooting at random in village streets in an effort to break any spirit of resistance that might still be present, and to prepare the way for house-to-house search. The manhunt spread through all the hills back of Taipei.

By March 17 the pattern of terror and revenge had emerged very clearly. First to be destroyed were all established critics of the Government. Then in their turn came Settlement Committee members and their principal aides, all youths who had taken part in the interim policing of Taipei, middle school students, middle school teachers, lawyers, economic leaders and members of influential families, and at last, anyone who in the preceding eighteen months had given offense to a mainland Chinese, causing him to "lose face." On March 16 it was reported that anyone who spoke English reasonably well, or who had had close foreign connections, was being seized for "examination."

Many mainland Chinese at Taipei were of course shocked by the brutality of this campaign, but few were surprised. One prominent person, visibly moved, told me that he had witnessed the notorious "Rape of Nanking" by the Japanese in 1937, but that this surpassed it, for the Nanking rape was a product of war, a wild outburst of wartime passion, whereas this was coldly calculated revenge, perpetrated by the Nationalist Government upon its own people.

The Nationalist Government would like to have the world forget the March Massacres. Prominent Nationalist officials have since then continued to brush aside the subject as the creation of propagandists — Communists, of course — forgetting that there were foreign witnesses in every part of the island.

Chen Yi's vindictive pursuit of students repeated his earlier behavior in Fukien Province, where he perpetrated similar barbarities. The mainland Chinese normally revealed a dread of any confrontation with the Japanese *or with forces efficiently trained by the Japanese.* In the student body on Formosa the Nationalists faced not only hot-headed youth who were potential leaders in the community (such as the Fukien students had been) but a large corps of students who had actually had years of drill and orderly training under Japanese instruction. This was a double threat. Basically, too, the leaders in Chen Yi's generation of military men were — and are — fundamentally anti-intellectual. The ignorant warlord mistrusts the "clever" intellectual.

We saw students tied together, being driven to the execution grounds, usually along the river banks and ditches about Taipei, or at the waterfront in Keelung. One foreigner counted more than thirty young bodies — in student uniforms — lying along the roadside east of Taipei; they had had their noses and ears slit or hacked off, and many had been castrated. Two students were beheaded near my front gate. Bodies lay unclaimed on the roadside embankment near the Mission compound.

If searchers, with student lists in hand, could not find a wanted boy at home, some member of his family — a father, grandfather or brother — would be seized and dragged off. Families were too terrified to make a wide search for missing members, or too confused to know where their bodies might be found.

Fifty students were reported to have been killed at Sungshan and thirty at Peito on the night of March 9. By March 13 I was brought a report (which I considered reliable) that more than 700 students had been seized in Taipei in the preceding five days.

The UNRRA Accounts Officer (a stouthearted New Zealand girl, Miss Louise Tomsett) visited Taipei, Keelung and Tamsui, and reported on conditions at Peitou, site of the UNRRA residence:

> I did not get into Taipei until Tuesday . . . to the Office, and then called at the MacKay Hospital . . . Everywhere I was told tales of looting, shooting, murder and rape, and [I saw] trucks loaded with heavily armed soldiery and bearing mounted machine guns patrolling the city. Then it was decided that it may become necessary to leave the island and I was asked to . . . see the British Consul, [Geoffrey Tingle, at Tamsui] and find out if we could leave heavy baggage in store there. Jim Woodruff drove me down . . .
>
> That same evening Hokuto [Peitou] seemed to have been raided, and heavy firing went on for thirty minutes, and afterwards Chinese soldiers searched the roads and bush systematically up past [the UNRRA hostel]. Large numbers of Taiwanese were on the move up to the hills and on a few walks I took

I found many people living out in caves. One man explained
that soldiers had shot his father so he had brought his family
up to relative safety away from the town. Apparently the soldiers did hunt some refugees out, as often — especially at
night — short bursts of firing could be heard.

Towards the end of the week I made one trip to Keelung —
buildings had been damaged and Taiwanese I spoke to told
stories of wholesale shooting and looting. I did see Chinese
police drag in the bodies of two men who had been shot, and
Taiwanese standing about told me that very many bodies had
been taken from the Harbor over the past week.[5]

For days the dead continued to be washed up in Keelung
Harbor. The wharves and narrow beaches were a favored execution ground. Ignorant Nationalist soldiery apparently expected the tides to remove the bodies, but they merely floated
about in the tidal currents within an enclosed port area. Foreigners observed small boats searching the harbor, towing
bodies in where grief-stricken families waited to search for
missing sons and brothers. Estimates varied of the number
killed at Keelung alone in these few days, but the lowest figure
placed the total about 300, and there is no reason to doubt this
as a minimum figure.

On one occasion as he drove into Taipei Dr. Hirschy of the
UNRRA staff saw a wounded man lying in the road, pleading
for help. Although it was forbidden to stop while moving into
the city, he and his aide took the chance. A Chinese officer and
his men stood nearby. Hirschy asked for permission to carry
the man into the hospital. The officer refused, but to save face
promised to have the man sent in at once. Six hours later, when
the doctor returned that way, the Formosan was still there,
dead.

On March 10 the Acting Director of UNRRA (a Frenchman,
M. Paul Clement) went on business to the Nationalist Army
Headquarters at Taipei and there in the inner courtyards
counted fifteen well-dressed Formosans, bound, kneeling, and

with necks bared, awaiting execution. At the other end of the island Mr. Allen Shackleton of New Zealand went to the local Garrison Headquarters at Kaohsiung to try to negotiate a truce of some sort in the midst of most atrocious acts of revenge and retaliation. General Peng Meng-chi was the Garrison Commander. In the grounds of the Headquarters Shackleton recognized a Formosan friend — a moderate leader who had done all that he could to *prevent* the outbreak of trouble between local Formosans and mainland Chinese, but now held as a "rebel." His crime, of course, was the fact that he was a prominent local leader who carried influence in the Kaohsiung community. Shackleton and his interpreter saw that he was cruelly trussed up. Sharp wires were twisted about his neck so that his head had to be held at an excruciating angle; when he tried to move, he was clipped under the nose by the bayonet of his guard. Obviously he was doomed.

The atrocities perpetrated at Kaohsiung were (if possible) even more revolting than the mass executions and torture used at Taipei to rid the Government of its most outspoken critics. For this General Peng Meng-chi is held responsible. The Generalissimo has since made him Commander-in-Chief of the Chinese Nationalist Army, but throughout Formosa he is still spoken of in secret as "The Butcher of Kaohsiung."

Late in the week of March 10 we began to note that the revenge motif had become general. Any Formosan who had caused any newcomer severe loss of face in the preceding eighteen months was now fair game, if the offended mainland Chinese could persuade a soldier or gendarme or a policeman to take action. Any government officer who held a grudge could be revenged.

On March 15 there came to me the wife and two infant children of one of my former students, a friend who had given offense early in 1946 by attempting to expose a case of corruption in a Government office. He had not played a prominent part in the activities of the Settlement Committee, for he knew he was a marked man in any case. Now as he was seized and carried off to oblivion he sent his small family to the American Consulate, certain that they would find protection. They had to be turned away.

The public prosecutor — a Formosan — who had directed proceedings against mainland police officers guilty of murder in Taichung in 1946, was now seized at Taipei by the convicts themselves, who had been released after March 8. The prosecutor was killed. The Formosan judge who had sat in this case was dragged from the Court offices and was reported to have been killed. The prominent doctor who had criticized the Tainan City mayor in a dramatic confrontation was slaughtered.

As the terror proceeded, even these tenuous involvements with the Government were no longer needed to "justify" vengeful murder. The Formosan lawyer who had won acquittal for the Japanese gynecologist Dr. Mukai in late 1945 was now seized and shot. At Keelung a minor employee of the Taiwan Navigation Company (an accountant), was taken out to the street in front of the offices and there shot before his assembled office colleagues; he had offended the Manager — an influential mainland Chinese — late in 1945 when he laughed and criticized the Manager's blundering attempts to drive an automobile.

At Kaohsiung there were incidents in which the victims' families were forced to witness cruel executions in the public streets. The nights in Taipei were made grim with the sounds of shooting, of screams, and occasionally of pleas for mercy heard as victims were driven along dark streets by the soldiery.

There were many instances wherein men threatened with death were able to buy survival or freedom. One Formosan who had exposed a twenty million yen peculation in the Government management of Textile Company accounts was seized but released when his father interceded with Pao Ko-yung, Commissioner of Mining and Industry, on the grounds that the son had once done Pao a favor, but such cases of favorable intervention were rare.

At Tamsui the British Consul and his staff observed the beginning of the terror in that seaside town. Several men were executed near the Consulate garden. A father reported that his son — a middle school boy — had been killed, and two of his companions badly wounded by a roving patrol. When the father sent an older son to recover the body, that son was seized, and neither he nor his brother's body were released to the father until he had paid over TY 3000 to the Nationalist soldiers who now controlled the town.

Doctors and nurses working at hospitals and emergency stations heard countless stories, and had bloody evidence of their truth lying before them. The Chief Medical Officer for UNRRA wrote later:

> Boys were shot down from bicycles as they rode. One man who was sitting in his home reading his evening newspaper had his money, watch and a ring removed from his person by soldiers who entered his home, and then shot him through the back. The next morning as he was being carried in a stretcher to the hospital by his family, they were shot at, even as they entered the front door of the hospital — a Canadian Mission hospital . . . A working man returning home was confronted by soldiers who had him raise his hands, then searched his person. Not finding any money they ran a bayonet through his leg; then as he fell to the ground they demanded that he stand up, which he could not do. So they shot him in the head and departed. But they only shot off his ear and he was able to tell of his experiences the next day in the hospital ward. Governor Chen Yi announced over the radio that everything was at peace again, and asked all Formosans to open their shops and resume work. The next morning a half-dozen Formosans were pushing a cart of fish to market when Chinese troops opened fire on them from the roadside, killing some and wounding others.
>
> In the city of Pintung where the inauguration of the brief people's rule was marked by the playing of the Star Spangled Banner on phonographs, the entire group of about 45 Formosans who were carrying on various phases of local government

were taken out to a nearby airfield from which, later, a series of shots were heard. A Formosan who, representing the families of these people, went to the military commander to intercede for their lives, was taken to the public square and, after his wife and children had been called to witness the event, he was beheaded as an example to the rest of the people not to meddle in affairs which did not concern them.[6]

He told of circumstances at Gilam, southeast of Keelung, where during the uprising the Chinese Mayor, his officials, and all local Chinese police and military personnel retired to a mountain hideout. In their absence the leading citizens carried on public affairs. A Formosan doctor — a surgeon and director of the local hospital which had been rehabilitated by UNRRA — took a leading role in the Citizens Committee established to govern the community in the absence of all mainland official-dom. But when Chiang's troops came in, the (Chinese) Mayor and his men came out of hiding. Scores of local citizens were arrested. The director of the hospital, another doctor, five lead-ing Committee colleagues, and more than one hundred "ordi-nary" Formosans were then executed.

To the last there was expectation that surely the United States would intervene, at Nanking or on the island, to stay the Generalissimo's revenge. Many UNRRA staff members re-ported this continuing hope born of desperation, and I shall not forget the wordless appeal in the eyes of four well-dressed young men who passed my gate and my protective American flag at midday on March 13. They were tied together by ropes attached to wires twisted about their necks, their arms were bound, and they were being hurried along toward the execution place on the banks of the Keelung River nearby. The ragged Nationalist soldier prodding them along at bayonet point saw the American flag on my jeep, and gave me the smartest salute he could manage. Here was the betrayal in its most simple terms; the Formosans looked to us for help, we armed and financed the Nationalists, and the Nationalists were making sure, if they could, that there would be no more appeals to the United States and "democracy."

Before we review the American position in this bloody affair, we must take note of Chiang Kai-shek's own "solution."

The Generalissimo's View of the Affair on Formosa

If there were any Formosans who still retained lingering trust in the Central Government, they were about to be disillusioned.

On March 10 at Nanking (less than two full days after the troops reached Formosa) the Generalissimo rose before members of the weekly Memorial Service (a Monday affair throughout the country) to defend Chen Yi and other members of the Government from public criticism. As usual he labelled all critics of his administration as "Communists." Here is the text:

Inasmuch as the cause of the unfortunate Incident which has occurred in Taiwan has been reported in various newspapers, I need not explain the details here. As a matter of fact, ever since Taiwan was reinstated last year, in view of the good public order in the Province, the Central Government has not chosen to send and station a large number of regular forces there. The maintenance of public order has been entrusted entirely to minor gendarme and police detachments.

For the last year our Taiwanese brethren in agricultural, commercial, and educational pursuits have sincerely expressed their law-abiding spirit and their support of the Central Government. Their patriotism and spirit of self-respect have never been less passionate than that of our brethren in any other province.

Recently, however, some Taiwanese who had formerly been conscripted and sent to the South Seas area by the Japanese and had engaged in the war, some of whom were communists, took advantage of the trouble incidental to the Monopoly Bureau's attempt to control cigarette stall-keepers and agitated the public. Thus they created a riot and submitted a request for the reformation of the government.

As the National Constitution is soon to be endorsed and, further, the administration of Taiwan ought to be put back on its normal lines as soon as possible, the Central Government has decided to grant as much authority to local governments as they are entitled to enjoy in accordance with the stipulations of the Constitution. Governor General Chen has already declared in compliance with instructions from the Central Government that the Government General of Taiwan should be converted into a regular provincial administration at a certain time in the future, and that the popular election of prefectural magistrates would be held within a certain period. All Taiwanese were very glad to accept this declaration. Therefore, the unfortunate Incident has already been settled. But unexpectedly the so-called Committee for Settlement of the February 28th Incident in Taiwan suddenly made impossible proposals which included the request that the Taiwan Garrison Command should be eliminated, that arms should be surrendered to the Committee for safe-keeping, and that Army and Navy personnel in Taiwan should all be Taiwanese. The Central Government naturally cannot consent to such requests which exceed the province of local authority. Moreover violent actions such as attacking government agencies were committed yesterday [March 9].

Therefore the Central Government decided to send troops to Taiwan for the purpose of maintaining public peace and order there. According to reports we have received, the troops have already safely landed in good order in Keelung yesterday evening. I believe that normal conditions can be recovered before long. At the same time, high officials are to be sent there in order to help Governor Chen in settling this Incident.

I have also strictly ordered the military and administrative personnel in Taiwan to calmly await the arrival of officials to be sent from the Central Government for the purpose of settling the Incident, and not to resort to any revenge action, so that our Taiwan brethren may be amicably united and cooperate.

I hope that every Taiwanese will fully recognize his duty to our fatherland and strictly observe discipline so as not to be utilized by treacherous gangs and laughed at by the Japanese. I hope Taiwanese will refrain from rash and thoughtless acts which will be harmful not only to our country but also to themselves. I hope they will be thoroughly determined to discriminate between loyalty and treason, and to discern between advantage and disadvantage; and that they will voluntarily cancel their illegal organizations and recover public peace and order, so that every Taiwanese can lead a peaceful and happy life as soon as possible, and thus complete the construction of the new Taiwan.

Thus only can Taiwanese be free from the debt they owe to the entire nation which has undergone so many sacrifices and bitter struggles for the last fifty years in order to recover Taiwan." [7]

This soothing statement, full of fatherly reproof and advice, was printed up in leaflet form and dropped over the principal cities of Formosa on March 12. This was the end, so far as the Formosans were concerned. So long as Chiang Kai-shek, his family, or his Party and Army govern Formosa, this "betrayal" will not be forgotten nor forgiven.

Obviously Chiang's remarks were not prepared for the Formosans (he could not care less what they might think, now that his troops were firmly in control) but for the public at Nanking, and for the historical record — the wonderful Chinese historical record of benevolent acts piously undertaken by paternal government and carefully set down for posterity to admire.

The body of his statement presented the official view of the Incident, made for the record. His commentary thereon revealed much of the Generalissimo's own character and conception of himself as Leader. Criticism of the Party administration is "treachery" and treason justifies the most harsh punishment. "Thoughtless acts" probably refers to appeals to the United States and the United Nations which might "be harmful to our country." And then there is the problem of "face" and of revenge for loss of it. Chiang could not bear to be "laughed at by the Japanese," and he knew the capacity of his own armed forces for revenge. This element of revenge for loss of face runs through all of the tragic story of Formosa after March 9.

We may never have accurate figures for the loss of life in the succeeding weeks, months and years. Each side exaggerated its losses in order to place the other in the worst possible light. It must be assumed that the bodies of hundreds were never recovered or identified. But by considering all the claims and the eyewitness accounts brought in by foreigners from every part of the island, we may reach an approximation. The mainland Chinese claims at that time ranged from a minimum figure of 30 to "more than 100" mainland Chinese killed. Many were beaten but not badly injured during the first few days of March.

Formosan leaders in exile charge that more than 10,000 were slaughtered in the month of March. I must assume that there could not have been less than 5000 and I am inclined to accept the higher figure. If we add to this the thousands who have been seized and done away with since March, 1947, on the pretext that they were involved in the affair, the number may reach the 20,000 figure often given by Formosan writers.

The Government has never relaxed its vengeful search; any "undesirable" can be picked up in 1965, charged with participation in the 1947 rebellion, and sent off to the notorious prison camp on Green Island (Lu Tao). According to the Chinese, it is used especially for the "Communist-inspired traitors" who sought external aid and intervention at that time of crisis.

XV

The Aftermath

The American Position at Taipei

SIX YOUNG FORMOSANS had appeared at the Consulate on March 8 to offer service as "guards." They lived far from Taipei, but they had heard that we were in danger. We had never heard of them before, but now discovered that they were members of an association of repatriated labor conscripts who had been captured in the Philippines, interned as POW's, and then sent home. They said they wanted to "repay American generosity."

But "This is China now" and I had no choice but to urge them to return at once to their homes in the distant countryside. We learned later that they suffered heavily for having shown readiness to help the Consulate at this time of crisis.

We were all in a most awkward position. As "official bodies" we were expected to deal only with members of Chen Yi's administration, but most of us found it difficult to be even coldly civil. The majority of the UNRRA Team members, too, found it repugnant to resume working relations with Chen Yi's men.

The foreign community had nothing whatsoever to fear from the Formosan people, but as the Chinese Nationalists came ashore on March 8 we were in some jeopardy. We had — officially — ignored the Government's anti-foreign campaign but we could not know in what degree the Formosans might resist incoming troops nor how far we might be drawn into a violent

crisis. Would we, for instance, give asylum to Formosan leaders if they came to us or would we — officially — deem that an
interference in a domestic Chinese quarrel? We had much
more to fear from the incoming Nationalist troops than we had
to fear from the island people. It was therefore agreed with the
British Consulate and the UNRRA group that we should be
prepared to evacuate the foreign population if need be. We
asked the American Embassy at Nanking to be ready for a crisis
message.

On Monday, March 10, an Embassy Attaché flew in to look
the situation over. At Taipei all Formosan eyes were on him.
Was America about to intervene at last? Would the Ambassador protest to the Generalissimo?

The American colonel, in full uniform and decorations, arrived on a Chinese Nationalist Air Force plane. An impressive
escort of high-ranking Chinese officers greeted him, piled him
into a jeep, and took him on a long tour of the city with a Nationalist military escort. He received the Nationalist salutes
smartly offered him here and there across town before he was
driven to the Governor's Office for what he believed to be a
routine courtesy call.

General Chen clearly indicated that he thought the uprising
a "blessing in disguise"; now he knew where everyone stood.
The colonel told me later that he drew then the conclusion that
Chen's opponents were doomed.

The local radio and press — now limited to one government
paper — reported the colonel's interview with Chen indicating
that an American "investigator" approved the Government's
measures and believed the local problem settled. Again it had
been demonstrated to the Formosans how easily visiting foreigners could be misled.

Meanwhile we had assumed that the visiting Attaché would
desire an opportunity to discuss the situation at the Consulate.
The Information Officer's wife prepared a luncheon for the
consular officers and the colonel. But quite unexpectedly and

without her consent the invitation was enlarged to include several of Chen Yi's aides, making certain that Chen understood where official American sympathies lay. There would be no Chinese criticism to taint the records at Nanking. On this, our hostess quietly refused to greet or to sit with the unwanted members of the party. The revolting cruelties which we had witnessed at our gate on the previous day were still too much with her.

That afternoon the colonel flew back to Nanking with his Chinese Air Force escorts. He had seen exactly what they wanted him to see. The Embassy at Nanking was certainly not much wiser in the event, but perhaps it did not matter.*

Settling the Incident, Nationalist Party Style

Control of information was of course a key to the management of this crisis. The outspoken *Min Pao* press plant was destroyed by repeated raids on March 11 and 12. On March 13 it was announced that all but two papers were banned because they had published accounts of the February Incident and of the Settlement Committee's activities, thereby embarrassing the Government.

At Shanghai on March 11 members of the Formosan Democratic League published demands that the United Nations establish a mandate in Formosa. The Minister of Information at Nanking (Peng Hsueh-pei) promptly branded the Formosan people "irresponsible and undisciplined," but noted that China would be lenient. This was not enough to silence mainland critics. The Shanghai press was filled with scathing condemna-

---

* I later learned from the colonel that he had not been sufficiently briefed on the gravity of the affair at Taipei, that his orders came to him too suddenly to retrieve his civilian clothes from the cleaners, and that the offer of transport by the Chinese Air Force was made in a manner which could not be turned down without awkward embarrassment. He had, in effect, been trapped into this compromising situation and regretted it.

tion of the affair, but none of it was reported in the Formosan papers. Major General Mao Ng-chang, former Director of the Intelligence Office of the Fukien Pacification Headquarters (hence presumably an old associate of Chen Yi) was appointed General Manager of the Government paper at Taipei, the *Hsin Sheng Pao*.

On March 14 it was announced that a general census would soon be taken. There was to be a thorough house-to-house search throughout the province. It was also learned that on this day the Government had begun examining Japanese remaining in the island. The majority were there at Government request or by Government order, but apparently many rumors had reached Taipei saying that "hundreds" of Japanese had suddenly come out of hiding in the hills and were now assisting Formosans in resisting mainland troops. These rumors were quite without foundation, but reflected clearly the nervous dread in which mainland Chinese faced any suggestion that a "Japanese element" might have to be overcome. They dreaded the element of discipline which the Japanese had introduced into Formosa.

It was now also announced that General Pai Chung-hsi, the Minister of National Defense, would be sent to Formosa to "hear the people" and assist General Chen Yi in settling the crisis.

General Pai reached Taipei on March 17, and at once issued a proclamation, urging the Formosans to "appreciate Generalissimo Chiang's love for the Formosan people" and to "preserve their law-abiding virtues."

The visiting General was lavishly entertained, taken on tour, and quoted in the press. He was deeply impressed, he said, by the progress which had been made on Formosa since the surrender; he thought the Taipei Zoological Garden a most remarkable place; he managed occasionally to imply that he thought the Formosans a poor lot, tainted by the Japanese, and unable to appreciate the blessings of reunion with the Homeland. On March 29 Pai broadcast a general report, leading off with a statement that during the Incident there had been 440 Army casualties, but that a total of only 1860 Formosan Chinese and mainland Chinese had been killed or injured. The remote causes of the rebellion were three, he thought; the Japanese had trained Formosans to dislike mainland Chinese, the island was spoiled by the presence of Formosan riff-raff schooled by Japan to be tools of aggression in China proper, and there was an "unavoidable" decline in the Formosan economy, causing unemployment. There were four immediate causes of the riots; the current monopolies had something to do with the decline of the economy, too many Formosan Chinese had been barred from office because of their incompetence, a few corrupt, inefficient Chinese officials had come into the island, and there were Communists about.

His "whitewashing" duties done, General Pai flew back to the mainland.

Meanwhile the mainland Chinese on Formosa were extremely uneasy. Some fifty thousand troops were reported to have come in to join thirty thousand who had been present on March 1. It was apparent to many foreigners that the mainland civilians were as afraid of their own undisciplined troops as they were of the rioting Formosans. To offset this and to "restore confidence," two misbehaving Nationalist soldiers were executed publicly, a gesture to demonstrate the "sincerity" of Party and Government.

But on Monday, March 24, seventy Formosans were executed at Chia-yi. It had become evident that Governor Chen was being given time in which to have his revenge, and was making good use of it.

Meanwhile even Chiang Kai-shek had to realize the public opinion throughout China proper was deeply aroused by events in Formosa. This was too close a parallel to the situation in Fukien under Chen Yi in the 1930's. In this present instance, China's foreign interests were involved; foreigners had witnessed the affair, and China's legal position in the island was by no means as firm as the Government pretended it to be.

Late in March the Nanking Government notified the mainland press that the Taiwan Incident was officially closed, and that rebels, gangsters, and Communists had been suppressed, hence the affair should no longer be discussed.

The Central Executive Committee of the Nationalist Party on March 22 adopted a resolution, by overwhelming majority, which censured Chen Yi and demanded his dismissal. Such a resolution was usually considered mandatory in all cases where the Generalissimo's personal interests were not deeply involved.

The Party Leader Chiang faced a dilemma, for Chen was a Chekiang general to whom he owed a great debt; the national interest called for action; Chen was identified with the so-called Political Science Clique which was supposed to be a "reform" group; and the United States Government, awkwardly enough, was demanding "reform" as a condition for even considering a new loan of half a billion U.S. dollars.

Chen was told to yield. On March 28 he offered his resignation as Governor of Taiwan. In order to "save his face" the Generalissimo did not formally accept the resignation until March 31, suggesting that Chen was not dismissed out of hand, and that the resignation was accepted with great reluctance.

Chinese Press Notices and Propaganda in the United States

The Newton stories in 1946 had alarmed the Nationalists. The propaganda agency at Taipei was developed thereafter as an agency for propaganda or "public relations" organizations subsidized by the Nationalist regime in the United States. Taipei was kept informed of all overseas press or radio notices (few enough) and of the general American reaction to events, personalities, and issues concerning China. The Governor's office in turn controlled all outgoing radio and cable dispatches, and routine "news releases."

One "pre-Incident" sample may suffice. In late December, 1946, as I prepared my gloomy predictions of impending violence on Formosa, Stanway Cheng's office nearby was preparing something of a cheerier nature. In January, 1947, the China News Service (a registered agency of the Chinese Government) released in the United States a four-page broadside which began in this vein:

REHABILITATION IN FORMOSA 80% COMPLETED
ONE YEAR AFTER CHINESE HAVE TAKEN OVER

After a week's visit in Formosa last October, President Chiang Kai-shek announced with considerable satisfaction that one year after its liberation 80% of the island's rehabilitation program had already been accomplished . . .[1]

At the moment this was released in the United States by the Governor's men, the Formosan economy, in terms of value and quantity of production related to total population, had reached the lowest point in some forty years.

Distortion of news sent from Taipei during and after the February Incident has been noted; a New Zealand member of the UNRRA group observed how smoothly handled this was — a credit to the School of Journalism which had produced the Information Service Director, if not exactly a great credit to the gullibility of the American public. As she wrote: "Each night [during the massacre] we listened to broadcasts from China and to one in particular from San Francisco, where the riots were mentioned and dismissed by China as terrorist and Japanese-inspired uprisings against lawful authority and the benign rule of China . . ."

In late March, while the bloody reprisals were at their height and the island was paralyzed by fear, an official of the United

States Department of Agriculture made his general observations known to the American press at Washington. He had just returned from an official survey mission, undertaken jointly by representatives of the State, War, and Navy Departments in cooperation with the Department of Agriculture. It was presumed that the Mission's recommendations would substantially affect the American aid program in Asia. Under the heading "Taiwan Seen as Bright Spot in the Far Eastern Food Picture," he was quoted at length. The fine statistics handed to him in Taipei showed that Formosa would export 350,000 tons of sugar in 1947. This pleased him, but someone had failed to tell him that in the best years the island had produced more than 1,400,000 tons of sugar, or that in the first year under Nationalist control the output was less than 30,000 tons, and might fall below that in 1947.*

The American food expert then continued:

> The most constructive efforts I saw in Chinese areas that I visited were going on in Formosa . . . There may have been disorders there recently, but it seems that the Chinese Government has sent some of its most efficient administrators to the Island. Being separated from the uncertainties of the Chinese mainland, the island was making distinct progress.[2]

On April 6 the China News Service handed to the American press a report of General Pai Chung-hsi's promises that there would be sweeping reform in Formosa. A month later the subject was referred to again under the heading "New Deal for Taiwan." Here is the official version of the March affair prepared at Taipei and released in San Francisco:

> General Pai also urged protection of the innocent, leniency to the rioters, and justice in the trial of the ringleaders. These

---

* The 350,000-ton figure — if it had any relation to realities — apparently referred to the pre-surrender sugar stockpiles which the Chinese were shipping out as rapidly as possible.

were conciliatory measures indeed, when one remembers that the islanders in their riots had killed and wounded over 1,660 government officials and their families, inflicted 440 casualties on the garrison forces, and had attempted to seize the island's government by force.

The riots seemed premeditated and well-organized. Fighting first broke out on February 28, raged on till March 4 when it spread to the entire island . . .

Fighting flared up again on March 8 when the rebels besieged government offices in the capital Taipei. A Central Yuan Commissioner sent to investigate the disturbances was ambushed. Chinese troops had to restore order, and in their efforts to bring the hostilities to a halt, had used rather stern measures during the first two days.

Foreign witnesses agree that native rabble-rousers had been busy fanning hostilities among the people against Chinese rule for some time, and as General Pai pointed out, the fifty years of Japanese education plus the activities of the Communist elements have further fostered their antipathy toward the Chinese.[3]

For some months after the March affair there appeared news notes and commentaries in the American press — especially on the West Coast — as correspondents in Hong Kong, Shanghai, Nanking, and Tokyo picked up stories from refugees and from UNRRA staff members leaving Formosa. For example, the *Portland Oregonian* (September 10) carried a story entitled "Corruption in Formosa Returns with Chinese." Under a caption reading "Chinese Rule of Formosa Held as Bad as Japs; People Demand U.S. Put in a Protest," the *Seattle Times* (November 15) noted, "one educated Formosan explained the sovereignty problem this way: 'I don't regard myself as a Chinese, even though China was our Mother Country. I am a Formosan.'"

At Taipei, however, the commentaries prepared in the Governor's office by an American-trained Chinese journalist, took on a vicious anti-American tone, venting a Chinese intellectual's reaction to American patronage. The propaganda which poured forth immediately after the March affair was exceedingly bitter and oddly enough some of it was printed in English. One example written with an attempt at heavy sarcasm, will suffice:

> The visit of two local [i.e. Shanghai] American newspaper-men [Tillman Durdin and Christopher Rand] to Formosa has been followed, as expected, by an outcry in the United States clamouring for the permanent separation of this island from China under American "trusteeship."
>
> In a typical and vivid editorial the influential *Washington Post* has described the Chinese administration in Formosa as a regime of unbridled brutality and "lust."
>
> It seems idle to answer these criminal and irresponsible charges against the long-suffering Chinese people. The coin of international and national morality has recently been much debased by America, and it is apparent to most people that the morality of the United States and the morality of the civilized races of the world are poles apart . . . Glib and complacent in that smug, debased international morality, of which America has become a byword, these "liberal" American newspapermen have conveniently forgotten that: (a) the economic handicaps under which Formosa is laboring were largely the inevitable consequences of the American bombing and destruction of factories, plantations, and communications . . .
>
> America, of course, does not owe any moral obligation whatsoever toward the Formosans (unless under a trusteeship), and positively insists that China fulfills her obligations for the damage for which the United States war machine was primarily instrumental . . .[4]

The Situation in the American Embassy, Nanking

I was ordered to report to the Ambassador. On March 17 General Pai Chung-hsi's plane taxied in at Sungshan field just as the Embassy plane prepared to leave for Nanking. General Pai was

welcomed with military bands and banners, but my reception
at Nanking was rather more subdued. A senior Embassy Secretary met me at planeside and bundled me off to an Embassy
guest-house. By mid-morning next day it was clearly apparent
that I had walked straight through the Looking-Glass, and was
not very welcome in some quarters beyond it; some members of
the Embassy Secretariat wanted to bury the embarrassing Formosan situation under as many papers as possible, others
wanted to have it aired and publicized to bring added pressure
to bear upon Chiang. And there were some important members
of the Embassy who seemed not quite sure where "Taiwan"
was. Obviously our reports from Taipei in 1946 had not carried
much weight; from the Embassy at Nanking the island seemed
far distant from the continental war front, and our Consul himself had consistently played down the gravity of events preceding the fatal clash.

Dr. Stuart had returned from a YMCA speaking tour to resume Embassy business. I had been his guest, briefly, at Yen-
ching University in Peking before the war, and now resumed our
acquaintance with a long review of the situation in Formosa.
He would like to have a well-documented written report, he
said, upon which to base further conversations with Chiang. I
received permission to consult the Embassy copies of my earlier
Taipei reports.

But first I made a round of courtesy calls. I was introduced
to the Military Attaché, who led off by observing that "since
the Nationalist soldiers had arrived, there would probably be
no further need to consider evacuation of American residents."
He brushed aside my comment that it was *because* of their arrival that we had considered evacuation. I was then subjected
to questions that seemed rather wide of the mark. For example,
"What about that large area on the south of the island which
the Communists have held since surrender?" I explained that
there was no "large area in the hands of Communists," and that
there were very few Communists on Formosa. I was bluntly

contradicted; his reports showed, the General said, that a large area had been held by Communists since the war. Again I observed that there was no such area on the island, that UNRRA representatives had worked in every part of Formosa, and that I myself had been everywhere since 1945. There was a long silence and a long, cold stare; then the General without further words turned back to his deskwork.

As I withdrew, wondering if I had suddenly become an "agrarian reformer," my companion, an assistant military attaché wondered *sotto voce* if just perhaps the General had confused the Island of Taiwan with the Island of Hainan, where indeed, the Communists held a large area. We agreed that it was just as well the Military Attaché had not sent a rescue plane to Hainan, hundreds of miles away, while we were being butchered, perhaps, by the Nationalists on Formosa.

In conversation I found the Ambassador full of sympathy for the Formosans, but also full of continuing trust in his friend Chiang Kai-shek. One day he noticed a copy of Theodore White's newly published volume *Thunder Out of China* in my hand, and said, shaking his head sadly, "These younger men do not understand the Generalissimo. They should — they *must* — give him just a little more time . . . a little more time . . . !" I promptly thought of the hundreds of young Formosans whose time had run out in the week of March 8. But here was the old, old missionary dream again — if we could just convert the Emperor, all of China would be saved.

In the course of the week's work on my Memorandum for Dr. Stuart I discovered that the Ambassador's private secretary was not an American citizen, but a national of the country to which the Ambassador was accredited. This circumstance may have no parallel in American diplomatic history. He was a man answerable to the Generalissimo and not to the American Government. Was he privy to the most secret papers crossing the Ambassador's desk? Had he seen my secret reports listing the names of leading Formosans who had come to us asking for help? Certainly they had been the first ones sought out and killed when the Nationalist troops came in.*

In discussing Formosa with Dr. Stuart, Chiang professed not to know details of the affair which I had reported to the Ambassador. He therefore invited Dr. Stuart to place in his hands a written account. My long résumé was therefore edited to become a "State paper." Some references to the American Consulate and to Formosan trust in the United States and the United Nations were removed in order not to inflame Chiang's well-known anti-foreign prejudices. Many qualifying diplomatic phrases were introduced ("It appeared to be . . . ," "It was alleged that . . .") in order to save the Generalissimo's face. Apparently it would never do to present him with an unvarnished record of the evidence of our own eyes. Quite properly we did not include my review of several possible alternative courses which lay ahead. The whole was translated into Chinese and in due course handed to Chiang.†

It was my view that if the Central Government wished to regain the confidence of the Formosan people, it would have to withdraw the punitive force, put an end immediately to venge-

---

* Dr. Stuart himself demonstrated the vulnerability of this strange situation in a report to the Secretary of State (Marshall) prepared at Nanking August 27, 1947. Lieutenant General Albert Wedemeyer had castigated the Chiang government in searing terms, in Chiang's presence, just before the Wedemeyer Mission left China. Says Stuart "On the evening of August 25 the Generalissimo called Phillip Fugh, the Ambassador's personal secretary, to his residence and quizzed him at some length with regard to the background of the Wedemeyer Mission. He wished to know whether the Ambassador had had any part in its organization or dispatch . . . The Embassy is not aware in detail of how Fugh handled this conversation except that he has informed the Ambassador that he was 'careful' and 'noncommittal'." (Dept. of State: United States Relations with China. Washington, 1949, pp. 825–826.) On Fugh's controversial position see Stuart's memoirs Fifty Years in China (N.Y. 1954), p. 293 and General Wedemeyer's Wedemeyer Reports. (N.Y. 1958) pp. 389–90.

† The English text appears in United States Relations with China, pp. 923–938. The original ran to 54 legal pages. In preparing it I drew heavily upon my December semi-annual political report from Taipei which had been endorsed and forwarded to the Embassy. But in the Embassy files I found also a brief, secret, unnumbered follow-up dispatch from Taipei which said in effect that the Embassy should not take my December predictions of impending crisis too seriously.

ful reprisals, and replace Chen Yi by a civilian Governor. The promised constitution would have to go into effect on Formosa whenever it applied in China proper. Reorganization of the Taipei government would have to take into very careful consideration the issues outlined in the Reform proposals handed by Formosan leaders to Chen Yi on March 7.

I noted that if the Generalissimo continued to support Chen Yi, or continued a harsh and heavy military occupation he might lose Formosa; the legal status of the island might be challenged and China's qualifications as an interim trustee might be called into review by the United Nations. I noted that all Formosan leaders who sought intervention by the United States or the United Nations were very keenly aware of Formosa's unsettled legal status, and would continue to raise the issue at every opportunity.

As for Communism, my comment on our failure to discover any significant Communist leadership or organization, and the universal lack of sympathy or interest in Communist propaganda would of course have been most unwelcome to the Generalissimo, for it contradicted fundamental KMT propaganda used in appeals for American military and economic aid. The American public had been led to believe that "All anti-Chiang critics are *ipso facto* pro-Communist"; in Formosa the facts could not be made to support that propaganda line.

On Formosan relations with China proper the original Memorandum had this to say:

> Until March 8 Formosan leaders showed a desperate eagerness to convince the world, the Central Government and the Generalissimo of their allegiance to China and their desire only to effect a political reform of General Chen's government. The landing of troops and the subsequent ruthless manhunt directed toward every critic of the Governor and his subordinates, despite specific pledges by the highest military authorities, appears to have convinced even the most conservative Formosans that the Central Government is not to be trusted any more than

General Chen's organization. Each act of brutality, each day of military suppression since March 8 has worn away faith, trust, and allegiance to the Generalissimo . . .

It is probable that when no help appears to be forthcoming from America, Formosan resistance leaders will look to the only other power in the Far East for support, and will . . . welcome communist intervention . . .

No area in China is so enthusiastically pro-American as this island, which completes the chain we influence, control, or occupy strategically from the Hokkaido through the Philippines. Its loss to us now by default may cost us heavily if we should need to occupy Formosa in the future.

I listed for the Ambassador seven different forms or degrees of intervention which had been suggested to me by thoughtful Formosans. The first and least promising was the "good offices" approach, in which the Ambassador (as Chiang's friend) would attempt to make sure that the Generalissimo had a true picture of the island crisis and its origin. The most extreme proposal called for creation of a United Nations trusteeship or protectorate. This should be set up for a stated period of time, and subject to review at a reasonable interval before the proposed terminal date, or until a local plebiscite would afford the Formosans themselves an opportunity to determine their permanent status.

Dr. Stuart adopted the mild ineffective "good offices" approach, and undertook that gingerly enough, in order not to offend the Generalissimo. The Ambassador, who favored the appointment of a civilian to succeed Chen Yi, told me that he had recommended T. V. Soong. Soong had declined, and the post would go to the internationally known lawyer and former Ambassador to Washington, Dr. Wei Tao-ming.

Before I left Nanking for Washington, I received the following letter from a former student, dated at Taipei, March 26:

You will get this, I hope, before you leave for America, and perhaps it will carry your mind back to this miserable Taiwan.

It may comfort you to know that Mr. —— is still alive, confined to the M.P. jail, but it is sad to tell you that Mr. ——'s father was seized and killed.

After your departure, every moment and every inch throughout this island, butchery, arrest and despoilment are occurred by the Government Army. Now the center of battle is moved to Musha, Kanshirei, and Koshun aboriginal districts. And after the suppression, to be sure, wholesale butchery, arrest and bribery of largest scale will follow. I can't know my life one second after. Oh! Terrible dark ages! Every people is trembling for fear. And every people hold the same opinion that Taiwan can only be relieved by you, United States.

Please do your best to emancipate this beautiful island from the mouth of those brutal pigs. Don't be deceived by the government's conventional counter-propaganda. Don't forget Taiwan, and please, remember that there are many people here praying fervently for [American help].[5]

Diplomatic Paralysis Sets In

From Nanking I flew to Peking. The Communists were near and a general exodus was taking place among those fortunate enough to have funds and influence to secure transportation. Returning to Shanghai I saw the immense disorder and confusion which had engulfed the old Concessions after foreign controls had been withdrawn. At Tokyo it was evident that the United State Forces had settled in for a long stay on the Western Pacific rim. There could be no question of the confrontation which was about to take place; Communist forces based on the continental landmass were pushing outward and gaining strength, and the United States was getting set in Japan, Okinawa and the Philippines to hold the line, if it could, along the sea frontier. Formosa, it seemed to me, was the Achilles' heel.

I returned to Washington on May 26, and at 5:30 in the afternoon sat down to discuss the Formosa crisis with the Director of the Office of Far Eastern Affairs in the Department of State.

After reviewing the "Incident," I presented my unpopular "imperialist" view. If we wanted to maintain American and United Nations interests along the Western Pacific frontier, Formosa would have to be in friendly hands to complete the chain. At that moment (1947) no one knew how long the Occupation of Japan might continue nor when the Treaty of Peace would be accomplished.

Despite official pronouncements, it was generally but privately conceded in Peking, Nanking, Shanghai and Tokyo that the Generalissimo faced almost certain defeat on the mainland. He had lost the confidence and support of the common people of China and he refused to take the American military advice available to him.

If Chiang were allowed to retreat to Formosa and establish himself there, we would be saddled with an enormous problem. Obviously we would be expected to continue to supply him with arms and economic support. If the Communists grew to giant stature on the mainland we would be committed to supporting a Tom Thumb on Formosa. This might be admissible if Chiang and the Nationalists enjoyed the support of the Formosans, but the March affair had embittered relations with the mainland beyond hope of recovery.

Why not intervene while we had a legal basis for doing so?

Why not insist on a United Nations or Allied administration until the Chinese civil war issues were settled? If we waited until after transfer of sovereignty took place at the Treaty Conference, we would be placed in an immeasurably more difficult position. Keep Chiang and the Nationalists on the mainland, or at least keep them out of Formosa. Give the Formosans the temporary trusteeship they seek; and then, if necessary, let Chiang take refuge there as a private citizen. By all means do not let Chiang lose Formosa as he was then losing the mainland. Why not make Formosa a policing base under Allied or American control, to be held until postwar Asia achieved a degree of political stability?

I was presenting my "imperialist" line of argument for the last time, I thought, in a quasi-official frame of reference. The Director of the Office of Far Eastern Affairs brought the discussion to a close and saw me to the door with remarks to the effect that no one in the United Nations and certainly no one in Washington would ever be interested in Formosa.

If he had added "as a colony," "as a trust territory," or even "as a moral responsibility" he might have been closer to reality. But he was voicing the Department's policy of "no-policy" for the island "Pay no attention to Formosa and there will be no Formosa Problem." Soon enough a policy-guidance directive was to state officially that Washington held Formosa to be "geographically, politically and strategically" part of continental China.

But somewhere in the Department there was a lurking uneasiness. On June 5 (the day of the great Marshall Plan address at Harvard) I was called to the Department and asked to prepare a one-page summary of my views, to be addressed to General Marshall. How could one possibly state the case for a right-about-face in basic policy and as justification, call attention to American vulnerability there and to the desperate Formosan search for help? I came away from that writing chore with an impression that someone in the Department thought it necessary to get these "imperialist" views before General Marshall, but that no career man in the Department wanted to have his name associated with them. My name, entirely unknown to General Marshall or the public, would carry no weight. If he wanted to pursue the subject, he would do so.

There were other tremors of interest, but they soon subsided. Senator Joseph Ball had me to lunch, Ambassador Warren Austin at the United Nations asked me to tell him of the March Affair, but nothing significant came of all this.

While going in and out of the State Department on these

empty errands I made the rounds of other Government offices which had become concerned with Formosa during the war years and now continued to show a lively interest in its future. If Chiang were defeated, what next?

The Navy was concerned lest this large island slip under Communist control, for it could dominate the seas lying between our bases in Japan, Okinawa, and the Philippines. The mere servicing of such a large maritime possession by the Communists would stimulate Chinese Communist development of military and merchant marine establishments. In naval offices we recalled with regret the Navy's proposal to place the island under an American naval administration *before* Japan's surrender.

At the Pentagon I found former colleagues who were eager for the latest information and an eyewitness report of the March Affair. At the moment they were more directly concerned with the impending collapse of Chiang Kai-shek's military positions throughout North China. From the Pentagon Formosa looked like an excellent offshore base, protected by a "moat." Here, too, there was regret that the United States was not taking advantage of Formosa's unsettled legal status to insist upon an American or United Nations share in the local administration. Lieutenant General Albert Wedemeyer was even then in China reviewing the unstable mainland military situation, and negotiating a proposal to create a special Sino-American training base upon Formosa.

But the War and Navy Departments moved in these matters only with the consent and approval of the Department of State, and here the "hands off" view prevailed. I found that it was not possible to suggest that America's long-range interests should take precedence over tender consideration of Chiang Kai-shek's face, and over Chinese interests in general. It was my view that a friendly, non-Communist and *non-Nationalist* Formosan population would serve our interests best.

There was more than a trace of vindictiveness in the counter-argument offered by some Foreign Service officers with "old China Hands" or mission background, and much of their argument echoed the arguments used on behalf of the Chinese in the mid-19th-century Formosa controversy, when foreigners wanted to bring order to the island by cutting it off from China proper. Clearly my disputants shared the Chinese view that Formosans were "tainted" by long association with the Japanese, and deserved little consideration, or that in a spirit of true missionary renunciation, we Americans must put Chinese claims and interests always before our own. There was a certain cold logic, of course, in the observation that the Formosan people, numbering then only six millions, were a minority too small to be considered in weighing the interests of the huge mainland Chinese population. There could be no suggestion of a separate Formosa.

XVI

The "Reform Administration"

General Chen Yi Rewarded

THE FORMOSANS WAITED in stunned bewilderment, mourning the dead. What next? Neither the ostentatious visit of General Pai Chung-hsi nor the shower of leaflets bearing Chiang's speech had done much to improve the tense situation.

In late March and April many nervous Chinese carpetbaggers slipped away to the mainland, taking with them what they could. The future was not bright here among such hostile island people. Some of the better immigrants also began to leave. They had come to Formosa in hope that here, at last, they could move forward in their professions. Now some thought it a good time to leave China altogether — a hard decision to make — moving on to Hong Kong, America, or Europe to begin life anew. Obviously Formosa was destined to go the way the rest of China had gone under Nationalist Party rule.

I shall quote from only one — an engineer — to suggest the views of non-Party men who wanted only peace for China, and an opportunity for national recovery. He also gives us a glimpse of mainland Chinese attitudes toward Formosa, toward Government, and toward the United States.

"You appreciate [he wrote] how many intellectual Chinese regard American support of the Chiang regime as the main factor in prolonging the Chinese people's agony . . ." On the subject of a Trust status for the island he was vehement:

> To the average Chinese such a solution would appear grossly unjust . . . Formosa is related to China by blood and history. It would therefore be a double wrong for the Americans to advocate severing Formosa from China on the grounds that the government they support in China is corrupt. [He refers here to Chen Yi as Chiang's agent] . . . within my life I have watched the Formosans drift away from us as a result of Japanese education and propaganda. The gap widened to such an extent that in 1941 I could scarcely pick out the Formosans who came across with the Japanese Army. Peace has hardly come long enough to allow the Formosans to reorient themselves. A further stretch of American administration would further alienate the Formosans from my people. The drift might be permanent and impossible to remedy.[1]

In commenting on Chen Yi's failure, he believed that the Central Government had too many agencies under its direct control — among them the Army, the Party, the Customs, and the Judiciary. This made it impossible for Chen Yi to get a firm grip on the situation. Then with great candor, he puts forward this view of government:

> . . . Under Chen Yi were some bad eggs, such as his Secretary General Keh, who happened to be supported by Chiang. Of course the masses of lower officials were of very poor quality. Lastly, I maintained that Chen Yi pursued a liberal policy which was entirely unsuitable for the task, for the simple reason that (1) the Central Government had made up its mind to milk Formosa, (2) discord produced by the independent bodies mentioned above were bound to undermine any good that Chen Yi might do for the Formosans, so that a strong hand from the start, coupled with a policy of white-washing (through the press, bribing the vociferous classes, i.e. the intelligentsia, school teachers, businessmen, etc.) would have done the trick, and the

world would never have heard about any misrule on Formosa.

I mentioned the last because such patterns of government have been practiced and are still practiced in China successfully. The main thing is to suppress undesirable news, and show a strong hand on every occasion. Any other man in Chen Yi's position would have proclaimed martial law, and warned the Formosan leaders of mass arrests, put them under strict surveyance, etc. instead of letting things drift into chaotic freedom . . .[2]

These comments illustrate the failure of well-educated mainland Chinese to comprehend the changes which had taken place among Formosans during three hundred years of frontier island life, and half a century of orderly technological development. They continued to treat Formosa as a backward hinterland province.

Chiang was just then begging Washington for another huge loan to keep his regime afloat. Some show of reform was required. Chen Yi would have to be replaced.

To sooth the barbarians at Washington, where the Weis in wartime had established a large reputation as genial hosts, Dr. Wei Tao-ming was named to succeed Chen, a choice bound to be received favorably. They could be assured of support among officials who sometimes mistook a foreigner's ability to speak English for a passionate devotion to democracy and the American Way of Life.

Chen was allowed to linger on at Taipei for six weeks. This gave him time to settle many old scores. The local economy was shaken as his men liquidated real properties and sought gold bars or American dollars to pack off to Shanghai.

Despite the fine talk of "reform" at Nanking, the reign of terror continued. Under the ancient Chinese "mutual responsibility" system (the *pao-chia* system), every community was organized in groups of ten households. Each household put forward a senior member who was held responsible for the behavior of all the individuals within his own household. From each group of ten household representatives, one member was put forward to represent them all in a second group of ten. This second group, therefore, represented and was held responsible for the behavior of one hundred households, and for every individual in the subordinate groups. For any infringement of the law, or for acts deemed offensive to the Army, the Party, or the Government, punishments were graduated to suit the occasion. These ranged from a mere public tongue-lashing (loss of face) through fines, confiscation of property, imprisonment and torture, to the extreme penalty, death. Thus the entire community could be squeezed without mercy to yield up information concerning an individual member wanted by the authorities.

Chen Yi brought the system to new refinement now by altering the base unit from ten to five households, thus making twice as many household heads immediately responsible in every community. This, coupled with the reward-system for stool-pigeons, made it extremely difficult for Formosan leaders who had gone underground to rally their forces.

A Formosan letter to UNRRA's Chief Medical Officer at this time notes the persistent hope that the United Nations might intervene, and alludes to the continuing manhunt in the hills and through the countryside.

I try my best in spreading the news and persuading the people that U.N. Trusteeship is possible. But under the present situation it is almost impossible to spread it wide enough. And it is very difficult to persuade the people that U.N. will take the problem because people think Taiwan is too small.

Several hundred are still in the mountains, but they are in difficult situation because food is very short there and some influential aborigines who were bribed by the Government do not cooperate with the Formosans.

Secret organization is now going on very slowly, but increasingly. Majority of people become very timid after the "blood bath". I hope they will quickly forget it. But the hatred is 100%.

If plebiscite is held I am quite sure that U.N. Trusteeship (especially U.S.A.) will get 100% support . . .

So-called "Purge of Towns and Villages" is practised and people are imposed with joint liability, and if one wicked person is found, all the people will be punished. Such a wicked system as the Dark Ages! [3]

Another Formosan writing at the time tells of the terrifying sudden night raids: "If . . . police happen to investigate in the midnight, which happen very often recently, and the change in number of the family is found, all member of the family, including the old and children, will be arrested, and the people also who guaranteed will be punished." [4]

From every part of the island UNRRA team members reported a continuing campaign of intimidation and revenge, settling old scores for the Army, the Party and the Government. Mainland Chinese who had been thwarted in buccaneering exploits in 1946 now sometimes enjoyed bloody reprisals. At Keelung seventeen prominent Formosans were arrested and told that they would die if they could not produce 100,000 yen or its equivalent value in rice. At Taipei thirteen men were forced to produce a total of 40,000 bags of rice within three days. Similar incidents elsewhere led the UNRRA observers to believe that confiscations were intended to deny supplies to refugees in the high mountains, and to enable the newly arrived troops to live off the land.

All criminal acts — including the depredations of Nationalist soldiers — were now blamed upon Formosans, diversifying excuses for arrest and execution. A Norwegian member of the UNRRA team wrote:

Monday the 14 April in Takao about 11:30 a.m., two brothers about 25 and 33 years of age were executed in the main square in front of the railway station. Helena [also] saw the gathering of people and the police just after . . . we found out . . . that the two were accused of being some of the ringleaders on the 28

February. The cruelty of it was, the two men's families were fetched and they had to attend the execution . . .

You will remember the man who tried to intercede for those arrested at Heito when the troops came in (Muriel's report). He, who had not participated at all, was led down to the square in front of the Provincial Hospital, had to kneel down, got tied up and shot. His wife and two children were forced to attend . . .[5]

On April 19 an UNRRA doctor — a South American — saw a score of well-dressed young Formosans being driven through the streets by Nationalist soldiers. Each man was trussed up and the lot were bound together, neck-to-neck, by heavy cords. They were headed toward the river on the outskirts of town and there could be no doubt that they would be tortured or dead within the hour.

Chen Yi was to leave on May 1. It was now decreed that April 26 would be set aside as "Thanksgiving Day" and that all school children would contribute tokens of thanks — money tokens, of course — for the protection which had been extended to them by the Nationalist Army in March. Every primary school child was assessed five yen; every middle school pupil was assessed double the sum.

Both the Protestant and Catholic schools protested this outrageous "thanksgiving" rite, but protest only added to their difficulties. Schools were closed just after the February Incident. As they resumed work, the mission authorities had to agree, in writing, to create new boards of directors on which mainland Chinese would form the majority. The boards thereafter would determine curriculum and have the power to hire and fire the faculty. The missions were denied permission to resume work at stations among the East Coast aborigines.

At about this time the UNRRA organization was astonished to learn that the Taipei Government (Yen Chia-kan, Finance Commissioner) had arranged a loan of forty-nine *billion* Chinese National Currency dollars — a credit to be available in

Shanghai — which was secured against a quantity of sugar, rice, and other Formosan products, and against an UNRRA shipment of 200,000 tons of fertilizer donated by Canada and the United States for use in Formosa. The UNRRA team wanted to know who was to use this credit on the mainland, and for what purpose. It was widely speculated that this might perhaps represent Chen Yi's final payoff insofar as Formosa was concerned.

Chiang Kai-shek showed his supreme indifference to public opinion. For the benefit of the barbarians at Washington he had made the gesture of reform in the appointment of Wei Tao-ming. General Chen Yi was called up to Nanking to become a Senior Advisor to the Government. When a suitable time had elapsed he was made Governor of Chekiang Province which has an area three times greater than the island of Formosa, and a population twice as great. It offered splendid economic opportunities. Moreover it had special importance in Chiang's eyes, for it held the tombs of his ancestors and the ancestors of Chen Yi. It was true Home Territory.

Dr. and Mrs. Wei's Reform Administration

General Chen Yi and his Japanese mistress had been content to live in a modest confiscated house on a side street, using the ostentatious Executive Mansion as a Government Guest House for conferences and parties. Governor and Mme. Wei preferred the official residence.* This grandiose structure — nearly as large as the White House in Washington — was set in park-like gardens. It had been built early in the century as a symbol of Japan's imperial authority and over the years had become a museum of sorts, filled with rare and curious objects.

Madame Wei — a colorful and forceful personality, to say

---

* This was the first Mme. Wei (1894–1959), who preferred to be known as Cheng Yu-hsiu, Tcheng Soume, or Soumay Tcheng.

the least — often boasted that she had been a bomb-carrying student revolutionary in her youth, but these days were now far away. It was soon seen that she dominated the Governor's office, and at Shanghai and Nanking she was sometimes dubbed the "Super Governor" of Formosa. She had prominent and powerful connections in the Central Government in her own right, and on Formosa enjoyed the presence of her nephew, the Deputy Garrison Commanding General, Niu Hsien-ming.

Soon after the Weis took office, there began to be extraordinary fluctuations in the money market. A few well-favored persons were said to have made fortunes. After commenting on the erratic exchange and the cynicism with which the Formosans looked upon Wei's "reform administration," one well-informed Formosan wrote:

> We hope that Governor Wei may not follow the way of Chen. But I have heard that many persons who are adherents of T. V. Soong followed Wei into the economic sphere of Taiwan. Now the Government are going to open the door of Industry under the name "Democratic policy" but how can we Formosans compete with T. V. Soong group or other mainland business men . . . ? [6]

All of Chen Yi's Commissioners vanished from the scene — all but one, Yen Chia-kan, Chen's Commissioner of Finance. The new Secretary General was Dr. Hsu Dau-lin, a legal expert trained in Germany and one-time secretary to the Generalissimo. As window-dressing, seven Formosans were named Commissioners, representing half of Dr. Wei's "cabinet." The titles were nominal, for none of the Formosan Commissioners was free to name his own subordinates, and in each case the Vice Commissioner was a mainland Chinese, the effective "boss." At the fourth level of administration many Formosans were named "vice directors," but each was in turn surrounded by mainland Chinese to make sure that all were kept in line. One familiar face lingered for a time on the edges of bureaucracy — Dr.

King, Chen Yi's Director of Public Health remained on Formosa to direct the drug manufacturing company in which Chen had had such manifest interest.

Governor Wei held office for eighteen months and two weeks. Given the conditions then prevailing on the mainland he faced a hopeless task. Many of his attempts at economic reform and social readjustment failed. The raw material stockpiles were depleted, and the technical organizations were disrupted by the post-Incident emigration of well-trained men. Unemployment increased as industrial production declined. Bank loans continued to be made principally for commercial purposes.

While the new Governor rustled papers on his desk and Commissioner Yen struggled to hold inflation in check, the economic confusion at Shanghai grew worse. Taipei had authority to adjust exchange rates for the local currency (Taiwan yen) against the wildly fluctuating Chinese National Currency (CNC), but it was extremely difficult. There could be no stabilization of economy on Formosa until the island was cut off from mainland chaos.

The UNRRA organization remained in being until December, 1947. By December, 1948, the Formosan economy as a whole had reached the lowest point of production per capita known since the island was ceded to Japan in 1895. In this sense, indeed, it had reverted to China. The population was increasing rapidly. In prewar days the annual export of foodstuffs and semi-processed goods had exceeded $50,000,000 in value; in 1948 goods worth scarcely $1,000,000 left Formosa through legitimate trade channels. The great Japanese sugar industry had passed into mainland Chinese hands, and now rice acreage was being reduced to make room for larger cane plantations.

Formosa was slipping back toward old Chinese habits of thought and behavior as well. The Formosan shopkeeper complained that he was no longer able to keep reasonably accurate accounts, for the immigrant Chinese refused to accept the "fixed price" system to which the Formosans had become accustomed. A single object in a merchant's stock in trade might bring ten different prices in a day, according to the shopkeeper's ability to haggle with ten different customers. The price tags attached to an object meant nothing now, and inventories yielded no reasonable basis upon which to estimate profit or loss. There were no limits to "squeeze" — the payments that had to be made to officials of Army, Party or Government to obtain licenses, privileges, or bare security in business.

Costly traditional religious practices long banned by the Japanese were resumed. These had often led families to bankrupt themselves providing ostentatious display for weddings, divination rites and costly funerals. Upon these expenditures the Japanese had placed limits which the older generation resented, but the younger generation — say those born after 1900 — had recognized them as an economic benefit. They were sorry to see them lifted. On the contrary the newcomers encouraged a return to traditional rites and ceremonies as a sign of "reassimilation" to China proper. It was all very colorful and quaint, according to visiting Americans, and it was duly recorded and published in the *National Geographic Magazine, Life Magazine,* and other pictorial journals, but it represented a marked retrogression, a return to 19th century Chinese standards.

The general incapacity of Governor Wei's administration may be summed up in the reports that the Government seriously considered abandoning the entire East Coast region south of Suao anchorage as "too difficult, too costly to administer, and populated only by aborigines." It was proposed to maintain contact with Hualien town by sea, but to give up the dangerous cliffside coastal road which the Japanese had constructed years ago to facilitate administration. The wretched state of the aborigines and the mixed-blood hill-people at this time has been recorded in Vern Sneider's poignant tale *A Pail of Oysters*, published by Putnam in 1953.

The Terror Continued

On his second day in office (May 15, 1947) Governor Wei announced that martial law was lifted forthwith, and that there would be no more arrests in connection with the February Incident. This again was window-dressing, the gesture of reform which Washington expected.

Arrests and executions continued. The civilian Dr. Wei had very little influence with either the Nationalist Army or the Nationalist Party goons. Heaviest pressure was brought to bear on Formosa's emergent middle class, the small landholders who had hitherto enough surplus to send sons and daughters to the higher schools on Formosa and the universities in Japan proper, and to invest in small business enterprises in the town. This was the class that had produced the leaders of early 1947.

The Government was particularly concerned with the higher schools, known to be centers of anti-Chinese feeling. The educational system was a shambles; at the Taiwan University in 1948 there were fifty mainland Chinese professors, eight Japanese professors and two assistant professors who were Formosans. Even the Formosan janitors had been dismissed to make way for carpetbaggers. Within the year no less than five deans succeeded one another in the University Law School and each change brought a change in staff. At one time the turnover was so confusing the Government asked the remaining Japanese professors to act as the property custodians, for they represented the only element of stability on the campus.

The hunt for student plots and for underground organizations was relentless. Stories were put about — but never verified — that the government had uncovered a conspiracy calling for island-wide retaliation upon mainland Chinese, an uprising to take place on August 22 (i.e. "8–22" the reverse of "2–28," the February 28 Incident). General Peng Meng-chi set October 31 as a deadline by which all "communists" must register. Peng and his aides let no opportunity pass to make clear that "interventionist" or "independence" sentiment was equated with "communism" and would be punished accordingly.

Prominent Formosans were compelled to sign up as members of a *New Culture Association,* declaring themselves emphatically opposed to the very thought of trusteeship. Provincial, municipal and local councils, schools and private organizations were expected to subscribe to these declarations. To hesitate was to lay oneself open to charges of Communist subversion. Signatures by the hundreds were recorded on manifestos opposing intervention and these documents were forwarded to Washington or New York to be used as evidence that no "true Formosan" desired independence or trust status for the island.

It became necessary for every family to look first to its own security and for the individual to think twice before endangering his family through rash conduct or indiscreet conversation. The Government offered attractive rewards for information lodged against anyone heard speaking of "intervention" or "independence." Soon it was said that wherever ten Formosans were together it had to be assumed that at least one was an informant in government pay. The story is told of a party at Kaohsiung at which someone asked the guests what they would do if an invasion took place. One indiscreet Formosan, remembering the enormous rewards reaped by a Formosan collaborating with the Japanese in 1895, said with a laugh that he would like to be a "second Ku Wen-hsing." A few days later he disappeared and was not heard of again.

Formosans who had been notably friendly toward foreigners became the objects of special police attention. It was useful enough to have Governor and Mrs. Wei cultivate foreign approbation at Washington, on the other side of the Pacific, but it was quite another thing to have Formosans confiding their woes to foreigners on Formosa. On the day Wei took office the Government newspaper published a thinly veiled hint that foreigners were not welcome and that they would be subjected to a more rigorous supervision. "We will therefore strengthen our investigation of passports, and foreigners' exits and entrances, and will control them during their stay in the island." [7]

Formosans with foreign friends now found their homes searched repeatedly and their relatives and local friends subjected to harassing interrogations. All were instructed to report to the nearest police station, at once, all foreign visitors who came to their attention and to render a full account of all topics discussed with them. A "Wanted" list of thirty names was posted. In an effort to bewilder foreign newsmen and to cast doubt upon stories which had already appeared in the foreign press the list included names of persons known definitely to have been slaughtered in early March. To suggest guilt by association well-known advocates of UN or American intervention were listed with Miss Snow Red and other known Communists. All were held to be "criminally responsible" for the March affair. They were warned to repent, turn themselves in, or face death. Governor Wei's amnesty pledges meant nothing to the Army.

Writing in June, 1947, Dr. Pierre Sylvain, an UNRRA agricultural specialist from Haiti, noted that Government forces were continuing to terrorize villages by holding "military exercises" in the narrow streets and alleyways — bayonets at the ready — which drove everyone indoors and served to remind them emphatically of their helplessness. Kaohsiung, he said, was under specially heavy pressure. Wealthy and moderately well-to-do farmers and townsmen everywhere were being held to ransom under pretext of investigating charges that they had participated in the March affair.[8]

But even under these conditions Formosans continued to appeal for help. The American Consulate was asked to sponsor a delegation of Formosans who wished to go to New York and Washington to plead their case. Writing to me, far away in America, an acquaintance said:

Plenty of the new Chinese escaped from the mainland have come to Taiwan almost every day and are disturbing and spoiling this beautiful island . . .

We understand the Chinese and Formosans are incompatible forever. We are hopeless now and can do nothing in Taiwan.

It is true that ninety-nine percent of the Formosan desire Taiwan be separated from China and they are very anxious to ask for the trusteeship under the United States. It is too heavy burden for Taiwan to support the national government's war coffers, and in fact we have no interest and loyalty to China. After the February 28 incident all of the Formosans excepting some puppet have thought the trusteeship is the only way to rescue Taiwan from the "Hell."

We believe we shall be able to carry out the democracy by ourselves under the aid of the United States, and of course we can do our best to cooperate with the U.S. in every way to defend against your enemy in the future . . .[9]

General Wedemeyer's Visit

General George C. Marshall had returned to the United States from his China Mission in January, 1947, convinced that there was no possibility of bringing the Communists and Nationalists together. The question "What to do about China?" was becoming the most important issue in America's domestic politics and foreign affairs. Marshall believed that the United States must reduce its commitments to the disintegrating Nationalist Government and so cut its losses in China's civil war. President Truman, on the other hand, was being harassed by savage charges that he was withholding military aid and thereby deliberately favoring the Communists. Before making final decisions, the President sent Lieutenant General Albert C. Wedemeyer to China once more to assess the military situation, the chances of Chiang's survival, and the practicality of further massive aid for the Nationalist regime.

It was a fact-finding mission. Before leaving China Wedemeyer flew to Formosa, so recently relieved of Chen Yi. Governor Wei sensed the General's lack of enthusiasm but did his best to convince him that Formosa was indeed a bastion of democracy. As usual the perennial "sample native," Huang Chaochin, was brought forward for a private interview as "spokesman for the Formosan people." Noting the "intervention" agitation, Wedemeyer assured Huang that the United States had no territorial ambitions in Formosa. Huang bowed himself out and promptly told the waiting press that the General had declared, "The United States has no interest in Formosa," thereby chilling the hearts of Formosan leaders who had hoped Wedemeyer would recommend an investigation of the situation on the island.

General Wedemeyer reported to the President that the Chinese were not using efficiently the aid we had given them, and while asking for enormous American dollar grants-in-aid had not drawn on their own resources. "Privately-held foreign exchange assets [of the Chinese] are at least $600 million, and may total $1500 million, but no serious attempt has been made to mobilize these private resources for rehabilitation purposes." [10] Wedemeyer detailed Chiang's incapacities as a military leader, the gross incompetence of his generals, and the corruption of the Nationalist Party and Government. He recommended complete American withdrawl from the Chinese Theatre and the formation of a five-nation "guardianship" for Manchuria, with Russian participation. But in strange contradiction, in the same document, he urged increased military and economic aid for Chiang on a massive scale, and the placement of American "advisors" at every level of the Nationalist administration. He would in effect transform Chiang into a "front man" or puppet.

For obvious reasons the Department of State could not release the *Wedemeyer Report* at that time. Every semblance of Nationalist administration in South China would have vanished overnight. The Department would not recommend placing part of China (Manchuria) under an international trust administration. The *Report* was shelved and kept secret.

Soon thereafter it was announced that the United States would help the Nationalists develop a military training program on the island.

This was a turning point, a recognition that Formosa, at least, could not and would not be written off if the Pentagon could prevent it. Five years had elapsed since a first Memorandum on the subject had been prepared in the Pentagon suggesting development of a postwar policing base in southern Formosa. Now it was about to be realized.

Formosan leaders heard the news with some bitterness; they had hoped for a direct American or United Nations intervention to cut them off from the civil war in China. As one wrote to me ". . . a reenforcement of the present Chinese troops garrisoning the island will be resented and open to misinterpretation."

The announcement loosed a spate of rumors that General Wedemeyer had also recommended increased economic aid and the construction of huge military and naval bases. The whole program, it was said, would be related to a general reconstruction program for South China, where T. V. Soong had become Governor of Kwangtung Province.

On October 3, at Hong Kong, the newspaper *Hua Shang Pao* carried banner headlines which read:

U.S. NAVAL AND AIR BASES ALL OVER TAIWAN

U.S. COLLABORATING WITH LOCAL GENTRY

PLOTTING FOR TRUSTEESHIP

TERROR HAS NOT ENDED, BUT PEOPLE CONTINUE STRUGGLE

According to the text, a Major in the United States Air Force had assured a prominent Formosan that the Nationalist Government would soon collapse, and that Formosans should prepare for the aftermath. The Communists would probably take over the mainland (the American had said), but Communism would not be good for the island. If Formosans wished to improve conditions within Formosa and required American aid, they should consult with the Director of the United States Information Service at Taipei.

Then — according to the Hong Kong story — the Formosan leader had a two-hour conversation at the American Consulate. The USIS Director noted Formosa's unsettled legal status, saying that it was still technically under General MacArthur, and that he would receive Formosan petitions for help. The United States expected to apply the terms of the Atlantic Charter here, giving Formosans an opportunity "to determine of their free will to which nation they will belong."

Continuing, the article alleged that the USIS Director pledged American help if the Formosans asked for it and were willing to free themselves from the Chinese government. Under an American Trust administration they would be permitted to determine the length of the Trust period. Meanwhile the United States would do all that it could to rehabilitate the island economy. Lastly (it was alleged) after the fall of the Nanking Government the United States would at once undertake to release all the so-called political criminals and those involved in the February Incident and its aftermath. Conscription would be abolished.

To this point the story rather clearly outlined the position and hopes of the leaders who wished to get rid of the Nationalists, but the story had been prepared by exiles who were now swinging over to the Communists, taking the view that anything would be better than the Nationalists, and that the revival of foreign concessions must not take place. In their view the proposed Sino-American training program was merely resurgence of old-style military imperialism. ". . . We can see that the United States is now trying her best to collaborate with the local gentry, and has started the trusteeship movement so as to prepare favorable conditions for her invasion of Taiwan." [11]

Soon after this the UNRRA group left Formosa. On the 15th of December Allen Shackleton (the Industrial Rehabilitation Officer) made a shortwave broadcast from Sydney, Australia, in which he gave an account of conditions on Formosa under Wei Tao-ming's "reform government." It was a strong indictment and was heard on Formosa where it provoked a furious reaction. Stanway Cheng's propagandists took the line that the British and American imperialists had the same ambitions which had fired the Nazis and the Japanese, but were more clever about it; America and Britain brought UNRRA supplies as deceptive gifts and offered "aid to China" as a decoy while plotting to annex, exploit and "enslave" Formosa.

On December 20 Governor Wei visited Nanking, was briefed, and came forth with the statement that all outside criticism of the policies and conduct of the Nationalists on Formosa was promoted by the intrigues of communists and "ambitious elements of a certain nation" who wanted to sever Formosa from China. He warned that the rumors of Formosan discontent would continue to spread until the Peace Treaty could be signed, but that China's claims to Formosa were unchallengeable.[12]

As 1947 drew to a close the United States found itself in a most awkward position of its own making. Our Information Service continued to pour propaganda into Formosa which pictured the United States as the world's foremost champion of liberty and of minority rights, but at the same time we were enlarging our commitment to support Chiang's disorderly Army. The Nationalists, on the other hand, were energetically seeking to destroy Formosan confidence in the United States.

Eight Catholic priests (who were not Americans) spent the long New Year holiday in villages far from Taipei, but they carried with them an American film series made available by the Consulate. They showed the films seven times and each showing drew large crowds. Of their experience the Fathers wrote:

The mayor of —— made a speech asking the people to be thankful to the Americans who, through me, gave them this golden opportunity of seeing such wonderful things and which never before had they seen, all the people applauded fervently.

Some people complain the talking of the films, which is Mandarin, and they would rather prefer the english talking. Anywhere the Formosan people is very enthusiastic about anything coming from the U.S., and not only that but also some people many times ask me when will the U.S.A. take control of this Island. They say that [they] hope the day of being free of the "Pigs" (as they call them) of the Mainland . . . Many people want to learn English . . .[13]

The anniversary of the Incident approached; Governor Wei prepared for trouble. Arrests and search on a large scale began again about February 20; a new Gendarme Force was established to strengthen the Governor's hand, and the island was held under close restriction at the ports. The day came and passed in an islandwide atmosphere of great tension but with no major incident. Formosans in surprising number were moved to write to foreign friends on that grim anniversary. Said one to me, "I have tried many times to write . . . but each time there has been something which prevented me from doing so — we are not enjoying the 'Freedom from Fear' here, you know." Said another:

One year has passed since those dark terrified days we had to have, and now still we are always in some worry, uneasy feeling what may be done [to] us by the capricious present leading power in China . . .

At the first anniversary day those from the mainland were threatened by the rumour that some of the islanders would break up and do the same thing as last year. On the other hand the islanders held the idea that they are standing at the very end of a cliff, and might be thrown into the deep valley by the present forces in this island, [who throw] over them the name

"Communists." Like this the public in the island are divided into two parties and watching each other . . .

But when [I realize] that one year has passed and still no definite moving outside to bring this island out to the center of the world for discussion, I would feel something down-hearted . . . And although there is no apparent [change in Formosa's international position] the unwillingness of converting themselves into the way of those from the mainland is still growing in the mind of the Formosan people . . .

There may be some underground movements in the island. But they are not in good organization or in good connections with each other . . .

In any way, the islanders are not blessed by the god of freedom, I guess . . .[14]

The writer then elaborates arguments for intervention which he hears discussed among his friends and questions Formosa's future relations with Japan. They fear that a prolonged civil war in China will reduce Formosa to absolute poverty and a state of administrative chaos. Will Japan then arrange to return, or will the United States establish a trust administration?

The mainland Chinese at Taipei were well aware of these sentiments and arguments. The circumstances brought into the open the basic Chinese contempt and dislike of all non-Chinese people. Here in Formosa it was galling to see the "inferior" island people so eager to invoke barbarian intervention. Worst of all, it was so apparent that the Nationalist regime, in order to survive, was indeed becoming entirely dependent upon American military and economic grants-in-aid. These deep-seated resentments sometimes welled to the surface.*

* This was a matter of face on a national scale, of wounded cultural pride tormented for 150 years by condescending foreign patronage which demanded that "backward" China exchange its traditional religious, social and political ideas for a mode of life and standards of value approved by the West. The subject cannot be explored here, but I believe the accumulated resentment — a century old — may lie near the heart of Peking's savage rejection of the West, her inhuman treatment of missionaries as symbols of the Western patronage, and the bitter determination to "destroy the United States."

October's Hong Kong story telling of Formosan interest in a trust status for the island, under American administration, had alarmed Nanking and Taipei, for it was too close to the truth.

Sun Fo: "Communist Agents in the American Consulate?"

A strong counterattack was required. To please Americans Governor Wei had decorated the façade of his "reform government" with many details, among them a Formosan chapter of Rotary International. Properly managed it could be used to disseminate suitable propaganda through worldwide distribution of club publications. One of the first "plants" was an address by Dr. Sun Fo, at that time President of the Legislative Yuan or "Premier," and son of the "National Father." This was a heavy gun, but heavy guns were needed.

Sun flew in from Shanghai, rose before the Rotary Club, and began his remarks by denouncing inaccurate reporting of conditions within Formosa by foreign newsmen who raised the question of Formosa's future status. Social conditions on the island (said Dr. Sun) were "most peaceful and orderly" and Dr. Wei's administration represented a very stable government and economy if compared with certain other regions in the world. At least 90 per cent of Formosa's population is of Chinese descent, he observed, and the similarity of cultural traditions shows how close Formosa is to China despite the Japanese half-century. "I deeply believe," he said, "that Taiwan will always be one of the provinces of China." As for conditions within Formosa, he assured Rotarians around the world that "all technical personnel in Taiwan have done their best in the last two years. All local industries are on their way to recovery." [15]

Dr. Sun then expressed his belief that a mere one hundred million dollars from the United States of America would bring everything in Formosa to peak production.

With this he flew back to Shanghai.

Having been well briefed at Taipei, on March 1 he called a

press conference. Again he led off by severely criticizing foreign correspondents for "inaccurate reporting." They had failed to interview responsible members of Government on Formosa and "leaders in various circles," said he. The persistent stories that Formosa wished to be separated from the fatherland were false; the newsmen "were fooled by people engaged in disseminating communist propaganda." Furthermore:

> The fact has been disclosed in the United States that the person engaged in this is an officer in the Press Office of the American Consulate in Taiwan. He misinterpreted the facts by taking advantage that these American reporters do not understand the local language.
>
> Some people infected by propaganda said that all the people sent by the Chinese Government to Taiwan either to take over the posts left by the Japanese or to work in Taiwan are incompetent and they have made a mess of the good foundation for reconstruction left by the Japanese. This is contrary to what I have seen in middle and southern Taiwan.
>
> We should also query our friendly nation [i.e. the U.S.A.] which should allow such a person [the USIS officer] undermining the U.S.–China friendship to remain in its government until the present moment . . . As to the Chinese working in the USIS as interpreters, translators and guides, it is hoped they will be investigated, impeached, and denounced by society.[16]

The American Embassy at Nanking and the Consulate at Taipei promptly protested, and as promptly everyone on Formosa from Governor Wei to the lowliest clerk in his Information Office denied advance knowledge of Sun Fo's text. The China News Service was obliged to send out a "correction" with orders that the story be deleted from the news-record files, but the damage was done.

The USIS Officer was the last American official left in Formosa who had actually witnessed the bloody March affair and was therefore "dangerous." He was on the eve of departure for a new post, so that Sun Fo's blast could be interpreted as a "success." But beyond this it was evident that Chiang's agents and friends on both sides of the Pacific had determined the basic line of propaganda which they have followed since that day: any critic of Chiang or of his Army, Party and Government is, *ipso facto*, a Communist, a fellow traveler, or a dupe of the Communists; anyone who suggests intervention on Formosa is open to grave suspicion.

As for the Consulate itself, it was a foregone conclusion that the Consular officers could never again expect interpreters, translators and guides to speak frankly on the subject of Formosan relations with the mainland Chinese.

American Bases for Formosa?

The creation of a Sino-American Military Training Program at Pingtung in southern Formosa marked a turning point in American relations with the island.

General Sun Li-jen inaugurated the program on February 19, 1948. His camps were orderly, his men disciplined, and no rumors accused him of graft and corruption. The Formosans soon saw that they had a military officer of new quality among them. American correspondents hurried over to have a look; Henry Lieberman wrote "The Training Group [camp] which is a going concern, is a much more orderly place than the new bases established here by the Chinese Air Force and Navy." Christopher Rand predicted that there would soon be an all-out Sino-American occupation of Formosa in order to hold it secure as a link in the Japan-Okinawa-Philippines chain.

But Sun's appointment had a certain ambiguity about it. He was then Deputy Commander-in-Chief of the Chinese Armies, and was without question the Chinese officer held in highest esteem by American officers who had worked with him in the China-Burma-India Theatre during World War II and later.*

* General Sun held a Purdue University engineering degree ('23), and had graduated from General Marshall's old school, the Virginia Military Institute ('27). He had served with General Joseph Stilwell, with great distinction.

As commander of the "New First Army" he had distinguished himself in the northeast; although Manchuria was lost, his personal reputation was high. Officers who served with him were said to make a special effort to stay in his commands, and when he was named to the Formosan operation, it was said that one hundred officers immediately crossed over to join him there and that three hundred waited impatiently in Shanghai for a summons to his staff.

None of this sat well with the Generalissimo whose capacity for vindictive jealousy is well known. He would brook no potential rivals in Party, Army, or Government. It was rumored that by sending General Sun off to distant Formosa — to a training camp ill-supplied with arms — he thought to diminish the possibility that this popular general could bring an army into the field on behalf of the anti-Communist "Third Force" of which there was much talk. It is more probable, however, that the Americans arranging for this joint enterprise simply insisted upon the assignment of the man who could do the job to best advantage.

The possible isolation of Formosa became a topic of wide speculation. A leading Shanghai editor sought comment on a number of key problems, including Formosan dissatisfaction under Nationalist Party rule. The fourth question read "If the northern and southern harbors in Taiwan should become free harbors, how will the United States, China and Taiwan itself be affected?"

The so-called C-C Clique (a powerful faction headed by Chen Li-fu) began to build up public belief that a massive new American aid-to-China program was assured, but that it was not on a grand enough scale. The C-C newspaper *Shun Pao* protested that any aid given to Formosa should be a separate and additional item in the American budget for overall aid to China. It also discovered that China needed a powerful Navy.

Here was something new, for the world had not heard of a Chinese Navy since the old Empress Dowager long ago used the Government's naval appropriations to build a marble boat in her Peking Palace garden.

Now it was suddenly realized that Formosa is an island, and that it might be good to have a Navy, and this in turn would require a large organization to handle the huge sums which quite naturally would be forthcoming from the United States. "What is of special interest to us," said the *Shun Pao*, "is that the United States is going to help us carry out fully our plan of building a naval base in Taiwan." [17]

Chen Li-fu was quick to scent rewarding possibilities; using attendance at a Moral Re-Armament Conference as an ostensible excuse, Chen flew on to Washington and New York, where he was received cordially by Congressmen, military men, and MRA enthusiasts.

But he found that the bloom had passed from the great Sino-American romance. On his return to China in September he complained that "Years of Communist propaganda in the United States have changed the American view of China. Traditional sympathy has become general disappointment."

We expressed our national disappointment in this instance by transferring to China a total of 131 naval vessels, valued at $141,315,000, under terms of Public Law 512 (79th Congress), approved on July 16, 1948. Chiang's naval bases on Formosa began to take on life.

Among Formosans the initial bitterness evoked by the new "Aid-to-Chiang" program gave way to resignation. A foreign doctor noted that "the people welcome the U. S. Army, still very small, here, in the belief that their presence lays some restraint on the Nationalist troops."

Were the Americans coming into Formosa to protect the rights and interests of the Formosan people, or were they coming in to confirm Chiang Kai-shek's hold upon them?

XVII

The Retreat to Formosa

How to Regain American Support?

BY MIDYEAR 1948 it was evident that the Nationalists would be swept out of North China. Chiang soon lost the great postwar advantages given him by American transport and supply, for he insisted on holding walled cities which the Communists promptly isolated by pouring through the countryside with fluid ease.

For a time it looked as though Chiang might be pushed aside by his own people. Criticism of his leadership was becoming open and direct. One of his most important rivals — General Li Tsung-jen — was elevated to the Vice Presidency. Intellectual leaders attempted to organize a non-Communist Third Force which could replace Chiang and the Nationalist Party and by drastic housecleaning in the Chinese administration regain the confidence and support of the American Government. Clearly fresh leadership was required if the Communists were to be kept out of South China. Washington considered the need to support the Third Force movement.

But if Chiang's military genius left something to be desired, his capacity for intrigue was undiminished.

Only American intervention could save him now and keep him on top. A renewed indirect aid program was not enough. At some point the United States forces must become directly involved.

Obviously the Democratic Administration was prepared to write off the Nationalist regime and wanted no more to do with Chiang. An effort must be made, therefore, to persuade the American people to force the Administration to come to Nationalist aid. "If you can't change the policies, change the policy-makers."

How this might be done is well illustrated in reports of the Senate Foreign Relations Committee which probed the "Activities of Non-Diplomatic Representatives of Foreign Principals in the United States." The Committee was interested in the methods employed by foreign governments to achieve political ends within the United States. In passing he explored the activities of one of the public relations firms hired by the Nationalists to influence American opinion at all levels. The terms of the contracts brought to light in the Hearings spell out the themes to be developed, the methods to be used and the costs, which were high.

Whether the Nationalist leaders provided the general outlines of the campaign to influence American public opinion, or whether it was provided for them by hired public-opinion analysts and public relations firms within the United States is here beside the point. If General Wedemeyer's estimates were correct, the Generalissimo's family and other favored Chinese had assets within the United States of not less than six hundred million and perhaps as much as a billion and a half dollars, ample funds upon which to draw for a massive pro-Chiang propaganda drive.

It is not difficult to see that the overall campaign was organized to secure support by three influential interest-groups. Each was persuaded that aid to Chiang was necessary for its own good and each therefore was ready to use the others or to draw on them for support. These three interest-groups were (a) the American military establishment, (b) the Republican Party, and (c) the world of Christian missions and its supporting churches.

The American military establishment was rather easily persuaded. The American public had become painfully aware of Russia's growing military strength. After midyear 1945 the United States had disarmed and demobilized in pell-mell eagerness to turn from war to peace but the Russians were making it clear that nothing short of world conquest was the Communist goal, to be attained by guile and subversion if possible, or by force if necessary. As this ugly truth was realized an extraordinary sense of uneasiness disturbed the American people. Among the leaders in the American military establishment were a number of "activists" who were convinced that war with the Soviet Union was inevitable and imminent. In their view the sooner we came to blows the less prepared the Russians would be. And here was Chiang Kai-shek, a Generalissimo in his own right, offering us an opportunity to roll back Communists in China to the very borders of Soviet territory in Asia.

To preserve Chiang's face, he was openly hailed as an Ally, a military hero, and the one man who had stood up bravely and boldly against the Communists. Chiang himself asked only for arms and "some" support by sea and air. It is difficult to believe that any responsible American military officer really believed that Chiang could "go it alone" or intended to try. The advantages of having Chiang as a puppet were obvious; as long as he was the nominal Chief of State we could use his territory and his manpower. For propaganda purposes therefore the "activists" military leaders in the American establishment adopted the Generalissimo as their "hero," represented to the American public as a military genius being sacrificed by selfish and possibly pro-Communist American policies. Less impressionable military men in Washington were quite correct in noting that Chiang Kai-shek controlled the only "friendly" military organization in being in the Far East; however shabbily supplied and managed at the moment, the Nationalist troops might be whipped into shape if a good man were given a real chance to do the job.

Considered solely in military terms, it was important to keep Chiang's military organization in being and the way open to make use of any territory he might control. He had to be given public support.

The military had the blessing and extremely vocal support of the Party of the Opposition, the Republican Party which represented the second of the two major groups to which the Nationalists addressed their propaganda. The Republicans had been out of power too long. Party leaders were in a state of angry frustration. No domestic political question generated enough force to take them into the White House, but in the "Aid Chiang" theme they found the perfect made-to-order foreign policy issue. Given the state of near-hysteria induced by fear of Russian expansion, it was not difficult to relate the "Aid Chiang" issue to the larger question of national security. The irascible Ambassador Patrick Hurley had set the tone for attack on the Administration in his letter of resignation. The Nationalist defeat in China was attributed to intrigues and pro-Communist sympathies in the State Department. Anyone critical of Chiang *ipso facto* showed himself sympathetic to the Communists. So the arguments went with growing bitterness until in McCarthy's heyday it was possible for him to suggest that General George Catlett Marshall was a traitor, and that loyalty to Chiang was a proper test of loyalty to the United States.

The more fanatic Republican attacks upon the Administration suggested that if Chiang were not saved, the whole structure of American society was doomed. Prominent Republicans soon discovered the publicity value of a clear identification with the Chinese drama — the noble Christian warrior standing alone against Communism in Asia, the beautiful lady in distress, and above all, a Moral Cause.

By making aid for Chiang a moral crusade against the Anti-Christ in Asia, the Chiangs tapped a most powerful source of strength for the Nationalist propaganda drive. Every American church missionary society in every parish in the land felt that it had a vested interest in the Chiangs' welfare.

For a century and a half the missionary world has been attempting to "save China" with pennies, nickels and dimes contributed each week to support missionary endeavor. Every contributor was encouraged to feel that he had a personal interest in the conversion of the Chinese to Christianity and to the American Way of Life. Centuries ago the Jesuits dreamed that if they could convert the Emperor the people at large would then embrace Christianity. In its new version, the Soongs and the Chiangs — China's most prominent families — were adopted as symbols of all that Americans desire for China — modern men and women professing devotion to Democracy and Christ. Nothing has ever been left undone to convince the American public that the Generalissimo and Madame Chiang are endeavoring with great personal dedication to transform China into a Christian country. Now — in 1948 — the godless Communist hordes, puppets of Moscow, were sweeping through the country. To withhold aid from Chiang would be a gross betrayal of trust.

Thus the Army, Party, and Church each had reason to believe that Aid to Chiang was of special importance to its own welfare. The assault upon the Democratic Administration's "disengagement" policies grew in bitterness and violence. Both the Army and the Party made extravagant promises and declarations; the very fate of the United States seemed to depend upon Chiang Kai-shek's survival.

The Generalissimo's own problem was fairly clear; how could he trade space for time to best advantage? He must hang on until the outbreak of World War III or until he could induce an open conflict between the United States forces and the Communist Chinese.

Chiang's Search for Assurance

Chiang's major problem now was to ensure that he was not pushed aside by his own people, and that any further American aid to China should remain entirely within his control.

After most acrimonious debate at Washington the United States agreed to continue an aid-to-China program on a reduced scale as part of the worldwide program underwritten by the Economic Cooperation Act of 1948. An agreement was signed at Nanking on July 3.

Very soon it became clear that this would be aid to Chiang alone and would not reach any of his potential rivals. On September 22 a Vice Minister for Defense was sent to Shanghai to speed the distribution of enormous quantities of UNRRA relief goods and of American supplies which had been held in the warehouses. With this began a great movement to Formosa of materials of every description. Dismantled Shanghai factories, too, began to make the crossing. On Formosa they could be stockpiled beyond a water barrier, wide and deep.

But Chiang's aides were confronted with a truly difficult question. Had Formosan agitation for intervention affected American public opinion to a serious degree? Was there really any danger of intervention? Would the United States or the United Nations move to deny Formosa to the Generalissimo?

To test American reaction to the interventionist idea and the trusteeship proposals, Governor Wei dispatched Stanway Cheng of the Information Office for a quick trip to the United States in the autumn of 1948, there to renew old friendships among fellow journalists and to consult with public relations firms retained to "guide" American opinion.

Soon a spate of stories appeared in the American press, stories bound to evoke public debate if there were any substantial interest in the subject. They were of great diversity. Some were obviously pro-Chiang in character, and some were highly critical of the Nationalist Party and Government. Taken all together, a common theme was apparent. "What would the United States propose to do about Formosa if the Nationalists were defeated on the continent?" "Has anyone paid serious attention to the Formosan clamor for intervention?" These were the essential questions.

Prominent columnists soon broke into a rash of stories. How they were stimulated to this sudden interest in the intervention idea I am not prepared to say. Harold Ickes condemned any thought of intervention as a form of "new imperialism." Since his story obviously carried an indirect reference to me in an inaccurate story, I approached him on it. A usually reliable source, he said, had given him the story; he would check it when he had opportunity. Meanwhile, his informant had assured him that any suggestion that the Formosans preferred to be ruled by the United States or Japan was "ridiculous and untrue." "The idea of an autonomous Formosan state [Ickes wrote] is a purely synthetic figurine." In his syndicated column he asserted that the idea of an American trusteeship was an American device through which "American imperialists" desired to exploit the suffering of the Formosans.[1]

Drew Pearson took up the plebiscite issue, but Constantine Brown's commentary most clearly revealed the source and purpose of this sudden spate of articles. Under the heading "Formosa Wants Protection from the Reds" he built the case for an appeal to the United Nations and a program making the United States the Trustee. On Formosa, he said, the vast majority of people are Chinese and that in a total population nearing six million, less than 5 per cent were Japanese. (Obviously he consulted a prewar source when boning up on the subject.) He then continued:

The move, which is said to be only of recent date, sprang from the fact that the inhabitants of Formosa fear chaotic conditions in the event the Nanking Government collapses, and the area south of the Yangtse River becomes the scene of civil war while the northern area falls into Communist hands.

The movement to ask for a U.N. Trusteeship is said to have been first conceived by the youthful Governor Wei Tao-ming, close friend of Chiang Kai-shek, who was China's ambassador to Washington until 1946.[2]

There were other notes and commentary planted about the United States, telling of Dr. Wei's liberal plebiscite proposal. It was obviously a ploy to draw American opinion on the subject, for word of such a proposal by Dr. Wei was never heard on Formosa itself.

Wei's public relations agents were playing a rather safe game; at best a plebiscite held under Nationalist Party auspices would surely show a desire for continuation of the Nationalist regime under American protection, and at worst a plebiscite conducted honestly under United Nations auspices would reveal a fervent desire to be sheltered from the mainland civil war. It would then be time enough to insist that Nationalist leaders remain in authority under UN protection.

Late in 1948, former members of the UNRRA Team who had served on Formosa were scattered over the world. They continued to exchange letters in which the majority deplored Washington's indifference to the state of affairs and to the fact that the Formosans themselves had no voice and no means by which to make their views known abroad.

Because of this, a former UNRRA Reports Officer and Economic Analyst (Edward E. Paine) joined me in preparing a brief five-page mimeographed statement entitled "Will America Face a 'Formosa Problem'?" in which we set forth some background notes on the plebiscite issue. It was not a text for publication but a reference data sheet. This we mailed off to 165 editors and columnists across the country.[3] Soon we ourselves had the answer to Dr. Wei's problem. It was "No"; the view that no one would "ever" be interested in Formosa seemed still to be a valid forecast. Notes of thanks came back to us from several leading correspondents, but our effort stimulated only one editorial — in the *Baltimore Sun*, on January 3, 1949. Clearly, the United States had little interest in the problem of the Formosan people. Where, indeed, *was* Formosa?

A Million Dollars for the Missionaries

Stanway Cheng having done his best to prepare the way, it was now necessary to make a really big play for American support. Time was running short for the Party and Army on the mainland.

Madame Chiang asked the American Government to provide a plane to carry her across the Pacific to the United States. She had urgent reasons to leave, for the Communists were closing in upon Nanking. She flew away on November 28, and on November 30 the American Embassy staff began to leave the capital city.

Madame Chiang had enjoyed an enormous success in wartime Washington.

In 1943 she had addressed the United States Congress and after crossing and re-crossing the country in dramatic appeal for American sympathy and support, had gone on to address the Canadian Parliament. That tour had been a triumph, but now, she discovered, things were very different.

On December 1 at Washington she was greeted by the Chinese Ambassador (Wellington Koo) and by her brother-in-law Dr. H. H. Kung. The State Department protocol office sent someone to greet her, but without enthusiasm. The magic was gone.

She had to wait nine long days before she was invited to tea by the President. There was considerable press notice, however, which helped to focus nationwide attention upon her mission. She asked all American Christians to pray for China. On the day before she was to be received at the White House it was announced in New York that an "anonymous Chinese Christian" had donated one million dollars to the relief and aid of American missionaries in the United States, including of course those thousands who had been forced to leave China and were at the moment telling of their experiences before missionary societies and churches throughout the land.

But Madame Chiang had not flown from Nanking to Washington merely for a cup of Presidential tea, or to encourage someone to give a million dollars to missions. She sought three things. She desired a clear-cut statement of continuing American support for the Nationalist Government. She sought material support on a massive scale, and she asked for an on-the-spot investigation of the situation in China to be undertaken by a top military figure.

It would have been tactless to name General MacArthur; this was left to the Chinese Foreign Minister (Wang Shih-chieh) then at Paris, who suggested "either General MacArthur or General Mark Clark." This politely gave the American President some latitude for choice, but not much.

Of far more interest, it was understood that she was prepared to offer the United States military bases on Formosa in return for these measures of assistance.

While Madame Chiang waited in Washington, a spate of rumors across the world predicted a Nationalist retreat to Formosa, but on December 8, China's delegate to the United Nations (Dr. Ting-fu Fuller Tsiang) issued a statement:

The Chinese Delegation herewith categorically denies and emphatically refutes the allegations that the Chinese Government plans to establish itself in Formosa, and that leading Chinese personalities refuse to transfer to Formosa, preparing "to seek to accommodate themselves to a new Communist regime in Nanking." [4]

General Chen Cheng Prepares the Island Refuge

On December 29, 1948, Governor Wei Tao-ming was abruptly dismissed. Within the week the Governor's Mansion was empty, stripped of its valuable furniture and curios. Dr. and Mrs. Wei left for Hong Kong en route to comfortable retirement in California.

Madame Chiang had been exceedingly busy in Washington and New York and it must be assumed that she found reason to be assured that the United States would not question Chiang's right to hold on to Formosa — if he could — even if he were defeated on the mainland.

To make the island secure, Chiang sent tough, loyal General Chen Cheng to govern there. Chen would see to it that Formosa was prepared for defense and he would show no quarter to any Formosan agitation for independence or UN intervention. There would be no further nonsense about plebiscites. This would be a military administration.

General Chen Cheng assumed office on December 29. There was no time to be lost, for things were going very badly. A great exodus from coastal ports had begun about December 15. This grew steadily in volume until it was estimated that as many as 5000 refugees were entering Formosa each day. Some who had unlimited resources and influence, for example the younger Soongs and Kungs, sent entire shiploads of personal property, industrial raw materials, dismantled factories and foodstuffs across to Keelung and Kaohsiung. The great majority made their way across the Straits as best they could, landing not only at the major ports but at the junk harbors, rivermouths and beaches wherever they came ashore. The confusion was indescribable and the pressure upon the native Formosans brought them again near the breaking point. There was also the problem of Communist agents entering in the guise of refugees.

General Chen closed the ports for a period of two weeks in

February in order to establish a checking system and the Generalissimo's son Ching-kuo was brought in to manage internal security, taking for the moment the title "Chairman of the Taiwan Provincial Nationalist Party Headquarters." Henceforth (in theory) only certified military personnel, government officials, "legitimate merchants" and their families would be permitted to enter Formosa.

Chen Cheng's new Government was designed to give employment to the greatest possible number of refugees who had any claim upon the Party, Army or Government. For the most part Dr. Wei's people were retained in the local administration, but upon it there began to be erected the rough outlines of a so-called "national" administration. Many new Commissions and Committees came into being, offering nominal employment, place and perquisites to the members. In due course there were to be found on Formosa about 1600 generals, nearly 200 admirals and enough bureaucrats to govern the whole of mainland China. Room had to be made for all of them, and all had to be fed by the Formosan people.

As the Communists moved southward in China the country people either welcomed them as a possible relief or resigned themselves to a simple exchange of one military dictatorship for another. Scholars, military officers and civil servants had to make a great decision; some went abroad to Hong Kong, to Southeast Asia, to Europe and America. Some went only across to Formosa, hoping that by a miracle they might soon return. Many declared for the Communists.

Among the prominent military and political figures faced with the necessity to choose sides was General Chen Yi, former Governor of Formosa and now, by Chiang's grace and favor, Governor of rich Chekiang Province.

In January, 1949, Chiang's agents discovered that Chen Yi was dickering with Hsieh Nan-kuang, the turncoat Formosan who had so bemused American intelligence officers at Chungking in wartime and had briefly represented the Nationalists at Tokyo during the Occupation. Now he was deeply committed to the Communists. It is alleged that Chen Yi was talking of a new form of Necessary State Socialism for Chekiang Province, under the Communist regime.

He was arrested on February 14 and flown promptly to Taipei. On March 3 the Formosans were told that Chen Yi had been seized and imprisoned and would be punished for his past misdeeds on Formosa.

The Formosans were skeptical, noting that Chen Yi had been rewarded very handsomely by Chiang and that he had been arrested only when it was discovered that he was about to betray his friend and patron the Generalissimo.

Generals Chen Cheng and Chiang Ching-kuo applied themselves to the internal security problem with ruthless thoroughness. No figures concerning arrests and executions can be considered reliable, but Formosan leaders estimated that at least 10,000 persons were arrested during 1949, some to be detained for harsh questioning, some to be sentenced to long terms, and some to die. The Governor himself is reported to have stopped in the street, ordered the arrest of Nationalist soldiers whose behavior displeased him, and on the spot to have shot them with his own side arms.

The security net spread wide, gathering in Communists, Democratic League members who advocated a "Third Force," Formosans alleged to have participated in the February Incident of 1947, and all known advocates of Formosan independence or UN intervention.

The year 1949 is remembered on Formosa as a year of terror. I shall quote only one letter addressed by an observant Formosan to a former UNRRA team member. This suggests the atmosphere at Taipei during General Chen Cheng's year-long administration:

> Situation both on the mainland and on the island changed drastically since I wrote you last. The former Wei Tao Ming's administration was comparatively stable than the present one.

But except some puppet Taiwanese were appointed to several government high positions, very little improvement has been made as far as the economic situation and the political positions of the islanders are concerned.

Situation deteriorated very quickly especially after the last fall, when the government forces were collapsed on the fronts of the mainland. More than half a million refugees of the corrupted government officials rushed to the island; many divisions of troops were sent [here] for reserve and training. The Taiwanese have to feed these scraps of people.

The c.c. Clique and secret police nest in the island. Their activities are mainly directed against the Communists and the U.S. Trusteeship movement. After General Chen Cheng was appointed as the governor, he adopted very severe oppressive measures just as he adopted in Manchuria.

There is a recent example. About a month and a half ago, a conflict occurred between the students of National Taiwan University and Normal College, and the police. The governor was in Nanking then. The conflict was localized and settled in favor of the students by the efforts of Mayor Yu and many representative Taiwanese.

The Governor heard this when he returned, he got very angry, and told his men "these rascals should be punished severely."

He took the step on 6th of April. On the midnight of 6th, all the dormitories of all the National Taiwan University and Normal College were surrounded by many armed soldiers and about thirty students were arrested. Next day several secret police went to the dormitory of Normal College to make further arrest and a conflict occurred between the students and the police, which resulted in the arrest on block of about 300 students of the Normal College.

The Normal College was ordered to be closed temporarily and reorganized.

Turning to the case of National Taiwan University the case was not so serious. Only about 25 students were arrested and the students held a meeting and decided not to attend lessons until those arrested were freed and their freedom guaranteed. The case was settled between the school and the governor that those who had no connection with the former conflict would be released and those who were suspected as offenders should be sent to court at once.[5]

Before the great flow of refugees was cut off nearly two million mainland Chinese had crossed to Formosa. This figure includes the Army conscripts who came under order and not by choice. (They were merely bundled aboard transports and put ashore on Formosa.)

For the most part the civilian refugees, too, had been fleeing before the tide of battle with little choice to make along the way. They looked with no favor on Formosa or the Formosan people. By tradition mainland Chinese considered the island a wild and barbarous frontier — certainly no place for a true Chinese to leave his bones, his ancestor tablets and family records, far from the family tombs. The Formosans, worst of all, had been tainted by the Japanese and were known to be hostile to mainland Chinese.

Thus by the very nature of things there could be little expectation that the refugees and the Formosans would easily intermix.

This was not always understood by foreign correspondents and American columnists; Clyde Farnsworth, for example, reported in the Scripps-Howard chain that "Formosa's indigenous Chinese have been drawn deeply into partnership with the mainland Chinese." The Formosans resented every new arrival. Too much had taken place in the past and the future seemed too uncertain. Other foreign correspondents were alert to the tensions created by this sudden weight thrust upon the island. A *London Daily News* correspondent noted:

> The Formosans, who did not take kindly to the arrival of the acquisitive Chinese following Japan's surrender, remained unimpressed by Nationalist military might. So far as the future fortunes of Chiang's regime are concerned, the natives are un-

interested . . . Prices have risen nearly one hundred percent in the past three months . . .

The Formosans are probably the only Orientals who wouldn't be sorry to see the Japanese back. That being impracticable, they would happily settle for the transfer of Formosa to General MacArthur's command. Rumors flood the island that should the Nationalist defense fall, the Americans will move to deny the island . . . to the Communists . . .[6]

A distinguished American correspondent (Tillman Durdin, of the *New York Times*) took note that

. . . robberies, depredations to property and other lawless acts [by the Nationalist soldiers] have not improved the attitude of the native Formosans to the mainlanders . . .

The traditional Nationalist practices and policies applied to the administration of Formosa and the prosecution of the anti-Communist warfare from here are proving to have about the same effectiveness as they have had on the China mainland . . .[7]

Chinese Theatre: The Generalissimo "Retires"

One must admire Chiang's consummate skill in discomfiting rivals within the Nationalist organization who thought that by replacing him they might create a fresh administration, recover Washington's confidence and support, and make a successful stand against the Communists, south of the Yangtze. He neatly trapped and destroyed them.

Although at the beginning of 1949 the Generalissimo saw that the Nationalist military position was hopeless, he himself was not prepared to sue for peace. Instead he expressed a New Year's wish for a peaceful settlement and said that he would not stand in the way if one could be arranged.

He knew, of course, that there was growing dissatisfaction

throughout the Government. On January 19, 1949, the Executive Yuan proposed a cease-fire and peace negotiations with Mao Tse-tung.

Two days later — on January 21 — he announced his retirement from the Presidency.

For the next thirteen months the world watched Chinese drama on the grand scale. It must be understood that one of Chiang's few important non-Communist rivals was General Li Tsung-jen, often critical of Chiang's conduct of the Government and of the war, and sometimes mentioned in Washington as a possible replacement for Chiang. In Chiang's eyes, Li had become a distinct threat to his own position. He had not been able to prevent Li's election to the Vice Presidency in April, 1948. Now, thought Chiang, let him bear the onus of defeat.

From January 21, 1949, until March 1, 1950, armies and bureaucracies, generals and prime ministers, civil servants and foreign diplomats were moved about on the Chinese stage by a shadow-man in black. In theory Chiang was in retirement, but it was a retirement designed to prove that he and he alone represented Nationalist China.

General Li was not "President" but merely "Acting President," and upon him the history books would place blame for Nationalist defeat on the mainland. On the day after Chiang "retired," Peking fell to the Communists.

Chiang's withdrawal from Nanking to the relative security of Formosa was carefully arranged to avoid any impression that he was fleeing from the enemy. As all proper sons should do, he first retired to the ancestral home at Fengwha in Chekiang, to "sweep the tombs of his ancestors." From there he went to Hangchow, then to Amoy, adopting the role of a retired scholar seeking a quiet place for meditation. He found it at last, at a beautiful hot-spring resort on Grass Mountain (Tsaoshan) just back of Taipei on Formosa.

It was an odd "retirement." On leaving the Presidency he reserved the privilege of resuming office at any time. He remained "Party Leader" (*Tsungtsai* or *Führer*), and he continued to be Supreme Commander of the Armed Forces. This left very little to Acting President Li. In these offices as Party Leader and Generalissimo his orders superseded the wishes of a mere Acting President of the civil Government.

The American public of course — and most American leaders — assumed that he had actually retired and that General Li was the President of China.

From Grass Mountain a stream of commands went to military officers scattered over South China, and to Government and Party officials. These often countermanded the orders of Acting President Li who was attempting vainly to regroup Nationalist forces below the Yangtze. For example, at Chiang's order the National Government's gold reserves were flown to Formosa, beyond Acting President Li's control, and an immense variety of assets — including the National Museum treasures — were transferred beyond the sea frontier. They were beyond Communist reach, to be sure, but they were also well beyond the reach of Chiang's principal non-Communist rivals.

To hold the line in South China — if it could be done at this late date — Li desperately needed military supply, money and strong support from abroad. But shipments of American arms and relief supplies en route to Chinese ports were henceforth diverted by Chiang's order to Formosa, going to Chiang and not to Li.

Li was also harassed by Sun Fo, President of the Executive Yuan, who ordered Government offices to move to Canton, to be supported there by a powerful clique led by Chen Li-fu. But Sun himself was under heavy fire for mismanagement and peculation and in March was forced to resign. He left at once for comfortable exile.

He was succeeded by General Ho Ying-chin. On April 6 the American Ambassador reported to Washington that "The Prime Minister (General Ho) is still hoping to secure a silver loan from the U.S. and suggested a lien on the island of Taiwan, or its products, as security." [8]

In this and other dispatches the Ambassador documented Chiang's efforts to interfere with Li's attempts to consolidate Nationalist forces in South China and to deny Li military and economic supplies held on Formosa.[9] On April 18 the Ambassador reported:

> General Pai Chung-hsi called on me this morning to report that the Acting President, in view of the latest Communist demands, will propose to the Generalissimo that, peace being impossible, he (Chiang) should either resume full responsibilities of the presidency, or leave China, turning over all authority and national resources to (Acting President) Li Tsung-jen. By such steps the Acting President will seek to force the Generalissimo to end by a clear-cut decision the present state of confusion which the latter, himself, has created.[10]

Nanking fell to the Communists on April 24. Acting President Li flew to Kweilin, to Canton, and then ultimately far inland to the old wartime capital of Chungking. He did not dare visit Taipei.

Chiang meanwhile used Formosa as a base from which to make very sure that although he was "retired" the world should understand that he was "China." It was a *bravura* performance. He arranged to be invited to the Philippines and to Korea, proposing a Pacific Union or a Far Eastern Anti-Communist Alliance, speaking for China as if he were still Chief of State. On April 27, when Nanking had fallen and Shanghai was about to go, he announced with a straight face that he was personally determined "to suppress the Communist rebellion." On June 20 he announced that all seaports in Communist-held China were closed to international trade.

Shanghai, one of the world's largest cities, fell to the Communists on May 27. Chiang had entrusted its defense to a favorite, General Tang En-po, whose idea of a proper stratagem was to erect a wooden palisade — a fence of stakes — for a distance of some forty miles about the city. It was a grotesque illustration of Tang's capabilities and of Chiang's "military genius."

The Communist occupation of Shanghai marked an end to an era in Formosan history. Since midyear 1945 Shanghai had formed the island's principal link with the mainland and had dominated its economic life. The fall of the great port city broke this tie; henceforth Formosa would resume its position in the maritime world, linked with Japan on the north, the United States across the Pacific, the Philippines to the south, and, through Southeast Asia, with distant Europe.

Shanghai was crowded with refugees who had not been able to make their way over to Formosa. On June 29 Chiang's planes, operating from Formosa, made a savage attack on the great city. Taipei described it as a successful strike against military targets; foreigners at Shanghai described it as an irresponsible general attack which did no damage to significant military objectives but killed and wounded hundreds of refugees in the crowded slums. European reporters noted that Chiang was in no position to follow through in any way and that the planes, fuel, and ammunition were all supplied by the United States. The Communists made great propaganda of it.

The British Government was deeply disturbed. Britain had vast interests at Shanghai which she hoped to salvage through negotiation with the Communists, and serious thought had to be given to the position and safety of the Crown Colony at Hong Kong. The Leased Territory shared a common land border with mainland China. What if the Communists at Peking demanded that London break with the United States in exchange for a guarantee of British interests in China and at Hong Kong?

The question of Formosa's legal status was raised in the House of Commons, and Taipei's standing in the United Na-

tions became the subject of serious debate. How long would
America's allies and friends be willing to go along with the pretense that Chiang truly represented China? Did Chiang in exile have a greater value to the United States than the British
Government and members of the British Commonwealth?

The influential *London Economist* observed that since Formosa had been surrendered to the Allies and General Mac-
Arthur was acting as Supreme Commander for the Allied
Powers — including the British Crown — perhaps it was time
to bring about reversion of Formosa to the Allied Command
pending the settlement of Formosa's status by treaty.

By midyear 1949 the Department of State at Washington
was paralyzed; it had lost the initiative for policy-making here,
for on the domestic scene it had little public support and it was
at loggerheads with the military activists. It could not take a
realistic approach to the problem in international discussions.

The Nationalists were in pell-mell retreat everywhere, but
for the benefit of their American supporters they announced
that they had "two million crack troops" ready to put into the
field which lacked only the necessary equipment. On August 1
the Retired President announced that he had reestablished the
headquarters of the Emergency War Council in his residence
on Grass Mountain, far indeed from the fighting front. The
Secretariat of the Nationalist Party had also established itself
there in the safety of the Formosan hills. Formosa's Governor,
General Chen Cheng, occupied a rather ambiguous position
vis-à-vis the Acting President and the roving "Central Government" on the continent. His loyalties definitely were with
Chiang.

Foreign governments were obliged to communicate with
General Li, the *de jure* Acting Chief of State. Chiang on his
part realized that he must remain closely identified with the *de
jure* Government of the Republic of China. To this end he flew
off from time to time to "confer" with the Acting President.

On August 20 the American Embassy in China was closed

without ceremony. Far across the world in Washington the State Department released the controversial "White Paper" entitled *United States Relations with China* with which it hoped to document its reasons for bringing the China Aid program to an end.

October 1 brought the Communist declaration that Peking was once again the capital of China. It was a fateful moment, opening a new era in modern history. Russia at once recognized the new Communist Government which styled itself the People's Republic of China. The Nationalists promptly "broke off relations" with the USSR, and Washington as promptly reaffirmed its recognition of the Nationalists.

The Retired President followed Acting President Li everywhere and continued to send along a stream of interfering messages and emissaries, disrupting the Acting President's plans and issuing orders to his subordinates. Li moved the capital to Chungking on October 12, and Chiang in due course flew in "to confer." On November 30 Chungking fell. The headquarters were moved to Chengtu. Chiang flew there.

Li was helpless, as Chiang intended him to be. At last, on December 7, the Acting President left China for Washington to see what might be done to secure direct American help and to "smother" Chiang Kai-shek. President Truman was prepared to receive Li as Nationalist China's Chief of State. Perhaps even at this late hour, with Chiang out of the way, the United States could help Li organize an effective defense in South China.

PART FOUR

FORMOSA BECOMES
"FREE CHINA"

XVIII

Turning Point

Saving Chiang in Washington

ON NOVEMBER 16, 1949, a *New York Times* editorial reviewed the Formosa Question, noted that the mainland Chinese appeared to be "somewhat" unpopular with the Formosans and that the island continued technically to be enemy territory and an Allied responsibility. Would a United Nations trusteeship solve the problem?

Chiang's partisans professed to be outraged by any suggestion that Formosa was not indisputably Chinese territory. On this point, more moderately, the Department of State found itself in agreement. Ambassador Phillip Jessup addressed the United Nations on November 28 stressing the Territorial Integrity of China as a "background for refusal to entertain the idea of taking over Formosa." American diplomatic missions abroad were quietly prepared to explain a policy statement which would signal the end of aid to Chiang.

Behind the scenes at the Department someone was giving thought to the possibility that the forthcoming declaration might bring Chiang's sudden downfall. What then? Suppose Washington had suddenly to intervene at Taipei? We might one day have to deal directly with the Formosan people.

In early December I was asked, very quietly, to name local leaders who might be "cultivated in the American interest."

There was only one possible response; the conservative For-

mosan leaders — the men who had sought our help in 1947 —
were now dead or in exile. Some time must elapse before a
new pattern of leadership emerged. Perhaps we had forfeited
Formosan trust by our official behavior during the March crisis
and thereafter.

But as the State Department moved to jettison Chiang and
abandon Formosa, American military leaders continued to urge
an opposite course. They could not stand by silently as each
Communist offensive on the mainland diminished the area from
which someday we might desire to mount a counterattack in
Asia. Speaking in behalf of the military interest, Hanson Bald-
win advocated a strong show of the Seventh Fleet in the
Straits of Taiwan and a large military aid mission to China
which should have authority to control the supply of American
arms to the Nationalist Chinese. Senator Alexander Smith of
the Senate Foreign Relations Committee urged the United
States to take over Formosa promptly and said in effect that his
proposal had General MacArthur's support. Smith had just returned from six weeks in Asia; "The feeling I got from Mac-
Arthur and the admirals was that they were unwilling even to
assume that we would consider letting Formosa fall into hostile
hands." Senator William Knowland proposed sending General
Wedemeyer back to Formosa as Chief of Mission. Furthermore
"Goodwill visits by American Navy task forces, including carriers, would have a stabilizing influence."

A number of Congressmen decided to form a "Committee to
Defend America by Aiding Anti-Communist China." Soon the
most extravagant claims were being made for Chiang's "military genius" and on behalf of his armies. The Nationalists
obliged by announcing that they had more than a million men
on the mainland waiting to spring to arms if they could be
given guns. Chiang was said to be preparing a "powerful striking force, poised to move against Communism." Chiang's partisans began to refer to Formosa in ringing terms as "Free China"
and a "bastion of democracy."

No one attempted publicly to separate the issues. The American military interest required the isolation and security of the island of Formosa. Chiang saw to it that they had to take him, too.

Despite General Wedemeyer's note that privileged Chinese had immense wealth abroad which was not being used in China's behalf, some leading members of Congress and many prominent Republican laymen were persuaded that if Washington would just send along enough money Chiang would promptly stem the Communist tide. The "Aid Chiang" bills and programs were of great variety. The 80th Congress had voted $125,000,000 for 1949. Senator Knowland urged huge additional expenditures. Mr. William Bullitt scaled down his earlier estimate of needs from the billions to a mere $800,000,-000. Senator Alexander Smith thought perhaps $200,000,000 might be helpful for the moment. Pat McCarran (a Democrat, but the Silver State Senator) proposed an aid bill of one and a half billion dollars of which the greater part (he hoped) would be sent to China in good hard silver dollars. Mr. Thomas Dewey demanded "much greater aid." Madame Chiang had asked for three billion American dollars to be advanced over a period of three years. It was suggested by one gallant Senator that she should be invited again to appear before the Congress to explain her needs. The Chiangs were assured that when the Democrats were unseated and the Republicans took over the Administration, nothing would be left undone to restore Nationalist authority on the mainland.

But the Chiangs had a problem; the American presidential elections would not be held until late 1952, and the Republicans could not possibly take over direction of policy until 1953. The Generalissimo had to find somewhere to await salvation.

Taipei, "Temporary Capital of China"

General Li's presence in Washington damaged Chiang's projection of himself as the "only possible savior of China." What if President Truman persuaded Acting President Li to break with the Nationalists and allow a Third Force to emerge in the civil Government in exchange for direct military aid to the generals who were still fighting in South China?

The Generalissimo neatly disposed of this danger. He ordered Li's Cabinet to fly to Formosa and there it convened on December 9. Chiang himself flew in next day, declared Taipei to be the "Temporary Capital of China," and set about reorganizing the shattered Party, Army and Government. Formosa was not the sprawling continent with its many unmanageable regional problems; here was a compact island, physically well organized, technologically well advanced, and susceptible to a very tight security control. Not even foreign newsmen might enter without permission, and if one reported "inaccurately" his permit could be promptly lifted. There would be no unauthorized broadcasting from the island. The hunt for "subversive" Formosans would be redoubled.

Here Chiang — always making a great show of eagerness to return to the mainland "alone, if need be" — could wait it out until the United States cleared the way for him to return to power in China.

Retreat to Formosa also enabled Chiang to slough off many embarrassing associates — not least among them his wife's money-hungry relatives. Dr. T. V. Soong declined the opportunity to settle on Formosa, preferring the Hudson River Valley near New York. Dr. H. H. Kung and his wife were already there. Madame Chiang's elder sister preferred to join the Communists at Peking.

For the moment the Communists had neither navy nor air force with which to cross over to Formosa. On the other hand

Formosa's communications were open to the West, to the source of arms and economic supply in America — if the American Government could be made to reverse its "hands-off" policy decision.

Chiang had enough armed forces with him to impose iron control upon the Formosan people. It was estimated that nearly half a million conscripts had been tumbled aboard ships in the last few weeks of the exodus and even Chiang could see that too many had come in. Soon some 25,000 had died of disease, another 150,000 were demobilized, and scores of generals and colonels were retired.

The Generalissimo's principal military rivals within the Nationalist organization — the generals who supported Acting President Li, for example, and a scattering of former warlords who had never been very much Chiang's men — were now being pushed back into the rugged southwestern provinces or down through Kwangtung and Kwangsi to Hainan Island. There the Nationalists were destined to make their last stand. Some of the defeated generals obeyed orders to cross over to Formosa, risking mild restraint or loss of face and influence. Some went abroad, for they could not trust Chiang. Some, taking their men and supplies with them, went over to the Communists.

Would a sufficient reorganization at Taipei provide Chiang's military friends in America with convincing evidence of "military vitality" and his Republican friends with evidence of "genuine reform"? It was worth a try.

On December 21 General Chen Cheng left his post as Governor of Formosa to assume the presidency of the Executive Yuan, the Premiership. From there the tough old general could continue to supervise the civil administration of Formosa as "one of the Provinces of China."

To succeed him, the Generalissimo brought forward Dr. Wu Kuo-chen, better known to a host of important American friends as K. C. Wu. To some qualified observers the choice was a measure of Chiang's desperation, for K. C. Wu was a genuine liberal, a man of highest personal integrity, and an accomplished administrator. He was a graduate of Grinnell College in Iowa and of Princeton University. He had wartime experience as Mayor of Chungking and as Vice Minister for Foreign Affairs. Most recently he had been Mayor of Shanghai. Soon enough on Formosa the island people began to say that at last, in Dr. Wu, they found a Governor who truly had their interests at heart.

Wu took office when Nationalist fortunes were at their lowest ebb.

On December 23 the Secretary of State at Washington let it be known to all American diplomatic missions overseas that in the Department's view "Formosa, politically, geographically, and strategically is part of China . . . Although ruled by the Japanese for fifty years, historically it has been Chinese. Politically and militarily it is a strictly Chinese responsibility."

On that day the Chinese Ambassador at Washington made a formal request for further military aid. The answer was "No," but on the same day the Department reestablished the Embassy to China at Taipei, in the dingy Consular Building. Dr. Stuart, the Ambassador, and his Chinese secretary Phillip Fugh remained in the United States, leaving the office in the hands of a chargé d'affaires.

On January 5, 1950, President Truman formally stated the "hands-off" policy. It was traditional practice, he said, to respect the territorial integrity of China. Formosa had been handed back to the Chinese under terms of the Cairo and Potsdam Declarations.

The United States has no predatory designs on Formosa or on any other Chinese territory. The United States has no desire to obtain special rights or privileges, or to establish military bases on Formosa at this time. Nor does it have any intention of utilizing its armed forces to interfere in the present situation. The

United States will not pursue a course which will lead to involvement in the civil conflict in China . . . Similarly, the United States will not provide military aid or advice to Chinese Forces on Formosa . . .[1]

The President's statement prompted a number of leading Republican leaders to speak of the rights of the Formosan people. Senator Taft was already thinking of an independent "Republic of Formosa"; Senator Alexander Smith suggested creation of "a joint political authority and military responsibility between ourselves, the Nationalists, and the Formosan people." Senator Vandenburg observed that "The rights of the Formosan people themselves must be consulted . . ."

Such liberal Republican voices were soon stilled, or drowned in the streams of abuse poured by the Opposition upon the Administration.

The Nationalists called President Truman's declaration a "betrayal," and basic Chinese anti-foreign sentiment came welling to the surface. There was bitter talk at Taipei and on January 9, hot-headed young officers aboard the Nationalist gunboat *Wuling* shelled an American freighter as it moved toward Shanghai.

What was Washington to do? If it moved to protect American shipping it would be condemned for "pro-Communist" policy, and if it meekly accepted Chiang's declaration of blockade, then it must recognize both belligerents. This in turn would create a new state of tension in Washington's relations with governments which did not recognize the Nationalists.

Across the world in New York the Russians moved to expel the Nationalist Chinese from the United Nations, holding that they represented only a band of refugees at Taipei. It was absurd to pretend that they were a "World Power." But China's delegate was at that moment Chairman of the Security Council, and Russia's motion was defeated. The Russians walked out of the Council (January 11). This act marked the beginning of the end of the Council's prime importance in the world organization. Would the Assembly, too, someday be torn apart on the Formosa Question?

On the next day the harassed Secretary of State (Acheson) made an address which defined a defense perimeter for American interests in the Western Pacific, a line running southward from the Aleutians through Japan and the Ryukyu Islands to the Philippines. Korea and Formosa were beyond the pale.

Formosa was a "continental" and not an "oceanic" problem. Chiang would be left to defend himself as best he could.

Reform! Reform!

What of the Formosans?

President Truman's policy statement had plunged Formosan leaders into despair. For the second time since Japan's surrender the United States had let pass an opportunity to intervene on behalf of the island people. On the day Secretary Acheson declared Korea and Formosa beyond the frontiers of American interest, a poignant letter was addressed to me which reflected the sense that the Formosans had been trapped and would bear Chiang's harsh police rule until the Red Chinese should take the island from him. The letter also disclosed how carefully Formosans scanned every dispatch from abroad and searched every public statement which might bring a ray of hope.

> Thinking that this may be the last chance that you can hear from me, I have decided to write you this letter . . .
>
> [I have been] looking forward to the time when I can see you again on the island "under brighter situation." But I am almost sure now . . . I have to give up my hope, as it is clear now that Formosa has been written off by the United States, and accordingly in another few months I shall find myself under the rule of the Chinese Reds, unless I succeed in getting away from the

island. It will be extremely optimistic to expect that the Nationalist forces on the island will successfully fight the Red invasion which is sure to be launched against the island any time after February.

As a matter of fact, Formosans are hopelessly disappointed at President Truman's statement on the fundamental policy toward Formosa. I wonder what the late FDR would have done if he were still alive. I think this is a situation he could not have dreamed of when he promised to give Formosa to "The Republic of China" (not to the "People's Republic of China"), apparently not paying any consideration to the will of the 6 million people living on the island.

Ever since the conclusion of the Shimonoseki Treaty the will of the islanders has never been respected at every crucial moment when the fate of the island was at stake. Since the shape of Formosa, as seen on the map, looks somewhat like that of a foot-ball, probably the people living on the island are predestined to be kicked around in the game of world politics.

I was very much surprised to read in one of the USIS news bulletins the following paragraph:

"Hamilton Butler (Detroit Free Press) while noting the strategic importance of the island (Formosa) declared: 'The permanent occupation of Formosa as an American outpost would not only get us into a lot of troubles with the islanders themselves, but would involve us in a course of action . . .'"
(Daily News Bulletin No. 140, dated December 17, USIS, Taipei)

I do not know on what ground Mr. Butler could make such a statement, and what kind of trouble he expected, but no Formosans would agree to his statement.

In contrast, an AP dispatch from San Francisco, dated January 4, 1950 quoted Mr. John J. MacDonald who had been the American Consul General at Taipei until last December as saying ". . . Most Formosans had hoped they might be taken out of the Nationalists control through a United Nations trusteeship, but seemed to have given up the hope of that recently when the Chinese Government fled to Formosa from the mainland and established its capital at Taipei. Now they seem to think it would be a good thing if the Supreme headquarters in Tokyo could take them over, provided they could get a guarantee that they would get their freedom later." I have never met any Formosans who objected to Mr. MacDonald's view.

Some Formosans think: "Politically Formosans are mere infants who need outside help in their struggle for survival as a free people. But the Formosans will not remain forever as political infants. If things are to be left as they are now, Formosans may some day grow up to be a formidable and sworn enemy of U.S. under the influence and guidance of the Kremlin."

I know, of course, that U.S. has a lot of other problems to take care of as the leader of freedom-loving peoples in the world, and that there is a limit to the capability of the United States. In this sense such Formosans may be called too self-centered.

Some other Formosans are of the opinion that on deciding her policy toward Formosa, the United States should have chosen between justice and injustice instead of between advantages and disadvantages, and they deem it unjustifiable that Formosans who dislike Communism should be left to fall behind the iron curtain simply because Formosa happened to have been Japan's colony for over fifty years, while Japan, one of the chief culprits in the last aggressive war, is made entitled to the blissfulness of democracy and freedom just because she may otherwise start another aggressive war. History will be the best judge.

While I am writing this letter, I hear the chorus of Japanese military song being sung by a bevy of Formosans marching along the streets and cheering up the Formosan youths who are going to be conscripted this year for the first time since the inauguration of the Chinese rule after V-J Day. The enthusiasm with which Formosan youths responded to the call to the ranks is mystifying, and in a way frightening to mainlanders on the island! I think you can understand why the enthusiasm.

I am fed up with such kind of local life as one can never tell when and where he may lose his life, in whatever outrageous way, but I still pray that present state of affairs may take, in time, a turn for the better. I would like to know your opinion, if possible . . .[2]

To the Formosan elite — men such as this one — Governor Wu now addressed himself with a reform program designed to reduce local bitterness and to secure Formosan support for the Nationalist organization. In his heart he knew that Chiang would not "reconquer" the mainland; it was going to be hard enough to hold Formosa, and the refugees were going to need the full support of the island people.

On January 13 Wu promised measures to promote local self-government. On April 5 it was announced that the Executive Yuan had granted the new Governor authority to hold popular elections for district magistrates and mayors. On paper, at least, this would give Formosans some degree of control over the local civil police, an objective which had been at the very heart of the demands presented to Chen Yi during the March crisis, 1947.

In Governor Wu's new cabinet or council of twenty-three Department Heads, no less than seventeen were prominent Formosans, including some who had been sharply critical of Chen Yi and had been long in hiding. Wu meant that they should have an effective voice in local government.

But when elections actually took place the Nationalist Party agents exercised their right to supervise the selection of candidates, the qualifications of voters and the conduct of the elections themselves. Formosans who were given place in Wu's Cabinet found themselves surrounded by mainland assistants, subordinates and advisors. Governor Wu did his best to liberalize the administration and mitigate abuses, but (as he later said) at every turn he met the secret police and security agents who were responsible to Chiang Ching-kuo.

Wu faced great odds. Iron-fisted General Chen Cheng was his immediate superior in the table of organization, Ching-kuo's security agents penetrated every civil and military office and inspired fear among the common people with frequent acts of brutality, unwarranted house-search and threatening interrogations. In economic matters the ghost of T. V. Soong lurked in the background. In the realm of finance there were two familiar faces. The former Commissioner of Finance for Governors Chen Yi, Wei, and Chen Cheng was Yen Chia-kan, now moved upstairs to become Minister of Finance in the "National" government. This in effect left him in control of local finance at the Provincial level. In his place Wu was obliged to accept Jen Hsien-chuan as Commissioner of Finance. Jen had been Chen Yi's Commissioner of Communications, and Yen's colleague in 1946 and 1947.

We are not surprised to learn that twice within the first fifty days in office (on January 11 and on March 9) Governor Wu threatened to resign. His first administrative crises involved a question of fiscal policy raised by the "professional Formosan" Huang Chao-chin. Huang, it will be recalled, also served in Chen Yi's administration and for his help during the March massacre had been rewarded with chairmanship of one of Formosa's largest banks. When Wu's reforms threatened to disturb long-established arrangements ensuring the proper flow of reward to the proper people, Huang protested vigorously, and Wu took the issue to the Generalissimo. Chiang knew that he had to maintain the new Reform Image for a time, and Wu won his point.

Chiang Returns to the Presidency

In spite of all these stirring reforms on Formosa, in which he had no part, Acting President Li continued to be a potential threat to Chiang. As he went in and out of clinics in America he conferred widely with Americans and with Chinese in America, seeking to crank up enthusiasm for a Third Force endeavor. At last it was arranged for Li to confer with President Truman on March 3.

On March 1, far away on Formosa, the astute Generalissimo announced that he had resumed the Presidency of China. Li's status in Washington promptly became that of a "former Acting

President" and his presence at the White House purely ceremonial.

Within a few weeks President Chiang arranged to have the
former Acting President impeached, *in absentia,* for "dereliction of duty." Li joined the Soongs and the Kungs in retirement on the banks of the Hudson River.

And so history books will show that without Chiang Kai-shek
at the helm China proper was lost to the Communists. Li must
take the blame and the Chinese people must wait for the Generalissimo to rescue them from Communist bandits and rebels.

To match Wu's reforms in the civil administration, Chiang
now decreed a show of reform within the Party and the Army.

With an eye to the effect in Washington, Chiang made Lieutenant General Sun Li-jen Commander-in-Chief of the Chinese
Armies and of the Taiwan Defense Command. No better
choice could have been made for propaganda purposes.

Sun promptly proposed a training program for Formosan
youths, saying that he had found them excellent material with
which to work. He would recruit 4500 in the first instance and
then use them in training a next recruitment of 35,000 men.
This was a radical step, for as the older mainland Chinese conscripts were mustered out they had perforce to be replaced by
Formosans. The new men might be eager to defend Formosa,
but would they be so ready to fight on the mainland?

Foreign correspondents gained the impression that General
Sun was quietly taking a realistic position. He would have all
he could do to prepare adequate defenses for the island itself;
to talk of "retaking the mainland" was window-dressing.

For Chiang the appointments of Wu and Sun were distasteful; for many years he had exercised his genius for creating factional checks and balances with consummate skill. He now
began a reorganization of the Party and Army which would ensure the succession to his elder son, "Crown Prince" Ching-kuo,
and place him in a position to check Sun and Wu or any other
liberals who might think of Formosa as a "second China," a
trust territory, or an independent entity.

Step by step the structures of the Army, Party, and Government were modified until General Chiang Ching-kuo became a dominant figure, next to his father in importance in these three sources of power. The Generalissimo was supreme in military authority. The Heir Apparent was gradually brought forward until at last he became Defense Minister, second only to his father in direct military authority. As *Tsungtsai* or Party Leader, old Chiang held supreme authority in all political matters, interpenetrating the Army with a system of political commissars attached to each military unit and controlling the Government by controlling appointments and supervising elections at every level of this "democracy." Here the Elder Son was brought forward in the Party as master of the Political Department in the Army and as a member of the elite Central Executive Committee which controls Party affairs. As President of the Republic of China, the elder Chiang enjoys special emergency powers — dictatorial powers in times of crisis and war. His son, as Defense Minister, dominates the civil authority under these emergency provisions.

The grooming of Chiang Ching-kuo to succeed his father took place over a number of years, but the process first began to be clearly indicated during the crisis in early 1950. The forced concessions to "reform" and the appointments of K. C. Wu and Sun Li-jen had to be offset behind the scenes. Ching-kuo's ultimate source of power lies in his control of the secret services of Army, Party and Government, and the political commissars placed at every level of the military organization.

This was Free China, the "bastion of democracy."

After he moved to Formosa in 1949 to prepare the way for his father, General Chiang Ching-kuo held the Formosans in line through a policy of terror. The losses of 1947 had been heavy; arrests, imprisonment and executions had continued throughout 1948, but Ching-kuo's advent in 1949 brought on a new era of fear throughout the island.

Anyone found objectionable to the regime, at any level, in

Party, Army, Government or private life, can be labeled "pro-Communist" and be done away with. Guilt by association is easy to arrange and false or malicious accusations are encouraged by rewards. Tillman Durdin comments on the "indiscriminate ferocity" of the campaign which began in 1949 and notes that in 1954 Chiang Ching-kuo boasted that he had broken up (as he put it) an average of thirteen "communist conspiracies" every month over a period of three and a half years. This chilling figure adds up to 550 "conspiracies" in all. Ten years later — in 1964 — it was estimated that Ching-kuo had 50,000 regular policing agents in the many organizations under his control, and that the number of paid informants active on Formosa might be ten times that figure.[3]

The Generalissimo's first concern was with the Army. Pell-mell retreat from the mainland and offshore islands brought into Formosa many officers whose loyalty Chiang questioned. Soon Ching-kuo's agents were naming scores of officers who were not deemed trustworthy and were said to be in communication with the enemy.

The purge which began in early 1950 ran for many months, with disclosures embarrassing to Americans who had so loudly proclaimed the strength of Chiang's military organization. Among the lieutenant generals taken up, tried and executed were the Chief of Military Conscription, the Vice Minister of National Defense, the Chief of Army Supply Services and the Commander of the 70th Division. Scores of less prominent military figures were seized and done away with.

Meanwhile on the mainland the Nationalist military record was one of unmitigated disaster. Hainan Island was lost on May 2, 1950, and on May 16 Chiang's forces abandoned the Chusan Archipelago lying between the Yangtze estuary and Formosa.

To divert attention from these reverses the Nationalist Air Force increased the number and range of its spectacular hit-and-run raids all along the coast. The Communists began to prepare for retaliation, a massive cross-channel drive that would put an end to Chiang.*

By midyear a sense of crisis gripped the Nationalists at Taipei. The great question continued to be "What will the Formosans do if the Communists attack?"

In a spectacular bid for favor Chiang at last ordered the execution of his old friend General Chen Yi. It was announced that he was being punished for his abuse of the Formosan people in 1946 and 1947. Rallies were organized, a ration of fireworks was issued to make a gala occasion, and on June 16, after a year in prison contemplating this event, Chen Yi was taken before the firing squad.

The Formosans were glad to see him go but as they set match to the firecrackers, not a few remembered Chiang's praise of Chen Yi for a "job well done" in March, 1947.

One week later the need for reforms seemed to have vanished.

Chiang Saved — But Leashed

Peking had taken seriously Washington's declaration of "no interest" in Korea and Formosa, considering it an open invitation to push into Korea and to cross the channel.

On June 25 the Communists entered South Korea. Chiang quite inadvertently had been saved by Mao Tse-tung.

President Truman promptly announced an abrupt change in American policy. On June 27 he served notice that the United States would resist Communist aggression in Korea and called upon the United Nations to act together there. He then said:

> In these circumstances the occupation of Formosa by Communist forces would be a direct threat to the security of the

---

* It has been reported that an epidemic swept the Communist base camps from which the cross-channel invasion was to take place and it had therefore to be postponed indefinitely.

Pacific Area and to the United States forces performing their lawful and necessary functions in that area.

Accordingly, I have ordered the Seventh Fleet to prevent any attack on Formosa. As a corollary of this action I am calling upon the Chinese Government on Formosa to cease all air and sea operations against the mainland. The Seventh Fleet will see that this is done. The determination of the future status of Formosa must await the restoration of security in the Pacific, a peace settlement with Japan, or consideration by the United Nations.[4]

This was in effect a blunt order telling the Generalissimo that he was under restraint, for his own good. The United States and the United Nations had quite enough to cope with in Korea, to which the President was determined to confine the fighting if it could be done. Members of the United Nations organization who were prepared to resist Communist aggression in Korea were not at all prepared to support Chiang's "comeback" ambitions in China.

Taipei had to accept Washington's blunt presidential order, but to save face Chiang promptly offered to send 30,000 Nationalist troops to Korea.

This was embarrassing, for the Joint Chiefs of Staff did not want to be hampered by Nationalist units of dubious quality and untested loyalty, nor did Washington want to give Peking an excuse to open a second front by striking at Formosa. General MacArthur at Tokyo was directed to reject Chiang's offer.[5]

The Generalissimo's chagrin was tempered by realization that now Formosa would probably receive massive economic and military aid.

XIX

Formosa's "Republican Decade"

Problems of Representation — and Misrepresentation

PRESIDENT TRUMAN'S POLICY statement on June 27 heartened many Formosan leaders. For a moment it seemed that the United States was about to approach the Formosa problem with fresh ideas. The decision to neutralize the island — to cut it off from the continent — meant perhaps that its value as a forward oceanic base had been realized and that henceforth it would take its place in line with bases on nearby Okinawa and Luzon. The President's allusion to Formosa's unsettled legal status raised a flicker of hope that it would come under the Allied Command at Tokyo or an American administration. Had not General Wedemeyer told the President there was reason to believe the "Formosans would be receptive toward United States guardianship and United Nations trusteeship"? There would be trouble with the Nationalists, of course, but in their state of total dependency this might soon be overcome by skillful diplomacy which would clear the way to develop Formosa's full potential in the Allied interest.

This was not to be. A propaganda campaign of unprecedented character and scale had been launched in the United States by the Nationalist Chinese. An alien group had determined to manipulate public opinion and to create irresistible pressures upon the Administration at Washington. If the policymakers there could not be forced to abandon the "neutrality" program then they should be forced out of office and an administration favorable to the Nationalists must be brought in. The Taipei Government, sustained by American grants-in-aid, subsidized the campaign directly or through public relations firms retained on contract.

A generation must pass and with it the principals who took part before the full significance and details can be established. For an intimation of the scale of operations and the methods employed the reader needs only examine sworn testimony presented before the Senate Committee on Foreign Relations in 1963.[1]

In time Washington yielded perceptibly — or appeared to yield — to the pressures generated by this campaign. This shook the confidence of our major allies, lowered American prestige in international affairs and substantially weakened Washington's position as a leader in the United Nations. The bitter test will come in full-dress UN debates on China and the Formosa Question.

In 1950 the Communist threat to Formosa was very real. The invasion of South Korea startled a complacent America which had so hastily demobilized its soldiers in 1945, put its ships in mothballs and dismantled its great air fleets while a cynical Russia had steadily enlarged its military establishment and moved to subvert or overrun non-Communist nations everywhere. The Kremlin promised to "bury" the capitalist world.

Chiang wanted much more than a safe neutrality behind the U. S. Seventh Fleet. He held his regime together at Taipei only by promising an early return to the mainland but he knew that only an American force could put him there. He wanted first an American commitment to train, equip and transport Nationalist forces to the continent. If a landing could be made in force he could feel assured that he would not be left dangling on the edges of China. An American commitment to move him to the beachhead would involve a moral commitment to support him all the way into the heart of China.

How to persuade the American people that most vital interests were at stake in this? How to keep the money and arms flowing to Formosa in ever-increasing quantity? How to draw the American armed forces into battle with the Communist Chinese on his behalf?

We may doubt that American military leaders were deeply impressed by Chiang's record as a military genius or were particularly interested in his political ambitions, but his interests ran closely parallel to larger American military interests. It had to be assumed that there would be war with Russia and its satellites. In Asia Moscow was supplying arms, industrial equipment and technical advice to Communist China on a massive scale. It would be advantageous to destroy the new Peking Government before it could mobilize continental manpower, natural resources and industrial potential. It was highly desirable to build up a threat somewhere on China's flank to relieve pressure upon UN forces in South Korea. Under these circumstances it was not difficult for Taipei to get a hearing and to gain champions in the American military establishment despite the fact the President was striving to confine the "hot war" to the Korean peninsula.

Chiang wanted a "hot war" on the China coast and so, too, did a number of his champions in the American armed forces. They scoffed when warned that a brush-fire on the China coast could quickly become a conflagration involving not only China but Russia as well. As for local political conditions affecting Formosa's security as a base of operations they knew they could leave that to the Generalissimo; Formosa was governed under martial law and the island looked like an excellent source for manpower.

Christian America was an easy target for Taipei's propaganda. China's conversion had been an American dream for a century and there was a deep emotional attachment to China mission programs. Churches in every township in America offered ready-made and inexpensive vehicles for the dissemination of news concerning the leading Christian family in

China. Missionary societies were active in parishes across the land already persuaded that a victory for Communists in China meant a triumph for the anti-Christ in Asia. Best of all, from Taipei's point of view, church membership and mission support involved Democrats and Republicans alike and an appeal could be made to pacifists as well as to the most militant patriots. If the enslaved Chinese people could be freed, mission work could be resumed.

The most important propaganda prize lay in the Congress and the organized political leadership of America. Congressmen who voted on grants-in-aid were also in powerful position to influence the Administration. They were at this period peculiarly vulnerable. They had to respond to the pervading sense of America's military insecurity vis-à-vis Russia; they could not ignore the argument that Chiang had a ready-made military establishment and was passionately eager to use it in defense of Freedom.

The domestic political situation was open for exploitation. The Democratic Party had been in office since 1933; the "Ins" were solidly entrenched and the "Outs" were desperate. President Truman's victory in 1948 left the Republican Party in disarray; repeated Democratic victories had demonstrated the extraordinary lack of Republican appeal on the usual campaign issues. The "Aid Chiang" debate came along as a godsend. It had distinct advantages, for it enabled the Republicans to charge that Democratic reluctance to increase aid and use Chiang suggested pro-Communist sympathies in the State Department. This was "evidence" that Communists were about to subvert the Government and destroy the American Way of Life. Anyone who opposed massive aid for the Generalissimo must be a fool blind to the Communist threat, a definite security risk, or a member of a Communist apparatus. A second great advantage rested in the distance at which Formosa lay, an island about which the American people knew nothing. This explains the success of the "Senator from Formosa" whose con-

stituents at home could not hold him responsible if things went
sour on that distant frontier.

The United States was saturated with propaganda but as we
wade through samples of it in review we notice what great pains
were taken to smother criticism of Formosa's internal administration and to divert American attention from the great majority of the population. Nothing is said of Formosan appeals for
intervention in 1947 and the March uprising is dismissed briefly
as the work of Communists and pro-Japanese elements on the
island. Nothing is recorded of the Formosan desire to be cut off
from continental China nor of the fruitless effort within the island to secure Formosan representation at all levels of government. The "Free Formosans" in exile at Tokyo are traitors deserving death.

MacArthur on Formosa

The Communist invasion of South Korea in 1950 revealed one
of the larger policy errors of 1945. Because there had been no
reservation of Allied interests in Formosa pending a general
postwar settlement in Asia or a satisfactory treaty, nothing could
be done there without the consent of the Generalissimo.

There was now let loose in the United States a flood of propaganda designed to convince the American public that Chiang
had a powerful military force ready to strike into the heartland
of China. The public was allowed to guess whether "potential
strength" meant strength *in being* (men well armed and well
organized but not yet tested in the field) or whether this meant
strength *which might be developed* from Formosa's man-power
resources. As the military arguments were elaborated, apparently three stages of action were foreseen — first, the island
would be prepared to defend itself from Communist attack and
invasion; secondly, Chiang would lead his "powerful striking
force" to the mainland opening a second front; and thirdly, the

United States would become involved and take over the operation.

It was proposed to base this grand strategy on an island landmass of less than 14,000 square miles in area (two thirds of it rugged mountain hinterland) served by two small ports of embarkation with minor subsidiary anchorages. Across the channel lay a continental landmass approaching 4,500,000 square miles in area. Formosa's population in 1950 was about 8,000,000, bitterly divided. No layman knew the approximate strength of Chiang's Nationalist Army, but the American public was assured that it was nearly first-rate and ready to go. Defense came first. One widely published report said in part, "U.S. military men believe that a Red invasion can be turned back by the U. S. Seventh Fleet together with the Nationalist Army of about 500,000 men who have been licked into shape by VMI-trained General Sun Li-jen." This is a sample of the propaganda spread abroad at a time when professional military estimates at Tokyo and Washington placed the number of effective Nationalist troops at about 50,000 men, enough (with Seventh Fleet support) to repel a Communist cross-channel invasion but with nothing to spare for continental ventures. We need not belabor the point; a significant number of prominent American military leaders were convinced that Chiang's forces must be used, that Formosa when prepared to defend itself must become a base for active attack. The only way to force the President's hand was to convince the public that a powerful and eager ally was being willfully neglected. On April 7, 1951, A. J. Liebling wittily examined the extraordinarily varied and extravagant claims which were then being published, summing them up in the *New Yorker* magazine under the supremely appropriate title "The Rubber-type Army." It was no laughing matter for the Administration, however. The Formosa Problem had become an explosive issue.

Lincoln's troubles with defiant Civil War generals pale beside President Truman's difficulties with the "activist" military leaders for whom MacArthur set the pace with a perfect sense of drama and timing, and with passionate, moralistic rhetoric. He wanted a second front to divert pressure upon his forces in Korea. Americans were encouraged to believe that failure to win a quick victory there might be attributed to politicians in Washington who refused to use every resource available to them. The important visitors who passed through Headquarters at Tokyo were flattered with private conversations and "confidential briefings" which did not remain confidential very long.

We remember that on June 29, 1950 — two days after Truman "quarantined" Formosa — the Generalissimo grandly offered to send 30,000 men to Korea and that the Joint Chiefs of Staff at Washington decided the risks were too great. They notified MacArthur of their decision. This meant a great loss of face for Chiang.

To soften the blow and to make his own position clear MacArthur found time to fly in person to Taipei. There, on July 31 before the news cameras he kissed Madame Chiang's hand in a gallant fashion and then behind closed doors conferred with the Generalissimo. He brought assurances that military advisors and weapons would soon be flowing to Formosa. On the next day, August 1, he flew back to Tokyo.

Months later MacArthur was sacked by President Truman because of his arrogant defiance of Presidential policies concerning Formosa. Since the President had refused to let him bring Chiang into the Korean War and the war was not won, the General had to convince the American public that a great military asset — the island of Formosa — was being neglected.

He was asked to address the Congress and to testify before the Senate Committees on the Armed Forces and on Foreign Relations. What he said there was important, for despite his conflict with the President it had to be assumed that he knew well the conditions prevailing in vital areas of his command and in Formosa. What he said would be listened to with the closest attention and — for the most part — would be taken at face value.

Here is a brief quotation from his testimony before the Senators in which he set forth what he claimed to be his observations during an overnight visit — his only visit — to Formosa.

> I superficially went through Formosa. I was surprised by the contentment I found there.
>
> I found that the people were enjoying a standard of living which was quite comparable to what it was before the war. I found a financial system which at that time was about as sound as anything in the Far East except Japan. I found representative government being practiced.
>
> In one legislative group I went into, I found of the 21 people there were 19 elected Formosans. I went into their courts. I found a judicial system which I thought was better than a great many of the other countries in Asia.
>
> I went into their schools. I found that their primary instruction was fully on a standard with what was prevalent in the Far East. I was surprised.
>
> I found many things I could criticize, too, but I believe sincerely that the standard of government that he [Chiang Kaishek] is setting in Formosa compares favorably with many of the democracies of the world.[2]

This was very personal and very authoritative but by any normal standard these were gross misrepresentations of fact. From the use of the personal pronoun "I" no less than seventeen times in twelve compact sentences one suspects that General MacArthur was at the moment concentrating more on the drama of his position rather than on the accuracy of his report. In any case the General had had a busy day on Formosa; the Senators were not reminded that these remarkable activities had been crowded into one overnight stop involving also ceremonial entertainment and important conferences.

Close scrutiny suggests that these remarks were carefully calculated to counter all questions concerning the internal situation. They reflected underlying concern with the unsatisfactory relations between the mainland refugees and the Formosans and some concern that word of the true state of affairs may

have reached Senatorial chambers. Coming from General Mac-
Arthur, however, these assertions had to be taken at face value.
No later reports on conditions within Formosa from official or
private sources could be expected to outweigh the General's
testimony.

Meanwhile, seven days after MacArthur's dramatized one-
day visit his Deputy Chief of Staff (Major General Alonzo Fox)
flew in from Tokyo to assess Chiang's military needs. With him
was a Survey Group which had orders to have nothing to do
with the State Department's representatives on Formosa. This
was one of many gestures to make it clearly understood that the
Supreme Commander dissociated himself from the policies of
the Truman Administration with regard to Formosa. The Chinese saw where their interests lay.

Three days after General Fox appeared Mr. Karl Lott Rankin
flew in from Hong Kong to take up duties as Chargé d'Affaires
at the American Embassy, Taipei. His memoirs, published in
1964 under the title *China Assignment,* reflect the difficulties
and embarrassments arising from this obvious division of American policy and representation on the island.[3]

On May 1, 1951, Major General William C. Chase established himself at Taipei as Chief of "MAAG," the Military
Assistance Advisory Group which henceforth dominated American activities on the island. It grew steadily larger until thousands of American military men — advisors and their aides —
were present, sent there to build up defenses and to prepare for
the war in China which might become necessary any day.

General Eisenhower's victory at the polls in 1952 was a resounding victory for the Nationalists. Now all the fabulous Republican campaign promises — or some of them, at least —
would be made good. The need for administrative "reform"
undertaken to please Washington in 1950 now lost its urgency.
As Eisenhower prepared to enter the White House the pub-
lisher of *Time, Life* and *Fortune,* visiting Taipei, let it be

known that General Eisenhower might soon "de-neutralize" Formosa, ending the quarantine upon Nationalist action in the Straits. A week before the inauguration at Washington General Chase at Taipei met correspondents at a grand military review to say "I make no promises and no prophecies, but I think business will pick up next year — and I think you know what I mean." [4]

The new President prepared to announce Chiang's "unleashing" in his first State of the Union message, but before it could be delivered the press was allowed to learn that the Seventh Fleet would be withdrawn from the Straits. The wraps were off. It now remained for the world to see what Chiang would do with his new freedom.

Hailing Eisenhower as a "statesman of towering stature" and noting that his inaugural address "breathed like a living thing with the spirit of justice and righteousness" Chiang praised the decision to de-neutralize Formosa as "not only judicious, but militarily and morally sound." [5] The Promised Land was just around the corner.

But there it stayed; Chiang and his splendid striking force, refurbished by MAAG and now unleashed, failed to leap across the Channel. He had promised so often to "go it alone" if only the Americans would permit him. But there was the small problem of naval transport, air cover and the need for massive logistic support. In every New Year's address to the people of "Free China" from 1950 until 1965 and on innumerable less festive occasions the Generalissimo continued to promise action which would liberate the mainland "soon."

The American Military Aid Advisory Group remained at Taipei; Parkinson's Law was at work; long after the Nationalist forces were reorganized and prepared to defend Formosa they continued to grow. American military advisors and supplies poured in until the island nearly foundered under the weight. By 1961 it was reported that Chiang had a military establishment of about 250,000 men, all said to be eager to recover the mainland. But by that time the aging mainland Chinese soldiers were being replaced by Formosan youths. At last the great majority of conscripts were Formosan natives, and for them the mainland is a foreign country in all but name. The total Nationalist Government budget for 1961 was $375,000,-000 of which no less than three fourths was spent to maintain this economically unproductive striking force. Of the total Nationalist budget no less than $250,000,000 was supplied by the American taxpayer.

At the end of the Formosa's Republican Decade Chiang's military establishment as a *defensive force* was too big for little Formosa, and as an *offensive force* was much too small for a significant continental campaign. Nevertheless the physical foundations had been laid for an important base. If the need to occupy it should arise it could be taken over by the United States. Provided, of course, it had not been handed over to Peking through direct negotiation.

The American Embassy's View of Formosa

General MacArthur spent one night at Taipei but managed to see everything on Formosa. The State Department's representative flew in to settle at Taipei, stayed seven years and managed to see considerably less.

In his memoirs Mr. Rankin notes that he never became a controversial figure; he served at Taipei throughout the McCarthy Era when every dispatch from the field was scrutinized by pro-Chiang Senators eager to "prove" communistic sympathy in the State Department. He was compelled to be circumspect; his reports therefore have a certain noteworthy blandness.

As Chief of Mission he supervised at least fourteen agencies having to do with support for the Formosan economy and the Nationalist military effort. Thousands of Americans were scattered over the island in excellent positions to report to, or through, the Embassy. A generous sampling of Mr. Rankin's own reports, notes and private letters appear in his volume, *China Assignment*, which runs to 343 pages. They are full of advice to the military on how to run the war in Korea and how to strengthen the military posture vis-à-vis the Communists in China, and there is even a note that Baedeker's *Travel Guide* for 1909 awards two stars to Yosemite National Park.

But we look in vain for a report on Governor Wu's administration, his attempts at political reform and his struggle to oppose Chiang Ching-kuo's *Gestapo*. The attempts on Wu's life are not noticed, and the Governor's name does not appear in the Index. It does appear once in the text, however, for Mr. Rankin felt called upon to chide the Governor for failure to notify him of Senator Knowland's arrival at the Taipei airport. General Sun Li-jen made the Index when he told the Ambassador that an invasion of South China would require American logistical support and United States naval and air cover, and once again in a notice that after Sun had been cashiered he appeared to be living contentedly in Taichung, tending his rose garden.

Military preparedness in "Free China" involved questions of internal security — not least among them the question of Formosan loyalty to the Nationalist regime and readiness in crisis to make a sacrifice on behalf of the American military interest. We look for Index references to the Formosan people; under "Formosans (*Taiwanese, or Chinese born in Taiwan*)" there are two page references, and only two, both to the same paragraph from a report to Washington. Here the distasteful word is placed in sanitizing quotes — "Formosans." Elsewhere in the text there are at least five un-indexed references to "Taiwan-born Chinese," "native-born Chinese," and "Chinese native to Taiwan." This is rather as if we were to refer to "America-born Anglo-Saxons" or "Canada-born Englishmen." On page 202 all caution is thrown to the winds in a note sent to Washington; here the distinction is boldly drawn with an observation that of all the people of Chinese race on Formosa, approximately 98

per cent are actually called Formosans, and that the majority
were born under the Japanese administration. Furthermore it
is admitted that the Formosans are better physical specimens,
have superior education, and enjoy higher living standards
than the mainland Chinese refugees. On another page there is
raised the ugly question of popular support for the Chiang
Government with the suggestion that the Generalissimo had
better prove that he enjoys popular support on the island before
he sets out to retake China. Noting the surpassing skill with
which Communist states arrange spectacular mass demonstrations, Mr. Rankin incautiously hints that there may exist on
Formosa a harsh and oppressive police system.

These remarks in the Embassy's reports to Washington are
more than offset by enthusiastic references to Free China as a
genuine democracy, a "rallying point for all freedom-loving
Chinese" and an island which had attained a degree of law and
order "probably unequalled elsewhere in Asia, yet without significant restrictions of freedom of movement." Other freedoms
are not mentioned.

One reviewer of these memoirs suggests that the Ambassador
may have stayed too long on Formosa and become "too much at
home in the old tiger's lair," and that by the end of his assignment Mr. Rankin rather fancied himself not the American
President's ambassador at Taipei but rather Chiang's representative at Washington.[6] Of later Embassy reporting to Washington perhaps the less noticed the better, for on excellent authority it is said that one of Mr. Rankin's successors ordered the
Embassy staff to avoid association with Formosans and —
above all — to avoid listening to Formosan complaints.

The Attack on the American Embassy in May, 1957

In the twenty years since surrender I have talked with scores of
Americans who have been involved in the Formosan problem

either at Taipei or at Washington. These conversations have left me with a profound impression that we are over-confident, that we flatter ourselves to think that Chiang is a willing puppet or, if a reluctant dragon, at least one who has become so dependent upon the United States for goodwill and military supply that in crisis he will always do our bidding. But if Americans at Taipei flatter themselves that they successfully "manage" General Chiang Ching-kuo by indirection, they should remember the sacking of the American Embassy on May 24, 1957. The official story of that strange affair is retold by Ambassador Rankin. The unofficial story has been retold by Captain William Lederer (USN, ret.) in *A Nation of Sheep* and by Formosans publishing at Tokyo.

On the night of March 20 an American Army sergeant shot and killed a prowler discovered in his garden at Taipei. An American military court tried the case, acquitted the sergeant on May 23, and flew him out of the island. The victim was described as a minor employee in a Chinese government agency and a reserve officer. In time-honored Chinese custom his widow demanded "consolation money" which was not promptly forthcoming. On the day following the acquittal (May 24) she took up a position in front of the American Embassy gates to scream hysterically that she had been denied justice. This, too, is a time-honored Chinese custom. According to the official story her noisy clamor attracted a crowd, the mob spirit took over, a stone was thrown, and soon the crowd poured into the Embassy compound. The American flag was torn down, cars were overturned and the offices were sacked. Some local employees and American officers were injured before they could retreat from the premises. The rioting began about one-thirty in the afternoon and continued with brief lulls until well after nightfall. Files were broken open, cipher books and coding equipment were tossed about, and confidential and secret papers were strewn through the building.

After many hours of uninterrupted rioting Chiang Ching-kuo's security forces took over the gutted Embassy. Ambassador Rankin returned from Hong Kong during the height of the riot. He visited the site during a lull in the affair but was asked by the Chinese to leave the premises; for they anticipated further violence. When he returned soon after daylight next morning, accompanied by Embassy officers, he was gratified to find the Chinese had been so helpfully attempting to restore order to chaos and to sweep up some of the debris within the building. Approximately fourteen hours had elapsed. The ladies of the American community promptly volunteered to assist in sorting scattered file materials. Some 90 per cent were recovered. No classified materials "of consequence" were missing and enough of the cryptographic material was recovered to satisfy the Ambassador that the codes were intact. Prompt official protests brought equally prompt apologies and indemnities.

The unofficial accounts add disturbing detail to this story and raise troublesome questions. According to Captain Lederer certain Chinese and Formosans and some foreigners had been warned of possible trouble days in advance. It is maintained that the dead "minor official" was a Major in one of Chiang Ching-kuo's secret organizations and that other members of Chiang's organizations were identified as ringleaders whose faces appeared in news photos made during the riot. The screaming widow is alleged to have been provided with a prepared text which she obligingly read into a recording apparatus conveniently at hand when the riot began.

Behind all this lay the odd circumstance that so spontaneous a riot took place precisely on the day when Madame and the Generalissimo were far away at a mountain retreat, the Ambassador was not on Formosa and the chief officers of the Army administration were across the channel on the offshore islands. In a city notorious for its elaborate secret services and policing agencies — all under Chiang Ching-kuo — why was a riot such as this permitted to go unchecked for hours? And why was not a strong police cordon established around the premises, leaving only Americans or Embassy employees to handle scattered cryptographic materials and secret papers? Was someone seeking for documents recording American views on the internal situation or confidential notes which might incriminate anti-Nationalists in communication with the Embassy?

The Missionary Picture

It is not possible to discuss the American idea of "Free China" without touching on the delicate subject of missions and upon the projection of the Chiang Family as great Christian leaders.[7]

Ambassador Rankin notes in *China Assignment* that the number of missionaries present on Formosa in 1950 was about thirty, and that it had risen to seven hundred in 1957. He observes that they were welcomed not only because of the benign influence they had upon the Chinese Government but also because of "evident international political advantages to Free China in cultivating the Christian Churches while the communists were persecuting them." It must be presumed here that "benign influences" upon the Chinese Government is a delicate allusion to Chiang himself.

The projection, in America, of Chiang as a great Christian leading a crusade against the Anti-Christ in Asia is an old, familiar and privileged theme. That is to say one does not question the Generalissimo's sincerity. The stories of his conversion are many and varied but all agree that it was one of the conditions laid down by the old matriarch of the Soong family before she would consent to the marriage of her daughter Mei-ling to the rising General Chiang.

When the Generalissimo accepted Christ there was great rejoicing in every parish in the United States. It was believed that this would have tremendous consequences for mission work throughout China and speed realization of the American dream that Chinese life everywhere would be reorganized according to Christian and American ideals. At the time of the marriage and the conversion the Soongs were the leading Christian family in China, and when it saw fit to ally itself with the most powerful general and chief political figure in the State all things, in time, seemed possible.

The Generalissimo and Madame Chiang have probably been spoken of, read about and prayed for in every missionary society and evangelical church in the United States. The warmth of this emotional approbation carries over easily into any political consideration of support for Nationalist China. The Party cannot be too bad if the Leader is a devout Christian and the Government cannot be too oppressive if it is guided by Christian hands. This was the background against which the Chiangs were elevated to heroic stature in time of war and revolution.

An appeal for the Christian leaders of China reaches all political groups in the United States. A review of press records over the years suggests that whenever a major China Aid measure is about to be brought before the American Congress a selection of stories reaches the American press concerning the Chiangs' rich spiritual life. Undoubtedly they regret this public intrusion upon their privacy.

The stories have a pattern. Favored correspondents who have been invited to breakfast sometimes have to wait until the Generalissimo has finished his morning meditation and devotions. Under these circumstances the story theme becomes "austerity." One fortunate correspondent managed to obtain a picture of the Generalissimo in sober scholar's gown holding an open text identified in the caption as a selection of Methodist "thoughts for the day." By chance the Generalissimo happened just then to be standing before a large statue of Jesus of the Sacred Heart, the well-known Catholic devotional figure.

Occasionally the Generalissimo does speak of the meaning of Christianity for China and of his concern for the native Christians of Formosa. One example will suffice. It is a quotation from a Christmas season broadcast, we are told, and appears in

the official *China Handbook 1953–54* (pp. 478–479). We learn
that the Generalissimo

> . . . exhorted the people of Free China to do their utmost to
> save their fellow countrymen and the Christians on the main-
> land by leading them out of the night and through the bitter
> winter by the strength of their own faith. "They must hold the
> shield of Love," he continued, "wear the armor of freedom, and
> God's sacred sword of Truth to fight Satan and to bring Jesus
> Christ's glory and happiness."

General Chiang Ching-kuo has followed the example of his
father and with his Russian wife and children is said to have
become a devout Methodist. They have been seen attending a
church service and the General, it is reported, has been observed carrying a dog-eared Bible with him on his travels.

XX

Behind the Reform Façade

Cooperation's Price Tag

THE NATIONALISTS AT TAIPEI need no reminder that one of the best-loved American saints is Santa Claus; but the Formosans think he may be something of a fraud.

The military policy change in June, 1950, brought with it a major adjustment of economic support programs. In a sense the Americans took over where the Japanese had left off, but there was an immense amount of work to be done to recover the losses which had been sustained in the tragic five-year interval. It should not be forgotten that fifty years of Japanese investment — an investment of administrative skills as well as money — had prepared the foundations for the Sino-American achievement. This is sometimes overlooked in the propaganda designed to put "Free China" before the world as a shining example of successful "international" cooperation.

From 1950 onward there was an outpouring of printed matter describing and praising projects undertaken with American initiative and paid for with American funds. Books, brochures, pamphlets and mimeographed throw-aways were usually paid for with program funds and were designed to keep the Congressional appropriations pump well primed.

The Rankin memoirs offer a summary of aid programs which

came under the Embassy's general supervision. The so-called
Conlon Report prepared for the Senate Foreign Relations Committee in 1959 provides a more detailed analysis.

When Mr. Rankin reached Formosa in August, 1950, there
were fewer than three hundred Americans on the island and the
available program funds were a mere $20,000,000. In 1952 a
total of $300,000,000 became available and by then Parkinson's
Law had begun to work. When Mr. Rankin prepared to leave
Formosa in 1957 there were about 10,000 Americans present in
an official capacity. There were other hundreds engaged in private enterprise. Commodore Perry's old dream of a Sino-
American administration of the Formosan economy, outlined in
1853, seemed about to be realized.

The Ambassador estimates that the total American investment in military and economic aid for the period 1950–1957
had reached two billion American dollars. The *Conlon Report*
notes that in terms of per capita investment Formosa received
much greater aid than any other country served by an American program anywhere in the world. For the Nationalists these
were indeed the Seven Fat Years.

With such an enormous investment in such a small area it is
not surprising that the total agrarian and industrial output rose
rapidly. Statistics presented to visiting Congressmen were usually set forth to show percentage increases after 1949. Few
opportunities were seized to note that production levels in the
period 1945-1949 had dropped far below prewar Japanese production levels and in some instances had sunk to the production
levels of 1895. Nor were VIP's often reminded that as total production moved back to prewar levels and then gradually surpassed them, the total population on Formosa had nearly
doubled since the surrender. By 1959 it was moving beyond
ten million with a growth rate of 3.5 per cent annually. Not
much was said of the fact that mainland refugees, members of
the armed forces, the government and the Party were non-
producers. All had to be supported by the Formosan farmer.

There was never much left at home when the tax-collector had taken his share.

Formosan friends who wrote to me at this time expressed deep appreciation of American effort to improve economic conditions but pointed out that the net result was to strengthen the hold which the refugees had upon the economy. The greater part of Formosa's industrial establishment had passed into mainland Chinese hands thanks to the postwar confiscation policies. Every American dollar used to subsidize the major industries became a contribution to the unnamed Chinese investors, shadowy figures in the background. The Formosans believed that chief among them was T. V. Soong and other members and associates of the "royal family."

There was undoubtedly a continuity of management of the national and local finance dating back to 1927. During the exodus of 1949–1950 Kung and Soong had left China for the United States and official retirement, but the men who assumed direction of economic affairs on Formosa had been their close associates for many years. O. K. Yui, a graduate of St. John's University at Shanghai, had been variously Managing Director of the Central Trust, Vice Minister and Minister of Finance in the National Government, Managing Director of the Bank of China and deeply involved with other large banking interests, all dominated by Kung and Soong. On Formosa Yui succeeded Yen Chia-kan at the Bank of Taiwan, then became Governor and at last Premier or President of the Executive Yuan. Yen, too, had become Minister of Finance, then Governor, and (succeeding Yui) Premier of the National Government. It was a game of musical chairs in which the Formosans were not invited to take part.

These were the men who continued to handle American aid to Formosa after 1950 as they had handled it in wartime China, working now very closely with the large American Aid mission.

Formosans agree that under Governor Wu there was a great improvement in the administration of law and of economic affairs. Foreign observers agree that graft, corruption and the grosser forms of nepotism were significantly reduced. It was standard practice, however, for mainland Chinese to imply to foreign visitors that Formosans were a rather backward or provincial lot, and that Formosa's technological development was for the most part a Chinese achievement since 1945. Under the circumstances members of the aid missions readily adopted the official line; aid propaganda brochures asserted that the United States was providing "Fuel for the Good Dragon" and mission members talked of their work in terms of the big push back to the mainland. Aid to the native Formosans was a side issue and they knew it.

On the mainland an abusive traditional Chinese landlord system had long been recognized as a prime source of peasant discontent. The Nationalists had talked of reform but for years had done nothing on a significant scale. The Communists exploited these unfulfilled promises to woo support among the landless peasants. Very late — after World War II — American advisors in China had persuaded the Nationalist Government to organize a Sino-American Joint Commission on Rural Reconstruction. It made little headway on the mainland, for its reform program disturbed too many great landholders who were influential members of the Nationalist Party, Army and Government. They would not tolerate change. The JCRR, as it was called, was transferred to Formosa during the great retreat.

In Formosa it could surge ahead with its land redistribution plans. The Formosan landholders were fair game; no one in the Government or Party hierarchy was hurt by land reform except perhaps those who had acquired extensive property under the Chen Yi and Wei administrations.

American aid-program literature gives exceptional prominence to two measures sponsored by the JCRR. The Land Rental Reduction Program which was written into law on May 25, 1951, said that henceforth the tenant-farmer shall not pay more than 37.5 per cent of his crop or crop-value as rental on his leasehold. The American literature calls this a magnificent achievement and a generous reform, but it usually implies that the Formosan tenant-farmer had suffered exorbitant rent-rates before the Chinese came in to liberalize the system. In point of fact the Japanese had established rent controls and land-courts before the war. The exorbitant rents being so handsomely reduced in 1951 had been exacted from the Formosan peasant *after* the Chinese took control in 1945.

The second great achievement, according to aid-program literature, was the so-called Land-to-the-Tiller program set in motion in 1953. Every farmer who held more than three hectares of middle-grade paddy field (about 7.5 acres) or six hectares of dry field was compelled to sell his surplus land to the Government. He was paid 70 per cent of the price in "land bonds" and 30 per cent in stock in government-owned industries — principally industries which had been confiscated in 1945.

Thousands of Formosans were grateful for the opportunity to become landowners or to add a little to their small holdings, even though they found it difficult to obtain chemical fertilizers and had very little rice left when the tax-collector was finished with them. But for thousands of Formosans the Land-to-the-Tiller program brought a sharp reduction in their modest standards of living. Many suspect that the program was designed as much to destroy the base of the emergent middle class (the class which produced the leaders of 1947) as it was to aid the landless peasant.

Few Formosans — very few — had great landholdings before 1945, but there were many who had enough income to support them in comfort at home, to invest in small shops or businesses in the towns, and to send bright sons and daughters on to higher schools and to the universities in Japan. Now they were forced to accept bonds and stocks which taken together could not produce income equal to the income lost when private land was taken up by the Government. Furthermore, they

were well aware that government-owned industries were generating salaries and dividends for the privileged managerial staff
who were predominantly Chinese. From one of my former students came a letter touching on the subject and dated August
28, 1953.

> . . . Taiwan has changed very much since [1945]. 90% of
> Taiwanese become poor and poor. I've lost all my fields during
> these years . . . the Government took up and sold them to
> "tillers." We can't pay daily expenses with salary, which is less
> than $50 a month. Thus we can't educate our children.
>
> There are two ways; one is to go abroad and don't go back to
> Formosa, the other is to get a job in American office, as Mr. ——
> did. As for me, I don't want [to stay] in Formosa where there
> is no freedom, no hope.[1]

I am inclined to accept this at face value, for in a letter to
Assistant Secretary of State Dean Rusk Ambassador Rankin
reported that "due to rapid population growth and to the much
more rigorous collection of taxes from the largely agricultural
population" some American experts in the Aid Mission were
convinced that "the average inhabitant of this island is worse
off economically than he was a year or two ago . . ."

Dumping the Liberals

While the tax-collector's rice sacks were being filled so bounti-
fully what was happening elsewhere in General MacArthur's
contented democracy, where representative government prevailed, the courts were in good order and the standard of living
so high?

The appointment of Dr. K. C. Wu to the governorship in the
last days of 1949 had been a desperate but successful effort to
restore American confidence and to ensure a continuing flow of
American aid. Dr. Wu had moved promptly, boldly and with

vigor to institute political as well as economic reforms. At the top of the list was his program to grant some measure of political expression to the Formosan people. He must gain the confidence of the native islanders. The Nationalist refugees would need Formosan help if the Chinese Communists one day moved against the island in force.

Wu's liberal views were well known. He was never a great favorite with the Generalissimo, and between the Governor and the Heir Apparent there was a wall of mutual dislike and mistrust. Now Wu, with great courage, dared to tell the Generalissimo of his son's extreme unpopularity. Ching-kuo had instituted a reign of fear throughout the island, using the secret services, the police and the political commissars in a ruthless attempt to secure absolute submission to Party, Army and Government. The Governor warned the Generalissimo that the Formosan majority were being estranged to a dangerous degree.*

General Chiang Ching-kuo on his part believed Wu was making dangerous concessions and that liberal gestures were no longer needed. Now that the Republicans had come to power in Washington (in January, 1953) American aid was assured; Wu had served his purpose. But more than that Ching-kuo had lost face before his father the Generalissimo. No liberal civilian could embarrass General Chiang Ching-kuo with impunity. Wu must go.

On April 3, 1953, the Governor narrowly escaped assassination. On April 10 he was dismissed but was given permission to leave Formosa. There was a second attempt on his life. It is said that when Madame Chiang learned of a plot to waylay Wu en route to the airport she intervened with the Generalissimo, pointing out what serious repercussions this would have in America.

Dr. and Mrs. Wu were required to leave their young son a

* Texts of Wu's later communications to the Generalissimo and to the National Assembly on this subject are to be found in *Appendix II*, pp. 480–486.

hostage at Taipei. The former Governor retired to Evanston, Illinois, and there kept silent for thirteen months. At last influential Americans persuaded the Generalissimo to permit the boy to apply for a passport and to leave Formosa.

When the lad was safely away Wu spoke out. In a series of "open letters" to the National Assembly at Taipei he sought to alert the Assembly to the need for genuine reform if "Free China" were to survive. He noted Chiang Ching-kuo's dangerous ambition to succeed his father despite constitutional provision for succession to the Presidency of China. His letters reviewed Ching-kuo's "political commissar system which was undermining the morale of the Army, a system which he and his father had borrowed from Red Russia. He reviewed Ching-kuo's abuse of police authority and his campaign to generate fear everywhere as a means to secure absolute obedience. He noted that neither the Formosans nor the mainland Chinese refugees had guarantee of individual rights, freedom of assembly and publication or the right of free speech. It was a powerful indictment.

The former Governor asked the National Assembly to publish his six-point analysis of the Taipei dictatorship. Chiang quite naturally suppressed it and accused Wu — rather belatedly — of "dereliction of duty," "corruption in office" and "treason."

From Evanston Wu replied that he would be glad to stand trial in an American or an international court but never in a court set up by Chiang. He then addressed a new series of questions to the National Assembly and the Generalissimo, each designed to illumine an aspect of the Gestapo organization which ensures proper public attitudes in "Free China."

In an attempt to rouse Americans to some recognition of conditions on Formosa the former Governor published a vigorous account of his experiences with Ching-kuo and in passing called Peng Meng-chi Chiang's "hatchet-man." The article entitled "Your Money is Building a Police State in Taiwan" appeared in *Look Magazine* on June 29, 1954. But this was the McCarthy

Era and the period of growing crisis concerning the offshore islands where — if Mr. Dulles were to be believed — Chiang Kai-shek was nobly defending American democracy. Wu's voice was drowned in the clamor for more aid for Chiang.

K. C. Wu's fate served warning that Chiang Ching-kuo would brook no opposition in high places. With the liberal Governor disposed of Chiang's security officers turned their attention to a liberal General who had been given prominence in the "reform" period, General Sun Li-jen, Commander-in-Chief of the Chinese Army.

American correspondents had heard Formosans say that Wu and Sun were two mainland Chinese leaders they felt they could trust to give Formosans a "fair deal." This praise had been dutifully reported in the American press. From there it went back to Taipei by way of the clipping services.

Sun freely expressed his belief that Formosan youths made good recruits and took pains to ensure fair treatment for them in the ranks. He, too, realized that one day the refugee Nationalists might need Formosan loyalty. He was also known to believe that Taipei should look first to the defenses of Formosa and should perfect them before venturing overseas to "retake" the continent. It was well known that among foreigners General Sun was the most popular Nationalist officer, that members of the American military mission considered him the finest professional in the Chinese Army and that he enjoyed Washington's full confidence.

Added up, these presented to Chiang Ching-kuo's eyes a most formidable challenge. Ching-kuo is not a regular Army man, a product of the Chinese military academies, but an interloper in the military establishment, raised to favor by his father. Even in 1955 he was holding key positions, however, and could ruin any officer and any member of the Government. He was master of the secret services, controlled the Youth Corps and the Veterans' League and was Director of the Political Department in the Army with commissars or spies in every subdivision of the military organization. From Ching-kuo's point of view if General Sun enjoyed American support and had the loyalty of the Formosan conscripts he was a dangerous man.

Sun made the mistake Wu had made. He found occasion to protest — politely, of course — that Ching-kuo's political commissars seriously interfered with regular Army operations, morale and discipline.

In midyear 1955 the Generalissimo had occasion to stage an elaborate military review in honor of General Maxwell D. Taylor, USA. The American Ambassador was present. Several reckless and dissatisfied young officers seized this opportunity suddenly to push forward with a petition in which they set out grievances. Chiang was furious. On the spot General Sun was relieved of his command, held responsible, and placed under restraint. Then followed an inquiry conducted chiefly by Chiang Ching-kuo's agents. General Sun soon found himself charged with "harboring Communists" in his vast military organization.

He was placed on trial knowing full well that whatever the "evidence" was it could be twisted readily enough and could lead to the firing squad. The court-martial, however, found him not guilty of Communist association or conspiracy but of "culpable negligence." None of Sun's American colleagues would have accepted a "red conspiracy" charge at face value hence he could not be done away with out-of-hand. It was certainly not wise to let him leave Formosa as Wu had done. He was sent off, under Chiang Ching-kuo's surveillance, to retirement at a small house far from the capital, where Ambassador Rankin observed him "tending roses."

A bit of truth was visible through the curtain of words surrounding the trial for the indictment had included not only charges of "culpable negligence" and "harboring Communists" but also an allegation that Sun had "built up a personal clique" for his own advancement.

To discourage any demonstrations of sympathy some three hundred of Sun's officers were arrested in the case — quite

enough to chill any desire in the Army to speak out or act thereafter in Sun's favor. The Generalissimo chose Ching-kuo's
trusted associate General Peng Meng-chi to take Sun's place as
Commander-in-Chief.

A Case for Mr. Dulles

After attending a meeting of the Committee on Foreign Relations one day Senator William Fulbright rose in the Senate
Chamber to declare with some heat that "What we want and
what we will support is the truth. What we want and what we
will support is a Secretary of State who will not treat us as children ready to clap in delight at every fairy story, however fan-
ciful."

He was speaking of Mr. Dulles and his views were shared in
many capitals around the world. From the public record it is
indeed difficult to know which story-of-the-moment to accept
when we search for his basic policies toward Formosa.

No American leader was more outspoken in his condemnation of Peking and all its works and none could surpass Mr.
Dulles in lauding the high moral purpose, dedicated leadership,
and world importance of Chiang Kai-shek and his associates at
Taipei. His record for "brinkmanship" needs no comment here;
who could doubt then that Mr. Dulles considered the Nationalists to be America's most important allies? The Secretary was
not one to walk softly.

As we sift through the record, however, we see that Mr. Dulles in truth thoroughly undermined Chiang's legal position on
Formosa and skillfully blocked his plans for a large-scale continental venture. While talking non-recognition of Communist
China it was he who flew to Europe to confer with China's Foreign Minister Chou En-lai. It was Mr. Dulles who arranged the
ambassadorial meetings in Europe through which Peking and
Washington continue to keep in touch and at which the Formosa problem can be discussed.

The conferences between ambassadors from Washington and Peking take place behind closed doors far from Taipei. The Nationalists resent them, wondering if their claims upon China proper and Formosa are being discussed or compromised in any way. Formosan independence leaders in exile likewise mistrust these meetings and wonder if Washington seeks a formula through which (after Chiang's death) the island may be "negotiated" into a state of neutrality and from a state of neutrality in due course be transferred to Peking, thus restoring "the territorial integrity of China."

It will be recalled that the State Department held unwaveringly to the view that China's territorial integrity must be respected and that Formosa must be restored promptly by treaty signatures. This was the official position on April 8, 1950, when Mr. Truman invited Mr. Dulles to become Foreign Policy Advisor to the Secretary of State. Then came the June crisis — the Korean affair — and the President's statement that "the determination of the future status of Formosa must wait the restoration of security in the Pacific, a peace settlement with Japan, or consideration by the United Nations." On September 8 Mr. Dulles was directed to negotiate the Peace Treaty. He had therefore to steer a diplomatic course through very choppy waters. It was an extraordinary performance, for henceforth his fervent public statements and his "brinkmanship" seemed entirely to support Chiang's territorial claims, but his official acts and hidden negotiations had quite a different purpose.

He soon found a formula which enabled him to circumvent or cancel out that unfortunate "territorial integrity" commitment. He first proposed that Japan should merely relinquish sovereignty there, after which the island's permanent status would be determined by the United States, the United Kingdom, Soviet Russia and China acting together on behalf of nations signing the Treaty. If these four Powers could not agree within one year the question should then be taken into the UN Assembly.

The Generalissimo would never accede to this and Communist China was not a member of the UN nor among the nations summoned to San Francisco. In midyear 1951 Mr. Dulles let it be known that the Nationalists, too, were not invited and would not sign the Treaty. Thus at San Francisco Japan was divested of her sovereign rights in Formosa. Title was surrendered to the forty-eight nations who signed the Treaty, to be held in trust by them until the final issue can be settled in the UN Assembly at some future time. The Treaty came into effect in 1952 and there the matter stands.

Taipei announced that it would not consider itself bound by any provisions affecting its interests. As for feeling bound by President Truman's earlier embargo on provocative cross-channel military action Chiang had long since displayed indifference. Ambassador Rankin notes that there were frequent hit-and-run forays to the China coast; Americans at Taipei conveniently looked the other way.

Upon entering office in 1953 President Eisenhower promptly fulfilled Republican campaign promises to lift the ban. It was well known, however, that he too wanted to minimize the dangers of a full-scale war along the China coast. Perhaps he thought Chiang's military advisors could control the situation by controlling military supply.

Chiang (and not a few of his American friends) had other ideas. He was determined to provoke an open conflict between the United States and Communist China. No other conclusion can be drawn from the pattern of subsequent events. Throughout 1953 the number of cross-channel raids increased in number. The Nationalist Air Force extended the range of attack to reach inland cities and industrial targets. Significantly there were no visible efforts to "go it alone."

Soon the world's attention was fastened on Quemoy and the Matsu base — the offshore islands. As Chiang built up his installations on Quemoy with an immense amount of publicity the Chinese Communists developed highways and railways leading into the coastal area and began a build-up there to block any Nationalist attempt to cross the Quemoy water barrier in force.

But still Washington would not agree to support offensive action on a large scale. The Nationalist propaganda campaign within the United States was being pushed to an extreme and was generating an extraordinary pressure upon the Eisenhower Administration. At midyear 1954 Chiang attempted to tip the scales by a move of extraordinary boldness. Nationalist naval units with air support captured a Polish freighter and a Russian tanker in waters near Formosa. This was not a hit-and-run strike against Communist fishing craft along the coast but an act of piracy on the high seas. This was brinkmanship of a new order.

At what point here would Moscow's obligations to Peking overweigh Washington's commitments to Taipei?

President Eisenhower looked at his military maps with a professional eye and decided that the risks were becoming too great. On September 9 Mr. Dulles flew into Taipei for a five-hour talk with the Generalissimo. He flew away again solemnly announcing that "China does not stand alone."

On December 2, at Washington, the Sino-American Defense Treaty was signed. In this new document the Nationalists promised to leap to the defense of the United States if it were attacked by a third party and the United States promised to defend Formosa and the Pescadores. It was reserved to the President of the United States to decide if the offshore islands — meaning Quemoy and the Matsus — were to be defended with American help.

Chiang seemed to have agreed that the head of a foreign state could make decisions vital to Free China's welfare. Mr. Dulles on his part had shrewdly moved to sharpen the line of demarcation in the Straits.

The Generalissimo was not to be thwarted; to maintain his regime intact at Taipei he had to prove that he was on the offensive and that return to the homeland was imminent. Vio-

lating the spirit and the intent of the new Treaty before it had
been confirmed by the Congress, he stepped up offensive action
far to the north in the Tachen islands lying between Formosa
and the Yangtze River estuary.

This renewed and heightened the sense of crisis and the dan-
gers of "brinkmanship" in early 1955. Under instructions from
Washington Chiang's American advisors informed him that
American naval units would help him withdraw from the
Tachens but would not support him there in offensive action.
Most reluctantly he ordered the evacuation of Nationalist
forces and with them, willy-nilly, brought off some 14,000
Tachen villagers who had no interest whatsoever in being "lib-
erated" in this manner. To them Formosa was foreign territory
but they had no choice.

On March 3 the busy Secretary of State again appeared at
Taipei to repeat and impress upon the Generalissimo the President's desire to reduce dangerous tensions in the area. For public reassurance there were formal statements and clouds of
rhetoric concerning partnership in defense of Free China and
the Free World. The Nationalists were assured again that if
Washington deemed an attack on Quemoy or the Matsus a direct threat to Formosa or the Pescadores then all restraints
upon Nationalist action would be lifted.

Mr. Dulles needed that clear-cut territorial definition if he
were to bargain with Peking. He let it be known by indirection
that Communist China might have the offshore islands if it
would not attempt to take them by force.

Thereafter there continued to be a great many verbal pyro-
technics and not a little smoke and fire concerning Quemoy.
But has Peking at any time been serious there? Certainly the
Communists would resist any Nationalist attempt to advance
beyond the water barriers, but otherwise the situation worked
well to Peking's advantage. If the Communists succeeded in
taking Quemoy they would be faced with the need to make
good promises to take Formosa as well and that endeavor would
certainly mean the quick destruction of Chinese cities and in-

dustrial concentrations everywhere in China. They gave some indication of their contempt for Chiang's position when they instituted the ridiculous Monday-Wednesday-Friday bombardment schedule at Quemoy as if daring Chiang to waste his resources on Tuesdays, Thurdays and Saturdays.

Meanwhile the Nationalists used Quemoy as a major propaganda resource. An enterprising Formosan once counted the published records of more than two thousand foreign visitors flown over from Taipei within a short space of time to see how seriously Chiang is determined to "retake" the continent. At Tokyo Formosans speak of the offshore islands as "Chiang's Quemoy-Matsu National Park." Mr. Dulles was photographed there, looking grimly impressed.

Formosan leaders in exile watched all of this with close attention. They appreciated Dulles's efforts to sever the links with the mainland but they were baffled by fulsome praise of Chiang's moral leadership in the Free World and of Formosa as a symbol shining before all freedom-loving peoples. They were aware of Mr. Dulles's occasional hints that UN action and a plebiscite might provide solution for the Formosa problem; none knew what form the plebiscite might take nor what choices might be placed before the Formosan people.

Getting at the Facts: The Conlon Report

As Formosa's "Republican Decade" drew to a close the Senate Committee on Foreign Relations at Washington determined to probe the realities of the American position in Asia if this could be done. A team of specialists was asked to bring in a report on the facts and an analysis of the problems.*

* The Conlon Associates group produced the study under the title *U.S. Policy — Asia*. Three University of California specialists were the principal team members. Professor Richard Park prepared the section on South Asia, Professor Guy Pauker wrote the section on Southeast Asia and Professor Robert A. Scalapino prepared the section on Northeast Asia, with subsections on "Communist China and Taiwan."

On November 1, 1959, the Senate Committee published the *Conlon Report*.[2] This dispassionate and orderly presentation provided a fresh breeze to disperse the clouds of diplomatic and military rhetoric through which the Foreign Relations Committee had been so long groping its way. The basic issues could never be quite so confused again.

The emergence of a strong Communist China was recognized by the reporting specialists. Peking was rapidly establishing its claim to be a world power. It could no longer be described in Chiang's terms as a temporary accession of "bandits." To the population of 660 millions there must be added each year millions more. A highly developed organization of economic manpower and natural resources was backing up an army in excess of 2,500,000 men.

Against this formidable power unit the United States had been persuaded to pit Formosa with a deeply divided population and an army far too small to make headway on the mainland, but much too large for the island economy to support. Formosa, to keep afloat, was wholly dependent upon heavy American subsidies.

The *Conlon Report* noted the unrealistic military ambitions of the dominant minority, and the gap between this minority and the Formosan natives. It warned of Communist appeals to homesick mainland Chinese, urging them to come home where — Peking said — "all will be forgiven."

On the other hand, the Formosans want to stay on Formosa and for them to talk of "return to the mainland" is meaningless. Among the Formosans communism has little appeal; the local ideal is autonomy or independence under a guaranteed neutrality.

The *Report* examines and deflates the argument that Formosa as "Free China," has appeal for overseas Chinese living in other parts of Asia; it is scarcely a "rallying-point for freedom-loving Chinese." It warned of the danger attending American insistence that Chiang's government is the "Government of

China" and that Taipei alone can be recognized in the United Nations.

In presenting policy alternatives the authors suggested that the United States should cancel commitments involving the off-shore islands and should see to it that the Nationalists withdraw. Disengagement there and a clear line of demarcation in the Straits are essential if policies are to be realistic and practical.

It was observed that if Formosa could be held neutral for a sufficient period the mainland refugees would be absorbed by the island people. On the other hand the *Report* warned that a serious crisis at some unexpected point might call for swift decisions at Washington. The succession problem is a major danger point.

An oblique reference to Chiang Ching-kuo and his clique was made in these words:

> In the event of a bargain between some political leaders on Taiwan and the communists, to be sure, the United States might be placed in an extremely awkward position whereby it would have to decide hastily whether it should intervene in an attempt to protect the Taiwanese right of self-determination.[3]

The *Conlon Report* proposed a Republic of Taiwan under an American guarantee of its defense and of assistance to all mainland refugees who would wish to return to China proper or go elsewhere overseas. To propose the transfer of Formosa to Communist China in seeking a general settlement in Asia without the consent of the people on Formosa would be an "immoral act" and would seriously undermine American relations with all smaller countries who look to the United States for aid in maintaining independence.

> The Taiwanese people themselves have given considerable indication of wishing to remain separate from the mainland and could be tested by plebiscite if this were agreed.

XXI

Two Chinas?

Red China's Formosa

I FIRST HEARD THE "Two Chinas" idea put forward in 1945 in an address at Princeton University. A senior officer in the Department of State suggested the possibility of a division within China — perhaps at the Yangtze River line — which would produce a Communist North and a Nationalist South. But from 1945 until 1950 the State Department held rigidly to the "territorial integrity" or "This is China now" thesis, and from 1950 until 1960 China proper was considered to be "overrun" and "occupied"; Chiang, as President of China, governed from a temporary capital in an unoccupied or free province. After 1960 there began to be serious talk of "two Chinas" and the talk was not Chinese. One wonders, when the suggestion for "two Chinas" is advanced at Washington or by China specialists, if it is always put forward in good faith. Washington knows that Peking will never recognize the existence of a second China, and neither will Chiang Kai-shek at Taipei. It is difficult to believe that the United Nations could be persuaded by the United States to recognize a "Big China" and a "Little China."

Communist leaders state most emphatically that the Formosan Problem must be solved and Peking's claims to the island must be recognized before there can be any consideration of other issues outstanding between the United States and China. They promise the Formosans "liberation."

The Formosans on their part think of it as a threat rather than as a promise. At the risk of repetition let us take note of some Communist activities on the island and propaganda relating to it.

The Generalissimo blamed the 1947 disturbance on "communists" and "Japanized renegades," but we had reason to believe that fewer than fifty professed Communists appeared during the March affair. Six years later — in 1953, three years after the Nationalists' retreat — Chiang Ching-kuo claimed that he had been breaking up "communist conspiracies" at an average rate of thirteen per month. On the face of it we have either to believe that an extraordinary number of mainland Communists had crossed over in 1949–50 or that an extraordinary number of Formosans had become Communists under Nationalist Chinese rule.

Neither was the case. Undoubtedly the number of Formosan converts grew larger in that period and we may be sure that Peking had sent in many crusading agents, but the explanation of Ching-kuo's boast lies elsewhere. He was charged with internal security; and merely exercised his power to pick up suspects without warrant. Anyone known to have expressed criticism of the regime was fair game. They were given the "communist" label, sentenced to long prison terms or disposed of with a bullet. Formosans who spoke of intervention or dared to talk of independence walked in special danger.

The only well-known Formosan Communist was Miss Snow Red whose presence and activities in the Taichung area we noticed on an earlier page. Her career deserves further remark, although her name may be the only romantic touch about her; she was tough in character and utterly dedicated to her subversive mission.

Hsieh was born about 1900 in the Taichung district and therefore as a young girl lived through the period of Japan's military campaigns to put down Formosan rebels in the foothills and exterminate aboriginal tribes in the mountains. In the early 1920's she joined in promoting the Home Rule Movement led by Lim Hsien-tang. When harsh Japanese police reprisals drove scores of young Formosan irreconcilables into exile she went over to Shanghai and there, in 1925, joined the Communist Party. Soon she followed Chiang Kai-shek's footsteps to Moscow where she studied at the Labor University. In the year that Chiang Ching-kuo went off to Moscow for an education (1927) Hsieh returned to Shanghai and soon slipped back into Formosa to work with an underground Communist cell directed from Tokyo. After at least three arrests the Japanese sent her to the penitentiary. Having served eight years of a thirteen-year sentence she was released because of extreme ill-health and allowed to go back to Taichung to live quietly under strict surveillance.

It was assumed then that she would soon die of tuberculosis. But she was tough in spirit and when MacArthur's amnesty order in 1945 opened the penitentiary doors for all political prisoners Miss Hsieh was ready to welcome her companions to Taichung district. Little was heard of them as conditions ripened for local rebellion in 1947. When it came members of the Taichung group attempted to establish themselves as leaders in attacks upon the homes of well-to-do farmers and local townsmen believed to be hoarding rice.

The Formosans were not yet hungry enough; this was not a doctrinaire class struggle according to Marx or Mao but a Formosan struggle against the mainland carpetbaggers. When the Nationalist troops came in on March 8 the Communists fled to the mountains. Some were caught but Miss Snow Red is believed to have left Formosa on July 16. Going over to Hong Kong she attempted to establish herself among the new exiles, with little success. In due course she went over to Shanghai and then on to Peking to become a leader among Formosan Communists in China.

Peking Prepares to Liberate Formosa

No one knows how many Formosans remained in the coastal cities in 1949. There were old, well-established Formosan communities in Shanghai, Amoy, Foochow and Canton. Some Formosans remained on the continent by choice, prepared to take a chance with the incoming Communist regime, but many anti-Communists were trapped at the ports, unable to find homeward transport.

To the long-established Formosan groups there had been added a very large number of young men who were labor-conscripts in the Japanese army, stranded in China in 1945 wherever Japanese forces had surrendered. Thousands then had no place to go and no means of livelihood and were often treated roughly by the Nationalists as "Japanized traitors."

In 1947 these two older Formosan groups in China proper were joined by the young men and women compelled to flee Formosa after the February uprising. Many were deeply embittered by what they considered an "American betrayal." Among them were exceptionally able youths who had worked desperately to attract American attention before the March affair and had then seen Chiang's troops roll through Taipei streets in weapons carriers bearing "U.S.A." clearly legible under thin coats of paint.

Communists everywhere promptly adopted the February 28 Incident, as it is called, as the chief rallying point in propaganda, claiming that the Chinese Communists brought it about. They called on Formosans to observe the anniversary as a testimonial to Mao's noble effort to free Formosa from the Nationalists, the "running dogs of American imperialism."

Soon the Formosans in China were being rounded up, registered, and sent off to be "re-educated." They were to be prepared for the "liberation" to come. Many were assigned to a

"Taiwan Recovery Training Corps" encampment near Shanghai.

Some may have joined up with dedicated enthusiasm but the majority had no choice; a Formosan reluctant to cooperate in the liberation work was a reactionary and for reactionaries there was no room in the New Order.

At the Hsin Chuang training camps internees were placed under guidance of professional Communists skilled in "re-education" techniques. They were promised a better life under Mao Tse-tung than they had ever known under Chiang Kai-shek, and for many of them any change would be a change for the better. The United States was charged with being in illegal occupation of Chinese territory and Chiang was described as Washington's puppet or straw-man.

Peking's early propaganda directed to Formosa was designed to appeal to mainland Chinese officers and men in the armed forces, urging them to sabotage Chiang's efforts and to "come home." But the Chiangs' very thorough purge of ranking officers and the elaborate development of the political commissar system among conscripts appears to have brought some shift in propaganda emphasis. Henceforth it was directed to the civilian refugees, urging them to return to the mainland and promising amnesty and employment. If they came of their own accord all would be forgiven. On one point Peking's propaganda was unwavering; all talk of UN intervention, of autonomy, trusteeship, or independence was condemned as "treason." Here Chiang Kai-shek and Mao Tse-tung were in complete agreement.

For a time Peking praised and encouraged the Formosans who had become active Communist leaders. The turncoat Hsieh Nan-kuang who had served Chiang in Occupied Japan worked now with the Central Communist Party organization at Peking and as an advisor at the Taiwan Recovery Training Corps base. The training program Director is reported to have been a Formosan woman named Chu Chen-tse whose principal lieutenants for field work divided the island into operational districts. Tsai Hsiao-chien was assigned to the important Taipei-Keelung area; Snow Red was sent back to her native Tai-chung, and Chen Shih-ming is said to have been appointed principal agent for the south. Chu Chen-tse in due course slipped into Formosa, was captured and executed.*

For a time Snow Red was a star performer for broadcasts and training programs with additional duties as Vice Chairman of the China Youth Federation. Formosans who were not selected for the Liberation Corps training were expected to show enthusiasm in other ways. Those who voluntarily sought to join the Party, and were permitted to do so, were also permitted to form a "Taiwan League for Democratic Self-Government."

Using Hong Kong as a way station Formosan Communists in China established communication with those in Japan and there, too, formed a "Taiwan League for Democratic Self-Government" so-named to embarrass much larger, vigorously anti-Communist Formosan groups in Tokyo. The prime purpose was to discredit appeals for United Nations intervention.

All refugee groups had by now adopted February 28 as the principal anniversary for an outpouring of propaganda and used the "2–28" designation as a slogan reference. The Nationalists and their American protagonists would like to belittle and forget the Incident but they do so at risk; the affair left a wound which will not heal in this generation.

But February 28 and its aftermath did cause some embarrassment. Communist propagandists had to explain away the fact that Formosans had made it very clear they wanted nothing to do with *any* mainland Chinese, either Communist or Nationalist. Moreover some of the new recruits to communism — refugees who had survived the March massacre at Taipei and the subsequent manhunt — had been prominent among the

* Information and rumor concerning the Communist organization and activities usually cannot be verified or directly documented. The account here must be read with this qualification in mind. GHK.

young men who sought American help in the weeks just before the Generalissimo sent in his troops.

An issue of the communist *China Digest*, dated February 22, 1949, carried a long commemorative article entitled "Taiwan: The Marble Ball and the Marble Lion" in which it was predicted that Japan, the United States and the Nationalist Chinese would struggle henceforth for possession of the island but that like the marble ball in the sculptured lion's mouth, Formosa can never be taken from China.

The author (Li Chun-ching) blames Formosan attitudes upon the United States, of course, writing of the secret agents of the U.S.A., including consular officials of the American Consulate in Taipei, "who did infiltrate into the insurgent crowds dishing out sweets and cigarettes and encouraged them with profuse applauds." According to this account a youth employed by the Consulate proposed intervention but was hissed and booed. The story of Li Wan-chu's alleged visit to the American Consulate which had been published at Hong Kong in 1947 was now republished in 1949 with suitable variations and on the expressions of Formosan dislike for all mainland Chinese the author had this to say:

> Ignorant mobs were not able to distinguish those who served in Chen Yi's mal-administration and the innocent ex-provincials, so, as a result, there were bound to be people who received undeserved blows. To conclude from this that the Civil Rebellion had anti-Chinese tendencies would be very erratic indeed . . .
>
> In a country so vast as China there is provincialism in every province. Only in this sense can one admit the regional feeling in the Rebellion. But the real object of their hatred was Chen Yi, the stooge of Chiang Kai-shek. People from the mainland unfortunately were identified with that evil regime by some ill-informed Taiwanese . . .
>
> The Civil Rebellion was mainly a display of the terrific energy of the Taiwanese. Even Chen Yi remarked with a sigh and admiration that "the Nationalist Government would long ago have

been crushed had all the Chinese in China proper possessed the same strength." [1]

Communist pamphlets and books began to be smuggled into Formosa. The unvarying theme was the wickedness of American imperialism and the unchanging aim was to disabuse Formosans of any hope for intervention.

The story of the "public opinion survey" which the American Office of Strategic Surveys attempted to make in late 1945 was retold with gross inaccuracy to prove how early the United States had planned to separate Formosa from the Mother Country. The "anti-American" demonstrations staged by Chen Yi's men in December, 1946 and January, 1947, were recalled in this Communist version:

> To protest against American imperialistic aggression of China, over 10,000 students in North Taiwan held an impressive demonstration on January 9, 1947, shouting "American troops, Get Out of China." In opposition to the despotic rule of the American puppet KMT the peoples of Taiwan Province launched the February 28th Movement two years ago and set in motion a vigourous armed uprising throughout Taiwan." [2]

A small volume entitled *Taiwan in Anger* (*Fen Nu ti Taiwan*) printed at Hong Kong in 1949, purports to tell the overall story of American effort to seduce the Formosan people. According to this, three officers working at the American Consulate (Kerr, Catto, and Conlon) were mere catspaws for the imperialists. By showing friendship for the island people, they hoped to establish intelligence sources and a Fifth Column. Kerr (it continued) created the "people's voice" calling for American control; Catto, through management of the USIS facilities, told the world about this and showed the Formosans what steps to take to secure American intervention, and Conlon later cleverly changed the propaganda line from a request for "American control" to a demand for "independence" which in the long run would come to the same thing.[3]

The Russians took up the issue on behalf of Peking. At Moscow the journal *Red Fleet* declared that "Formosa was, is, and always will be the national territory of China," and *Isvestia* proclaimed that with Japan's capitulation in 1945, Formosa automatically reverted to China. "Clearing this island of Nationalist Party reaction — this is the internal affair of the Chinese people."

After the Bandung Conference Peking's propaganda developed what might be called the "sweetness and light" approach, appealing to the tired and disillusioned mainland Chinese refugees to come home voluntarily. This was during the period when Chiang Ching-kuo is alleged to have been in secret communication with Chou En-lai, Peking's Foreign Minister. In 1958 the bombardment of Quemoy and Matsu was resumed and with it there came a slight change in propaganda. The mainland Chinese refugees were urged to realize that the United States was promoting the Independence Movement in order to deprive the Nationalists of Formosa. Here was an obvious attempt to drive a wedge between the Nationalists and the Formosans; behind it lay a hardening of attitudes toward the Formosans at Peking and the attempt on Formosa to form an Opposition political party bringing together Formosans and non-Nationalist or independent and liberal mainland refugees.

It will be remembered that for a brief period Mao Tse-tung encouraged the "Blooming of the Hundred Flowers" of criticism. The Formosan Communist "flowers of criticism" proved to be thistles; numbers of the most prominent Formosan Communists in China were denounced as "rightist, counter-revolutionary, and tinged with regional nationalism." In other words Peking had discovered that the island brothers in their midst were possibly more Formosan than communist. Party leaders began to see that Formosans feel themselves to be an island people who might accept communism, but want it on their own terms.

"Little China" — the Chinese Liberals' Program

Liberal Chinese refugees watched Chiang Ching-kuo's elevation with great uneasiness. Each promotion and each new act of violence brought warning of a day when he would rule. A struggle for the succession could spell disaster at Taipei. Within the Army there are factions which support Ching-kuo and others which oppose him. Within the Party are elements which would accept his leadership and others which would not. Within the Government the same dichotomy exists. As for the mass of nondescript refugees — the ricksha men, the factory workers, the peddlers — most of them find themselves too preoccupied with the daily struggle for a livelihood to give much thought to factions within the Government and Party organizations. They live in keen competition with Formosan natives who are their rivals in the marketplace for food and labor.

The Formosans, too, are divided roughly into the nonpolitical majority of laborers and farmers who accept passively any administration under any political label provided it is not too harsh and greedy, and those who would welcome relief from the Nationalist administration. Some dream of quieter days under the Japanese and some dream of a Formosa governed by Formosans. No Formosan is interested in "returning" to the mainland and none welcomes the prospect of a bloody sacrifice on behalf of the Nationalist regime.

All refugees are aware of a degree of isolation and of the latent hostility with which they are regarded by many of the island people. Among them, however, are many intellectuals who realize the danger and insecurity of their position. They are an elite, a minority within a minority, who realize that they will not return to their homes on the continent and that they must come to some accommodation with the Formosans to form a new island society.

A significant number fear Chiang Ching-kuo's rise to power and he is well aware of this. Outspoken liberals must oppose an extra-legal succession or must flee once more, if they can, to other lands.

Meanwhile they have offered to cooperate with Formosan leaders. Should they form a coalition with the Formosan majority Chiang Ching-kuo's chances to become the recognized master of Formosa would be diminished. Here would be the foundations for a new society, a "second China" or an independent Formosa living under UN guarantees.

A statement published by Formosan exiles at Tokyo in 1962 summarizes the conclusion that both Chiang Ching-kuo and Peking fear such a union of liberal refugees and Formosan leaders:

> The Formosans are against the Communists and do not want to merge with Communist China. Chiang Ching-kuo and Communist China know this fact better than anyone else. The communist's China consequently fears the Formosans and Chinese liberals more bitterly than [they fear] the Nationalist Government.
>
> When the Formosans and the Chinese liberals in Formosa gain strength, "peaceful liberation" through internal changes [brought about by Chiang Ching-kuo] which Communist China is aiming at, is less likely to occur. The Nationalist regime, that is, the unshakeable dictatorship of Chiang Ching-kuo in Formosa, is therefore considered to be a necessary step toward the "liberation" of Formosa by Communist China.[4]

The formation of a liberal Opposition Party with a mass basis offered the only possibility of genuine reform at Taipei in 1957 and only this could offer some hope that the succession, when it takes place, will be by a liberal elective process. It was a forlorn prospect from the outset but was thought worth the attempt.

For many years Chiang Kai-shek permitted two small, impotent organizations to provide political window-dressing for the benefit of foreign critics. They are sometimes spoken of contemptuously as "house-pet" parties. Neither the Young China

Party nor the Democratic Socialist Party carried any weight in Formosa. They had been "tamed" on the mainland. Here in Formosa changed circumstances (and the Generalissimo's total dependency upon the United States) gave them some hope. The key to the problem was freedom at the polling booth.

In 1957 some thoughtful members met with a number of independent non-Party liberal refugees to discuss problems of the forthcoming Assembly elections. They prepared an appeal for clean campaigning, addressed to the Generalissimo.

The elections held on April 21 revealed no change; as usual the Nationalist Party had swept the polls. At this time the total mainland Chinese refugee civilian population numbered only 1,014,228, whereas the total Formosan majority numbered 8,676,022.* As matters stood, Nationalist Party candidates took twenty of twenty-one contests for the offices of county magistrates and city mayors, and for the Assembly seats, took forty-four in a total of sixty-six.

One month later the moderate reformers met again to consider election returns. It was proposed to found a "Society for the Study of Local Autonomy in Taiwan." The Government promptly compelled the group to change its name to "The Society for the Study of Local Autonomy in the Republic of China."

Things moved along at a slow pace until midyear 1958, when the distinguished Dr. Hu Shih, former Ambassador to Washington, lent his support to the movement and seventy-eight prominent persons petitioned the Government for permission to form a new political party. There was no response for a period of five months, and then the answer was "No." When the group continued to discuss its problems the members began to be subjected to petty personal harassment. Nevertheless, once again they changed the organizational name and submitted a new petition.

Now Chiang Ching-kuo's agency, the Garrison Headquar-

---

* All figures on the refugee population are open to question, for many persons arrange to escape registration, and the Government is most reluctant to provide evidence of the "unfavorable" ratio of refugees to island people.

FORMOSA BECOMES "FREE CHINA"

ters, began to growl. Newspapers were forced to publish a "communist's confession" which purported to show a link between the organizing group and a mainland Communist agent. Of necessity the Society became inactive, for the warning was clear.

Many months later the American presidential campaigns opened a new prospect in Formosa. The Democratic candidate, Mr. Kennedy, made it known that (in Mr. Dulles's famous phrase) an "agonizing reappraisal" of American policy toward Chiang Kai-shek might be necessary. According to Formosan accounts, Mr. Kennedy's success was greeted with such enthusiasm on Formosa that "even uneducated Formosan pedicab men" celebrated in the streets. A meeting of intellectuals gathered to hail the victory was broken up by the Nationalist police.

The New Year, in any case, brought new hope, and the liberals began to meet again. Now they looked to Formosans for support as well. A prominent mainland Chinese named Lei Chen, editor of the fortnightly magazine *Free China*, took the lead in seeking out influential Formosans who could assist in forming a new Opposition Party. The time seemed ripe to expect another show of "reform" on Chiang's part. Lei Chen's move was a significant step toward coalition among all elements opposed to dictatorial Party rule.

On March 3, 1961, a new Memorandum was prepared for the Generalissimo, stressing again the need for clean and free elections. Again there were elections and again the Nationalists smothered the contest by patrolling every polling booth and manipulating the rules for registration. In twenty-one contests for the offices of District Magistrate eleven Nationalist Party candidates appeared before the public unopposed.

With contumacious persistence the group proposed to found a "Society for the Discussion of Better Elections." It will be realized that each of these attempts generated publicity drawing fresh island-wide attention to the issue. Now seven notable mainland Chinese joined thirteen Formosans to appeal for an end to Government subsidies for the Nationalist Party, an enlargement of personal liberties, a decrease in military expenditures, and a decision by the Government to use only peaceful means in recovering the mainland. They wished to preclude the danger of massive Communist retaliation upon the island people.

Premier General Chen Cheng chose a press conference for his reply. He had an eye upon the new Democratic Administration at Washington. The Government would welcome the birth of a powerful Opposition Party, he said. "The [new] Party should follow the example of the United States." But having said this, he attached reservations and warnings to establish necessary pretexts for suppressive action to come. "If unqualified politicians or ruffians should organize the Party or if the objectives of the Party are not clear" the Government would be forced to withdraw permission.

The military, of course, felt not the least bound by promises made when General Chen spoke in his civilian role as "Premier." Soon the Government-controlled press began to express disdain for the proposed new Party, calling it "unnecessary" and "reactionary." Next Chiang Ching-kuo's agents professed to have found evidence that the Party had Communist connections and support. Then began a campaign of heckling interference at Party conferences, forced cancellations of scheduled public meetings, and at last came a ban on all activity.

By this time Taipei had discovered that there was no imminent danger of a drastic change in policies at Washington. Aid continued to flow across the Pacific. There was no need further to placate the liberals who proposed this new Party on Formosa. The organizing members began to be watched, searched, questioned under various degrees of physical hardship and exposed to damaging economic reprisals. At last Lei Chen, the editor, was arrested with three colleagues. One who "confessed" that he had been a Communist years before was sentenced to twelve years' imprisonment. Lei Chen was sent up for ten years and the others received somewhat lighter terms. With this the journal *Free China* ceased to be a "voice" for the opposition, and the proposed new Party collapsed.

One by one Chiang Ching-kuo eliminated prominent men who represented potential leaders for an aroused coalition. Each removal was to be construed as a warning for all members of the class or profession in which the victim moved. And with each of these cases the victim's fate became a little more severe. Perhaps it was not intended to be so neatly arranged, but this was the net effect. Dr. Wu, representing the liberal elements in Government administration, was forced into exile. General Sun Li-jen who saw merit in the Formosan recruit and attempted to ensure fair play within the military system was stripped of his offices, subjected to house arrest, and kept under surveillance, always within easy reach of Ching-kuo's agents. Lei Chen, editor and representative of the liberal political independents, received what was in effect a life sentence for a man of his years.

All of these men were mainland Chinese who were well known abroad, each case attracted considerable attention in the United States, but upon the Formosan leaders, unknown overseas, fell the heaviest reprisals.

When Lei Chen was seized a young Formosan named Su Tung-chi courageously came forward to sign a petition seeking clemency for the elderly journalist. Su was of a prominent family in the Yunlin area, a graduate of Meiji University in Tokyo, and a very popular leader in his home district. He had held several appointive posts and had been elected repeatedly to local public office despite Nationalist opposition. He was thirty-nine years old and the father of five young children.

On September 19, 1961, Su's home was raided at two o'clock in the morning by security officers. Su was taken away at once to Taipei and his wife dragged away first to the local police offices and then on to Taipei to be subjected to the third degree. The police who searched the house for "incriminating evidence" turned up among other things several old copies of Lei Chen's *Free China* fortnightly, a copy of the *Chuo Koron* (a Tokyo publication in the forbidden Japanese language) and six back numbers of the *Reader's Digest* in the Japanese-language edition.

There follows a tale of compelling sadness, of inhuman treatment and persecution which dragged on for months. On the first arrest Mrs. Su had been compelled to leave four children unattended while she took the fifth and youngest baby with her to face the dread interrogation. Although she was ill and nearly deranged with worry the police were merciless in attempting to secure her signature to a "confession" accusing her husband of treasonable activity. She was released and rearrested no less than three times and was arrested again when she refused to keep silent concerning her experience. At last she was given a life sentence.

Su meanwhile was charged in a military court with having twice plotted rebellion. No details were released. Scores of arrests were made throughout the countryside to deter any public agitation on his behalf. He was sentenced on May 18, 1962, and is believed to have been executed sometime in July.[5]

With this act Chiang Ching-kuo's Taiwan Garrison Command gave ample warning to all Formosans that not the least opposition to the Nationalist Party, the Government or the Army would be tolerated, on pain of death. It has been suggested that after 1960 he was turning his attention to the so-called Anglo-American liberals — all potential members of a Sino-Formosan coalition, the necessary matrix for any independent Formosa or UN Trust administration. Criticism of America and "American imperialism" was stimulated in the schools by political agents. Well-known figures alleged to be in Chiang Ching-kuo's pay were encouraged to publish vicious attacks upon scholars having strong academic affiliations and friends in the United States. Before his death Dr. Hu Shih was an object of attack. The eminent archaeologist Li Chi was abused in print and Professor Huang Chu-kuei, Chairman of the Political Science Department in the National Taiwan University, was actually set upon and beaten in the streets.

As we sketch here the violence which smothered attempts to promote solidarity among the liberal refugees and the Formosan people we can sense the growing crisis as each month brings Formosa nearer to the day of the Succession. What then?

XXII

Free Formosa

The Search for Independence

FORMOSANS IN EXILE find opportunities sometimes to remind Americans of the year 1776. After one hundred and fifty years of haphazard colonial administration by agents of the British Crown the colonists demanded reforms including the right to home rule and representation. The demands were met by military action. During the rebellion and for long thereafter the colonists were bitterly divided among themselves but out of these difficulties and hardships a new nation was born.

The parallel is obvious — at least to the Formosans who lead in the search for independence. It is no accident that in the United States the United Formosans for Independence group made its headquarters at Philadelphia and that the organization's basic principles are these:

> *United Formosans for Independence* is dedicated to the establishment of a free, democratic, and independent Republic of Formosa in accordance with the principle of self-determination of peoples.
> We repudiate, therefore, all forms of totalitarian dictatorship, Chinese Communist or Nationalist.

The "smallness" of Formosa and the lack of experienced leadership are sometimes cited to belittle Formosan appeals for autonomy. Formosans answer that the American rebellion took place when the colonies had a population of less than four million, all told; Formosa had a population exceeding six million in 1947. As for area and wealth, technological development and educational facilities, the island exceeds many states represented in the United Nations. As for proximity to continental China, the Straits of Formosa are at least four times as wide as the Straits of Dover which make England an oceanic rather than a continental entity.

Leadership presents the great difficulty. Under the Japanese administration many individuals developed high competence in banking and land management, transport services and publishing, sugar manufacturing and forest industries, law and medicine, but none had been employed at the higher levels of administration in posts requiring general coordination of all these civic interests. The massacre was a numbing blow. Fortunately among those who survived and managed to slip away were many who had absorbed the ideals of the old Home Rule Movement. For years they had been thinking of the problems of local representative government.

These men — the old Home Rule Association members and men who were graduated in law, medicine and literature at the leading Japanese universities before 1945 — form the "elder statesmen" of today. In 1947 the Home Rule Movement became a search for independence.

Emerging Independence Leadership

For the men and women who escaped in 1947 Hong Kong offered the most secure temporary retreat. There British law kept both Communist and Nationalist agents under some restraint. Shanghai on the other hand was still Nationalist territory and Japan was under an Occupation in which the Nationalist Government took part. Some fortunate exiles had personal investments or bank accounts in Hong Kong, or could turn for help to friends and relatives already in residence there. Many were destitute and had to seek immediate employment in the crowded settlement.

What to do next? There were factions and quarrels, divisions and disagreements. We have already taken note of the disillusioned Formosans who went over to the Communists and soon enough made their way to the China mainland. Others plunged into intensive work on behalf of intervention, autonomy or independence. Some turned away from active participation but contributed what they could to finance dedicated leaders. Many simply sank into obscurity, glad to be alive, but ready to forego any further risks.

One characteristic which sets the Formosans apart from the mainland Chinese is a deeply emotional attachment to the island. I had often noted this when I was teaching in Formosa before the war and now it was demonstrated again and again. I will quote here from one of many letters which I received from Hong Kong, this one written in April, 1949, when the latest negotiations between the Nationalists and the Communists had broken down.

Now the fire opened again between Communists and Government, and some papers say about Formosa's future. I believe most of Formosans got tired of more than three years misgovernment.

Some one says "Formosa is Chinese, so that they cannot speak of Independence." [But] if it is true, we can say that it is the same American between England, [i.e. Formosans are "Chinese" in the same sense that Americans are "English"].

I believe that if United States want to help China, at first she must hold Formosa. If Formosans can build their own regular Government they not only can defend [themselves against] Communist, but also can help South China . . .

Now I am in . . . Hong Kong, because I do not like to go back to Formosa to see so much unpleasant circumstance. But if I can do something for Formosa I will do my best.

I expect you can do something for Formosa in near future, and your old students will welcome you again at our memorable beautiful island.[1]

For some time the Crown Colony continued to be an important way-station for persons slipping in and out of Formosa and passing from Shanghai to Japan. But the Colony, then in a most precarious position on the borders of Communist China, could not afford to permit Communist, Nationalist or Free Formosan organizations to stir up trouble within British territory.

Chiang knew this, and attempted therefore to prejudice the position of the exiles. Agents were hired in Kowloon and Hong Kong to stage trouble-making "incidents" (some of them of a serious and violent nature) which were then blamed on Formosan leaders. Through formal channels the Generalissimo demanded the extradition of individuals known to be seeking intervention. The British Government took no action. In due course, when the Occupation of Japan came to an end, many Formosans at Hong Kong removed to Japan, offering a rather bleak commentary on the "liberation" of Formosa.

Shanghai was a particularly dangerous place for advocates of intervention. There both Communist and Nationalist agents attempted to silence Formosan demands for UN action. At the time of the February Incident there had been thousands of islanders in Shanghai, but when news came of the uprising hundreds at once took passage for Keelung. We have seen on an earlier page that those left behind were ultimately forced to declare for Communism or face extinction.

Joshua Liao happened to be in Shanghai and Thomas was on Formosa when the uprising took place, putting an end to their dreams of local political education, reform, and reunion with China through federal arrangement. Their lives were spared, but their lands were lost, their families were endangered, and they were exiles once again.

In mid-March Thomas escaped to Hong Kong, where he urged local Formosans to assist incoming refugees. In August he addressed a petition to Lieutenant General Wedemeyer, asking for American help to secure relief for the island. At the same time his group at Hong Kong attempted without success to find some common basis upon which to work with the pro-Communist Formosan exiles. The doctrinaire Red leaders would accept no terms but their own; Formosa must be liberated by Communist force according to classic prescription. They would tolerate no appeals to the United States. They were then more interested in "proving" Marxist doctrine than in seeking freedom for their own people.

At Shanghai, late in the year 1947, Joshua Liao was arguing strongly *against* the proposal that trusteeship was the solution of the problem. This, he felt, would be a confession that Formosans were unable to govern themselves and it would delay indefinitely the day of Home Rule. A trusteeship, he said, was a prolongation of colonialism in a new guise. He still hoped Chiang Kai-shek would initiate the drastic reforms that were required to convert Formosa from a political liability to an economic and political asset for China. These views he published at Shanghai in early January, 1948, together with an analysis and outline of steps to be taken to achieve federal status. He wanted Formosa to stay within the Chinese frame of reference but to have freedom to develop as rapidly as its favorable geographic and economic position would permit. He proposed a provincial constitution modeled on the system of state constitutions in the United States.

On the eve of the first anniversary of the February Incident Joshua was suddenly thrown into prison at the Woosung Garrison Headquarters in Shanghai, accused of having instigated and participated in the Incident. He was charged with advocating American intervention and trusteeship and he was accused of association with radical (i.e. pro-Communist) Chinese. The first and second of these charges were patently untrue and the third was true only in the sense that Communist agents and sympathizers constantly sought to persuade him to cast his lot with them. When word of his arrest spread, his non-Communist associates fled Shanghai to gather around the younger Liao brother at Hong Kong.

An influential American brought the case to the attention of Dr. K. C. Wu, then Shanghai's Mayor. Wu in turn persuaded the Garrison Command to release Liao after an imprisonment of one hundred days, and he, too, left for Hong Kong.

In August the Liaos sent a group of younger Formosans to Japan to rally exiles there and to prepare appeals to foreign governments and the United Nations. The prison experience had brought home to Dr. Joshua Liao the futility of appeals to President Chiang Kai-shek.

The men going to Japan were instructed to develop public understanding there, using pamphlets, the daily press and public rallies to advance these arguments:

1. Formosa should be treated as Korea was then being treated. Formosans should be given American aid in establishing independence as an island people.
2. There should be a United Nations investigation of the misgovernment and maltreatment of Formosa after 1945. The record would justify intervention.
3. Formosans come of a mixed race, having no natural political bond with any nearby country.
4. Having suffered for half a century at the hands of the Japanese, Formosa should be represented at the Peace Conference. The island is not merely a piece of real estate to be handed about without reference to Formosan interests.

The fundamental argument was simple: Formosa belongs to the Formosan people. The Manchu Government in 1895 had no right to cede Formosa to Japan. Formosa had been sacrificed to save Peking. Now it was being sacrificed to serve Chiang Kai-shek's interests.

One theme used by the exiled group especially angered the Chinese at Taipei, and one suspects that not all Formosans were happy about it. This was the argument that Formosans are not pure Chinese but are a mixed race. Although Nationalist leaders might call the Formosans a "degraded people" when addressing them in anger, for world propaganda purposes the Nationalist claim to "instant reversion" rested on the assertion that the Formosans were Chinese in blood, language, and social institutions. They were members of the Han Race. It was unthinkable that the Formosans should now claim to have Indonesian, Malay, Spanish, Dutch, British, French, and Japanese blood flowing in their veins. Taipei would admit only to the presence of some aborigines of Malay or Indonesian extraction — a mere 150,000 of them — a primitive minority to which the mainland Chinese were bringing cultural salvation.*

To establish a clear Formosan identity the exiles began to employ a romanized form of the Amoy dialect when transliterating names from the Chinese characters instead of using the system employed by the Nationalists.

In the period 1947 to 1949 it was extremely difficult for them to sink faction and personal prejudice in a common cause. China itself presented such a vast drama of confusion no one quite knew what to expect or what course to advocate. Acrimonious debate led to the formation of ineffectual splinter groups upon which foreign newsmen began to comment unfavorably in stories for the American public. The pro-Chiang press was delighted to exploit the weakness.

In mid-summer 1948 the Liaos promoted formation of a "League for the Re-Emancipation of Formosa" which sent its first petition to the United Nations in September. It was an appeal for intervention, a temporary trust status, and an opportunity to prepare for independence. With this came the end of all attempts to work with the Leftists.

The League foundered in factional strife and bitter disputes

---

* At the United Nations China's representative Dr. Tsiang assured newsmen that there were only 150,000 "native Formosans" and that all others were Chinese.

between Dr. Thomas Liao and Miss Snow Red who insisted that only Communist China could and should give aid to Formosa. As one Formosan wrote to me, "Hence, the factions of Dr. Liao and Miss Chia cursed each other while the League was dying, and all left Hong Kong."

As the Nationalists retreated across the face of China in May, 1949, and world attention focused on Chiang's "retirement," Joshua Liao published a long statement predicting mutiny among unreliable Nationalist troops on Formosa. To prevent the extension of civil war to the island, he said, it would be necessary to bring in American forces to keep the Nationalists quiet and prevent a Communist sweep across the channel. A Formosan self-defense corps should be developed to enable island people to defend their homes and to act on behalf of the United Nations.

To Dr. Phillip Jessup at the United Nations he sent assurances that Formosans were prepared to fight for spiritual liberty as the Irish had so long fought to obtain independence, but he hoped it would not require so many years to achieve Formosan autonomy.

Thomas Liao flew to Manila to seek support among leaders there who had every reason to be deeply concerned with Formosa's fate. A series of articles soon appeared in the Manila press, and on October 14 the Philippines Minister at Tokyo and Representative in Korea (Dr. Bernarbe Africa) spoke up, advocating a plebiscite for the Formosan people. Said he:

> The days when subject peoples are considered attached to the land as chattels are over. People are now considered more important than the land in which they live, and it is unfair to transfer them like personal property from one country to another.

When it became apparent that the Formosan Independence leaders were beginning to attract some international notice the Communists struck out at them with familiar invective. The Nationalists, on the other hand, for a brief period adopted a "soft" line, appealing to them to come home and take positions in the government at Taipei. Chiang's men were "running scared" at that moment in 1949; the big "reform" under Dr. Wu and General Sun was about to be advertised to the world.

In December the exiles at Tokyo addressed a seventeen-page appeal to the Supreme Commander for the Allied Powers asking for an immediate occupation of Formosa by Allied troops pending preparation for a plebiscite under international auspices.

This was embarrassing to SCAP, but coming as it did from unofficial bodies it carried no great weight. It was more embarrassing, however, to have a veritable flood of letters sent out from Independence Movement headquarters at Tokyo, addressed to an extraordinary variety of world figures — to Trygve Lie of the United Nations, to Jawaharlal Nehru, Sir Benegal Rau, Carlos Romulo, Dean Acheson, General Marshall, Senator Taft, and many others.

Some of these letters sought formal disavowal of the Cairo promises, some appealed for application of the terms of the Atlantic Charter, some asked for prompt action to stay Chiang's vengeful pursuit of all critics within Formosa and virtually all of them asked for a plebiscite. A plebiscite, they said, should offer them freedom to choose between (1) retention of the *status quo*, (2) union with Communist China without violence or (3) a United Nations trust status leading to complete independence.

Said Joshua Liao, "We'll obey the majority, but Chinese who came since V-J Day are not entitled to vote!" In the last letter I received from him before his death at Hong Kong in 1950, he wrote:

Dear George:
. . . Regarding the Formosa Problem, still ideas should be preferred to weapons for a solution. There's no reason why it

could not be solved to the satisfaction of all parties concerned
— not only the Formosans and Chinese, but also the surrounding democratic peoples like the Filipinos, the Koreans, the
Americans, the Englishmen, and the Japs who intend to become
"democrats." . . . Time is on our side, I fairly believe. The
Korean patriots waited 35 years. We won't have to wait so
long . . .

Japan as a Refuge from Both Chiang and Mao

Henceforth the Independence Movement activity centered in
Tokyo, with active groups in other metropolitan areas — Na-
goya, Kyoto, Osaka, Kobe and Fukuoka. By 1949 it was estimated that more than one thousand Formosan expatriates
were entering Japan each month. Some came in legitimately
enough "on business" and then soon summoned their families to
join them. Many were smuggled in.

All Formosans who had been born on the island between
June, 1895, and September, 1945, could undoubtedly claim Japanese citizenship by birth. All who took refuge in Japan had
been educated in the Japanese primary schools and thousands
were graduates of Japanese higher schools and universities.
They had no great difficulty in settling into community life and
easily found places in Japan's burgeoning postwar economy.
Some faded into the general community, assuming Japanese
names. The majority entered quietly into the business and professional life of Japan's large cities. Estimates of the total
number of Formosan exiles there run from 25,000 to 75,000. No
reliable census is available. From this substantial well-educated
urban group the Independence Movement draws sympathy and
some cash support.

On the whole this large group of exiles was not unwelcome,
for they gave little trouble; they had no desire to return to Formosa as long as Chiang was in control and they certainly had

no desire to serve the Communists or to be dominated by them.

Their presence offered asylum for individuals fleeing from Chiang Ching-kuo's agents and so from time to time the Nationalist Embassy and the Chinese Consulates made it very difficult for the Japanese Government. We may anticipate our story to illustrate the point.

Just before President Eisenhower visited Taipei in 1960 a youth named Ko Shih-lin was arrested on Formosa. According to the Formosans in exile, he was distributing leaflets urging people to petition Eisenhower to intervene on behalf of the Formosan people. According to the Nationalists, he was plotting to assassinate President Chiang and Vice President Chen Cheng.

By a twist of luck the young man escaped and managed to stow away on a Swedish Maersk Line freighter at Keelung, sailing for Kobe, Japan. En route he was discovered. When the Swedish ship entered Kobe harbor he was handed over directly to officers aboard a Nationalist ship, the *Chung Chao,* lying at anchor there. This, of course, took place within Japan's territorial waters.

Ko was a prisoner aboard the Nationalist ship when it sailed for Keelung. As it moved southward a violent storm forced it into Kagoshima Bay for shelter and there Ko, handcuffed, eluded captors, leaped overboard and swam ashore. It was an extraordinary feat. When he sought help to have the handcuffs removed the local police had no choice but to arrest him for illegal entry. He was tried in the Kagoshima District Court.

The circumstances of the case attracted wide attention. The Nationalists, surprised that their erstwhile prisoner was alive, demanded that he be turned over to the Chinese Consul at Nagasaki. The Japanese knew well what his fate would be. Exercising their right to try him for illegal entry, they gave him a sentence of six months in jail, promptly suspended the sentence, and placed him on probation for two years. They did not order deportation. The Nationalists clamored for custody. Meanwhile many Formosans and Japanese petitioned the Minister of Justice, who canceled Ko's sentence, granted him political asylum, and directed that he be released.

This newsworthy incident dramatically advertised in Japan the truth that conditions within Formosa were producing a new generation eager for autonomy or independence. Taipei continues to press Tokyo on every technicality which may bring about the arrest and deportation of Formosans, and to Japan's embarrassment operates an elaborate Embassy and Consular intelligence apparatus in the metropolitan areas.

Japanese sympathies tend to lie with the Formosans on many counts. Chiang and his pretentions as a military genius have always been held in contempt. From a Japanese point of view, the Generalissimo is a puppet. Among the technical problems is the fact that the majority of Formosans living in Japan have a special right to claim political asylum by virtue of birth under the Japanese flag.

Beyond this, Tokyo must be deeply concerned with the question of Formosa's ultimate fate. Can it be settled in the United Nations before the advent there of a Communist Chinese member?

The "Provisional Government" at Tokyo

Among the voluntary exiles in Japan was the aged Lim Hsientang. We recall that he had been the living symbol of the Home Rule Movement for nearly forty years. His position was unique. All literate, adult Formosans knew with what great courage he had devoted his life and his fortune to the public welfare and the search for an honorable and effective Formosan representation in local government. They remembered that in the 1920's the Japanese police on Formosa had slapped Lim's face in public in an attempt to humiliate him, they had fined him, jailed him and persecuted his associates in an attempt to silence reasonable appeals for representative forms of government and political equality for the Formosan people. After 1930 wiser heads at Tokyo and Taipei had brought him into the Japanese Governor's Council and at last began to grant the forms if not the substance of local elective representation. In a belated and desperate wartime effort to woo Formosan loyalty, the emperor had appointed Lim to the House of Peers.

The Chinese knew his position, and in 1945 summoned him to Nanking to represent Formosa at the formal Surrender ceremonies. But as soon as Chen Yi took office it became apparent that Lim was to be ignored. He withdrew to the background, and not long after the March massacre he went up to Tokyo, pleading an illness which required medical attention in Japan. While not publicly disavowing the Nationalist Party regime, he prolonged his visits to Japan, and in his last years saw the development of a Formosa Independence Movement under a new leadership in a new generation.

This retreat to Japan was interpreted as a bitter rebuke to the Chiang organization at Taipei. When word of his death at last reached Formosa it was promptly suppressed, and Lim's son was sent at once to bring the ashes home to Taichung. There the event was announced and the funeral held. Then Chiang's agents began to spread rumors that Lim had led a dissolute life in his later years and was not at all the model of devotion to Formosan welfare which the public had so long believed him to be. On the contrary (so the allegations went) he had been a notorious "running dog" of the Japanese.

The active Independence Movement leaders were all marked men. Taipei was embarrassed and furious when these "degraded" people left Hong Kong and turned back to Japan for security of life and freedom of speech. Unfortunately for themselves, Dr. Liao and his associates were indiscreet, or politically naïve, for they set about organizing political action in Japan to secure the overthrow of a government at Taipei which was a "Great Power" member of the Allied Control Commission.

Thomas Wen-yi Liao entered Yokohama from Hong Kong in

February, 1950, to begin a tour of major cities. At a rally in Kyoto he made an attack upon Chiang Kai-shek which the watching Nationalist agents could not ignore. In mid-March an association of Tokyo newspapermen invited Liao to speak in the city's principal auditorium (Hibiya Hall), thus offering an important opportunity to state the case for intervention.

On the day before the lecture he was suddenly arrested by American military policemen, taken before a Military Court, tried on charges of illegal entry, and sentenced to six months' imprisonment to be followed by deportation.

In this abrupt fashion he learned that he was in MacArthur's Japan and that words spoken against Chiang Kai-shek were tantamount to *lèse majesté*. The sentence was imposed and imprisonment began within twenty-four hours of his arrest.

While he languished in Sugamo Prison for war criminals his case began to attract the attention of prominent Americans at Tokyo. There was a prolonged debate, for all knew that deportation to Formosa was a sentence of certain death for Dr. Liao.

A compromise was reached; when released Liao was not hustled off to the port but was placed under a mild house arrest in Tokyo, which he agreed to accept. As the case was being discussed with some acrimony in the American community Liao quietly disappeared, to remain out of sight until the Peace Treaty came into effect and neither General MacArthur, his successors, nor his democratic ally at Taipei were in a position to press effectively for extradition. Japan granted him political asylum.

While he was imprisoned Liao's associates went ahead with plans to organize a Taiwan Democratic Independence Party, naming Liao the Chairman, *in absentia*. It is beyond the scope of this account to trace the complex stories of faction and compromise, grouping and re-grouping which took place thereafter. There was pressing need to achieve solidarity of purpose and planning, but progress was slow.

When the series of international crises developed in the Formosan Straits — when Mr. Dulles was practicing brinkmanship with such daring disregard of Allies other than Chiang Kai-shek — the British became especially concerned because of the vulnerable Crown Colony nearby, and because of the dangers of general war. They sought a legal basis for interference. Anthony Eden wrote that "The Allies approved Chiang's occupation, but this did not constitute legal transfer." The *London Times* published a series on the legal status of Formosa, and Canada's Foreign Secretary (Lester Pearson) proposed an international conference to treat the problem.

Dr. Liao felt the need for a more substantial symbol of resistance within Formosa and of the vitality of the Independence Movement overseas. He insisted that the Formosans themselves must be represented and heard in any negotiations concerning the island's future.

On September 1, 1955, Liao's Party formed a Commission of thirty-three members which in turn sought out exiled representatives for each of the twenty-four principal cities and districts of Formosa to constitute a "Provisional National Congress of the Republic of Formosa." In the following year, on February 28, 1956, this "Congress" inaugurated a "Provisional Government." Not unexpectedly, Dr. Liao was named First President.

A flag was designed and adopted and a great many slogans were developed while the leaders waited through long days and weeks and months for a major change in world affairs to bring them forward. Late in 1956 Dr. Liao produced a volume in Japanese entitled *Formosanism* designed to provide a theoretical basis and doctrinal text. It was eagerly read by Formosans everywhere in exile. It gave them much to consider in reviewing the island history, but it drew heavily on a certain mystical element not much to the taste of younger men. They were not fired by great admiration for the old 17th-century freebooter Koxinga who had founded the Kingdom of Formosa and claimed to be a "Ming loyalist." The younger men were not prepared to spend money and energy on parades and rallies throughout Japan honoring a dubious 17th-century hero. Moreover, Koxinga's little island kingdom of long ago had not survived.

New Voices Overseas

Dr. Liao's associates began to drift away from him, turning to younger leaders. Formosan students overseas began to meet seriously for discussions of the future, rather than the past. They were conscious that the leadership and technical skills required to replace the aging refugees on Formosa would have to be found in their own rising generation. They were also aware of a growing sense of discontent and frustration among contemporaries who were being graduated but were leaving the schools to find no employment worthy of their education and capacities.

In 1950 there were about fifty Formosans studying in the United States. By 1960 there were at least 554, and the number grows steadily. Small scattered campus clubs began to merge, forming three larger regional affiliations in the western states, the Middle West and on the eastern seaboard. In 1960 they agreed to form an overall body which they called simply Formosan Clubs in America, a non-political organization devoted to the welfare and intellectual growth of all Formosans studying in the United States.

But where there are students there must be political discussion. A group calling itself "Formosans for Free Formosa" began to meet quietly in the Philadelphia area. As the Formosan foreign-student population grew in numbers the group grew with it. The majority came directly from Formosa and were not the sons of exiles in Japan. They had passed very stiff competitive examinations at Taipei and knew that for every moment of residence abroad most of them were under close surveillance by Chinese Embassy agents and by fellow students whose

Government scholarships were designed to place informers in their midst. In 1960 the Philadelphia group discussing Formosa's political fate reorganized to make itself known publicly as the United Formosans for Independence which has been cited and quoted on earlier pages. Soon it was publishing a quarterly journal, the *Ilha Formosa*, or *Beautiful Island.** To this was then added a small newsletter for students, called the *FORMOSAgram*. The leaders of the so-called "UFI" acknowledged indebtedness to Dr. Liao in Tokyo, and were in a general way committed to support the "Provisional Government" group.

In 1963 Formosan students in Canada organized as a League for Self-Determination of Formosans. In 1964 a much weaker student group with political interests made its appearance at New York. Under the name Formosan Readers Association, it proposed to distribute reading materials in Japanese and English in a periodical pamphlet entitled *Taiwan Lang* or "The Formosan."

An "Appeal for Justice"

Although Tokyo remained the center for protest and publication, and the rallying point for all Formosans opposed to the Nationalist regime, Dr. Liao's "Provisional Government" group began to lose support. The "Provisional President" had become too dogmatic, too inflexible, too sure that he alone was qualified to represent Formosan interests before the world. He was indeed the only expatriate Formosan well known abroad.

To brighten that image Liao left Japan to travel briefly in Europe, Canada and the United States, but while he was renewing friendships and making himself known to persons who might one day be concerned with the Formosan Question, a strong secessionist movement set in at Tokyo. New organiza-

* The original Portuguese name by which the island was first known to the Western World.

tions appeared whose leaders competed for recognition and support. Problems of "face" and faction produced many splinter groups, weakened by an inability to agree on procedures. The most important new organization was the Taiwan Chinglian Hue, the "Taiwan Youth Association" which presented itself to the public in 1960, in February, the month now consecrated to the memory of all who died in 1947. The Hue founded a monthly Japanese-language journal, the *Taiwan Chinglian* or "Taiwan Youth" to keep Formosans in Japan and the Japanese public informed of events bearing on the Independence Movement. A second journal for the same purpose, the *Toklip Taiwan,* carried the same material in romanized Fukien dialect. For the benefit of foreign readers the Hue called itself in English "The Formosan Association" which published the *Formosan Quarterly* and its successor, the *Independent Formosa.*

Formosans living abroad who call openly for the downfall of the Chiang regime, a plebiscite under UN supervision, and a government of Formosa by Formosans, obviously place themselves in an extremely vulnerable position. In September, 1964, came a sharp reminder of Chiang Ching-kuo's attitude toward Formosan intellectuals tainted by democracy and critical of the Taipei dictatorship. A distinguished young professor of the National Taiwan University and two of his former students were seized one Sunday afternoon as they were drinking tea and discussing Formosan problems. The Garrison Headquarters merely announced that they had been arrested for "destructive activities"; foreign press dispatches said that they were accused of "Independence Movement agitation." For a period of five months nothing more was heard of them and it was rumored that they were dead.

But across the world questions were raised in New York and Boston, and in London. There were letters to the press and queries behind the scene at Washington, for Dr. Peng Ming-min is well known as an authority on International Law relating to air-navigation and space and in his earlier days had distinguished himself in the schools of Japan, Canada and France.[2]

Suddenly the Taiwan Garrison Headquarters announced that Peng and his friends had been tried on charges of "treasonous conspiracy to bring about local rebellion" but that as an act of clemency their lives had been spared; they would serve long prison terms.

This "clemency" gesture was widely interpreted to mean the Chiangs at Taipei had been reminded that Peng's fate was a matter of international interest and was drawing attention to Formosan unrest under Nationalist rule. Professor Peng and his friends were spared as the editor Lei Chen had been spared, and as former Governor Wu and Lieutenant-General Sun Li-jen had been spared because each was well known abroad and each had influential friends in America. Lesser critics of the regime who have no friends at Washington — Su Tung-chi for example — find no such support and vanish without significant notice.

But what to do about Dr. Thomas Liao, living beyond reach at Tokyo? In the United States and Canada Liao was widely accepted as the principal spokesman for all the Independence Movement organizations and all Formosans determined to prevent General Chiang Ching-kuo's extra-legal succession to the dictatorship at Taipei. Liao's existence as a symbol of Formosan discontent would become a major embarrassment in 1966 when presidential elections must be held on Formosa. The aging Generalissimo was expected to retire only if he could ensure the succession to his son. All pretense of democratic processes would be swept aside if need be to ensure the dynastic succession, but it would be easier and safer if an appearance of legitimacy could be arranged. Steps must be taken to prevent violent local protests and possible international intervention. Taipei must not become a "second Saigon." General Chiang Ching-kuo must be elected in a contest from which Formosan voters cannot be barred in great numbers. They must therefore be prevented from voting against Chiang Ching-kuo en bloc. They must be persuaded that the Independence Movement crusade preached by the exiles in Tokyo has become a lost cause.

In 1963 Dr. Liao lost the support of his oldest and closest

associates who declared that they could no longer agree with his policies nor accept his dictatorial manner. Soon others drew away to associate with the newer organizations and younger men. Liao began to speak openly and very bitterly of "Formosan ingratitude."

Taipei promptly recognized an opportunity to create confusion. In 1964 Chiang's agents approached Liao with offers of an amnesty, a welcome at Taipei, a high post in the Nationalist Government and perhaps a choice of presidencies among important companies other than the sugar and power companies — T. V. Soong's old interests.

Before these tempting offers Liao hesitated a long time. Should he allow chagrin, anger, family interests and personal ambition to outweigh his obligation to a "cause" so long maintained and so important to the Formosan people?

The dawn of 1965 brought the election year (1966) very close, but still Liao hesitated. Taipei felt urgent need to neutralize the Independence Movement organizations at Tokyo and to create confusion among the electorate on Formosa. A cruel trap was prepared for Dr. Liao.

In February, 1965, Liao's sister-in-law was sentenced to fifteen years' imprisonment on conspiracy charges and a favorite nephew was condemned to death for "treason." Liao, at Tokyo, was then given to understand that the nephew's life would be spared and the sentences reduced if he would return to Taipei and give open support to Chiang. Moreover his own large properties would be restored to him. It is alleged that Liao was also told that he might be asked to serve as Special Advisor to the Chinese Delegation at the UN, that he might be offered the governorship of Formosa, or that General Chiang Ching-kuo might even ask him to become his vice-presidential running mate in the forthcoming campaign.

Without forewarning his associates, Dr. Liao flew to Taipei on May 14. There he at once pledged ardent and unwavering support for Chiang Kai-shek and began to publish a torrent of articles explaining his dramatic new position. The Nationalists applauded and the controlled press gave credit for this coup to the wisdom of General Chiang Ching-kuo.

Liao's foreign friends were baffled by this turn of events. In Japan, Canada and the United States Formosan exiles met to discuss the implications of Liao's defection. None would condemn him for attempting to save the life of his nephew, unless, perhaps, the nephew himself feels betrayed. Some optimists at Tokyo believe that Liao "entered the tiger's cave to capture the tiger" and that he hoped to strengthen underground organizations in anticipation of a presidential election crisis.

Chiang Ching-kuo was not unaware of this possibility. A few days after Liao's appearance at Taipei Chiang's security forces conducted an island-wide house-to-house check of unprecedented thoroughness. Letters and documents taken up in the search were expected to yield private comment on the Liao affair.

Meanwhile the exiled Formosans pondered the future. Would Liao's support of Chiang Ching-kuo split the Formosan vote disastrously in the forthcoming election? Would this enable Chiang Ching-kuo to succeed "legitimately"? And if he becomes President by means of a rigged election will he then turn from Washington to Peking?

An exiled Formosan put the issue in these terms:

Chiang Ching-kuo is a Chinese nationalist more than a Nationalist. His chief mission is to see that the island always remains a part of China. When he takes over the mantle of power from his father, he is expected to enter an all-Chinese negotiation for the permanent settlement of Formosa.[3]

During his father's lifetime will he promise Formosan neutrality to both sides "in the interests of World Peace"? Upon his father's demise will he follow General Li Tsung-jen into the Communist camp? Does he prefer a future in association with a powerful China and an arsenal of nuclear weapons under Chinese control or will he be willing to continue forever dependent upon a fickle American Congress for arms and political support? As a Chinese trained from his youth in Communist totalitarian methods would he be more comfortable as a puppet dependent upon Peking?

Formosan exiles fear and mistrust elections held under the Taipei Government. What (they say) will the United States do if a rigged election leads ultimately to a declaration that Formosans desire to revert to China? What will Washington do if Taipei asks the United States to withdraw from its position on the island?

In an "Appeal for Justice" addressed to the American people Formosan leaders have warned that unqualified support for Chiang since 1945 has damaged American prestige although, in a future crisis, the United States may need the goodwill and local cooperation of the Formosan people.

> More than frequently we are tempted to accuse the U.S. of hypocrisy in declaring her opposition to any form of dictatorship and, at the same time, supporting the Chiang Government, one of the most dictatorial regimes in Asia. Yet we earnestly believe that the true interests of the United States lie in Formosa itself, and that her support of Chiang is only temporary. It is this belief that has kept alive our confidence in the U.S. and our hope for eventual support from Washington for our cause of independence.
>
> We demand, in short, an immediate U.N. Trusteeship over the island, to ensure the freedom of campaign in which all the inhabitants will hear the voice of every faction and determine in a plebiscite that follows, the future of the island. We are confident that the overwhelming choice in such a plebiscite will be independence.[4]

APPENDICES

Appendix I

The Thirty-two Demands

Presented by the Settlement Committee to
Governor-General Chen Yi at Taipei, March 7, 1947

I. REFORMS REQUIRED TO ENSURE EQUALITY
FOR FORMOSANS IN LOCAL GOVERNMENT

1. A provincial autonomy law shall be enacted and shall become the supreme norm for political affairs within this province, so that the ideal of National Reconstruction of Dr. Sun Yat-sen may be here materialized.

2. The appointment of Commissioners shall have the approval of the Peoples Political Council after new elections have been held. The Peoples Political Council shall be newly elected before June, 1947.

    In the meantime, such appointments shall be submitted by the Governor-General to the Committee for Settling the February Incident for discussion, approval or rejection.

3. More than two-thirds of the Commissioners shall be appointed from those who have lived in this Province for more than ten years. (It is most desirable that such persons only shall be appointed to the Secretariat and to the Departments of Civil Affairs,

Finance, Industry and Mining, Agriculture and Forestry, Education, and Police Affairs.)

4. Unarmed gatherings and organizations shall enjoy complete freedom.

5. Complete freedom of speech, of the press, and of the right to strike shall be realized. The system requiring registration of newspapers to be published shall be abolished.

6. The Regulations in force covering the formation of popular organizations shall be abolished.

7. The Regulations governing the [Nationalist Party] scrutiny of the capacity of candidates for membership in representative organs of public opinion shall be abolished.

8. Regulations governing the election of members of various grades in representative organs of public opinion shall be revised.

9. A Political Affairs Bureau of the Settlement Committee must be established by March 15. Measures for its organization will be that a candidate be elected by representatives of each village, town and district, and then newly elected by the prefectural or city Peoples Political Council. The numbers of candidates to be elected in each city and prefecture are as follows:

Districts (Hsien)		Cities	
Taipei	3	Taipei	2
Hsinchu	3	Hsinchu	1
Taichung	4	Taichung	1
Tainan	4	Tainan	1
Kaohsiung	3	Kaohsiung	1
Hualien	1	Keelung	1
Taitung	1	Changhua	1
Peng-hu		Chia-yi	1
(The Pescadores)	1	Pintung	1

10. The Office of the Governor-General shall be converted into a Provincial Government. Before this reform is approved by the Central Government, the Office of the Governor-General shall

be reorganized by the Settlement Committee through popular elections so that righteous and able officers can be appointed.*

II. REFORMS REQUIRED TO ENSURE SECURITY OF PERSON AND OF PROPERTY

1. Popular election of prefectural magistrates and city mayors shall be held before June of this year and at the same time there shall be new elections of members to all prefectural and municipal political councils.†

2. The posts of the Commissioner for the Department of Police Affairs, and of directors for all prefectural or municipal Police Bureaus ought to be filled by Formosans. The special armed police contingents and the armed police maintained by the Railway Department and the Department of Industry and Mining shall be abolished immediately.

3. No government organs other than the civil police can arrest criminals.

4. Arrest or confinement of a political nature shall be prohibited.

5. All chiefs of local courts of justice and all chief prosecutors in all local courts of justice shall be Formosans.

6. The majority of judges, prosecutors and other court staff members shall be Formosans.

7. More than half the Committee of Legal Affairs shall be Formosans, and the Chairman of the Committee shall be mutually elected from among its members.

III. REFORMS REQUIRED TO ENSURE A REVISION AND LIBERALIZATION OF ECONOMIC POLICY, AND A REFORM OF ECONOMIC ADMINISTRATION

1. A uniform Progressive Income Tax shall be levied. No other

---

* *Item I–10:* A Formosan lawyer indicated to me at the time that this measure was put forward to provide for the interim period leading to the peace treaties and the legal transfer of sovereignty to China; until then, he believed, a legal Provincial Government could not be established by the Central Government.

† *Item II–1:* This was desired to establish control over the police systems and to ensure the supremacy of, and respect for, the courts which had suffered great loss in 1946.

sundry taxes shall be levied except the Luxury Tax and the Inheritance Tax.

2. Managers in charge of all public enterprises shall be Formosans.

3. A Committee for Inspecting Public Enterprises, elected by the people, shall be established. The disposal of Japanese properties shall be entirely entrusted to the Provincial Government. A Committee for management of industries taken over from the Japanese shall be established. Formosans shall be appointed to more than half of these Committee posts.

4. The Monopoly Bureau shall be abolished. A system for rationing daily necessities shall be instituted.

5. The Trading Bureau shall be abolished.

6. The Central Government must be asked to authorize the Provincial Government to dispose of Japanese properties.

IV.   REFORMS AFFECTING MILITARY ADMINISTRATION ON FORMOSA

1. The military police shall arrest no one other than military personnel.

2. As many Formosans as possible shall be appointed to Army, Navy, and Air Force posts on Formosa.

3. The Garrison Headquarters must be abolished to avoid the misuse of military privilege.

V.   REFORMS AFFECTING SOCIAL WELFARE PROBLEMS

1. The political and economic rights and social position of the aborigines must be guaranteed.

2. Workmen's protection measures must be put into effect from June 1, 1947.

3. Detained war criminals and those suspected of treason must be released unconditionally.*

---

* *Item V–3:* This was designed to secure the immediate release of wealthy and prominent Formosans who had been held for more than a year on vague charges of "treason" and "war crimes," apparently on the grounds that they could not have acquired great wealth without "treasonous alliance" with the Japanese. They were paying continuous "installment" ransom to ensure their lives and the security of their extensive holdings.

VI.   SUBORDINATE DEMANDS, SUBJECT TO COMPROMISE

1. The abolition of the Vocational Guidance Camp [an internment camp for persons the Government decides to make over into "useful citizens"] and other unnecessary institutions must be determined by the Political Affairs Bureau of the Settlement Committee, after discussion.
2. The Central Government must be asked to pay for the sugar exported to the mainland on order of the Executive Yuan.
3. The Central Government must be asked to pay for 150,000 tons of food exported to the mainland, after estimating the price in accordance with the quotation at the time of export. [This was designed to recover, if possible, some of the costs of the Settlement Committee interim administrative work.]

Appendix II

Dr. K. C. Wu's Views on the Police State and General Chiang Ching-kuo

[These extracts, reproduced with Dr. Wu's permission, are from letters addressed by Dr. Wu to the National Assembly at Taipei, and to Generalissimo Chiang.]

In an open letter to the National Assembly dated February 27, 1954, Dr. Wu appealed for consideration and debate upon six cardinal points. The first concerned the dangers of one-party rule.

> But the operations of the Kuomintang itself are financed, not by contributions from Party members, but by the Government treasury, or, in other words, by the citizens of China. This practice is not to be found in any modern nation save the Communist and totalitarian states. Speaking from inside the Kuomintang, it is also modeled after the so-called "centralized democratic system" of the Communists. That it is "democratic" is totally false. That it is "centralized" is sadly true. In order to put genuine democracy into practice, we must have at least two major political parties . . . The present methods adopted by the Kuomintang in government are entirely devoted to the purpose of perpetuating its power. It is directly contrary to the fundamental principles of modern democratic government.

Dr. Wu's second point concerned the devastating influence of Chiang Ching-kuo's agents upon Army morale.

The armed forces of a nation should belong to the nation so that they will not be made loyal to only one party or to only one person, thus creating forces for feudalism and possible civil strife . . . But inside the armed forces of our country now, there is not only Kuomintang organization operating in secret, but there is also a Political Department. The so-called Political Department is entirely modeled after the system of political commissars of the Communists. Ever since the establishment of the Political Department promotions in the Armed Services have not been based on the merit of the individual but on his relations with the Political Department. Not to speak of the unjustifiable position of the system itself, the Political Department, through the abuse of power, has almost totally wrecked the morale of the troops . . . I have talked with many an intelligent man in the services . . . Their reaction toward the activities of the Political Department has reached such a point that they cannot be worse. Some even went so far as to say "If fight we must one day, we shall have to kill the agents of the Political Department first." If we want to employ these troops just for the purpose of giving reviews and parades, it may be feasible. If we want to use them to fight for the recovery of the mainland, I cannot help shuddering at the thought!

On the activities of the secret police — his third point — the former Governor had this to say:

During my more than three years' administration . . . hardly a day passed without some bitter struggle on my part with the secret police. They interfered with free elections. They made numberless illegal arrests. They tortured and they blackmailed . . . the secret police of our country at present, relying on their special backing, have so abused their powers that they have no regard whatever for law. The people are reduced to such a state that they only dare to resent, but not to speak in the open. If this method is used to ensure the positions of some high authorities, it may be understandable. If we desire to secure the full-hearted support of the people . . . this is utterly impossible.

Turning to the absence of any guarantee of individual rights, he wrote:

As the secret police are rampant, so Formosa has become virtually a police state. The liberties of the people are almost totally suppressed. While I was Governor of Formosa I did my utmost to inculcate the principles that arrests cannot be made without sufficient evidences of crimes and searches cannot be conducted without due process of law. But as my powers were limited, even now I can hardly tell how many innocent people were, and have been illegally held and molested. Every time when I think of this, I cannot but feel an ache in my heart.

Commenting on the absence of press freedom he noted that "Papers have been ordered to suspend publication and reporters have been put into custody from time to time." As for Thought Control, Dr. Wu observed:

The establishment of the so-called "anti-Communist and Save-the-Nation Youth Corps" is really taken after the Hitler Youth and Communist Youth [organizations]. Whether the organ operates under the Kuomintang or the Government (this has never been clarified) I am even now too stupid to comprehend. When I was Governor it demanded financial support from the Provincial Government and met with my refusal. Since then how the organ has been financed is a matter which needs serious investigation. Ever since the establishment of the Youth Corps, principals and superintendents of schools have been forced to become its officers and the students its members, and persistent pressure has been applied to the principals and superintendents to make adjustments in the teaching staffs of the schools in order to regiment the thoughts of the students all the more. To have such an evil way to guide our youth will no doubt leave harm to our posterity for a long time to come.

Dr. Wu asked the Assembly to publish his "six points" and his recommendations concerning them, and notified the Generalissimo that he had done so.

Chiang suppressed the document. An outburst of official propaganda accused Wu of dereliction of duty, corruption in office, and treason. Wu responded in a series of letters to Chiang. The first (March 20) included twelve groups of questions, each group designed to illuminate the issues which he had addressed to the Assembly. For example, the former Governor asked Chiang:

How many secret police organizations are there in our country? What are the limitations on their powers? Who are in charge of them on the surface? Who is it that really controls them behind the scenes?

Ever since March 1, 1950, the date on which Your Excellency was restored to the Presidency, up till now what is the actual number of people who have been arrested and put into custody by the secret police?

Are there, or not, secret jails and detention houses in Formosa? Can they be open to inspection and investigation?

Have the secret police, or have they not, interfered with elections in Formosa? Have they or have they not made illegal arrests?

Ever since March 1, 1950, how many newspapers have received orders to suspend publication? And how many newspaper reporters have been arrested? What are the facts pertaining to each case and on what legal grounds were the orders given?

Does the Youth Corps operate as a branch of the Government or as a branch of the Kuomintang?

If it is supposed to operate under the Government, then under what Ministry and why is its organic law not passed by the Legislative Yuan? If it is supposed to operate under the Kuomintang, then why is it that Central News Agency reports that its expenses are budgeted in the National Government?

As for Chiang's attempt to discredit Wu with charges of corruption and dereliction of duty over a long period of years, Wu asked why Chiang had made him Mayor of Shanghai (1946–1949) and Governor of Formosa (1949–1953).

> Why was I not dismissed? Why must I resign so many times before my resignation was accepted? Why did Your Excellency yourself pay me high praises . . . ?
> Why did Your Excellency ask one of your most intimate confidants to write to me on November 20th last year, asking me to return to become your Secretary-General?

As late as February 8, 1954, the Generalissimo had sought to persuade Wu to return to Formosa, but on February 7 the former Governor, in exile, had ventured his first public criticism of the regime. He reminded the Generalissimo of these things, and then spoke frankly of his mistrust of Chiang Ching-kuo, the heir-apparent. In a letter to Chiang dated March 28 he revealed the heart of the matter.

> When I was in Formosa I gave freely my opinions to Your Excellency on many occasions. I shall just narrate two instances here to refresh Your Excellency's memory.
> In 1950 . . . I chose a leisurely moment of yours to make a serious proposal. I advocated that the Kuomintang should not be supported financially by the Government Treasury, but by contributions from Party members and that ways and means should be found to encourage the growth of an opposition Party so that we might lay a solid foundation for a two-party system in our politics. Your Excellency did neither agree nor disagree. But as events prove later, Your Excellency has assumed exactly the contrary position.
> Then in February, 1952 when I wanted to resign in my struggle for the establishment of the rule of law in Formosa, I spoke to Your Excellency these words: "If Your Excellency loves Ching-kuo your son, you must not let him head the secret police. For no matter whether, relying on your backing, he abuses his powers or not, he will become a target of hatred among the people."
> At that time, Your Excellency cried repeatedly that you were having a headache and asked me not to speak any more. But

after that, Your Excellency has put more trust in Ching-kuo. Not only has he been permitted to control the secret police and the armed forces, but he has also been given control of the Kuomintang and the Youth Corps. Because of such outspoken criticisms, evidently, an attempt on my life was made on April 5, 1953, a few days before my resignation as Governor of Formosa was finally accepted.

After citing instances in which other important critics suffered, Dr. Wu concluded:

I beg to be permitted to draw the following conclusions: (1) For those who make outspoken criticism in Your Excellency's presence, there is a possibility that attempts may be made on their lives; (2) For those who speak privately against Your Excellency, there is a possibility that their careers may be ruined and their reputations damaged; (3) For those who spoke critically of the Government and Your Excellency prior to their coming into Formosa, even though they may have remained discreetly silent ever after, there is a possibility that they may be arrested by the secret police and held incommunicado without trial . . .

On April 3, 1954, he sent on a letter to Taipei which probably never reached the irascible Generalissimo's eye. He took note of Chiang's public reputation, and then said:

Your Excellency has been known as a great and determined Anti-Communist, despite all reverses and disasters . . .

But the trouble with Your Excellency is your own selfishness. When we were on the mainland you had regard only for your personal political power. In Formosa, after the situation over there has become more secure, Your Excellency has become obsessed again with the idea of transmitting the power to your son. Your love of power is greater than your love of the country. And your love for your son is more than your love for the people. Because of this, Your Excellency has pursued the absolutely wrong course of seeking to control the Kuomintang by yourself, control the Government by the Kuomintang, control the Army by the Political Department, and control the people by the secret police. Your Excellency made that mistake once before, and the mainland was lost. How can Your Excellency make the same mistake again to deprive us of the chance of ever recovering the mainland, and, when it comes to worst, of even defending Formosa effectively? . . .

The situation of our country is, indeed, exceedingly grave. While dark clouds threaten from the outside, there is serious dissension and eruption inside. In order to avert this impending crisis, it is imperative that Your Excellency should do something spectacular . . . [by way of genuine reform].

In recent years another great obstacle to any political progress in our nation is Chiang Ching-kuo, Your Excellency's son. I shall not speak any more about what he stands for and what he does, and the bad reactions of the people . . . It is an undisguisable fact that Ching-kuo was trained in Soviet Russia for some fourteen years, and has no understanding whatever of the modern democratic government. In my humble opinion, it is necessary that Your Excellency, in order to reveal your absolute unselfishness, should not allow Ching-kuo to remain any longer in Formosa at this juncture, either staying in the limelight or behind the scenes . . . He should not return to Formosa until after the recovery of the mainland . . . Your Excellency may [then] become cleared of any charge . . . that you entertain any ulterior motive of setting up a dynasty.

NOTES

Notes

Introduction

For general histories of Formosa see James W. Davidson, *The Island of Formosa, Past and Present* (New York, 1903), 710 pp., and Fr. José Maria Alvarez: *Formosa: Geográfica e Históricamente Considerada* (Lisbon, 1930), 2 vols., 568 pp. & 530 pp.

On the Dutch colony in 17th-century Formosa, see William Campbell, ed., *An Account of Missionary Success in the Island of Formosa, published in London in 1650, and now Reprinted with Copius Appendices* (London, 1889), 2 vols., 330 pp. & 337 pp.

For Commodore Perry's "Grand Design" see F. L. Hawkes, ed., *Narrative of the Expedition of an American Squadron to the China Seas and Japan, in the Years 1852, 1853, and 1854, under the Command of Commodore Matthew C. Perry, United States Navy* (Washington, 1856), Vol. II, pp. 178–180.

On the 19th-century confrontation of the maritime nations with China concerning Formosa, W. A. Pickering tells the British story: *Pioneering in Formosa: Recollections of Adventures Among Mandarins, Wreckers, and Head-hunting Savages* (London, 1898), 283 pp. Edward H. House tells of *The Japanese Expedition to Formosa in 1874* (Tokyo, 1875), 231 pp. John Dodd published *The Journal of a Blockaded Resident in North Formosa During the Franco-Chinese War 1884–5* (Hong Kong, 1888), 229 pp., outlining the French position and local reaction.

An elaborate record of American diplomatic and consular effort to compel China to establish orderly government on Formosa is preserved in the microcopied records of the Department of State, preserved in the National Archives, which include diplomatic and consular correspondence of American representatives in Amoy, Foochow, Shanghai and Peking with Washington in the 19th century.

See especially General C. W. LeGendre: *Is Aboriginal Formosa a*

Part of the Chinese Empire? (Shanghai, 1874), 20 pp., 8 maps, and his report to Washington, printed at Macao in 1871 (141 pp.) entitled *How to Deal with China: a Letter to DeB. Rand Kheim, esq., Agent of the United States.*

For an elaborate summary of conditions within Formosa just before World War II, see the U. S. Navy's *Civil Affairs Handbook Series,* 1944–45 (11 volumes), printed at Washington for the Office of the Chief of Naval Operations.

I. The Cairo Declaration

1. Samuel Eliot Morison, *The Rising Sun in the Pacific, 1931–April, 1942* (Boston, 1948), Part II, "The Philippines and Nearby Waters," esp. pp. 168–170. This work is Volume III of *History of United States Naval Operations in World War II,* 15 vols.
2. See G. H. Kerr, "The Kodama Report: Plan for Conquest," *Far Eastern Survey,* Vol. XIV, No. 14 (N.Y., July 18, 1945), pp. 185–190. Original text in *L'Echo de Paris* (Paris), January 11–13, 1905. Full translation of the original issued in mimeograph form by the Institute of Pacific Relations, New York, 1945.
3. William D. Leahy, *I Was There* (New York, 1950), p. 213.
4. Robert Sherwood, *Roosevelt and Hopkins* (New York, 1948), p. 774.

II. "Island X"

1. See Robert Ross Smith's "Luzon vs. Formosa (1944)" in *Command Decisions,* published by the U. S. Dept. of the Army, Office of the Chief of Military History (New York, 1959), pp. 358–373.
2. Patrick J. Hurley, quoted in *United States Relations With China,* State Department publ. 3573, F.E., series 30, p. 86 (Washington, August, 1949).

III. The Surrender on Formosa, 1945

1. [U. S. Govt.] *Imperial Rescript Granted the Ministers of War and Navy. 17 August 1945.* Reproduced in facsimile as Serial #2118, in *Psychological Warfare, Part Two, Supplement #2 CINCPAC–CINCPOA Bulletin #164–45.*
2. Lin Wen-kuei, Letter to the *Fourteenth Air Force Association Bulletin* (Springfield, Mo.), Vol. I, No. 2 (August 1948), pp. 2–3.

IV. Americans in Uniform

1. Hanford McNider, Brig. Genl., USA: *Commendation of [Formosan] Prisoners of War,* HQ 158th Regiment Combat Team, Luzon, P. I., August 23, 1945, 1 p. mimeo.

2. G. H. Kerr: "Some Chinese Problems in Taiwan," *Far Eastern Survey,* Vol. XIV, No. 20 (October 10, 1945).

Chapters V and VI

Materials for these chapters were drawn from private journals, from UNRRA reports, and from the Taipei press which published, piecemeal, the so-called "Take-Over Report," an accounting of properties transferred by the Japanese Property Custodians to Chinese officials in 1946.

VII. Unwelcome Witnesses

1. *Washington News* (Washington, D. C.), March 21, 22, and 28, and *Washington Post* (Washington, D. C.), March 29, 1946.
2. *Hsin Sheng Pao* (Taipei), August 7, 1946.

VIII. The UNRRA-CNRRA Story

1. *The Summary of UNRRA–CNRRA activities and observations is based principally on the following:*
   (a) Twenty-four personal letters addressed to Paine and Kerr by UNRRA–CNRRA team members.
   (b) Twenty weekly reports from the Formosa Regional Office to the Office of the Economic and Financial Advisor, China Office (Shanghai) UNRRA; 133 pp., mimeo.
   (c) *Special Reports to Walter D. Fitzpatrick, Director, Taiwan Regional Office,* by E. E. Paine, Reports Officer, n.d.
   (d) *Summary Report,* Taiwan Regional Office (Taipei), Sept. 15, 1946, 15 pp.
   (e) *Reports on Industrial Rehabilitation,* by Allen E. Shackelton (UNRRA–New Zealand), Taipei, 1946, 14 pp.
   (f) Reports on the Work of CNRRA, Taiwan Regional Office (April 1, 1946), CNRRA's Emergency Sanitary Engineering Project (September 11, 1946) and on Public Welfare Projects (August, 1946), Taipei, 27 pp. mimeo.
   (g) *Special Report on Government–CNRRA Handling of Hainan Repatriates.* UNRRA–Taiwan Regional Office (Taipei, Oct. 11, 1946), 2 pp.
   (h) *Report on the February 28 Incident and Subsequent Events to 15 March 1946.* UNRRA–Taiwan Regional Office (Taipei, March 17, 1947), 9 pp.
   (i) *History of the UNRRA–Taiwan Regional Office* (Taipei, n.d.), 15 pp.
   (j) Allen E. Shackleton: "Formosa — Unhappy Golden Goose," *World Affairs* (Quarterly Journal of the UN Association of New Zealand), Vol. 4, No. 2 (June 1948), pp. 28–29.

2. Edward E. Paine (UNRRA Reports Officer): *Notes on the UNRRA Program, 1946–1947* (n.d.), 10 pp. mimeo.
3. Ira D. Hirschy, M.D. (Chief Medical Officer, UNRRA, Taiwan): "The World is Sick, the Cure is Difficult," *Plantation Health* (Honolulu, Hawaii), Vol. XII, No. 2 (April 1948), pp. 9–15.
4. Mary Mumford (Public Welfare Officer, UNRRA, Taiwan), letter dated July 6, 1948.
5. *Hsin Sheng Pao* (Taipei), May 2, 1946.
6. Mary Mumford, *loc. cit.*

IX. The Formosans' Story: A Year of Disenchantment

1. *Hsin Sheng Pao* (Taipei), May 2, 1946.

X. The Search for Recognition

1. *Jen Min Tao Pao* (Taipei), June 13, 1946.
2. *The Formosan Magazine* (Taipei), Vol. 1, No. 1, September, 1946, pp. 2–3, 38–39.
3. *Min Pao* (Taipei), October 28, 1946.
4. [U. S. Govt., Office of War Information] *The Story of the United States Government . . . How it Started . . . and How it Works . . .* (Washington, D. C., n.d.), 39 pp., illus.
5. Stanway N. W. Cheng, ed., *The New Taiwan Monthly* (Taipei), No. 1 (October, 1946), p. 2.

XI. On the Eve of Disaster

1. Allen E. Shackleton (UNRRA–New Zealand), *Formosa Calling*, p. 43, typescript of article published at London, n.d., 82 pp.
2. *Ta Ming Pao* (Taipei), January 20, 1947, quoting a Central News Agency dispatch from Nanking.
3. *Ta Ming Pao* (Taipei), January 20, 1947, quoting an earlier Central News Agency dispatch from Nanking.
4. *Taiwan Youth Report* (Taipei), January, 1947, p. 23.
5. *Ta Ming Pao* (Taipei), January 20, 1947.

XII. The February Incident, 1947

1. *Hsin Sheng Pao* (Taipei), March 2, 1947.
2. *Hsin Sheng Pao* (Taipei), March 3, 1947.
3. *Hsin Sheng Pao* (Taipei), March 5, 1947.

XIII. Town Meetings, American Style

1. *Hsin Sheng Pao* (Taipei), March 5, 1947.
2. *Ibid.*
3. Letter to Kerr from a former student, dated at Taichung, March 7, 1947.
4. *Chung Wai Jih Pao* (Taipei), March 6, 1947.
5. *Ibid.*
6. [U. S. State Dept.] *United States Relations With China*, pp. 933–935, with supplementary notes by the author of the quoted "Memorandum on the Situation in Taiwan" (G.H.K.).
7. *Ching Hua Jih Pao* (Tainan), March 5, 1947.
8. *Min Pao* (Taipei), March 6, 1947.

XIV. The March Massacre

1. *Hsin Sheng Pao* (Taipei), March 9, 1947.
2. Taiwan Garrison Headquarters, *Communique No. 131* (Taipei), March 9, 1947.
3. *Hsin Sheng Pao* (Taipei), March 11, 1947.
4. *Hsin Sheng Pao* (Taipei), March 11, 1947. Text also air-dropped by leaflet over Formosan cities.
5. Letter from Louise Tomsett (UNRRA–New Zealand) to Kerr, dated June 7, 1948.
6. Letter from Ira D. Hirschy, M.D. (Chief Medical Officer, UNRRA–Taiwan) to E. E. Paine (UNRRA Reports Officer), n.d.
7. Generalissimo Chiang Kai-shek, addressing the Weekly Memorial Services at Nanking, March 10, 1947. Text dropped by leaflet over the cities and towns of Formosa.

XV. The Aftermath

1. China News Service release (San Francisco, January 1947), mimeo., 1 p.
2. China Press (Shanghai), quoting a UP dispatch, March 27, 1947.
3. China News Service release (San Francisco, May 3, 1947).
4. Stanway N. W. Cheng, ed., *The New Taiwan Monthly* (Taipei), No. 1, October, 1946.
5. Letter to Kerr from former student, dated Taipei, March 26, 1947.

XVI. The "Reform Administration"

1. Letter from N. P. Koh (CNRRA) to E. E. Paine (UNRRA) dated July 20, 1948.

2. Letter from N. P. Koh (CNRRA) to E. E. Paine (UNRRA) dated June 15, 1948.
3. Letter to Dr. Ira D. Hirschy (Chief Medical Officer, UNRRA) dated Taipei, April 14, 1947.
4. Letter to Edward E. Paine (UNRRA Reports Officer) dated Taipei, May 4, 1947.
5. Letter from Hans Johansen (UNRRA–Norway) to E. E. Paine, dated Taipei, April 17, 1947.
6. Letter to Kerr from Taipei, dated June 16, 1947.
7. *Hsin Sheng Pao* (Taipei), May 1, 1947.
8. Dr. Ira D. Hirschy quoting Dr. Pierre Sylvain (UNRRA–Haiti) in letter to E. E. Paine (UNRRA–USA), dated at Shanghai, June 27, 1947.
9. Letter to Kerr from Taipei, dated September 6, 1947.
10. [U. S. State Dept.] *United States Relations With China,* "Report to President Truman by Lieutenant General Albert C. Wedemeyer, U. S. Army," September 19, 1947. Part II, "China-economic," p. 770.
11. *Hua Shang Pao* (Hong Kong), October 3, 1947.
12. *Chuan Min Jih Pao* (Taipei), December 20, 1948.
13. Letter from a Catholic priest on Formosa to an American friend, dated January 17, 1948.
14. Letter to Kerr, dated March 2, 1948, at Taipei.
15. *Chung Hua Jih Pao* (Taipei), February 27, 1948.
16. Central News Agency release (Shanghai), March 2, 1948; and *Hsin Sheng Pao* (Taipei), same date.
17. *Shun Pao* (Shanghai), February 14, 1948.

XVII.   *The Retreat to Formosa*

1. Harold Ickes, "Man to Man," *New York Post,* December 6, 1948.
2. Constantine Brown, *Seattle Times,* November 19, 1948.
3. E. E. Paine & G. H. Kerr, *Will America Face a Formosa Problem?* December 15, 1948. 5 pp. mimeo.
4. *New York Times,* December 9, 1948.
5. Letter to E. E. Paine (UNRRA) dated at Taipei, April 23, 1949.
6. Hessel Tiltman (*London Daily News*): "Formosa a Frail Gibraltar for China's Chiang." Reprinted in the *Washington Post* (Washington, D. C.), June 8, 1949.
7. Tillman Durdin, *The New York Times,* August 23, 1949.
8. [U. S. State Dept.] *United States Relations with China,* p. 404. Ambassador Stuart to Washington, April 6, 1949.
9. *Ibid.,* pp. 288–307.
10. *Ibid.,* pp. 288–307. On Chiang's betrayal of Acting President Li see especially pp. 302–304.

XVIII. Turning Point

1. Joseph W. Ballantine, *Formosa: A Problem for United States Foreign Policy* (The Brookings Institution, Washington, D. C., 1952), p. 120. President Truman's "hands off" policy statement, January 5, 1950.
2. Letter to Kerr, dated at Taipei, January 12, 1950.
3. Tillman Durdin, "Taiwan and the Nationalist Government," unpublished ms. prepared for the Council on Foreign Relations symposium on The United States and China in World Affairs, 1964.
4. [U. S. State Dept.] *Bulletin,* Vol. 23 (July 3, 1950), p. 5. President Truman's statement of policy neutralizing Formosa and declaring its legal status unsettled.

XIX. Formosa's "Republican Decade"

1. [U. S. Govt.] U. S. Senate Committee on Foreign Relations: Hearings. 88th Cong., 1st Sess., *Activities of Non-Diplomatic Representatives of Foreign Principals in the United States,* Part 7 (March 25, 1963) (Pp. 677–825); Part 10 (July 10, 1963, pp. 1425–1518), *passim.*
2. [U. S. Govt.] *Congressional Record,* "Hearings before the Senate Committee on Armed Services and the Committee on Foreign Relations" (82nd Cong., 1st Sess. 1951), "Military Situation in the Far East," p. 23.
3. Karl Lott Rankin, *China Assignment* (Seattle, Washington, 1964), 343 pp.
4. *China Handbook 1953–54* (Taipei, 1953), "Chronology of Major Events (1911–1953)," p. 478.
5. *Ibid.,* pp. 481–482.
6. Mark Mancall: "Too Much at Home in the Old Tiger's Lair," *New York Herald Tribune Book Week* (Nov. 15, 1964), p. 6.
7. On the missionary background of Chiang's appeal to Americans see especially Harold Isaacs, *Images of Asia: American Views of China and India* (New York, 1962), pp. 124–148.

XX. Behind the Reform Façade

1. Letter to Kerr, dated at Taipei, August 28, 1953.
2. [U. S. Govt.] *Congressional Record* — Proceedings and Debates of the 86th Cong., 2nd Sess. (Extract reprint, 1960) "Conlon Associates Report on Communist China and Taiwan. Extension of Remarks of Hon. Charles O. Porter of Oregon, in the House of Representatives, Tuesday, January 19, 1960."
3. *Ibid.,* p. 23.

XXI. Two Chinas?

1. Li Chun-ching: "Taiwan: the Marble Ball and the Marble Lion," *China Digest,* Vol. V, No. 9 (Hong Kong, February 22, 1949), pp. 4–8.
2. *Ibid.*
3. Chuang Chia-nung, ed., *Fen Nu ti Taiwan* ("Taiwan in Anger") (Hong Kong, 1949), p. 153.
4. [Editorial] "The Time for Reappraisal," *Formosan Quarterly,* Vol. I, No. 2 (Tokyo, 1962), p. 30.
5. —— "Councilor Su Tung-chi Sentenced to Death," *Formosan Quarterly,* Vol. I, No. 1 (July, 1962) pp. 17–18.

XXII. Free Formosa

1. Letter to Kerr, dated at Hong Kong, April, 1949.
2. [Editorial] "We Appeal to the World on the Arrest of Professor Peng Ming-min," *Independent Formosa,* Vol. III, No. 3, (Tokyo, Oct., 1964), pp. 1–2.
3. ——"Formosa Inside Out," *Ilha Formosa,* Vol. I, No. 3 (Philadelphia, Winter issue, 1964), p. 22.
4. [United Formosans for Independence] *Appeal for Justice* (Philadelphia, March, 1960), 3 pp. Mimeo.

INDEX

Index

INDEX